PARADOX AND POLARITY IN THE FICTION OF JOSEPH CONRAD

PARADOX AND POLARITY IN THE FICTION OF JOSEPH CONRAD

Stephen K. Land

St. Martin's Press   New York

© Stephen K. Land 1984
All rights reserved. For information, write:
St. Martin's Press, Inc., 175 Fifth Avenue, New York, NY 10010
Printed in Hong Kong
Published in the United Kingdom by The Macmillan Press Ltd.
First published in the United States of America in 1984

ISBN 0-312-59597-2

Library of Congress Cataloging in Publication Data
Land, Stephen K.
Paradox and polarity in the fiction of Joseph Conrad.
Includes index.
1. Conrad, Joseph, 1857-1924—Criticism and interpretation.
2. Paradox.   3. Polarity in literature.   I. Title.
PR6005. 04Z7646   1984   823'.912   83-40160
ISBN 0-312-59597-2

Contents

PART VI   AN OVERVIEW

Acknowledgements

I am grateful to the Trustees of the Conrad Estate and to the Trustees of the National Library of Scotland for permission to quote from Conrad's letter to William Blackwood dated 6 September 1897 and catalogued as MS 4657, ff. 81–2.

S.K.L.

Introduction

Each of Conrad's full-length novels and most of his shorter stories are written around some variant of a common structural framework, a core of conceptual interrelations and interactions of character types. This is not to say that Conrad continually rewrote the same story, or that he failed to develop over the thirty years of his career as a novelist; on the contrary, working with the structural framework he set up, Conrad was constantly experimenting, rearranging the components of his fictional universe to achieve different effects, so that almost every one of his longer works is in some significant way an advance on its predecessor. The first purpose of the present study is to trace this development.

Certain motifs, character types, situations, and even particular characters obviously recur across several of Conrad's works. Thus, the treasure which Almayer seeks in *Almayer's Folly* reappears as Kurtz' ivory in *Heart of Darkness*, as the silver of the mine in *Nostromo*, as Allègre's fortune in *The Arrow of Gold*, and as Peyrol's hoard in *The Rover*; the guilty outcast Willems is duplicated in Jim and echoed in Razumov and Heyst; and the colourful figures of Schomberg, Ellis, Lingard and, of course, Marlow, are each present in more than one of Conrad's stories. Some of these repetitions are symptomatic of the underlying common pattern, but the pattern consists not simply in recurring characters and situations but rather in a set of conditions and associated motifs which constitute the Conradian fictional universe, the common set of laws, circumstances, and concepts under which Conrad's plots unfold.

The details of the pattern shift and change from one story to the next, although once seen it is recognizable in all but the least significant of Conrad's fictional works. Its chief constituents can be briefly outlined, bearing in mind that not all of these elements occur together in all of the stories, and that there are many highly significant variations which remain to be considered.

(*a*) In most of the novels there is a central figure whom we will call the *hero*, meaning simply that his career and actions are the focus of the plot.

(*b*) The action of the story is initiated by, and generally flows from, some specific and readily identifiable *exertion of will* on the hero's part, which may consist in some deed or (as in the later novels) in an attempt to avoid the commitment of decisive action.

(*c*) Because of his own shortcomings and of the difficulties inherent in his circumstances, the hero, unable to achieve his aims through his initial efforts, accepts a *compromise*, taking what amounts to a moral shortcut to his goal, frequently entailing some form of betrayal or dereliction of duty.

(*d*) The primary law of Conrad's universe is that the hero's compromised exertion of will contains or brings about its own negation; the very act in pursuit of a specific goal entails its own frustration. This, the fundamental constant of all Conrad's major fiction, is the *paradox*, frequently imaged in an overtly contradictory character or situation, that purposive action is self-nullifying.

(*e*) In most of the stories the hero's exertion of will and compromise take place in the context of a *dualism* of antagonistic forces. The hero is caught between two opposing worlds or parties, sometimes (as in the Malayan and African stories) objectified as conflicting racial cultures, sometimes (as in the political novels) represented in a dialect of conflicting ideologies. His actions stand in relation to this dualism, either as an expression of commitment to one side or the other or as an effort to maintain a neutral middle path against the encroachments of both. It is through the dualistic setting of Conrad's plots that the paradox finds expression.

(*f*) In some of the stories the means whereby the hero exerts his will is objectified, usually in the form of a quasi-talismanic *treasure*. This may be an actual hoard of gold, silver, or some other valuable commodity, such as the mine in *Nostromo*, Kurtz' ivory, or Peyrol's booty, or else a merely speculative fund, such as Lingard's treasure in *Almayer's Folly* or Heyst's secret store in *Victory*, the existence of which may be doubtful or even false.

(*g*) The goal of the hero's exertion of will varies from the dubious strivings of Almayer and Willems to the dignified public aims of Charles Gould. From the time of the political novels onwards, moreover, it becomes not so much an action as an attempt to avoid action and to maintain neutrality. Most of the later heroes, notably Heyst, Anthony, George, and Peyrol, are men whose exertion consists primarily in withdrawal from society, normally a withdrawal to the isolation of the sea. In the earlier stories, where the hero's strivings are directed towards some positive goal, there is frequently a female figure associated with this objective, union with whom therefore becomes part of the hero's purpose. In the later stories, however, where the hero's aim is withdrawal, the female figure generally appears not as a reinforcement of his intention but as a distraction from it. In either case we will call the female the *heroine* of the story, using the term in the plain and traditional sense to indicate the woman with whom the hero falls in love, although we shall have to stretch this sense to cover a few cases where the heroine is a daughter-figure to the hero and where the love between them is consequently not sexual. Heroines are variable features of the pattern; Conrad changed their rôle considerably in about 1910, and he not infrequently constructed stories from which they are wholly absent (e.g. *The Nigger of the 'Narcissus'* and *The Shadow-Line*).

(*h*) Where the heroine is present she is frequently opposed, in her tendency towards the hero, by a contrasting female who is representative of a hostile orthodoxy. In the earlier novels, where the heroine belongs to one of the two worlds of the dualism, this second woman is of the other world, representing the counteractive pull upon the hero. In the later novels, where the heroine is independent of the dualism, her opponent remains simply an extreme representative of conventional values and, as such, antagonistic to her interest in the hero. This second woman we call, for want of a better term, the *anti-heroine*. Such are Joanna in *An Outcast of the Islands*, Kurtz' fiancée in *Heart of Darkness*, and Therese in *The Arrow of Gold*.

(*i*) The anti-heroine usually opposes the hero's exertion of will, particularly in so far as this is a striving towards the world of the heroine, and she sometimes, as most obviously in the cases of Joanna Willems and Linda Viola, has a hand in his final catastrophe. The hero is more directly opposed, however, by another male character, who stands in much the same relation to him as does the heroine to the anti-heroine. This man, moreover, has some prior claim upon the heroine, either as a husband, established lover, or close male relative, and is often sexually jealous of the hero. Such men are Omar in *An Outcast of the Islands*, Cornelius in *Lord Jim*, and Mr Travers in *The Rescue*. This figure we will call, for obvious reasons, the hero's *rival*.

(*j*) The rival, like the anti-heroine, usually has a hand in the hero's ultimate failure, but the hero's chief antagonist in the

Conradian universe is a figure distinct from both of these, who comes in some way from the hero's past, from a world or party the hero has deserted, and who is frequently portrayed as a hostile *alter ego*, a man who reflects a number of the hero's essential qualities but who is none the less his opponent in some crucial matter. Such men are Brown in *Lord Jim*, Jones in *Victory*, and Blunt in *The Arrow of Gold*. Because he is generally the immediate cause of the hero's downfall, and because the downfall (except in the one or two cases where Conrad permits it to be averted) is presented as an inevitable reaction to the hero's initial exertion of will, we refer to this figure as the (agent of) *nemesis*.

These in brief are the chief elements which, with their inter-relations as defined, make up the Conradian universe. The hero's exertion of will and compromise usually precipitate a dualistic conflict of interests in the paradoxical consequences of which he becomes enmeshed. He is often engaged at the same time in pursuit of a heroine. His interest in the heroine provokes a rival, who already has some claim upon her, although the hero is generally successful in pushing him aside. In many of the stories the union of hero and heroine is also resisted by an anti-heroine. Most import-ant, however, is the fact that the hero's exertion is invariably countered by the figure of nemesis, who is prevented from causing the hero's destruction in only one or two of the stories.

The most prominent feature of the structure, at this high level of abstraction, is its tendency to counterbalance conflicting forces: hero and rival over the heroine, heroine and anti-heroine over the hero, and hero and nemesis, action and reaction, through the whole of the plot. In addition, most of the stories are woven across a clear conceptual dualism of implacably opposed interests. The overall feeling, although this naturally varies from one novel to the next, is one of heroic impotence, of human striving in a universe whose condition of finely balanced conflict is such that no lasting progress or achievement is possible.

The heart of the structure is the anomaly that purposive action is self-defeating. This we shall call the Conradian paradox, as it is the metaphysical core of most of his fiction. The paradoxical condition is brought into operation in almost every case by a recognizable moral ambivalence in the hero's initial exertion. His conduct, however disinterested or well-intentioned, usually involves or implies some form of avoidance or betrayal, for which, in the end, he suffers defeat. In order to pursue his original goal he is obliged to cut corners, to make a moral compromise, and in Conrad's strict and inflexible universe such an offence, however understandable and however harmless the outcome, demands retribution.

The present study aims initially to show how this pattern is present in most of Conrad's works, suggesting in each case that a view of the story in terms of the pattern provides a useful approach to a grasp of Conrad's purposes and craftsmanship. More important, by considering the stories chronologically in order of their composition, it aims to present a view of Conrad's development as a novelist in terms of certain progressive changes he made in successive handlings of the pattern. Thirdly, and as a result, it strives towards an overview of Conrad's fictional work, in which fundamental constants can be distinguished from salient developmental trends, and by means of which some understanding of Conrad's craft as an architect of complex fictional structures may be obtained.

Such goals raise certain procedural issues. Discussion of development presupposes a clear picture of Conrad's chronology, a picture which is in fact clouded by his tendency to work on more than one piece at a time and by the failure of his publication dates to reflect invariably the order of his compositions. Not only are there such notorious problems as *The Rescue* (begun in 1896 but not completed until 1919) and *The Black Mate* (which Conrad once said was his first story, although Jessie, his wife, asserted categorically that he wrote it in 1908), but we also know of several cases (that of *Chance*, for instance) where Conrad had ideas for specific stories many years before he began in earnest the work of writing them out. None the less a fairly definite chronology of the longer works (apart from *The Rescue*) can be obtained if we confine ourselves to composition dates, to the periods in which Conrad was working more or less continuously on material which emerged as particular novels. Most of the longer works then fall into a clear-cut sequence, occasionally overlapped by shorter stories written while the novels were in progress. A rough chronology of titles is provided in the Appendix.

A more serious procedural problem is raised in the objection that when dealing with structures or patterns in fiction one can, by means of a sufficient volume of persuasive explanation, show virtually any pattern to be present in almost any work. The undertaking, after all, is not remotely analogous to that of unpacking a miscellany of tangible objects from a box, at the end of which operation the items, discrete and palpable, may be produced for exhibition. How are we to know that the shapes we find in a story are genuinely aspects of its construction and not mere retinal shadows seen in the dark? The answer, short of a vast deal of theorizing, must be pragmatic: the pattern is there, in each case, to the extent to which it provides a coherent and unified approach to the story without bypassing features which, on a careful reading of the work, appear to be important, and without emphasizing features which are apparently trivial. Such an answer, which consists essentially in an appeal to the intelligent reader's intuition, leaves open the possibility that the pattern might be less present in some stories than in others. It also avoids any claim to exclusiveness; the validity of other patterns, as well as of other different critical approaches which may be of help towards an understanding of Conrad's work, is unchallenged by the present discussion.

The very nature of the undertaking excludes consideration of any work of which Conrad was not sole author. No mention is made, therefore, of his collaboration with F. M. Hueffer (Ford), or of the three novels which they jointly produced. Nor are Conrad's non-fictional writings discussed.

The edition of Conrad used is the 'Kent' edition published in twenty-six volumes by Doubleday of New York in 1926, which has the same pagination as the contemporary edition published by Dent in London. These, the popular collected editions of Conrad, are still those most commonly found in libraries in England and the United States. Page references are given parenthetically in the text.

Part I The Early Works

1 *Almayer's Folly*

Almayer's Folly, Conrad's first novel, bears a striking resemblance in the structure of its plot to the story told in the four operas of Wagner's *Ring*. Conrad, who knew Wagner's work, may well have been influenced by it when undertaking his first substantial work of fiction, although it would be a complicated matter to argue this in detail. It remains possible, for instance, that Wagner's actual influence on Conrad was at second hand, through the French *symbolistes*, or that similarities in their work arose from a common cast of thought, which found a degree of expression in the writings of Nietzsche and Schopenhauer. The present purpose, however, is not to argue any historical connection between the writings of Conrad and Wagner, but rather to illustrate the first appearance of the Conradian pattern through comparison with a familiar work by another author. An outline of the *Ring* story is given in the following paragraphs.

Wotan, chief of the gods, awakes and sees that the fortress Valhalla, from which he plans to govern the world, has been constructed for him while he slept by the giants Fasolt and Fafner. In return for their labours Wotan has contracted to give them Freia, goddess of love and beauty and keeper of the golden apples of eternal life. The giants demand their payment, but Wotan cannot keep the bargain without depriving himself of youth and immortality. His counsellor, the crafty fire-spirit Loge, induces the giants to accept instead the Rheingold, the treasure stolen from the river-daughters by the dwarf Alberich who, having complied with the condition and foresworn love, has forged from the gold the Ring which bestows measureless power upon its wearer. Aided by Loge's trickery Wotan steals the treasure and the Ring from the dwarf and, after a personal struggle, delivers both to the giants in exchange for Freia's freedom. The giants at once dispute possession of the Ring, and Fafner, having slain his brother, takes the whole treasure for himself. The gods meanwhile enter Valhalla.

Wotan's rule is not secure while the Ring is held by another, yet because his government rests upon the principles of law he cannot wrest the Ring from the giants, to whom he gave it in settlement of a debt. He therefore creates a race of heroes, the Walsungs, led by Siegmund, whom he hopes will take the Ring from Fafner and make Valhalla secure. Fricka, Wotan's jealous wife, shows him that the plan must fail because Siegmund's independence is illusory. Even the sword, Nothung, with which Siegmund was to slay the dragon, was conveyed to him and endowed with its power by Wotan himself. Wotan is forced to abandon the plan and sends his favourite daughter, the Walküre Brunnhilde, to ensure the Walsung's death. But Brunnhilde is so moved by the devotion of Siegmund for his sister-wife Sieglinde that she reverses Wotan's decree and allows them to escape. In great anger Wotan himself slays Siegmund and pursues the terrified Brunnhilde, whom he punishes for her disobedience by casting her asleep on a mountain top surrounded by a wall of flame, to be released only by a hero brave enough to pass through the fire.

Meanwhile Sieglinde has fled to the forest where Fafner, in the form of a dragon, guards his treasure. There she is safe from Wotan, who will not trespass on the giant's ground, and there she dies giving birth to Siegmund's son, Siegfried. The child is brought up in the forest by the dwarf Mime, Alberich's brother, an unpleasant character whose object is to use Siegfried to obtain the Ring for himself. Unlike Siegmund, Siegfried has grown up independent of Wotan's will, and as a sign of his independence he reforges the sword, Nothung, which Wotan had shattered in Siegmund's last fight. Armed with this, and unmoved by Mime's deceptions, Siegfried slays Fafner and takes the Ring. He then sets off to seek Brunnhilde's mountain. Wotan watches, proud of the youth who is his grandson and whom he expects to accomplish the task for which the Walsungs were created. On the path approaching Brunnhilde's rock the god confronts the hero, but Siegfried will have nothing to do with him. In the ensuing quarrel Siegfried's sword cleaves Wotan's spear, and the hero passes on through the fire to awaken Brunnhilde.

Siegfried and Brunnhilde live for some time on the mountain, and Siegfried gives her the Ring as a token of his love. Leaving her still guarded by the flames, he goes into the world seeking adventure and comes to the castle of King Gunther on the Rhein. Gunther, weak but hungry for fame, is dominated by his half-brother, Hagen, son of the now-dead Alberich. Guided by Alberich's spirit, Hagen plans to regain the Ring by drawing Gunther and Siegfried into an elaborate plot. Siegfried is given a magic potion which causes him to forget his past life and to fall in love with Gunther's sister. In return for her hand he is induced to fetch Brunnhilde, of whom he now has no recollection, down from the mountain to marry Gunther. This he does, much to Brunnhilde's surprise and confusion, taking back the Ring from her. Seeing him with Gunther's sister at the castle, and knowing nothing of Hagen's trick, Brunnhilde thinks Siegfried has betrayed her for another woman, and in revenge she plots with Hagen to murder him. Gunther joins the conspiracy, because he sees that Siegfried has been Brunnhilde's lover, contrary to their bargain. Accordingly a hunting party is organised by Gunther during which Hagen, with Brunnhilde's help, finds an opportunity to stab Siegfried to death.

Wotan meanwhile, seeing that things are now beyond his control, has withdrawn to Valhalla to await the end. He orders the World-Ash-Tree to be cut down and its branches piled around the fortress. Waltraute, one of the Walküren, aware of Wotan's gloom, visits Brunnhilde on the mountain before Siegfried's return, in an effort to persuade her to give up the Ring; but Brunnhilde refuses to relinquish the love-token Siegfried has left her, even for the preservation of the gods.

After the fatal hunt Siegfried's body is brought back to the castle, where Hagen and Gunther fight over it for possession of the Ring. Gunther is slain, but before Hagen can take the Ring from Siegfried's body Brunnhilde, who has now learnt the whole truth from the Rheinmaidens, sets light to Siegfried's funeral pyre and rides into the flames. The fire leaps up to heaven, where Valhalla itself is burnt away, and the waters of the Rhein run over the bodies, sweeping Hagen away as he tries to capture the Ring.

The *Ring* story is centrally concerned with the figure of Wotan, whose action in arranging the construction of Valhalla as a fortress from which he can govern the world initiates the drama. Yet Wotan inhabits a dualistic universe; the heaven of the gods is reflected in Nibelheim, the underworld home of the Nibelungs (dwarves) where, at the same time as Wotan plans Valhalla, Alberich steals the Rheingold and forges the Ring of power.

The story exhibits the primary features of the Conradian pattern: a hero whose attempt to impose control on his world is shown to be self-defeating because of the reactions it evokes in the context of a dualistic universe. Wotan's exertion of will, his attempt to stabilize and govern the world from Valhalla, is paradoxical from the first because, in order to build and possess the fortress, he is obliged to consign the Ring into the independent hands of Fafner. As long as the Ring is at large in the world the policy of Valhalla fails of achievement. Throughout the drama the symbol of Wotan's rule, the spear he carries, on the shaft of which are engraved the laws by which he governs, is countered by the ungovernable, law-breaking force of the Ring. Every move which the gods make to restrain or control this power is answered by a corresponding move from the Nibelungs. There is no way out, as Wotan finally realizes, but resignation, the suppression of the will and its submission to the natural flow of events.

The resemblance between the *Ring* story and the Conradian pattern comes into sharper focus when we turn to the details of its exposition. Like Conrad, Wagner associates the hero's ideal, the goal of his striving, with a prominent female figure, who may be labelled the heroine of the drama. This is Brunnhilde, Wotan's beloved daughter, the child of his extra-marital love, to whom he refers as his "will" (*Wille*). The failure of Wotan's plan is marked by his separation from Brunnhilde, the embodiment of his will, whom he is obliged to repudiate after the death of Siegmund.

Brunnhilde is opposed by Fricka, Wotan's legal spouse, who argues against his policies and persuades him, against his will, to order Siegmund's death. Fricka, a conservative figure representative of established values and obligations in opposition to the hero's ideals, functions in a manner analogous to that of the Conradian anti-heroine.

Brunnhilde is rescued from the fire-bound enchantment under which the god has placed her by Siegfried, who achieves this in open defiance of Wotan and takes the Walküre as his bride. Having captured the Ring from Fafner, Siegfried refuses to bend it to Wotan's service and remains an independent, untameable power. His role as Wotan's rival, both politically and in a sublimated sexual sense, becomes clear when he carries off Brunnhilde and consigns the Ring to her keeping.

Fricka stands opposed to Wotan's attempt to realize his ideal through the agency of Brunnhilde and the Walsungs. Siegfried steals Brunnhilde from captivity and establishes himself as a power beyond Wotan's control. In addition, Wotan is opposed throughout by the Nibelungs, represented first by Alberich and later by Hagen, a race coeval with, and inherently antagonistic to the gods. Wagner does not develop in detail the alter ego motif exhibited by many of Conrad's fictional antagonists, as between Brown and Jim or Jones and Heyst, yet in a general way Alberich ("Schwarzalberich") is the dark counterpart of Wotan ("Lichtalberich"), and Nibelheim is the inverted image of Valhalla. Collectively, therefore, the Nibelungs correspond to the Conradian nemesis.

Finally, the Ring itself, together with the Rheingold from which it is forged, has a place in the drama broadly analogous to that of the treasures of silver or gold in Conrad's fiction. The silver of the mine in *Nostromo* is perhaps Conrad's closest approach to the Wagnerian symbol, his fictional hoards in general being less prominent and having less specific associations. None the less there is a recognizable similarity of function, both the Ring and several of the Conradian treasures providing motivating forces in their respective stories and serving as catalysts within the structures of their plots.

The structural correspondences between the plots of *Der Ring des Nibelungen* and *Almayer's Folly* are close enough to make plausible the suggestion that Conrad had Wagner's work in mind as he wrote his first novel. Almayer, like Wotan, makes a determined attempt to take direction of his world by gaining control of a treasure, an attempt which is frustrated by interaction of the very forces which his efforts have set in motion. Most of the subsidiary figures from the *Ring* story – the heroine, anti-heroine, rival, and nemesis – have clear counterparts in the plot of Almayer's tale.

The central figure, Almayer himself, is "gifted with a strong and active imagination" (p. 10), the cast of mind which makes him, like Jim and Gould among other Conradian heroes, particularly able to conceive his world as being other than it is, and therefore liable to take measures to change it. The faculty of imagination, as Conrad presents it in *Lord Jim*, is a dangerous blessing, both noble and destructive. It may function, however, on various levels: heroically, as with Jim; idealistically, as with Gould; or selfishly, as with Kaspar Almayer. Almayer's imagination leads him to no dreams of glorious self-distinction or politico-economic reorganization, but to a simple vision of "opulent existence" (p. 10), in pursuit of which he enters into partnership with Tom Lingard.

The consideration, the indolent ease of life – for which he felt himself so well fitted – his ships, his warehouses, his merchandise (old Lingard would not live for ever), and, crowning all, in the far

> future gleamed like a fairy palace the big mansion in Amsterdam,
> that earthly paradise of his dreams, where made king amongst
> men by old Lingard's money, he would pass the evening of his
> days in inexpressible splendour (p. 10).

The goal for which Almayer strives, egocentric and materialistic,
consists in the acquisition of wealth and the eventual pursuit of idle
extravagance in a European city.

Almayer's means to this end is his partnership with Lingard, to
secure which he has been obliged to marry the Captain's "adopted
daughter", a Malay girl captured in childhood by Lingard from a
crew of pirates, who remains, despite a convent education,
fundamentally hostile to white men's ways. This is Almayer's
compromise, for in spite of the "shame" (p. 10), he marries the girl,
planning as he does so to find some way of releasing himself from her
(p. 23). At the same time he accepts Lingard's stipulation that he
shall reside in Sambir as local manager of the company's business.
Here is the beginning of the paradox Almayer faces; his goal is
European civilized magnificence, but to win it he must ally himself
to Borneo, to the jungle, and to obscurity.

From the outset Almayer is obsessed by the contrast between
Sambir and the European world in which he imagines himself.

> He absorbed himself in his dream of wealth and power away from
> this coast where he had dwelt for so many years, forgetting the
> bitterness of toil and strife in the vision of a great and splendid
> reward. They would live in Europe, he and his daughter. They
> would be rich and respected. Nobody would think of her mixed
> blood in the presence of her great beauty and of his immense
> wealth. Witnessing her triumphs he would grow young again, he
> would forget the twenty-five years of heart-breaking struggle on
> this coast where he felt like a prisoner (pp. 3-4).

The world in which he desires to live is in all ways significant to him
the antithesis of that in which he must live in order to obtain his end.
As the years pass, moreover, a series of accidents progressively
postpones his departure. Trade declines in the face of competition
from the Arabs, and Lingard disappears. In the relatively recent
past before the story's opening Almayer's hopes were revived by
news that the territory might soon fall under the control of the
British Borneo Company. Anticipating expansion and an influx of

capital he began building a new house for the reception and entertainment of the company's agents. "He spent every available guilder on it with a confiding heart" (p. 33). The Borneo Company temporarily replaced Lingard as Almayer's means to a fortune and a passage to Europe, but once again the scheme foundered, no annexation occurred, no Europeans came up the Pantai, and Almayer stopped work ·on the shell of the new house which, christened "Almayer's Folly" (p. 37), provides the story's title. It stands for the paradox and futility of his aspirations, this "half-finished house built for the reception of Englishmen" (p. 36) in the middle of a Malayan jungle. He uses it thereafter as a place of withdrawal from the unpleasant realities of his situation; the "solitude of his new house" provides a retreat from the "scathing remarks and bitter cursings" of his wife (p. 40), and it is there that we first encounter him, standing on its "loose planks" (p. 12) dreaming of wealth and power.

Almayer's one source of pleasure in Sambir is his daughter Nina. Born two years after Almayer's marriage, shortly after his settlement by the Pantai, she was removed at the age of six by Lingard to receive in Macassar the benefits of a European education. As she grew to womanhood away from home Nina was made miserable by her guardians, who envied her beauty and despised her mixed parentage, and she therefore returned ten years later to her parents in Sambir, to become the focus of her father's ambitions. Almayer at once made Nina his reason for seeking a better life and enshrined her as the intended beneficiary of his opulence. From this time forth she is the central figure and sustaining force of his imaginary world. His later explanation of his motives, although angry and self-pitying, is basically honest: "it was for you," he says to Nina,

for your happiness I was working. I wanted to be rich; I wanted to get away from here. I wanted to see white men bowing low before the power of your beauty and your wealth. Old as I am I wished to seek a strange land, a civilization to which I am a stranger, so as to find a new life in the contemplation of your high fortunes, of your triumphs, of your happiness. For that I bore patiently the burden of the work, of disappointment, of humiliation amongst these savages here (p. 101).

Nina is the heroine of the story, the climax of which comes with her defection, her desertion of the hero's dream.

Nina's part in this respect is comparable to that of Brunnhilde. Each daughter embodies her father's hopes of achievement, Nina as object, Brunnhilde as agent, and each is eventually parted from her parent. The difference is that whereas Brunnhilde disobeys Wotan by persisting in pursuit of the goal he has been himself forced to relinquish, Nina, who never cared much for Almayer's ideal world, abandons it abruptly as soon as she is offered an alternative. In the one case it is the father, Wotan, a complex and developing character, who changes his position, while in the other case the father remains constantly self-absorbed as the daughter, Nina, grows away from him. The effect is the same in both cases; the failure of the father's self-defeating pursuits is imaged in his deliberate and ritualistic divorce from the daughter with whom he had identified his goal.

As the story opens Almayer anxiously awaits the overdue return of Dain, his new partner and most recent hope of escape. Dain had arrived unexpectedly on the scene some time before in command of a trading vessel. The arrival is opportune for Almayer who, having discovered from an old notebook left behind by Lingard the likely location of a fabled source of gold up river, is seeking a means to obtain the treasure for himself. Dain proves friendly to Almayer, his boat and crew offer a means for the treasure-hunt, and the treasure is to be Almayer's passport to Europe. As a condition of his help, however, Dain insists that the local ruler, Lakamba, be made party to the undertaking and that, in order to finance the expedition, the three – Almayer, Dain, and Lakamba – should first cooperate in a profitable but illegal deal in gunpowder. It is to complete this precondition that Dain has gone to sea. The expedition up river to seek the gold is planned for his return.

What is in the event the last of Almayer's several schemes for the achievement of his ideal thus involves him more deeply in the very situation from which he wishes to escape. In order to win his goal he must ally with Dain who, although friendly and apparently a man of honour, is none the less a native belonging to the Malay aristocracy of war-lords and pirates with which Mrs Almayer associates herself. The ominous connection is emphasized by the instant respect and approval which Dain, unknowingly, inspires in Almayer's wife, who calls him a "great Rajah . . . a Son of Heaven" (p. 51). Yet Almayer blindly thinks of his association with Dain, much as he thought of his marriage some twenty years before, as an essentially temporary alliance, a concession to the exigencies of the situation which will be justified and terminated by the achievement of his ends.

The compromise demanded of Almayer intensifies when he is forced into a reconciliation with Lakamba in order to stage his expedition. Lakamba represents the least impressive aspect of Malay culture, much as Almayer, who is surprisingly like him, exhibits some of the less desirable characteristics of western man. A former warrior-adventurer who, by intrigue, crime, and accident, has become rajah of Sambir, Lakamba as we find him is well into middle age, indolent, rapacious, and unscrupulous. By keeping his distance from the rajah, Almayer has hitherto maintained something of his integrity. The reconciliation engineered by Dain, hollow as it is, signals a further stage in Almayer's involvement with the context from which he wishes to escape. That this association is also ominous is suggested by the reappearance thereafter of Lakamba's minister, Babalatchi, in Almayer's compound (p. 59).

The agreement with Dain, moreover, involves Almayer in illegal activities which invite the disapproving attention of the Dutch authorities. Importing gunpowder is forbidden by the colonial government in Batavia, which is in the process of pacifying and subjugating the region. An earlier visit from a Dutch naval vessel had already intimated to Almayer that he was suspected (unjustly at first) of such dealings (p. 36). His engagement in Dain's enterprise at this point results later in the appearance of a man-of-war on the Pantai and the holding of a commission of inquiry within the otherwise empty walls of Almayer's Folly.

Almayer's last effort to wrest control of his fate from the hands of adversity thus intensifies the paradox of his situation. His goal is Europe and respectability, to obtain which he becomes increasingly entangled in the disreputable affairs of Sambir. Worse still, the agent with whom he allies himself, Dain, whom he sees as his potential saviour, not only fails to bring Almayer the treasure but also steals away his cherished daughter. Dain plays a role here analogous to that of Siegfried in the *Ring* story. Just as Wotan creates the Walsungs to be the agents whereby he will regain the Ring and so control the world, so Almayer enters into partnership with Dain to obtain the treasure which will enable him to live as he wishes; but just as the Walsungs, in the person of Siegfried, refusing to follow Wotan's plans, ally with his daughter against him, so Dain abandons Almayer and escapes taking Nina with him. In both cases an older father-figure expects help from a younger man, who in the event establishes his independence by carrying off the beloved daughter. Beyond this level there are, of course, many differences; Siegfried and Wotan have a special relationship which has no parallel in *Almayer's Folly*, and Nina's background is quite unlike that of Brunnhilde. The differences of character and detail, however, do not affect the common role of Dain and Siegfried as rivals to the heroes.

From the time of her return to Sambir Nina, whose life in Singapore had been generally unpleasant, turns increasingly to her mother's world, which finds expression chiefly in tales of native warrior-heroes.

> Mrs. Almayer's thoughts . . . were usually turned into a channel of childhood reminiscences, and she gave them utterance in a kind of monotonous recitative – slightly disconnected, but generally describing the glories of the Sultan of Sulu, his great splendour, his power, his great prowess, the fear which benumbed the hearts of white men at the sight of his swift piratical praus. . . . And listening to the recital of those savage glories, those barbarous fights and savage feasting, to the story of deeds valorous, albeit somewhat bloodthirsty, where men of her mother's race shone far above the Orang Blanda, [Nina] felt herself irresistibly fascinated, and saw with vague surprise the narrow mantle of civilized morality, in which good-meaning people had wrapped her young soul, fall away and leave her shivering and helpless as if on the edge of some deep and unknown abyss (pp. 41–2).

When Dain appears, a rich itinerant prince of her own people followed by a piratical crew, Nina recognizes him instantly as "the ideal Malay chief of her mother's tradition" (p. 64). They are at once mutually attracted.

Dain's arrival completes Nina's movement away from any interest she might have felt for Almayer's vision of opulent life in Europe. Not that Nina has no love for her father – on the contrary, she shows affection for him (pp. 103, 141) and restrains Dain from attacking him – but she has come to despise the European ways which he idealizes. Her perception sharpened by her dual background and experience of both peoples, Nina sees the white man's world as one of passionate, cunning materialism, in no way morally better than that of her mother's people.

It seemed to Nina that there was no change and no difference. Whether they traded in brick godowns or on the muddy river bank; whether they reached after much or little; whether they made love under the shadows of the great trees or in the shadow of the cathedral on the Singapore promenade; whether they plotted for their own ends under the protection of laws and according to the rules of Christian conduct, or whether they sought the gratification of their desires with the savage cunning and the unrestrained fierceness of natures as innocent of culture as their own immense and gloomy forests, Nina saw only the same manifestations of love and hate and of sordid greed chasing the uncertain dollar in all its multifarious and vanishing shapes (p. 43).

The novel bears out Nina's observation, as most of the white men in the story are obviously in pursuit of selfish material ends. Lingard is a pirate, the Dutch presence in the region (including that of Almayer) is directed at economic exploitation, and the society represented by the Vincks in Singapore is one of bourgeois commercialism. It is no wonder that to Nina "the savage and uncompromising sincerity of purpose shown by her Malay kinsmen seemed at least preferable to the sleek hypocrisy, to the polite disguises, to the virtuous pretences of such white people as she had had the misfortune to come in contact with" (p. 43). With this perspective, Nina falls inevitably under her mother's influence and is prepared to respond enthusiastically to Dain's advances.

A dualism is created in *Almayer's Folly* from the antithesis and confrontation between European and Malayan cultures. The novel turns upon the contrasting movements of Nina and Almayer across this duality; Almayer, trapped in Borneo, struggles increasingly to escape to Europe, while his daughter, having received a poor impression of European ways, returns to Sambir and identifies herself finally with the native people. The black–white racial dualism introduced in *Almayer's Folly* continues through most of Conrad's early works (*An Outcast of the Islands*, *An Outpost of Progress*, *Heart of Darkness* and *Lord Jim*), but, like the political dualisms of some of his later novels, this racial antithesis is never a simple matter of one set of values being contrasted favourably or unfavourably with another. We cannot say that any of these early stories present *either* a view of white civilization as decayed in contrast with the primitive integrity of the blacks *or* a sense of the white man's

civilized standards as corrupted through exposure to the unrestrained savagery of the jungle. Both views are present, each
undercutting the other. The ways of the jungle are both fascinating
and abhorrent; white civilization is both a bastion of moral strength
and a façade of hypocrisy.

In *Almayer's Folly*, as in most of the subsequent novels, the
Conradian conceptual dualism has a mirror-like effect in which,
upon scrutiny, each side appears as a distorted but inescapably
recognizable image of the other. The harder we look at the two races
portrayed in Conrad's first book, the more difficult it becomes to
isolate any significant moral difference between them. Dain is
matched as a pirate-adventurer by Lingard, Lakamba is no less lazy
and acquisitive than Almayer, and the "cunning" which repels
Nina among the whites (but which the white men in the story
conspicuously fail to exhibit) is thoroughly countered by the
machinations of Babalatchi. Conrad himself, in the "Author's
Note" to *Almayer's Folly*, drew attention to the similarity of the two
worlds.

> The picture of life, there [i.e. "in those distant lands"] as here, is
> drawn with the same elaboration of detail, coloured with the
> same tints. Only in the cruel serenity of the sky, under the
> merciless brilliance of the sun, the dazzled eye misses the delicate
> detail, sees only the strong outlines, while the colours, in the
> steady light, seem crude and without shadow. Nevertheless it is
> the same picture.

The mirror effect involves not only the revelation of virtual moral
equivalence between the two juxtaposed parties, but also a degree of
patterning among the characters and events, such that the foremost
figures and actions of one party are often counterbalanced by
similar but opposing persons and pursuits of the other.

The mirror effect is vital to the paradox of Conrad's plots, since it
entails that any significant move towards either pole of the dualism
will be countered by an equal but opposite move towards the other.
There is again a corresponding principle in the Wagnerian
universe. As Wotan conceives Valhalla, Alberich forges the Ring;
the gods retire to their sky-fortress while Fafner sleeps with the Ring
in a cave; and when Wotan begets the Walsungs to act as his agents
in the Ring's recovery, Alberich similarly begets Hagen, who is
Siegfried's antagonist in the final encounter. The outcome in the

Ring story is a cycle; all action is countered and negated until the story ends and the original harmony is restored. Conrad's universe is generally less serenely organized, leaving us with a sense of paralysis, a futility against which human assertion, although sometimes dignified and worthy, is ultimately vain. Thus, in *Almayer's Folly*, every move the hero makes towards his European goal at the same time binds him more firmly to Sambir. Almayer's partnership with Lingard initially involves marriage to a Malay woman, and we later note that at the point where Almayer optimistically begins work on his new European-style house his native wife re-emerges to torment him (p. 33). When Almayer begins his plans to hunt for Lingard's treasure Mrs Almayer and Babalatchi begin to plot against him (pp. 38–39), and as Almayer finds an ally in Dain he is at the same time obliged against his will to enter into illicit dealings with Lakamba (pp. 59, 62).

The Conradian hero generally becomes enmeshed in this conflicting dualism by electing to pursue his ideal through some specific morally ambivalent act, often involving a kind of deception, desertion, or betrayal. These initial deeds present at first sight a bewildering variety – Willems' betrayal of Lingard, Wait's malingering, Jim's "jump" into Patusan, Gould's repossession of the mine, Verloc's attempt upon the observatory, Razumov's betrayal of Haldin, Anthony's rescue of Flora – but they can usually be seen to involve the seizing of an "opportunity" (to take the term applied in *Lord Jim*) which, if not exactly unlawful in all cases, is at least an easy option or an unearned advantage, for which the hero will at some time be called to account.

The moral flavour of these acts varies with the degree of sympathy which the hero's objectives can command. Gould and Jim, for instance, begin with relatively elevated aims which circumstances oblige them to modify, whereas Willems and Verloc, in their different ways, are motivated primarily by self-indulgence. In most cases the moral evaluation remains ambivalent, because Conrad's universe eschews clear ethical alternatives. The aims and actions of the heroes are generally complex; altruism is tainted with selfishness, idealism with materialism, liberality with intolerance, self-effacement with imposition. Conrad does not take sides unreservedly for or against his heroes, just as he avoids commitment to either pole of the conceptual dualisms against which most of his stories are set.

Almayer, along with some of the heroes of Conrad's other early stories, is an extreme case, because his initial action is without redeeming features and clearly reprehensible in both its immediate circumstances and its purposes. In order to share in Lingard's fortune Almayer accepts marriage with a native woman, whose race he despises and with whose values he has no sympathy, while at the same time agreeing to reside for an indefinite period among her countrymen in a place for which he has no liking. His only significant reason is his avarice and his failure to satisfy it in the white world. These early stories are atypical of the Conrad canon, because the usual moral ambivalence, the conflict of feelings about the hero's actions, is largely absent. Almayer, although a rounded figure commanding our understanding and more than a touch of sympathy, fails to sound the discord of contrasting values which was to be the keynote of Conrad's mature work. Almayer's fate, foreseeable and deserved, illustrates only the folly and moral degeneracy of his initial endeavour. Not until Wait and Kurtz did Conrad begin to build networks of appreciable moral tension around his central figures, a move which, as we shall see, entailed a new approach to his overall fictional pattern.

The mechanics of a typical Conradian plot consist essentially in an initial exertion of will from the hero precipitating a situation in which his every significant step towards his goal is met by an opposing force, until a catastrophe occurs in which the goal is lost completely. This design to some extent dictates the way in which the stories are unfolded. The movement of a Conradian story characteristically requires a slow, protracted beginning, setting out the hero's motives, the circumstances of his initial act, and the early stages of the contrapuntal tension of the contextual dualism. This is followed by a dramatic acceleration of narrative pace into the catastrophe. The first, usually longer stage is frequently covered retrospectively or through a complex of interior narrators, while the second stage, the catastrophe, is almost always told directly and without subnarrative interference. Such, with variations, is the procedure in *Lord Jim*, *Nostromo*, *Chance*, and *Victory*, and the same method is discernible already in *Almayer's Folly*.

The hero generally precipitates the catastrophe by continued striving in the context of mounting tension, but in its accomplishment he is largely passive, suffering the state of affairs he has created to release its own energy. The active figures at this stage are his opponents, the rival, the nemesis, and the anti-heroine, frequently enmeshing in their doings the heroine, from whom the hero is to be divorced as a result. Again *Almayer's Folly* sets the pattern which most of Conrad's later long novels follow; after a lengthy and largely retrospective narration has brought the story to the point of Dain's return to Sambir, Almayer is deprived of all means of effective action while the plot of Dain, Nina, and Mrs Almayer unwinds swiftly before his eyes.

The mainspring of the catastrophe in Conrad's first novel is the heroine's dual racial background, combined with her ultimate decision to desert her white father for a native lover. Nina is taken from her father by Dain in a plot concocted largely by Mrs Almayer, who functions as the anti-heroine in that she opposes the relationship between the heroine and the hero. This aspect of the pattern in *Almayer's Folly* is unusual in that the hero and heroine are not lovers but father and daughter, and that the anti-heroine is not therefore the heroine's sexual rival. Nina is none the less the focus of her father's wishes, to which Mrs Almayer stands in direct opposition. As Nina's mother, Mrs Almayer has no hostility towards the heroine, but is vitally concerned to separate her daughter from the hero. Her jealousy of Nina's affection for Almayer comes out most strongly when she prevents the girl from turning back to take a last look at her father before joining Dain in flight (pp. 150–1). The Almayer–Nina–Mrs Almayer relationship in Conrad's first novel is atypical, in that the hero and heroine are not lovers but father and daughter, but is very close to the Wotan–Brunnhilde–Fricka relationship in Wagner's *Ring*.

Mrs Almayer devises the trick whereby Dain eludes captivity and escapes with Nina, an achievement which gives her great satisfaction, because it brings Nina the kind of marriage she herself had wished for, with a strong man of her own people. With Nina's desertion the wheel has come in a full circle for Almayer, the woman he married for money having deprived him of the daughter for whose sake the money was to be spent. Appropriately Mrs Almayer herself leaves the white man at this point, taking refuge with Lakamba, her former lover. With the daughter's departure the plot, unwound, has no further momentum, and the marriage which began Almayer's career is finally dissolved.

The reason why Conrad made the hero and heroine of his first novel father and daughter instead of lovers, as they are in most of the subsequent stories, extends into his whole conception of the plot. He could have made Mrs Almayer the heroine and Lakamba the rival, a course at which he glances in making these two past lovers. (In the later stories both Jim and Kurtz are white men whose heroine-lovers are native women who embody their respective ideals.) Nina is a much more active figure than any of Conrad's later heroines until Flora de Barral, in that the catastrophe depends primarily upon her movement from her father to his rival, a conscious choice in the pursuit of which she takes a dynamic part. Nina's choice involves a movement between the black and white worlds of which Mrs Almayer would be incapable, but which is open to her half-white daughter. The weight which Conrad's first novel places upon the heroine's decision between two opposing worlds, in both of which she has a place, virtually requires that the role fall to the child of a mixed marriage rather than to a woman of pure descent.

The heroine's dynamism in *Almayer's Folly* is matched by the hero's unusual passivity in his new environment. Subsequent heroes in the novels of Conrad's first phase strive arduously to create and reshape the worlds to which they withdraw. Jim and Kurtz are obvious examples. Almayer's one object in Sambir, however, is to get away. His only effort to shape his new home in the image of his ideal is the house, his "folly", which remains a hollow ruin. Beyond this, the story of his life in the jungle, contrasting sharply with the careers of Kurtz, Jim, and even Willems, is one of continuous decline into apathy. Most of Conrad's early heroes, moving into new worlds, attempt to take possession and to build there what they had been unable to realize elsewhere, but Almayer makes only the vaguest gestures in this direction.

Almayer's failure to establish any dynamic relationship with his black environment may be another reason why the heroine of his story is a daughter and not a lover. Conrad's heroines, up to and including Miss Haldin in *Under Western Eyes*, are associated not only with the heroes' ideals but also with the environments or ways of life against the background of which the heroes' fates are decided. Aissa, Jewel, and Mrs Gould are clear examples. The hero's creative possession of his environment is generally symbolized in a love relationship with the heroine. That there is no such creative possession in *Almayer's Folly* may be another reason for the non-sexual relationship of Nina and Almayer.

The love between Nina and Dain is the immediate cause of the novel's catastrophe, but the ultimate cause is the hero's final and greatest effort to achieve his ideal. Almayer's last attempt to leave Sambir is his alliance with Dain, whose abiding interest turns out to be not with the father's plans but with the daughter. The last phase of Almayer's self-defeating struggle thus consists in his introduction of the man who will rob him of the child upon whom he has centred his ideals. The means whereby Almayer engineers this phase of the plot is Lingard's treasure, the first in a line of Conradian hoards which function as catalysts in the action of his novels. Almayer's supposed knowledge of the treasure's whereabouts prevents Lakamba from killing him and elicits Dain's promise of assistance. It is in order to obtain the treasure that Almayer joins Dain and Lakamba in the powder-smuggling venture, which leads directly to Dain's loss of his ship and to his departure as a fugitive with Nina. As a motivating force Lingard's treasure has a function comparable to that of Wagner's Rheingold, and is echoed in Conrad's later novels by the silver of Gould's mine, Heyst's supposed fortune, Kurtz' ivory, and Wait's money.

Like the Rheingold and Nostromo's silver, however, Lingard's treasure is a symbol of paradox, being both the ostensible means to achievement and a counteractive force. Wotan desires the gold to secure Valhalla, but finds that his possession of the fortress is conditional upon his relinquishing the treasure, by the power of which his plans will be brought to nothing. Gould, similarly, finds his ideals corrupted by the "material interests" generated by the very silver upon which his success depends. Lingard's treasure, a less complex image in Conrad's first novel, works in a recognizably similar way, as both a means whereby the hero might at last achieve his end and as the force whereby that achievement is frustrated.

Almayer sees the treasure as a means to realize his hopes for Nina, whereas in fact his very attempt to possess it brings about her flight into the world from which he wishes to remove her. Not only does Almayer introduce Dain, his rival for Nina, in order to obtain the treasure, but he also becomes so engrossed in his schemes and visions concerning the gold that he begins to lose contact with his daughter at the very time when she is falling under Dain's influence.

For the last fortnight Almayer was absorbed in the preparations, walking amongst his workmen and slaves in a kind of waking trance, where practical details as to the fitting out of the boats were mixed up with vivid dreams of untold wealth, where the present misery of burning sun, of the muddy and malodorous river bank disappeared in a gorgeous vision of a splendid future existence for himself and Nina. He hardly saw Nina during these last days, although the beloved daughter was ever present in his thoughts. He hardly took notice of Dain, whose constant presence in his house had become a matter of course to him now they were connected by a community of interests (pp. 62–3).

In a sense Nina is for Almayer an alternative to the treasure, much as Freia in Wagner's *Rheingold* can be restored to the gods only in a carefully measured exchange for the coveted gold. On two occasions in *Almayer's Folly* Nina is the subject of a comparable transaction, first when Abdulla offers Almayer three thousand dollars to purchase her as a wife for Reshid (p. 45), and again when Dain does in fact give Mrs Almayer a small fortune for clearing his way to her daughter (p. 66–7). Nina is shown in this way to be herself a valuable commodity, which Almayer eventually loses as a result of his pursuit of the treasure.

Conrad's first major work therefore concerns a hero (Almayer) whose object in life is ease and opulence and who exerts himself to this end by accepting Lingard's offer of partnership. The action is a compromise, because it involves the hero in an unhappy interracial marriage, and it therefore precipitates a dualistic conflict in which the hero becomes helplessly enmeshed. He wants to escape the black world, to which he has allied himself, and to return to the white world, but he finds that every move he makes to get away from Sambir involves him more deeply in its affairs. Using Lingard's treasure as his putative means, Almayer makes a last attempt, enlisting Dain as his chief agent, but Dain deserts the white man and instead runs away with his cherished daughter. The loss of Nina, the story's heroine, leaves Almayer without further incentive. He abandons his plans and eventually dies. Related in this brief and simple way, *Almayer's Folly* is closely comparable to Wagner's *Ring*. In both stories the hero's initial endeavour creates a dualistic conflict which results in his own separation from the heroine and in the final defeat of his hopes.

Almayer's Folly is a simpler story than most of Conrad's later novels. Central to it is Almayer himself, whose character and situation are less intricate than those of his successors. His ideals are largely selfish and exclusively material, and as a result his exertion of will, his acceptance of Lingard's terms of partnership, is a morally straightforward act of greed. It follows that there is a virtual absence of moral tension in Almayer's act. Where the later novels present a deep moral and ethical impasse, *Almayer's Folly* is concerned with the more general and superficial irony of the self-frustration of planned endeavour.

For the same central reason the story is lacking in certain structural features common to the later novels. The hero's relation to the heroine is not sexual, and there is no confrontation between the hero and an agent of nemesis. Conrad's next novel, *An Outcast of the Islands*, moves in the direction of the subsequent works chiefly by giving its hero a goal more enlarged than mere personal gain, by pairing him sexually with the heroine, and by confronting him with a retributive figure from the world he has deserted.

2 *An Outcast of the Islands*

Conrad's second novel is superficially very close to his first, employing the same setting, many of the same characters, and the very similar central figure of a white man joined to a native woman in the isolation of the jungle. There can be no doubt that the author was conservatively reworking the material of his first novel, taking as he did so several significant steps towards the burst of mature writing that was to begin with *The Nigger of the 'Narcissus'* in 1896.

Willems' career in *An Outcast of the Islands* is similar to that of Almayer in *Almayer's Folly*. Both men are initially clerks working humbly for Hudig in Macassar while desiring better things for themselves. They are further alike, and distinct from most of Conrad's later heroes, in that their ideal consists chiefly in personal advancement and gain. In pursuit of their respective personal goals both men advance by contracting interracial marriages with the "daughters" of wealthy capitalists; Almayer takes the adopted Malay protégée of Lingard, while Willems marries the half-caste Joanna, who turns out to be the natural child of old Hudig. In each case the marriage begins a train of events which leads to the hero's isolation in Sambir, a black world which contrasts as an inverted mirror image with the white world of his origin. Both men then continue their strivings in a hostile jungle context to the point where the tensions they create bring about their deaths. Both men, in their closing stages, project their ideals on to a female, Almayer's Nina and Willems' Aissa, who is in each case a native of the Malay world; and in each case there is both an anti-heroine opposing the native woman's association with the hero and a male rival for the heroine's affections.

An Outcast of the Islands exhibits immediately the constant features of the Conradian pattern: a hero who, in striving towards a goal, makes a dubious, compromising move and finds himself caught as a result in a dualistic universe where his every significant action is countered or frustrated. Willems' ideal, very like Almayer's, is self-aggrandisement, in pursuit of which he embarks upon a career which receives its first real impulse when, at Hudig's behest, he marries Joanna, a half-caste woman who is later revealed to be his employer's daughter. This move is very close to the compromise made by Almayer in agreeing to wed Lingard's adopted child. Both men take women to whom they are personally indifferent in return for the patronage and promises of a powerful, wealthy father-in-law, and in each case the marriage of convenience involves the compromise that the woman is of a race regarded as inferior by the local whites. The marriages, emblematic of paradox, announce Conrad's major theme, the inherent self-frustration of human endeavour, for in each case the hero, in pursuit of social elevation, contracts a marriage which, although profitable, is felt to be socially degrading.

Almayer's marriage is immediately bound up with his deportation to Sambir, and that of Willems is the first cause in a sequence of happenings leading to the same end, entailing the drain on his resources occasioned by his wife's poor relations, his peculation of Hudig's funds to maintain his position, and his eventual discovery, shame and self-exile. Willems exhibits a deep-rooted moral laxity which both prompts his marriage and brings about his subsequent misadventures. He is a typical Conradian hero in that, unable or unwilling to work towards his goal by means of unaided effort, he seeks and finds dubious short cuts which bring him a measure of success but which at the same time compromise his aims. His failure as a seaman is symptomatic of this laxity. "The boy [young Willems] was hopelessly at variance with the spirit of the sea. He had an instinctive contempt for the honest simplicity of that work which led to nothing he cared for" (p. 17). The same desire for an "easy berth", clearly recognizable in Wait, Jim, Verloc, and the young hero of *The Shadow-Line*, causes Willems to fall into the arranged marriage with Hudig's daughter and later leads him to embezzlement as an alternative to self-discipline.

Willems' attempt to achieve wealthy respectability in Macassar lands him ironically in Sambir and activates the mechanism of a dualistic situation by which he is eventually destroyed. The antithesis of black and white worlds, the jungle of Sambir and the gardens of Macassar, works in much the same way here as it does in *Almayer's Folly*. The hero sees the black world as the mere negation of everything he desires – obscurity instead of fame, squalor instead of opulence, savagery instead of civility – but is none the less obliged, as a result of his own initial choice of indirection, to make this the scene of his endeavours. At the same time, however, the black world is seen by the reader to be not a simple opposite to the white, but an inverted image of it, a restatement in a minor key. Willems' situation in Macassar, in which he attaches himself to a woman, steals from her father, and is eventually confronted with his crime, is closely repeated in Sambir, where he "steals" Aissa from Omar, betrays Lingard's secrets in order to keep her, and is marooned in punishment by Lingard on his return. Moreover Willems' movements in Sambir, principally his usurpation of Lingard's authority and association with Aissa, are countered from the white world by the successive arrivals of Lingard and Joanna. The dynamism of the plot consists essentially in the tension created by the antithetical tendencies of these two worlds, a situation first precipitated by the hero's strivings and only resolved by his death.

The root of the chief structural difference between *An Outcast of the Islands* and *Almayer's Folly* is Willems' active and, in a sense, constructive relation to the black world. Almayer in Sambir merely declines, his one object being to escape to the white world of his dreams. Willems, on the other hand, in a way which looks forward to *Lord Jim*, begins by rejecting the white world, turning his back on Almayer in Sambir and on Lingard's promise of reinstatement in Macassar, and making himself an outcast rather than face humiliation among his own people. The immediate result is a considerable intensification of the paradox which centres upon the Conradian hero. Almayer exemplifies the relatively simple irony that human endeavour is self-defeating; he is a morally weak character whose willingness to accept easy options in pursuit of his goals places him in a situation in which every step forward is taken at the expense of two steps back. Willems is the same, but with the significant addition that he is not without unusual abilities; his eventual failure is the result not simply of weakness but also of a distinctive quality which, in its function, is akin to the idiosyncratic brilliance which sets apart Kurtz and Jim from the run of humankind. Willems, precisely because of the same laxity of principle which prompts him to make fatal compromises, is a highly successful businessman in Macassar before his fall. In Sambir, where Willems re-enacts a "black" version of his Macassar life, this same ability and lack of scruple enables him to become temporarily a leader and arbiter of local destiny. The hero of Conrad's second novel is more complex than Almayer in being not only flawed but also exceptional, and the mirror-world of Sambir reflects not only his failure but also his achievements. Willems, as the man of great promise who turns out to be unsound, prefigures the line of more developed paradoxical heroes which begins with Wait and Kurtz.

Willems in Sambir is therefore not simply an outcast but also, as Aissa calls him, "the great man of the place" (p. 70). It is this aura of unspecified greatness that attracts Aissa to him.

> To her he was something new, unknown and strange. He was bigger, stronger than any man she had seen before, and altogether different from all those she knew. He was of the victorious race. With a vivid remembrance of the great cata-strophe of her life he appeared to her with all the fascination of a great and dangerous thing; of a terror vanquished, surmounted, made a plaything of. They spoke with just such a deep voice – those victorious men; they looked with just such hard blue eyes at their enemies. And she made that voice speak softly to her, those eyes look tenderly at her face. He was indeed a man (p. 75).

Aissa is the symbol of Willems' success and the embodiment of his ideal in the black world, just as is Joanna in the white. Joanna emerges from the cultivated gardens and social milieu of Macassar, much as Aissa is identified with the jungle background in which Willems finds her, the "very spirit of that land of mysterious forests" (p. 70). Each woman comes to Willems finally as a reward for the exercise of his commercial acumen, in helping first Hudig and then Abdulla to promote their trades, the same sharp practice which also, in each world respectively, involves him in theft and betrayal.

Both Joanna and Aissa are first attracted to Willems by his reputed greatness, and each woman becomes in turn the auditor of his self-glorifying monologues. Joanna in Macassar was made to get up at nights when Willems came home late and to listen to him "explaining . . . how great and good he was" (p. 9); in Sambir Willems tells Aissa the story of his life, which "she made up for herself into a story of a man great amongst his own people" (p. 75). Each woman in turn, as receptor of Willems' view of himself and as his reward for practical achievement, signifies his goal in life, one in the white world, the other in the black. The structure of the story, with the Sambir episode at its centre, confirms Aissa as the heroine in terms of our pattern. Joanna, a drab figure of passionless conventionality and Willems' lawful wife, is a typical anti-heroine, returning at the end of the story to preside over the hero's final

divorce from Aissa. Joanna's object at that late stage is to fetch
Willems back to the world he has deserted, the world of their
marriage, his business connections, and white respectability. The
way in which she takes residence in Almayer's European-style
"office", a place long disused and with no practical function in
Sambir, is symbolic of her role and purpose in the story.

The difference between Almayer and Willems as Conradian
heroes manifests itself in the dynamic relation which the latter
establishes with the black world, taking a native woman as his lover
and effecting a radical change in local politics in a manner
prefigurative of Kurtz and Jim. The heroine is here, as she was to be
in most of the later novels, the hero's lover, not his daughter.
Through the heroine, and through his active involvement with
native life, the hero takes possession of the black world as a possible
place for the realization of his ideal. Willems' new relation to the
black world is represented symbolically after his first meeting with
the heroine.

> Willems never remembered how and when he parted from Aissa.
> He caught himself drinking the muddy water out of the hollow of
> his hand, while his canoe was drifting in mid-stream past the last
> houses of Sambir. . . . His face felt burning. He drank again, and
> shuddered with a depraved sense of pleasure at the after-taste of
> slime in the water (pp. 72–3).

The drinking of the river water, something Almayer would not have
done, is a sign of Willems' initiation into his new world.

His relationship with the heroine, symptomatic of Willems' over-
all position in Sambir, is ambiguous and ultimately unsatisfactory.
He is himself a man of paradox, a man of exceptional cleverness yet
with weaknesses which render him stupid and, like the typical
Conradian hero, he is caught in a paradoxical situation between
two worlds. Whatever he does proves unsatisfactory, and whichever
world he choses for his efforts finally throws him back to the other.
Willems' relationship with Aissa has, for him, the character of
demonic possession.

> As she spoke she made a step nearer, then another. Willems did
> not stir. Pressing against him she stood on tiptoe to look into his
> eyes, and her own seemed to grow bigger, glistening and tender,
> appealing and promising. With that look she drew the man's soul

away from him through his immobile pupils, and from Willems' features the spark of reason vanished under her gaze and was replaced by an appearance of physical well-being, an ecstasy of the senses which had taken possession of his rigid body; an ecstasy that drove out regrets, hesitation and doubt, and proclaimed its terrible work by an appalling aspect of idiotic beatitude (p. 140).

As Willems falls increasingly under Aissa's spell he senses a gradual "flight of [his] old self" (p. 69), a loss of "individuality" (p. 77). "He seemed to be surrendering to a wild creature the unstained purity of his life, of his race, of his civilization. He had a notion of being lost among shapeless things that were dangerous and ghastly" (p. 80). Just as Willems' deeper sexual instincts, of which he seems scarcely aware, make him dissatisfied with Joanna, so, conversely, his sense of the white world's civilized proprieties makes him ashamed of and resistant to his desire for Aissa. He feels "contempt for himself as the slave of a passion he had always derided, as the man unable to assert his will. This will, all his sensations, his personality – all this seemed to be lost in the abominable desire, in the priceless promise of that woman" (pp. 128–9). He is unable to live in peace with either heroine, unable to rest content in either world, because of the pull exerted by the other. His death follows fittingly from the final meeting of these two complementary but opposite female figures.

Aissa herself, although attracted to Willems on account of his supposed greatness, is strongly antipathetic to the white world of his origin. "What is that land beyond the great sea from which you come?" she asks him. "A land of lies and of evil from which nothing but misfortune ever comes to us – who are not white" (p. 144). The antagonism between the two worlds, itself a reflection of Willems' conflicting desires and paradoxical inclinations, is manifested in Aissa's hatred of whites, which makes it impossible for Willems to resolve the situation by taking her back to civilization. She will neither let him go alone nor accompany him.

The hostility of the black world, muted towards the hero in Aissa, is given free rein in the character of Omar, the heroine's father and Willems' rival for her affections. The conception of the rival figure has changed considerably from that in *Almayer's Folly*, a change to some extent conditioned by the hero's more dynamic relation to the heroine and the black world. Omar is not, like Dain, brought into the story as the hero's agent, but has a pre-established claim on the heroine which the hero dislodges, inviting reprisal. In this respect

Omar is in line with most of the later Conradian rivals: Cornelius in *Lord Jim*, Schomberg in *Victory*, Ortega in *The Arrow of Gold*, Mr Travers in *The Rescue*, and Scevola in *The Rover*.

The rival's role is typically a small one, but may none the less be a factor in bringing the catastrophe upon the hero, usually as a result of an attempted act of jealous vengeance after the hero's intervention has carried off the heroine. Omar is aroused by what is, from his point of view, Willems' "theft" of Aissa. Almayer points this out, indicating at the same time the parallelism between this theft and Willems' appropriation of Hudig's funds in Macassar. " 'So you did steal,' he went on, with repressed exultation. 'I thought there was something of the kind. And now, here, you steal again. . . . Oh, I don't mean from me. I haven't missed anything. . . . But that girl. Hey! You stole her. You did not pay the old fellow. She is no good to him now, is she?' " (p. 89). Omar, the "old fellow", who is blind and on the verge of death, therefore makes a pathetic attempt to kill Willems, which is easily prevented by Aissa but which shows Willems for the first time the underlying falsity of his position in Sambir.

> It was the unreasoning fear of this glimpse into the unknown things, into those motives, impulses, desires he had ignored, but that had lived in the breasts of despised men, close by his side, and were revealed to him for a second, to be hidden again behind the black mists of doubt and deception. It was not death that frightened him: it was the horror of bewildered life where he could understand nothing and nobody round him; where he could guide, control, comprehend nothing and no one – not even himself (p. 149).

From this point, even although he keeps his bargain with Abdulla in order to avoid separation from Aissa, Willems is desirous of escape from Sambir, recognizing the fatal hostility towards him which Omar embodies. Willems enjoys a temporary relief when, after bringing the Arab ship into the river, he becomes momentarily a man of local prestige, witnesses Omar's death and burns down the old man's hut. But Willems cannot sustain his position in the black world, which is founded on betrayal and deception, and the old hostility reasserts itself in the plots of Abdulla and Babalatchi, both of whom profess the highest regard for the departed Omar and are scandalized by the relationship between the white man and Aissa.

When Aissa finally shoots Willems as he attempts to leave her, she is prompted by "the whisper of the dead Omar's voice saying in her ear: 'Kill! Kill!'" (p. 359).

The first great structural advance Conrad takes in his second novel is to deepen the pardadox inherent in the central figure, making Willems not only an instance of the futility of human endeavour but more specifically a man who fails just because his exceptional qualities, his "cleverness" and companionability, are inextricably mixed with his weaknesses, his lack of clear moral principle and love of self-inflation. As a direct result of this change in the hero, his relation to the heroine is also altered, as are the roles of the heroine and the rival. The second advance to be observed in terms of the structural pattern is the introduction of a new figure, the agent of nemesis, who appears in order to block the hero's way at the end of the story, in explicit or symbolic reprisal for some act of offence the hero has committed in pursuit of his goal, coming in order to confront him with an adverse moral view of his conduct. This figure functions by means of the dualistic mechanism operative in most of Conrad's novels; he comes from the world or party the hero has abandoned or betrayed, and acts in such a way as to restore the moral balance which the hero's compromise has upset. The essence of his task is forcefully to remind the hero of the standards or principles he has deserted and, whether deliberately or unintentionally, to institute a corrective punishment, which generally involves the hero's fall and destruction. The figure of this type later becomes an *alter ego* in the sense that, coming from the hero's former world and representing to him what he has done, the nemesis is either, like Marlow in *Heart of Darkness*, the kind of man the hero should have been, or, like Brown in *Lord Jim* and Jones in *Victory*, a contorted image of the man he has become.

Lingard is recognizable as a nemesis figure in *An Outcast of the Islands* when his part there is compared to the line of similar roles in the later novels. There is no very clear *alter ego* relationship between Lingard and Willems, but Lingard does meet the criteria of coming (back) into the story after the hero has committed an act of betrayal, of himself representing a simple (and therefore somewhat limited) moral code which the hero has abandoned, and of proceeding to a confrontation and pronouncement of judgment against the hero. Lingard is a heavy-handed creation in *An Outcast of the Islands*, a novel whose chief structural flaw is the way in which, contrary to Conrad's usual practice, the pace slows and drags in the second movement of the story (i.e. after Lingard's re-entry). Lingard is best regarded as a sketch for the more complex *alter ego* relationships which occur climactically in many of the later novels.

A precondition for the development of the nemesis figure in the Conradian pattern is the hero's commission of an act for which retribution is in order. Almayer's selfish pursuits in the first novel do no real harm to anyone but himself, and his eventual collapse follows from the situation he himself creates, not from the intervention of the outside world. Willems is different, for in his strivings he betrays and defrauds first Hudig and then Lingard. Lingard's final confrontation with Willems is essentially a response to provocation, which ends in an explicit judgement and sentence of the offending hero. Willems is the first of a line of Conradian heroes who attempt to achieve their ideal by committing some real or reputed offence, usually in the nature of a crime, against the world or code they are abandoning. Lingard is the first of the counteractive figures who are generally responsible for ending the heroes' careers.

Lingard sees himself as a "doer of Justice"(p. 224). "Justice only! Nothing was further from his thoughts than such an useless thing as revenge. Justice only. It was his duty that justice should be done – and by his own hand" (p. 223). As the man who had introduced Willems into this world Lingard feels obliged to oversee the imposition of restraint upon his dangerous protégé. His rigid insistence upon what he sincerely believes to be a just and impartial solution distinguishes Lingard from many of the more complex figures Conrad later created for this role, men like Brown and Jones, who are themselves criminals and embittered outcasts from society. Lingard, Conrad's first essay in the nemesis type, is by contrast a figure of disarming and almost incredible simplicity. His heavy-fisted enactment of a naive notion of justice is one of the weaknesses which sets *An Outcast of the Islands* apart from Conrad's major work. Lingard plays his part explicitly, confronting Willems openly as accuser and judge, where later nemesis figures, beginning with Allistoun, perform this function implicitly, symbolically, whilst pursuing overt aims which may be very different. It was precisely the development of the *alter ego* aspect of this figure which added a new metaphysical dimension to Conrad's work in and after *Heart of Darkness*.

The nemesis figure generally exposes the weaknesses of the hero's moral position and therewith the unresolved anomalies in his relation with the heroine. In this story the latent misunderstanding between Willems and Aissa is brought to the surface by Lingard's condemnation of the hero to perpetual confinement in Sambir, and Willems' true nature as a man without friends or influence is revealed by Lingard's conduct towards him. The heroine, who typically embodies the hero's ideal and glorified image of himself, is naturally resistent to the "truth" which Lingard brings from what is to her an alien world.

Here, then, is a second group of structural developments in *An Outcast of the Islands* which, like the first group already mentioned, follows from the increased moral complexity of the central figure. We have seen that the new dynamism of Willems, compared to the relative passivity of Almayer in *Almayer's Folly*, results from his endowment with positive, active powers, and involves corresponding developments in the roles of the heroine and the rival. Similarly the deepening of the other side of the hero's paradoxical nature by making him guilty of specific acts of betrayal in the very exercise of his abilities opens the way to the first introduction of the nemesis into the pattern. The chief structural differences between Conrad's two first novels therefore have a common root in the deepening and complication of the hero's moral nature.

When we compare Willems to such of his successors as Jim, Gould, or Razumov, he seems a pale and unsophisticated creature, lacking the depth and intensity of conflicting motives which characterize the mature Conradian hero; yet traces of the basic structural ingredients of the later heroes can be found in him. Although neither his abilities nor his flaws are great or singular, he is a figure of paradox whose special qualities, his cleverness, his business sense and companionability, are also the cause of his crimes, his thefts and betrayals. His goals remain largely selfish and his offences, in human terms, rather small misdemeanours, but the conflict within the paradoxical central character stands none the less at the focal point of the story.

An Outcast of the Islands is in many ways a transitional work, itself a rather poorly structured piece, standing chronologically between the highly-crafted but much simpler *Almayer's Folly*, and the first product of Conrad's literary maturity, the superb *Nigger of the 'Narcissus'*. Key concepts lacking in the first novel are here introduced: the hero's paradoxical nature, his positive achievement (symbolized in his relationship with the heroine), his concomitant act of criminal betrayal, and the consequent retribution (embodied here in Lingard, the prototypical Conradian nemesis). These elements are handled here with some uncertainty – Willems, compared to the later heroes, lacks depth and intensity, Aissa is an exaggerated and unoriginal creation, while Lingard's part is excessively protracted – yet they are the essential ingredients of the greater novels which were to follow.

3 The Short Stories of 1896

An Outcast of the Islands was completed in September 1895, and published in the following year. Conrad's next major work was to be *The Nigger of the 'Narcissus'*, which occupied him from June 1896, to February 1897. Between these two he wrote three short stories, *The Idiots, An Outpost of Progress*, and *The Lagoon*, and a fragment of what promised to be a full-length novel entitled *The Sisters*. From this time forward it became Conrad's practice to compose short stories between, and sometimes during, his labours on longer pieces, primarily in order to earn money and to keep his name before the public. With few exceptions the short stories do not have the stature of his major fiction and were regarded by himself as of less importance. They cannot be put aside form a study of his creative development, however, because there is clear evidence that Conrad did not always set about the composition of his shorter pieces in a different frame of mind from that in which he approached a novel or novella. Conrad's method as a writer of fiction was usually to begin with a single episode – often an event which he had witnessed or of which he had read – and to build a story around it. Many of the longer novels, including some of his best, are known to have grown from what were initially conceived as short stories concerning such episodes. *Lord Jim* began with the tale of the ship abandoned at sea by its officers, *Chance* is first mentioned in 1898 as a short story called *Dynamite*, *The Secret Agent* grew from Conrad's interest in the attempted bombing of Greenwich Observatory, and *Nostromo* began as a story of the incident of the lighter of silver. Conrad himself was generally unable to predict whether a new story would remain a short piece confined to a single incident or whether it would evolve into a longer and more complex work. It is therefore not surprising that many of his short stories are related thematically to his longer writings and can in some cases be seen as essays involving structural features being developed concurrently in the novels.

Of the four stories written in 1896 one can be set aside. *The Idiots*,

which arose from Conrad's encounter with a group of children on
his honeymoon holiday in Brittany, bears no significant relation to
the structural pattern we are examining. Of the remaining tales, *An
Outpost of Progress* belongs to Conrad's sequence of stories concerning
the isolated white man making and breaking his fortune in a
primitive jungle environment, a sequence which begins with
Almayer's Folly and *An Outcast of the Islands* and includes *Heart of
Darkness* and *Lord Jim*. Both this story and *The Lagoon* present
miniature versions of the pattern Conrad had evolved in his first two
novels.

An Outpost of Progress concerns a pair of unimpressive heroes of
much the same general type as Almayer and Willems, morally weak
men, used to the comfortable materialistic standards of white
civilization, who are prepared to compromise when an easy means
to prosperity is offered them in the jungle. Kayerts and Carlier are
promised quick profits as managers of a jungle trading station, the
same fundamental situation as that of Almayer and, later, of Kurtz.
Their compromise involves paradox in that they accept a life of
hardship, isolation and savagery in expectation of eventual luxury
and social elevation. Two conflicting ways of life, represented
respectively by the black and white worlds, are thereby brought into
play, in much the same way as in the earlier novels; the white
civilization of the heroes' origins, which they remember and
endeavour to emulate, contrasts with the alien, primitive standards
of the jungle around them.

The tension between the two worlds, the strain upon the central
figures as white men in a black environment, in their case very much
as in that of Willems, results in a criminal act. Just as Willems,
through the machinations of Babalatchi and Aissa, is made to
betray Lingard in order to maintain himself in Sambir, so Kayerts
and Carlier become accessories to the sale of slaves in order to
preserve their station against a band of armed blacks.

Once again the two worlds are not simple opposites, and the
white men are not simply corrupted by the black environment to
which they are transplanted. Like Willems, they bring their
weaknesses with them and give way under the pressures of the
transplantation. The black natives are, like the whites, a mixture of
peaceable men and ruthless opportunists; the slavery transaction,
initiated by the black Makola, is eventually accepted by Kayerts
and Carlier with the conviction that the European director of their
company has often "seen worse things done on the quiet" (p. 109).

The two worlds are morally more or less equivalent, and black and white levels of conduct, here as in *Almayer's Folly*, are to be compared rather than contrasted. In what may be a significant aside, Conrad says of the language of the black slavers that it was like "something not exactly familiar, and yet resembling the speech of civilized men" (p. 97).

The crime of Kayerts and Carlier, which follows from their initial paradoxical choice, is but one step in a decline which deepens steadily as the tension of their situation grows. Like Almayer and Willems, although in a more general and cursory way, they become enmeshed in the alien world.

> It was not the absolute and dumb solitude of the post that impressed them so much as an inarticulate feeling that something from within them was gone, something that worked for their safety, and had kept the wilderness from interfering with their hearts. The images of home; the memory of people like them, of men that thought and felt as they used to think and feel, receded into distances made indistinct by the glare of unclouded sunshine. And out of the great silence of the surrounding wilderness, its very hopelessness and savagery seemed to approach them nearer, to draw them gently, to look upon them, to envelop them with a solicitude irresistible, familiar, and disgusting (pp. 107–8).

Like Willems, they suffer an increasing loss of their "old selves", and like Kurtz they drift into an animal way of thinking, which is the very opposite of the ideals with which they began. Carlier "talked about the necessity of exterminating all the niggers before the country could be made habitable" (p. 108).

Sick and demoralized, the two men drift into a series of trivial personal disputes, in the last of which Kayerts mistakenly shoots and kills his companion. Before the body can be buried the company director returns with his steamer, and Kayerts hangs himself in fear and remorse. The catastrophe which concludes the story is a recognizable short version of the usual Conradian ending, in which a figure from the hero's former world arrives to pass (in this case merely to witness) judgment. The director, rather like Lingard in *An Outcast of the Islands*, is a man of their own world whom the heroes wish to imitate and appease but whom, in the event, they offend by their conduct. The final picture of the hanged body of Kayerts "irreverently . . . putting out a swollen tongue at his Managing

Director" (p. 117) encapsulates much the same mixture of insolence and suicidal self-loathing as that with which Willems confronts Lingard.

This short story thus exhibits several features of the structural pattern of *An Outcast of the Islands*: white heroes whose moral weakness leads them to compromise in pursuit of their goals; a compromise which activates a dualistic tension between two opposing but equivalent worlds; a tension which drives the heroes to criminal action, to moral degeneration, and eventually to death; and the final return of a figure of authority from the world whose standards they have offended. Absent from the story are any traces of the heroine and, consequently, the rival. Here, as in *The Nigger of the 'Narcissus'*, the heroes' goals in the story are not imaged in a female character. As there is no heroine representing what the heroes desire, so there is no active anti-heroine to oppose their compromise. The anti-heroine is only vestigially present in Kayerts' daughter Melie, "a little girl with long bleached tresses and a rather sour face" (p. 108), whose interest he professes to serve and whose portrait is the focus of his later remorse, but who does not herself appear in the story.

From the point of view of Conrad's development, however, the most important feature of *An Outpost of Progress* is one that appears here for the first time and is central to most of the stories of his next phase. Hitherto we have spoken generally of the hero's goal, the object in pursuit of which he accepts a compromise, precipitates himself into a paradoxical situation, and becomes a criminal or traitor. In the earlier cases of Almayer and Willems this goal is largely personal, not extending significantly beyond the gain and prestige desired by the hero for himself and his immediate family. In most of the novels of Conrad's next phase, on the other hand, the hero's goal is also an "ideal" in the sense of a pursuit which is, at least in part, altruistic and which involves an element of rationalized ideology, however suspect or insincere this at times may be. *An Outpost of Progress* is the first of Conrad's stories in which the heroes exhibit ideals in this wider sense. The ideology, still perfunctory and shallow, consists in Kayerts' and Carlier's belief in the concept of "progress" enshrined in the title, an explicitly European (white) notion, which they first encounter in "some old copies of a home paper".

That print discussed what it was pleased to call 'Our Colonial

Expansion' in high-flown language. It spoke much of the rights and duties of civilization, of the sacredness of the civilizing work, and extolled the merits of those who went about bringing light and faith and commerce to the dark places of the earth. Carlier and Kayerts read, wondered, and began to think better of themselves (pp. 94–5).

Although the issue is not dwelt upon in the story, *An Outpost of Progress* is typical of Conrad's later work in exhibiting the ironic contrast between stated ideals and actual motives, an issue which was to be the keynote of *The Nigger of the 'Narcissus'* and *Heart of Darkness*, both written within the next two years, and which was to dominate the political novels of Conrad's middle period.

An Outpost of Progress is particularly close to *Heart of Darkness*, not only because it adopts the same jungle trading-post setting, but also because it exposes the same dichotomy between the ideal of "progress" and the facts of exploitation and extermination. Beside Mr Kurtz' movement from the composition of enthusiastic missionary treatises to the wish to "exterminate all the brutes" we can place Carlier's decline from the concept of "colonial expansion" to talk about "the necessity of exterminating all the niggers" (p. 108). In many ways *An Outpost of Progress* is a sketch of the material Conrad reworked in much greater depth in the later story after he had realized, perhaps through writing *The Nigger of the 'Narcissus'*, the potential for "horror" in the gulf between human ideals and human actions.

While *An Outpost of Progress* looks forward to the greater works to follow, *The Lagoon*, written immediately after it in the late summer of 1896, is a less adventurous piece which offers only a generalized reflection of the plot pattern Conrad had already established. *The Lagoon* concerns a Malay hero who, with the assistance of his brother, abducts from his tribe the woman he loves. As the three are making their escape the hero, Arsat, elects to save himself and his lover by abandoning his brother to be slain by their pursuers. In the course of the story, an unspecified time afterwards, the woman dies of an illness, and Arsat vows to return to avenge his brother and, presumably, to be himself slain in so doing. On a superficial level the story is close to that of Willems, who betrays Lingard, his benefactor, in order to keep Aissa, his lover, and later confronts Lingard, loses Aissa, and is killed as a result.

A few phrases in *The Lagoon* hint at the deeper implications developed in the longer works. In order to obtain the woman, for instance, Arsat sacrifices his place among his own people to become, like Willems, an outcast. "We are cast out," says his brother, as they take to the water in flight, "and this boat is our country now" (p. 197). Again, the act of abduction, although the two involved are lovers, is a "theft" of which the men are ashamed, admitting the paradox that, although brave and desirable, what they have done is also cowardly and disgraceful.

> My brother wanted to shout the cry of challenge – one cry only – to let the people know we were freeborn robbers who trusted our arms and the great sea. And again I begged him in the name of our love to be silent. Could I not hear her breathing close to me? I knew the pursuit would come quick enough. My brother loved me. He dipped his paddle without a splash. He only said, "There is half a man in you now – the other half is in that woman." (p. 198).

Here we have the same dual perspective of the hero's acts and objectives which, in the longer stories, grows into the dualism of opposing worlds or ideologies and is reflected in the figures of the rival, nemesis and anti-heroine. None of these figures is involved in *The Lagoon*, nor is any dualistic mechanism evolved to develop the paradox inherent in the hero's action, and for these reasons the story remains simple and without Conrad's usual psychological interest.

A further structural indication of the relative slightness of this story is the want of any firm connection between the hero's efforts to obtain his goal and the catastrophe, which in this case consists in the death of the woman and Arsat's decision to go back to face his enemies. Normally Conrad makes the catastrophe either explicitly or symbolically a consequence of the hero's actions, as the coming of Jones and the death of Lena are consequences, through Schomberg, of Heyst's retreat to the island and rescue of his heroine. In *The Lagoon* there is simply an unspecified time lapse between Arsat's betrayal of his brother and the death, from natural causes, of the woman.

The Sisters is an incomplete fragment comprising only seven short chapters. A few of the names and circumstances of the fragment were taken up and reworked in *The Arrow of Gold* twenty years later.* *The Sisters* is chiefly remarkable as Conrad's essay in Byronism, its hero, Stephen, being the vague but intense type who searches vainly through the world for the correlative to his aspirations.† This is not a type Conrad uses again and is one very different from those both of the earliest heroes, the relatively sad and mean figures of Almayer and Willems, and of the heroes of the first mature phase, the paradoxical personalities of Wait, Kurtz and Jim. It was almost certainly the uncongeniality of its hero that obliged Conrad to put *The Sisters* aside.

Even so, Stephen has the chief characteristics of the early Conradian heroes. His story begins when he leaves his own people to make a new life in a new and alien context, which he does at the cost of a considerable moral compromise. Stephen leaves his eastern home and the parents who love him to pursue the life of an artist in the West, but he is able to do so only by living on his father's money, while rejecting the paternal life-style as materialistic and unfit. There is an inherent paradox here, which Conrad was presumably planning to elaborate in something like the way in which he developed the inconsistencies of Wait and Kurtz. Stephen is like Kurtz in adopting a highly idealistic way of life which in fact rests upon egoism and the material exploitation of others.

The heroine of the story would almost certainly have been Rita, although, since the fragment ends before she meets with the hero, her status cannot be asserted with finality. She has, however, the chief characteristics of the early heroines, Nina and Aissa, her immediate predecessors, women caught between two cultures and jealously watched by possessive father-figures. Rita oscillates between the working-class peasant background of her own family, the Ortegas, and the extravagant middle-class world of her patroness, Madame Malagon. This motif, the placement of the heroine between two worlds, was to be developed in the last three novels, but it has its roots in the racial conflicts suffered by Nina and Aissa.

The twelve months or so after the completion, in September 1895, of *An Outcast of the Islands*, were a period of uncertainty and variety of experiment. With two long and closely similar novels

---

* *The Sisters* was first published in 1928 and has recently reappeared in *Conrad's Congo Diary and Other Uncollected Pieces*, ed. Zdislaw Najder (New York, 1978).
† Najder indicates several allusions and similarities to Byron's *Childe Harold* (*Congo Diary*, p. 70).

complete behind him, Conrad was evidently unsure of what path to follow for the future, and he consequently spent some time essaying different modes of fictional writing. The year 1896 saw the production of another Malayan tale in the manner of *Almayer's Folly*, namely *The Lagoon*, of a glance towards *Heart of Darkness* in *An Outpost of Progress*, of the stark but inconsequential tale *The Idiots*, and of two abortive efforts at longer pieces, *The Sisters* and *The Rescuer* (later finished off as *The Rescue*), along with the start of *The Nigger of the 'Narcissus'*. The next year, 1897, gave rise to another Malayan tale, *Karain*, and to an attempted study of domestic marital relations in *The Return*.

No other period of Conrad's career can exhibit anything approaching the range and variety of these stories. He was evidently searching for a direction, a path which, as a developing novelist, he might follow, still trying alternatives and glancing down a number of different avenues. He finally settled upon the line indicated by the paradoxical hero, the figure which made its first full appearance as Wait in *The Nigger of the 'Narcissus'*. The decision, subsequently confirmed in the heroes of *Heart of Darkness*, *Lord Jim*, *Falk*, and *The End of the Tether*, was neither sudden nor easy. Even after the completion of *The Nigger of the 'Narcissus'* in February 1897, Conrad continued to experiment diversely in *Karain*, *The Return*, and *Youth* before coming back to what was to be his true course in *Heart of Darkness*.

Conrad's two first novels, *Almayer's Folly* and *An Outcast of the Islands*, along with the stories and fragments prior to 1897, seen in the perspective of his whole career, are the products of his literary apprenticeship. Compared to most of the work which followed, they are both experimental and uncomplicated. What we shall call Conrad's first mature phase begins after these works with his first true masterpiece, *The Nigger of the 'Narcissus'*.

Part II The First Phase of Maturity

4 *The Nigger of the 'Narcissus'*

With *The Nigger of the 'Narcissus'* we come to Conard's first mature piece of work. *Almayer's Folly*, on which he spent at least four and a half years, is a highly finished novel, but remains none the less, relative to the rest of the Conrad canon, very much an introductory, experimental production. *An Outcast of the Islands*, although somewhat longer, was scarcely more than one year in the writing and bears the marks, in its structural anomalies, of being a less certain, more tentative piece. In these two novels, and in *An Outpost of Progress*, Conrad experimented with the fictional structures and concepts which, with some radical changes of style and technique, were to form the basis for the great works of his early period – *The Nigger of the 'Narcissus'*, *Heart of Darkness*, and *Lord Jim*.

From the structural point of view the change initiated in *The Nigger of the 'Narcissus'* which most strongly distinguishes the novels of this phase from the earlier writings is in the conception of the hero, a change which can be seen as an elaboration of features already implicit and developing in the characters of Willems, Kayerts and Carlier. Willems, compared to Almayer in *Almayer's Folly*, is a deeper character, both in having a dynamic side to his nature and in being prepared to commit definite acts of betrayal. The paradox, relatively superficial in Almayer, becomes significantly moral in Willems, who sees himself as obliged to become criminal in pursuit of desirable aims. A further step is taken in *An Outpost of Progress*, where Kayerts and Carlier subscribe to an altruistic ideology while, at the same time, committing acts of criminal inhumanity in its pursuit. The next step, achieved spectacularly in *The Nigger of the 'Narcissus'*, was to universalize this paradoxical hero, whose acts involve their own frustration and whose ideals, while attractive in principle, prove disastrous in practice.

Conrad achieves this by emphasizing the impersonally idealistic potential of the hero's goal. The central figure may remain, like Almayer and Willems, fundamentally self-involved, but his object-

49

ives and desires now acquire a sympathetic, or at least plausible aspect, which makes them capable of being (and likely to be) taken up by others. The hero becomes a man of reputation, not only in the rather narrow sense in which Willems is concerned about his social standing, but in the wider sense of exerting a real influence upon the thought and conduct of the group of which he is a member. James Wait, the central figure of *The Nigger of the 'Narcissus'*, is the first of a line of these men of (often inflated) notability, whose way of life or expressed ideal exercises a widespread fascination. Among Wait's successors in this respect are Kurtz, Jim, Nostromo, Verloc, Razumov, Heyst and George.

At the same time, just as the hero's ideals are invariably seen to have their hollow side, so his reputation in the story is regularly exposed as being partly (but usually not altogether) undeserved. The paradox which the hero embodies is now reflected chiefly in his public persona within the story, and not solely, as with Almayer and Willems, in the course of events for which he is responsible. In James Wait Conrad created the first of a line of heroes, each of whom images in himself the paradoxical nature of his ideals and actions. Wait is a man of outstanding appearance, voice and physique who immediately impresses the officers and crew of the *Narcissus* as a most promising seaman and yet proves to be virtually inactive, sick, dying, and a pernicious influence upon both the men and the voyage. His appearance, words and bearing, the surfaces of his life, conceal a deception, much as his ideals are seen in the event to be in part a specious covering for brutal selfishness.

The typical hero of this new phase is a man of high repute, an idealist whose overt goals are shared by a number of his fellows. Yet his ideals are flawed in practice, just as he himself conceals behind his public exterior an inner weakness, a tendency to compromise; and for this reason, like the earlier heroes Almayer and Willems, he encounters a paradoxical situation in which his efforts towards achievement are systematically frustrated. Unlike the earlier heroes, however, he images in himself, in his own person, this central Conradian paradox, being at once both strong in appearance and weak in fact, reliable and yet deceptive, attractive but dangerous.

Along with this development in the figure of the hero goes an expansion of the Conradian paradox into ideological dimensions, an extension first hinted in *An Outpost of Progress*. The earlier novels display a relatively simple paradox in which the hero's purposive movements towards his personal goal are regularly met by counter-movements within the structure of a dualistic universe. In *The Nigger of the 'Narcissus'* and in most of the novels which follow it, the paradox is primarily ideological. The hero's goal now entails a philosophy or way of life to which he openly subscribes in the story, and this is shown to have consequences, both theoretical and practical, contrary to what he desires and expects. The ideal of civilized progress, for instance, in *An Outpost of Progress* and in *Heart of Darkness*, leads in the event to primitive brutality, and the notion of liberal egalitarianism advocated by Wait in *The Nigger of the 'Narcissus'* results in anarchy and attempted murder. Conrad's concern with ideological motifs in this phase of his career is the stepping-stone to the great political novels of his next phase, which are set overtly against backgrounds of doctrinal conflict.

The ideological dimension of the central paradox is an aspect of the universality of the Conradian hero. Once the hero becomes representative of a recognizable – although not necessarily pro-found or specific – body of doctrine or code of conduct, then he can also become both a symbol of a cause within his story and, for the reader, a figure of more than merely psychological interest. Almayer and Willems, although not badly drawn, are insipid beside most of the later heroes, largely because, lacking the ideological dimension and remaining primarily personal in their pursuits, their fates have no very broad or compelling significance.

James Wait is the structural hero of *The Nigger of the 'Narcissus'*, both because he stands at the centre of the paradox, the ideological conflict between the human desire for equality and the demand for discipline and hierarchy imposed by the needs of a sailing ship, and because the story effectually begins with his entry and ends in the aftermath of his death. His personal aim is fundamentally to secure himself an easy passage by feigning sickness and resting idly while others do the work of the voyage. Through the agency of Donkin, however, Wait becomes a figurehead for the cause of common human rights to every available comfort, a cause which places egalitarianism and the bond of sympathy above the demands of discipline. Yet Wait really is ill and dying, apparently from consumption, and his own (and the crew's) half-belief that he is a healthy man cleverly deceiving the officers is a wishful self-deception induced by the fear of death. In the course of the story the crew becomes demoralized by the confusion of ideas Wait rep-resents and, having taken great risks to rescue him during a storm, rises to the point of mutiny in defence of his interests against the

Captain's orders. Finally, when the Captain faces the crew, they back away from the logical conclusion of their course and return to duty, while Wait dies and is buried at sea as the voyage nears its end.

James Wait, along with Nostromo, is one of Conrad's most nebulous, symbolically complex, and highly-charged heroes. The paradox he embodies is multifaceted. At the simplest level it is the anomaly of the easy option which, ironically, must be exercised in circumstances of unusual hardship. Just as Almayer, wanting luxury and European society, works out his destiny in the poverty and isolation of Sambir, so James Wait, needing rest and comfort, takes a berth as an able seaman aboard a sailing vessel on a voyage around the Cape. This is his compromise. Wait, like Almayer and Willems, takes himself into a context to which, in his condition, he does not belong. He is a sick man deceptively committed to a place which demands health and strength. This aspect of the paradox is reflected in his appearance, that of a powerful seaman, which prompts the mate, Baker, to seize upon him: "Those West India niggers run fine and large – some of them. . . . Ough! . . . Don't they? A fine, big man that, Mr. Creighton. Feel him on a rope. Hey? I will take him into my watch, I think" (p. 20). Yet Wait's physique is all the while deceptive, as is hinted by his cough, "metallic, hollow,   and   tremendously   loud   [which]   sounded like . . . explosions in a vault" (p. 18), and by his progressive loss of strength. The paradox is reflected also in his name, Wait, which comes to suggest a *weight* or burden on the ship, imposing a *wait* or delay which hinders the return voyage.

In the earlier stories a dualistic antagonism is activated by the hero's paradoxical compromise; both Almayer and Willems precipitate a conflict of black and white worlds by using dubious means to attain their ends. In *The Nigger of the 'Narcissus'* the dualistic conflict again follows from the hero's act, in this case from Wait's very joining the ship, but is ideological rather than racial in character. The imagery of black and white is retained superficially, Wait being a single black man among whites in an apparent inversion of Conrad's earlier interest in white heroes isolated in black communities, but in fact the purely racial antithesis has little function in the story. The conflict to which Wait's compromise gives rise is essentially political, a struggle between the extremes of liberal democracy, tending in Conrad's view to anarchy, and a hierarchy of command based upon mutual responsibility and the requirements of a common task. In *The Nigger of the 'Narcissus'* the action is confined to a ship at sea, a rather special case in which the breakdown of discipline has immediate and obvious consequences; but the dualistic conflict which Conrad first develops here between popular rule and traditional authority is recognizably the same as that which was to reappear in his political novels, *Nostromo, The Secret Agent* and *Under Western Eyes.*

The ideological dualism which results in mutiny on the *Narcissus* is initiated by Wait through the paradox he embodies and through his influence over the crew. In this influence over his fellows, which is almost mystical, Wait is comparable to several later heroes who, sometimes without wishing it, find themselves and their careers of unaccountable interest to the world. Wait, like Nostromo, revels in the fascination he exercises and turns it to his own ends. His power over other minds is symbolized initially by his pervasive, echoing voice. "The deep, rolling tones of his voice filled the deck without effort" (p. 18), and his words, "spoken sonorously, with an even intonation, were heard all over the ship" (p. 19). In this respect he is closest to Kurtz, another dying preacher of hollow but reverberating ideals.

Yet Wait holds sway over the crew of the *Narcissus* not so much by what he says as by the paradox he represents. Wait is, first of all, an apparently strong and healthy seaman who claims to be sick and weak, although as the voyage progresses he becomes also, and increasingly, an obviously dying man pretending that his debility is a mere sham. In a way that cannot be fully rationalized and remains partly mysterious, this pattern of trickery and self-deception causes confusion among the crew, upsetting their established notions and, in particular, disturbing the discipline of the ship. Wait's efforts to maintain two conflicting stories, to be at once a healthy object of respectful envy and a moribund recipient of ease and sympathy, touches upon the mystery of mortality itself, presenting the vital mind with the anomaly of its own extinction. Observing his inescapable presence and being constantly reminded of the real or pretended approach of death, the men of the *Narcissus* abandon their customary unaffected ways and become a group of pensive, unsettled individuals.

Was he a reality – or was he a sham – this ever-expected visitor of Jimmy's? We hesitated between pity and mistrust, while, on the slightest provocation, he shook before our eyes the bones of his bothersome and infamous skeleton. He was for ever trotting him out. He would talk of that coming death as though it had been already there, as if it had been walking the deck outside, as if it would presently come in to sleep in the only empty bunk; as if it had sat by his side at every meal. It interfered with our daily occupations, with our leisure, with our amusements. We had no songs and no music in the evening, because Jimmy (we all lovingly called him Jimmy, to conceal our hate of his accomplice) had managed, with that prospective disease of his, to disturb even Archie's mental balance. Archie was the owner of the concertina; but after a couple of stinging lectures from Jimmy he refused to play any more. . . . Our singers became mute because Jimmy was a dying man. For the same reason no chap – as Knowles remarked – could "drive in a nail to hang his few poor rags upon," without being made aware of the enormity he committed in disturbing Jimmy's interminable last moments. At night, instead of the cheerful yell, "One bell! Turn out! Do you hear there? Hey! hey! hey! Show leg!" the watches were called man by man, in whispers, so as not to interfere with Jimmy's, possibly, last slumber on earth (pp. 36–7).

The outcome is a gradual erosion of discipline as the crew becomes so wrapped up in the problems Wait poses as to question the very fundamentals of maritime regulation, which they had previously accepted without reflection. "All our certitudes were going; we were on doubtful terms with our officers; the cook had given us up for lost; we had overheard the boatswain's opinion that 'we were a crowd of softies.' We suspected Jimmy, one another, and even our very selves" (p. 43).

Wait's condition is related to the ideological theme of the tale through the notion, actually fallacious but maintained by Wait himself and propagated by Donkin, that the black man has discovered a foolproof way to beat the system, to get a paid passage in return for little or no work. When Donkin asks, Wait replies that he has played this trick before. "Last ship – yes. I was out of sorts on the passage. See? It was easy. They paid me off in Calcutta, and the skipper made no bones about it either. . . . I got my money all right. Laid up fifty-eight days! The fools! O Lord! The fools! Paid right off!" (p. 111). To the crew this view of Wait represents an ideal of undisciplined luxury, an ideal closely akin to the indolent, materialistic goals of Almayer and Willems. Under the influence of Wait and Donkin the men of the *Narcissus* "dreamed enthusiastically of the time when every lonely ship would travel over a serene sea, manned by a wealthy and well-fed crew of satisfied skippers" (p. 103).

The dream of reconstituting life aboard ship as a liberal democracy makes one side of the story's ideological dualism. The other side is provided by the established hierarchy of the ship, the officers and the master, Captain Allistoun. The antagonism between these two polarities is related to the conflict of black and white worlds represented in the earlier novels. In both cases the hero in his black world stands for a basically selfish indolence, which is opposed by the strict requirements of the white world of his origin with its demanding insistence upon the responsibilities he has neglected.

Allistoun's role in *The Nigger of the 'Narcissus'* is comparable to that of Lingard in *An Outcast of the Islands* as the authoritarian representative of the old world (there the white world Willems has abandoned, here the established disciplinary order the crew has disregarded), who appears at the climax of the story to cut short the hero's career. Apart from the nemesis and the hero himself, however, the other figures of the pattern at first sight appear to be absent. There is obviously no heroine in this story, and therefore no anti-heroine either, perhaps only for the straightforward reason that the setting of the tale does not allow for female characters. The remaining figure of the pattern, the rival, is present in the story and offers an interesting case. This position is in fact occupied by Donkin, which seems at first unlikely because no real rivalry develops between himself and Wait until near the end of the book, through most of which Donkin acts as Wait's friend and spokesman. It is, indeed, chiefly through Donkin's agency that the enigmatic figure of the sick man is translated, for the crew and for the reader, into ideological terms. Donkin is the prototypical Conradian malcontent, the first in the line which includes Cornelius, the Monteros, Verloc's anarchists, Schomberg, Ortega and Scevola. He is a fountain of dissident rhetoric, the voice of the crew's vague aspirations, the instrument which focuses their discontent upon Wait and directs it into channels of action. Yet Donkin is also, in a sense, Wait's murderer, who gloats over the dying hero and leaves the story with his stolen gold in his pocket.

The rivalry between Donkin and Wait does not manifest itself in the usual sexual mode because there is no heroine in this story. Their eventual antagonism has its source rather in Donkin's bitter envy

and his greed for the dying man's money. Yet it is of interest that the
final quarrel between them is precipitated when Wait offers Donkin
unsolicited confidences about his amorous experiences.

> "There is a girl," whispered Wait. . . . "Canton Street girl. –
> She chucked a third engineer of a Rennie boat – for me. Cooks
> oysters just as I like. . . . She says – she would chuck – any toff –
> for a coloured gentleman. . . . That's me. I am kind to
> wimmen," he added, a shade louder.
>   Donkin could hardly believe his ears. He was scandalised –
> "Would she? Yer wouldn't be any good to 'er," he said with
> unrestrained disgust. Wait was not there to hear him. He was
> swaggering up the East India Dock Road [. . . .] He cared for
> no one. Donkin felt this vaguely like a blind man feeling in his
> darkness the fatal antagonism of all the surrounding existences,
> that to him shall for ever remain irrealisable, unseen and
> enviable. He had a desire to assert his importance, to break, to
> crush (pp.149–50).

Conrad uses Donkin's jealousy of Wait's woman to introduce the
scene in which Wait slowly dies while Donkin abuses him and steals
his savings from his locker. Neither the jealousy nor the "treasure"
have any great place in the story, but they remind us of rivalries
elsewhere in Conrad's novels, involving a woman to whom the hero
is attached and an actual or imagined store of gold. It is almost as if
Conrad could not drop these elements from his plots, even when he
had no real need of them.

   Donkin figures in the story initially as the embodiment of the
crew's latent discontents. The scene of his arrival makes this clear, as
the men stand around observing his destitute appearance, beginning to respond to his self-pitying ingratiation, and eventually
dressing him in a miscellaneous bundle of clothes donated by them
collectively, a scene which represents their guarded acceptance of
his attitudes. The crew none the less maintains a reasonable distance
from Donkin, a rationally critical stance towards his conduct,
through the first stage of the voyage. They acquiesce, for instance, in
Mr Baker's beating of the insolent seaman on one occasion (p. 40),
and even assist the mate in silencing Donkin's protests against
authority during the storm (pp. 76–7). After the storm, however,
the crew's view of the rebel changes as the men become conceited

and more accepting of Donkin's large claims for their rights and merits.

> We decried our officers – who had done nothing – and listened to the fascinating Donkin. His care for our rights, his disinterested concern for our dignity, were not discouraged by the invariable contumely of our words, by the disdain of our looks [. . . .] We were men enough to courageously admit to ourselves our intellectual shortcomings; though from that time we refrained from kicking him, tweaking his nose, or from accidentally knocking him about, which last, after we had weathered the Cape, had been rather a popular amusement (pp. 100, 102).

Behind this change of heart towards Donkin lies the rescue of Wait, that ritual act of identification with the principle of paradox, which leaves the crew open to the miscreant's insidious suggestions. From this time Donkin dresses mostly in Wait's cast-off clothing (p. 102) and takes on the role of high priest to Wait's divinity.

> The little place [Wait's cabin], repainted white, had, in the night, the brilliance of a silver shrine where a black idol, reclining stiffly under a blanket, blinked its weary eyes and received our homage. Donkin officiated. He had the air of a demonstrator showing a phenomenon, a manifestation bizarre, simple, and meritorious that, to the beholders, should be a profound and everlasting lesson (p. 105).

From this point to the climax of the story, the mutiny, Donkin leads the crew, using Wait's influence to work upon their feelings.

It is only after the mutiny has failed and discipline been restored that the true relationship between Donkin and the hero comes to the surface. Both men are fundamentally selfish in their motives and essentially concerned to find an easy passage for themselves by imposing upon the officers and crew. The failure of the mutiny, which results in Wait's confinement and Donkin's loss of face, explodes the veneer of cooperation between them, leaving Donkin, aggrieved and bitter, prepared to turn on Wait as his only remaining victim. The two are competitors for the territory, for the misplaced sympathies of the crew, much as in Conrad's other stories hero and rival jostle one another for local influence and the heroine's affections.

Donkin remains Conrad's most expanded presentation of the rival figure, usually a secondary, less central character, such as Omar in *An Outcast of the Islands*, Cornelius in *Lord Jim*, and the Monteros in *Nostromo*. The reasons for this and for several other unusual structural features of *The Nigger of the 'Narcissus'* probably lie in Conrad's new exploration here of the ideological dimension. For the first time he was making the central conflict of his story a specifically conceptual one, a dualism in which two opposing philosophies are brought into play by the initial compromise of the hero. Wait, although befriended by Donkin and made a figurehead in the crew's revolt, remains essentially passive and self-concerned; other characters are therefore needed to present and verbalize the ideological polarities of the story. Conrad gives the two roles to the rival and the nemesis respectively; Donkin becomes the chief advocate of individual rights, while Allistoun, as Captain of the ship, stands for traditional authoritarianism.

Donkin and Allistoun are paired, as contraries, in several ways. The mutiny aboard the *Narcissus*, which stems ultimately from Wait's presence, is essentially a confrontation between these two, in which Donkin attempts to murder the Captain, fails, and is obliged to back down. Donkin and Allistoun are the only two aboard (apart from Singleton, who is lashed to the wheel) who are explicitly excluded from participation in Wait's rescue during the storm, and both similarly decline participation in the black man's funeral. (Allistoun is initially present but hands over the duty of conducting the service to Baker. He leaves unnoticed to resume his place on the bridge, from which he shouts an order as soon as the last word has been read (p. 160). Donkin was "too ill to come" (p. 159).) Allistoun's reason for aloofness on these occasions is clearly his non-involvement in the confusions for which Wait's presence is responsible. It is important to see that Donkin is no less aloof from Wait, despite their superficial friendliness during the middle stage of the voyage. Donkin uses Wait, rather as Dain uses Almayer, as long as their interests coincide, but turns against him the moment it becomes clear that the game is lost. Donkin is no more Wait's ally than is Allistoun. Wait himself, like all major Conradian heroes, is a man alone, caught between conflicting forces which he comprehends only in part and which he is, to his own undoing, largely unable to reconcile.

Donkin and Allistoun are not simply contraries, however, for they occupy different roles in the Conradian pattern, Donkin as the hero's rival and Allistoun as the figure of nemesis. In the earlier stories, where the central dualism is presented in broadly cultural rather than ideological terms, the rivals (Dain and Omar) are characters whom the hero meets in the world of his compromise, the world in which he finds himself after having abandoned or betrayed the code of his own world, while the nemesis figure (Lingard), representing the standards which the hero has deserted, comes from the abandoned world to confront the hero with his dereliction. In *The Nigger of the 'Narcissus'*, where the action takes place almost entirely on board a ship at sea, to whose company belong all the characters, this geographical definition of the pattern cannot be applied. (It recurs in several of the later novels, especially in *Lord Jim*, *Nostromo*, *Under Western Eyes*, *Victory*, and *The Rescue*.) There is here no literal way in which Wait moves from one "world" to another, as do Almayer and Willems, nor does it help to talk of Donkin and Allistoun as inhabitants of different "worlds" in other than a conceptual sense.

The chief figures none the less retain other defining characteristics. Wait, having chosen the moral compromise of the easy option by shipping aboard the *Narcissus*, there meets in Donkin the *reductio* of the course he has chosen. Donkin, the adopted spirit of the ship's crew, represents in his weak and insidious personality the logical conclusion of Wait's line of action universally applied. Like other rivals, he appears as the inescapable concomitant of the hero's paradoxical policy. Just as Willems' alliance with Aissa involves him with Omar, and Gould's attempt to reactivate the concession obliges him to deal with the Monteros, so Wait's attempt to gain an easy passage raises the spectre of Donkin, a spirit which eventually engages him in a vital struggle. Allistoun, who confronts Wait with the reality of his situation by sentencing him to remain on his sickbed, and who reasserts the balance which Wait's intrusion into the scheme of things has upset, is clearly not, like the rival, a figure brought into being by the hero's action, but is rather a member of a higher order, whose values are independent of, and prior to, the hero's coming.

In its employment of these key roles in their usual interrelationships *The Nigger of the 'Narcissus'* is on common ground with the earlier stories, despite the new dimension introduced by its ideological focus. Several features of the pattern first employed here, such as the use of the rival and nemesis figures to present opposite poles of the conceptual dualism, were to recur in many later stories. The comparable later novels, however, show an advance over *The Nigger of the 'Narcissus'* with respect to the nemesis figure, for Conrad's attitude to Allistoun remains largely uncritical. The Captain's key decisions, which appear on scrutiny to be arbitrary and of no great profundity, are invariably and highly improbably justified in the story by unforeseeable events. His refusal to cut away the masts in the storm proves correct when the ship, against all odds, rights itself; his impetuous command that Wait shall remain in his cabin – which, he says, "came to me all at once, before I could think" (p. 127) – commits him to a dangerous course of action but is appropriate to the story's deeper meaning; and his risky confrontation with Donkin after the mutiny is, by good luck, ended without mishap. During the storm Allistoun is portrayed as a superhuman figure engaged in a personal struggle with the elements. Conrad's only concession to realism is to show the Captain as "subdued by his captivity" (p. 168) once he leaves his ship and falls subject to the bureaucracy of landsmen.

The unreserved adulation of Allistoun, since he represents one side of the conflict and since Donkin, his adversary, is without redeeming features, affects the conceptual balance of the story. Even Lingard in *An Outcast of the Islands*, the Captain's immediate precursor, is allowed fallibility, as is shown by the collapse of his house of cards (p. 196), which images the failure of his entire jungle enterprise. Allistoun's unique impeccability makes *The Nigger of the 'Narcissus'* Conrad's only novel which approaches moral univocality. Whereas even the earlier stories played black and white worlds each against the other, this tale is unreserved in both approval of Allistoun's authority and condemnation of Donkin's revolt. Later comparable works, such as *Nostromo* and *The Secret Agent*, subtly undercut the representatives of established social order; only the most superficial readings can overlook the limitations of Gould and the Assistant Commissioner and the respective establishments for which they stand. Allistoun is fully vindicated, however, and *The Nigger of the 'Narcissus'* has in consequence a firm moral basis in what Conrad presents as the ethos of the sea.

Conrad's romantic view of life under sail gains the upper hand over his judgment here, just as it topples his prose into several protracted purple passages of praise of the sea and sailors, which perhaps appealed more to his original *fin de siècle* audience than they do to the present-day reader. Allistoun, seen in the context of Conrad's development, is a blind alley, a Neanderthal evolution with no descendants. His own immediate ancestor, the Lingard of *An Outcast of the Islands*, is himself encumbered with an aura of divinity relieved only by the failure of events to fall out in accord with his wishes. Allistoun, similarly presented as an ideal seaman and commander, masters his world absolutely so long as his ship remains at sea. Future occupants of this role of the nemesis figure, and (where these are different) future representatives of traditional authoritarian stability, were to be portrayed more critically. In no other major novel did Conrad allow himself an unreserved endorsement of either side in the story's conflict. The flourishing line of descent from the Lingard of the early tales is not that of Allistoun but that of such flawed and self-doubting characters as Marlow in *Heart of Darkness* or Blunt in *The Arrow of Gold*, characters who reflect and share in the feelings of the hero they confront.

For all its splendour, therefore, and despite the strongly positive feelings the author retained towards it throughout his life, *The Nigger of the 'Narcissus'* is neither typical nor exemplary of Conrad's mature work, because it lacks the moral neutrality and ambivalence which generally characterizes his fiction. Even the earlier novels had staunchly refused the reader the comfort of firm foundation in either the black or the white perspective, and the later stories, particularly the political novels of the middle period, were to make clear Conrad's fundamental scepticism.

The uncritical, romantic tenor of *The Nigger of the 'Narcissus'* is related to the search for a narrative point of view, in which Conrad was engaged at the time of its writing. The earlier stories were written in third-person narrative, but in *The Nigger of the 'Narcissus'* Conrad experimented for the first time with a first-person narrator. The first-person voice surfaces only occasionally in the story and is often lost sight of, sometimes relating information to which, as one of those on board, the narrator could not have had access. This narrator, moreover, is never identified, but remains an anonymous member of the group with no particular role in the plot (except that he is one of the five who free Wait from his cabin during the storm). These uncertainties of voice were to be resolved suddenly in Conrad's next important works, *Youth* and *Heart of Darkness*, with the discovery of Marlow, an identifiable narrator-character within the stories.

When Conrad took up once again his central preoccupation with the fictional pattern it was to the role of the nemesis figure that he gave renewed attention. In *Heart of Darkness* Allistoun's successor is none other than Marlow himself, a very different character, assuming the task of confronting the errant hero and restoring the balance that the hero's action had upset. Conrad was evidently sufficiently dissatisfied with Allistoun to replace him with a different personality type, a man open to doubts and uncertainties who participates in the temptations and the guilt of the hero. The result is an immediate restoration – and, indeed, intensification – of what we now recognize as the typical Conradian scepticism, questioning equally both of the conflicting sets of values presented in the story. For this reason *Heart of Darkness* is conceptually much more demanding than *The Nigger of the 'Narcissus'*.

Conrad thus addressed two areas of weakness in *The Nigger of the 'Narcissus'* with a single solution. Marlow in *Heart of Darkness* provides not only a firm technical centre for the narrative voice but also a sympathetically human and fallible figure for the nemesis role. Marlow not only introduces fallibility into the authoritarian nemesis role but also becomes the voice for that distinctive Conradian ironic scepticism which was to be the hall-mark of the greater novels, but which is often lost beneath the romanticism of the early stories, with their tendency to glorify such figures as Lingard and Allistoun.

In *The Nigger of the 'Narcissus'* Conrad identifies truth with one side of his dualistic universe. The dialectical structure remains unchanged, and the hero is still obliged to die, caught between the conflict of forces his initial act has unleashed; but in this story the values are shifted as one party is vindicated in the cosmic struggle and allowed to bring his ship-world intact to a safe harbour. Wait dies, releasing the *Narcissus* to bear her reclaimed crew under their victorious Captain to a good pay-day. With the partial exceptions of *Chance* and *The Rover*, all of Conrad's other longer works have more or less Wagnerian endings, in which either the hero is defeated or the endless cyclical struggle between the two sides is emphasized. *The Nigger of the 'Narcissus'* is unique in its positive (albeit nostalgic) conclusion, for which the reason is again Allistoun.

Allistoun has access to what the story recognizes as Truth, and is able to display it effectively when he confronts the false rhetoric generated among the crew by Wait and Donkin. Wait is the first of Conrad's heroes to sit at the centre of a web of verbiage – propaganda, doctrines, precepts, rumours, philosophies, gossip – in terms of which the stories' dualistic struggles are conducted. Allistoun is unique in being able to perceive and produce the facts which lie beneath this confusion. This he does when he confronts the crew on deck, in the light of day, with the belaying-pin with which Donkin had attempted to murder him during the dispute under cover of darkness. Exhibition of the belaying-pin, "the only tangible fact of the whole transaction", has the effect of confronting the crew with the true nature of their conduct, much as Allistoun has already faced Wait with the reality of the black man's moribund condition.

> He made a quick stride and with a swing took an iron belaying-pin out of his pocket. "This!" His movement was so unexpected and sudden that the crowd stepped back. He gazed fixedly at their faces, and some at once put on a surprised air as though they had never seen a belaying-pin before. He held it up. "This is my affair. I don't ask you any questions, but you all know it; it has got to go where it came from." His eyes became angry. The crowd stirred uneasily. They looked away from the piece of iron, they appeared shy, they were embarrassed and shocked as though it had been something horrid, scandalous, or indelicate, that in common decency should not have been flourished like this in broad daylight (p. 135).

Just as Allistoun has previously made Wait face the truth of his death by confining him to his cabin, so he now forces the crew to see the murderous nature of their undertaking. The logical end of their uprising is the death and destruction represented by the belaying-pin, just as death is to be the end of Wait's career.

Allistoun's "fact" is unambiguous and convincing. Having been confronted with the belaying-pin and made witness to Donkin's replacement of it, the crew returns to duty with no further trouble. Facts in Conrad's later fiction, like the silver of the mine of *Nostromo*, are generally nebulous symbols meaning different things at different times and to different people. Allistoun exhibits his fact and has its truth accepted by his universe; harmony is restored aboard the *Narcissus*, which then comes safely to port. Rarely if ever again was Conrad to display such certainty.

5 *Heart of Darkness*

The transition to *Heart of Darkness*, like that between *An Outcast of the Islands* and *The Nigger of the 'Narcissus'*, is marked by several short stories which can be seen as essays in the structural concepts Conrad was evolving. Each of these explores one of the principal structural or technical features which developed more fully in the next major work. The first of these stories in sequence of composition after *The Nigger of the 'Narcissus'* is *Karain: A Memory*, which belongs to the spring of 1897. It is a slight piece, unusual among Conrad's stories because of its happy ending, although there are dark overtones, and the telling is tarred with the brush of heavy nostalgia which also marks the near-contemporary tales, *The Nigger of the 'Nircissus'* and *Youth*.

As Conrad was aware, the plot-kernel of *Karain* is virtually identical with that of *The Lagoon*. In both, a Malay warrior-hero slays his comrade (a brother in one story, a best friend in the other) in order to win a woman and later, the woman having fallen away, tells the story to a sympathetic but uninvolved white audience. Both stories are stark encapsulations of the prototypical Conradian situation: the hero, to obtain the woman who represents his ideal, sacrifices his friend in an act for which he can never forgive himself, and so loses his goal in the very moment of winning it. The most obvious differences between these two tales, both written within a twelve-month period, are that *Karain* has a happy, even somewhat humorous ending, whereas *The Lagoon* is tragic; and that the focus of the story in *Karain* is the nemesis, the real or imagined ghost of the hero's friend and victim, who pursues him until exorcised improbably by an image of Queen Victoria.

The nemesis has no part in *The Lagoon* but, as we have seen, appears as Lingard in *An Outcast of the Islands* and as Allistoun in *The Nigger of the 'Narcissus'*. The tendency of *Heart of Darkness* and of Conrad's subsequent work suggests that he was consciously dissatisfied with these two characters, particularly with Allistoun, at least to the point of searching for a different mold in which to cast the figure. The emphasis in *Karain* upon the ghosly avenger is further evidence of that pursuit.

Two points of present interest stand out in this otherwise unarresting story. First there is the figure of Karain, the typical Conradian hero who, behind an impressive, manly, and martial exterior conceals a guilty secret. Karain, in his local magnificence, is akin on the one hand to Willems and Wait, and on the other to Kurtz and Jim. His past crime, actually heinous, is treated in the tale as little more than a misdemeanour, understandable and even sympathetic, which could and should be forgotten. The situation between Karain and his white friends is close to that between Jim and Marlow. In both cases the story presents a grossly criminal act for which the hero's responsibility, as he relates the events afterwards, is minimized. Jim's Marlow, like Karain's friends, then has the task (unsuccessful in his case) of liberating the hero from his "ghosts".

The second point is that in making the nemesis an avenging spirit, slightly comic but none the less fearsome, Conrad has taken a step towards the more sinister occupants of that role who were to appear in his later fiction. The motif of supernatural vengeance, muted to mere just reprisal in Lingard and Allistoun, now comes to the fore, even although its operation in this story is probably imaginary. The way is thus prepared for the uncannily demonic *alter ego* figures of Gentleman Brown and Mr Jones.

The Return, completed September 1897, is one of Conrad's oddest works, "a left-handed production" as he described it in his Author's Note to *Tales of Unrest*. It concerns, essentially, the change of perspective experienced by the hero when he learns that his wife has been on the verge of infidelity. Although she returns (hence the title) and convinces him that the indiscretion existed only in intention and will not be repeated, he finds, to his own surprise, that he cannot resume his old way of life with her. The story turns upon the contrast revealed to him by the shock of his wife's conduct between his former middle-class, convention-governed existence and a deeper, non-conventional reality which he has hitherto overlooked.

> In the pain of that thought was born his conscience; not that fear or remorse which grows slowly, and slowly decays amongst the complicated facts of life, but a Divine wisdom springing full-grown, armed and severe out of a tried heart, to combat the secret

baseness of motives. It came to him in a flash that morality is not a method of happiness. The revelation was terrible. He saw at once that nothing of what he knew mattered in the least. The acts of men and women, success, humiliation, dignity, failure – nothing mattered. It was not a question of more or less pain, of this joy, of that sorrow. It was a question of truth or falsehood – it was a question of life or death (p. 183).

The crucial distinction here, between conventionalized falsehoods and a nebulous substratum of truth, was already part of Conrad's conceptual scheme in *An Outpost of Progress* and *The Nigger of the 'Narcissus'*, and was to be more obviously so in *Heart of Darkness*. It remained integral to much of his best fiction, usually coming into play at the point where the hero is confronted by the nemesis, revealing to him a truth about himself or about the world, which has been up to that point obscured. An obvious case here, close in time, is Kurtz' final awareness of the "horror" of the gulf between his ideals and his actions, but we might also cite for comparison the unpleasant and often violent visitations of truth upon almost any of the later Conradian heroes.

The Return, unlike Conrad's major fiction, works largely in terms of explicit generalities with only the thinnest dramatic realization, and fails as a story because these broad generalizations are worked out laboriously in the hero's mind by the narrative voice. Conrad himself wrote of the tale, however, that "psychologically there were no doubt good reasons for [the] attempt", (Author's Note), reasons which we may plausibly connect with his work on the nemesis figure and on the hero's moment of truth in such near contemporary stories as *The Nigger of the 'Narcissus'* and *Heart of Darkness*.

The third and best short story intervening between these two acknowledged early masterpieces is *Youth*, completed in June 1898. It owes its success to Conrad's discovery of the narrative voice of Marlow, which freed him at once, although not permanently, from the worst of the purple prose of the early Malayan stories and *The Nigger of the 'Narcissus'*, and from the lumbering omniscience of *The Return*. At the same time, the sceptical, fallible intelligence of Marlow helped Conrad to redress the balance which his own romantic involvement with the personae of such figures as Lingard and Allistoun had been in danger of upsetting. The effect of this discovery, when applied to the Conradian fictional pattern, is to be seen in *Heart of Darkness* and *Lord Jim*.

Youth has no plot; it is, as Conrad said in his Note, "a record of experience" and is superbly crafted. None the less it is presented as an illustration of the fundamental principle of the Conradian universe: the paradoxical futility of human endeavour.

> You fellows know there are those voyages that seem ordered for the illustration of life, that might stand for a symbol of existence. You fight, work, sweat, nearly kill yourself, sometimes do kill yourself, trying to accomplish something – and you can't. Not from any fault of yours. You simply can do nothing, neither great nor little – not a thing in the world – not even marry an old maid, or get a wretched 600-ton cargo of coal to its port of destination (pp. 3–4).

Here, in essence, is the situation of the Conradian hero from Almayer through Wait and Kurtz, through the protagonists of the political novels to Heyst, Lingard in *The Rescue*, and Peyrol, a state of affairs in which every effort to achieve a personal goal is largely frustrated by its own inevitable consequences.

Such is the situation of Kurtz, the hero of *Heart of Darkness*, who endeavours, like Kayerts and Carlier, to carry enlightenment into the jungle, but finds that the very elevation of his thinking, when exposed to the native environment, becomes twisted to its opposite, a cult of manic despotism and exploitation. Kurtz is very close in function and symbolic value to Wait; both are numinous figures of outstanding reputation among their fellows, both are physically impressive men given to verbal sonority, yet both conceal fatal illness behind their façade of strength, and both are ultimately exposed as vessels of corruption. The paradox of Kurtz is apparent from the passage in which Marlow's first view of him is described.

> I saw the man on the stretcher sit up, lank and with an uplifted arm, above the shoulders of the bearers. . . . I resented bitterly the absurd danger of our situation, as if to be at the mercy of that atrocious phantom had been a dishonouring necessity. I could not hear a sound, but through my glasses I saw the thin arm extended commandingly, the lower jaw moving, the eyes of that apparition shining darkly far in its bony head that nodded with grotesque jerks. Kurtz – Kurtz – that means short in German – don't it? Well, the name was as true as everything else in his life – and death. He looked at least seven feet long. His covering had

fallen off, and his body emerged from it pitiful and appalling as
from a winding-sheet. . . . I saw him open his mouth wide – it
gave him a wierdly voracious aspect, as though he had wanted to
swallow all the air, all the earth, all the men before him. A deep
voice reached me faintly. He must have been shouting. He fell
back suddenly (pp. 133–4).

The tall man, called "short", is sick and dying and yet still, by the
power of his voice, controlling the balance of events.

Like Wait, Kurtz is surrounded by men who propagate his
reputation, and is himself the source of a body of rhetorically
inflated doctrine. Like Wait's powerful influence over the crew in
The Nigger of the 'Narcissus', Kurtz' "voice", his written and spoken
words and the words spoken concerning him by other characters, is
the mainspring of his story's plot. "The point," as Marlow observes,
"was in his being a gifted creature, and that of all his gifts the one
that stood out preeminently, that carried with it a sense of real
presence, was his ability to talk, his words – the gift of expression, the
bewildering, the illuminating, the most exalted and the most
contemptible, the pulsating stream of light, or the deceitful flow
from the heart of an impenetrable darkness" (pp. 113–14). Here is
the heart of the paradox of Kurtz. Just as Wait represents an
appealing notion of liberal humanitarianism which leads in practice
to a deadly anarchy, so Kurtz preaches widely an ideal of progressive paternalism which manifests itself in greed and depravity.

Kurtz, as Marlow understands, was "a gifted creature". "This is
the reason why I affirm that Kurtz was a remarkable man. He had
something to say. He said it. . . . He had summed up – he had
judged. 'The horror!' " (p. 151). This famous dying summation of
Mister Kurtz is the logical conclusion of a process that begins with
the attempt to propagate an ideal, an ideal which Kurtz, unlike
Marlow, dares to pursue to its natural end. The ideal attracts
Marlow, but Kurtz "had made that last stride, he had stepped over
the edge, while I [Marlow] had been permitted to draw back my
hesitating foot" (p. 151). The hero is of unusual stature precisely
because he is without the inhibitions of ordinary mortals, represented by the insecure Marlow, who remain within the narrow bounds
of their moral conventions. Kurtz is in this the descendant of
Almayer and Willems, prepared to cut corners in order to win his
goals, but whereas their aims are personal and unimpressive Kurtz'
ideals have universal scope. Once again Kurtz most resembles Wait,

committed regardless of consequences to a general goal with wide
ideological ramifications.

Largely because of the similarity between the heroes, *Heart of
Darkness* is very close to *The Nigger of the 'Narcissus'* in its conceptual
structure. In both stories the central figure is the paradoxical hero,
gifted and flawed, powerful yet dying, whose presence generates a
conflict between two opposed but inseparable principles. Both
heroes, Wait and Kurtz, are men of wide and varied influence
among their fellows, and their respective acts of will – Wait's
attempt to find an easy passage and Kurtz' efforts to regulate the
lives of savages – are therefore of wide significance in their stories.

Both heroes act in a context of dualistic conflict; Wait enters a
world in which hierarchical authority (represented by Allistoun) is
challenged by self-interest (Donkin), and Kurtz, in a very similar
way, operates in the context of a power-struggle between idealists
(with whose party Marlow is identified, not altogether correctly, by
others) and materialistic self-seekers (such as the Manager). The
ideological conflict of *Heart of Darkness*, a recognizable growth from
the small seed in *An Outpost of Progress*, is announced by Marlow in
his introduction.

> They [the Roman conquerors] grabbed what they could get for
> the sake of what was to be got. It was just robbery with violence,
> aggravated murder on a great scale, and men going at it blind –
> as is very proper for those who tackle a darkness. The conquest of
> the earth, which mostly means the taking it away from those who
> have a different complexion or slightly flatter noses than
> ourselves, is not a pretty thing when you look into it too much.
> What redeems it is the idea only. An idea at the back of it; not a
> sentimental pretence but an idea; and an unselfish belief in the
> idea. . . . (pp. 50–1).

The redeeming "idea", which Marlow here opposes to the common
human reality, is the structural successor of Almayer's dream and
Willems' inflated self-image, and is closer yet to the utopian
longings inspired by Wait.

The respective efforts of Kurtz and Wait to institute a new order,
to move away from the *status quo* in pursuit of an "idea", result
ironically in their arrival at an extreme opposite to their intentions.
This, in both cases, is because the hero makes a fatal compromise,
takes a moral short cut, which involves him in paradox from the

very outset of his endeavour. Wait, who by his appearance promises to be an ideal seaman, seeks an easy passage aboard a sailing vessel and destroys the harmony and discipline of his ship. Kurtz, a gifted and high-minded explorer setting out to elevate the savages, puts himself above the usual code of conduct and ends by participating in pagan brutalities.

The over-all point here, as in the earlier novels, is the systematic self-frustration of purposive human action, the vaguely Schopenhauerian principle that man's efforts to improve his condition are inherently unproductive. The case of Kurtz demonstrates specifically the psychological rule that pursuit of an enlightened ideal of rational conduct is not a rejection of the animal, appetitive aspect of man but rather its intensified application. Kurtz fails to escape the passion which activates such men as the Manager just because he tries too hard, too passionately, to do so. Man cannot shed his animal nature; his means of survival, as Marlow realizes retrospectively, is not to seek a pure "idea", but rather to master his passions, to subordinate and apply his appetites to the discipline of the task in hand.

> They [the savages] howled and leaped, and spun, and made horrid faces; but what thrilled you was just the thought of their humanity – like yours – the thought of your remote kinship with this wild and passionate uproar. . . . Let the fool gape and shudder – the man knows, and can look on without a wink. But he must at least be as much of a man as these on the shore. He must meet that truth with his own true stuff – with his own inborn strength. Principles won't do. . . . You wonder I didn't go ashore for a howl and a dance? Well, no – I didn't. Fine sentiments, you say? Fine sentiments, be hanged! I had no time. I had to mess about with white-lead and strips of woollen blanket helping to put bandages on those leaky steam-pipes – I tell you. I had to watch the steering, and circumvent those snags, and get the tin-pot along by hook or by crook. There was surface truth enough in these things to save a wiser man (pp. 96–7).

Kurtz' failing lies in his abandoning the discipline, the requirements and responsibilities, albeit conventional, of the civilization he represents.

Kurtz, like Wait, has thus betrayed his calling, broken the rules of his profession. The reasons for the hero's compromise, in both cases, remain largely implicit and unexplored. Wait's background prior to his arrival aboard the *Narcissus* is unknown, by which time he has already embarked upon his fatal course. Kurtz, too, is revealed as a fully-formed character in mid career. The histories and motives of the earlier heroes, Almayer and Willems, on the other hand, are expounded at some length. Having made his central character a figure embodying paradox, a man whose flaw is the very quality which makes him extraordinary, who is drawn into compromise by precisely the virtues which should, on the face of things, set him above it, Conrad was at first unwilling to subject to open scrutiny the biographical, psychological connection between the gift and the weakness.

In the case of Kurtz, however, Conrad does give a glimpse of this fatal connection in the document which the hero composed at the outset of his career, before his appearance in the story, and to which we are introduced in Marlow's summary.

But it was a beautiful piece of writing. The opening paragraph, however, in the light of later information, strikes me now as ominous. He began with the argument that we whites, from the point of development we had arrived at, "must necessarily appear to them [savages] in the nature of supernatural beings – we approach them with the might as of a deity," and so on, and so on. "By the simple exercise of our will we can exert a power for good practically unbounded," etc. etc. From that point he soared and took me with him. The peroration was magnificent, though difficult to remember, you know. It gave one the notion of an exotic Immensity ruled by an august Benevolence. It made me tingle with enthusiasm. This was the unbounded power of eloquence – of words – of burning noble words. There were no practical hints to interrupt the magic current of phrases, unless a kind of note at the foot of the last page, scrawled evidently much later, in an unsteady hand, may be regarded as the exposition of a method. It was very simple, and at the end of that moving appeal to every altruistic sentiment it blazed at you, luminous and terrifying, like a flash of lightning in a serene sky: "Exterminate all the brutes!" (p. 118).

Marlow tacitly observes here Kurtz' transition from "altruistic sentiment" to brutality by way of an exalted sense of his own idealism, his awareness of the "power for good" in "the simple exercise of [his] will". This very will towards the realization of ideals, unrestrained by practical considerations and propelled by "magnificent" rhetoric, takes Kurtz "over the edge" from which Marlow draws back. Kurtz' flaw consists in his lack of the normal human limitations of circumspection and practical sense, which hold a man like Marlow under control. "Mr. Kurtz lacked restraint in the gratification of his various lusts, . . . there was something wanting in him – some small matter which, when the pressing need arose, could not be found under his magnificent rhetoric" (p. 131). Because of this lack, in a move comparable to Almayer's compromise and Wait's signing aboard the *Narcissus*, Kurtz takes the easy option, the short cut, of applying his ideals without regard to the moral considerations and inhibitions which would occur as difficulties to the more ordinary man. Kurtz' greatness, which is also the seed of his destruction, is his adoption for himself of a standard which denies human limitations, a characteristic which distinguishes him from the earlier heroes, including Wait, but which makes him the immediate ancestor of Jim, Nostromo, and Heyst.

The dualisms in the respective stories of Wait and Kurtz are closely related. In both cases traditional values, the hierarchical discipline of the sea (represented by Allistoun) and accepted European morals (represented by Marlow), which may be grouped together under Marlow's concept of "restraint", are opposed by the licence of unrestrained egocentricity, by anarchy aboard the *Narcissus* and by the "unsound methods" of Mister Kurtz. The psychological and conceptual antitheses of order and chaos, authoritarianism and individualism, restraint and licence, which are discernible in *The Nigger of the 'Narcissus'* and *Heart of Darkness*, and which are thinly anticipated in *An Outpost of Progress*, were to emerge in a new key in the political novels of Conrad's second phase.

The structural resemblance between these two stories does not end with the heroes and their conflicts. The rival and nemesis figures of the two tales are also markedly similar. In *The Nigger of the 'Narcissus'* the rival is Donkin, the advocate of licence, whom the hero encounters at first as a colleague, when he embarks upon his enterprise, but who becomes the jealous opponent who finally presides over the hero's dissolution and steals his treasure. In very much the same way the Manager in *Heart of Darkness*, another senior employee of the company which also employs Kurtz, stands for an unrestrainedly opportunistic approach, resents the threat of Kurtz' advancement and, in the end, takes the dying hero captive aboard his steamer and assumes charge of Kurtz' hoard of ivory. The Manager does not kill Kurtz, any more than Donkin kills Wait, but both heroes are in the care of their hypocritically disapproving rivals at the time of their demise, and both rivals benefit immediately from the heroes' removal. One function of both rivals is to show by contrast the elevation of the respective heroes. Both Donkin and the Manager are engaged in pursuits much the same as those of the heroes in their later stages, yet, while the heroes are fallen supermen, the rivals remain petty, selfish individuals.

The rivals here, as in most of Conrad's longer stories, are brought into play as a result of the heroes' commitment to compromise. Just as Wait, having taken his deceptive place aboard the *Narcissus*, inevitably encounters Donkin, his fellow crewman, so Kurtz, practising his ideals in the employ of the company, inescapably provokes the envy of the Manager, on whose territory he encroaches. It is in these two stories that the rival's role crystallizes, after its uncertain beginning in the characters of Dain and Omar, as that of a man motivated by personal jealousy who acts against the hero so as to contribute significantly to his collapse. Donkin and the Manager are the precursors of Cornelius, the Monteros, and the Schomberg of *Victory*.

The nemesis in *Heart of Darkness*, the character who, at the story's climax, arrives from the world the hero has deserted to confront him with his dereliction, is none other than Marlow himself. Marlow's function here, as a figure in the plot, is very similar to that of Allistoun in *The Nigger of the 'Narcissus'*; both are experienced sea commanders of traditional outlook whose task is to arrest the errant hero in order to restore a moral balance. Yet it is in the area of this role that Conrad most obviously develops *Heart of Darkness* beyond the scope of the earlier tale. Symptomatic of novelty is the fact that whereas Allistoun, although powerful, has a relatively small part, Marlow, as the storyteller, occupies the foreground. The deeper effect of this shift of perspective is to focus centrally upon the relationship between the nemesis and the hero. Conrad was never to use precisely this device again, writing the story entirely from the nemesis figure's point of view, but the relationship it developed was to remain central to his fiction.

The relation between the nemesis and the hero is first given prominence in the confrontation of Lingard and Willems in *An Outcast of the Islands*. The most significant new feature introduced into this aspect of *Heart of Darkness* is the mysterious bond between Marlow and Kurtz. Before they meet Marlow is attracted by what he hears of Kurtz, and as events develop he assumes the role of guardian of Kurtz' reputation (pp. 138–9) in his anxiety that the Manager and his party should not be able to discredit the fallen idealist. Matters come to a climax when Marlow discovers that Kurtz has escaped from the steamer to rejoin the savages. Rather than organize a general pursuit, which would involve the further revelation of Kurtz' dark secrets, Marlow elects the dangerous course of following him alone. "I did not betray Mr. Kurtz – it was ordered that I should never betray him – it was written I should be loyal to the nightmare of my choice. I was anxious to deal with this shadow by myself alone, – and to this day I don't know why I was so jealous of sharing with any one the peculiar blackness of that experience" (pp. 141–2). As a result, the climax of the story is the coming face to face of these two men alone in the jungle, a difficult and dangerous moment in which Marlow must persuade Kurtz to give up his savage life and return to Europe.

The comparable confrontations in the earlier stories, those between Lingard and Willems and between Allistoun and Wait, although they have the same effect of terminating the hero's active career, have little of the same intensity. Marlow speaks of meeting with Kurtz in the jungle as the foundation of an "intimacy" which was "to endure – to endure – even to the end – even beyond" (p. 143). The experience goes further than Marlow's sympathy for Kurtz, his approval of the "idea", which makes him run risks and tell lies in order to preserve Kurtz' reputation. It is also something of a vicarious struggle, for Marlow finds that, in watching Kurtz examine the fascination of the jungle, he had also "to go through the ordeal of looking into it myself" (p. 145). The close personal bond created in this story between the nemesis and the hero, emphasized as it is by the fact that Marlow himself tells the tale, is a large step towards the mysterious *alter ego* relationships between Brown and Jim, Jones and Heyst, and Jörgenson and Lingard.

A smaller but noticeable difference between *The Nigger of the 'Narcissus'* and *Heart of Darkness* is the reintroduction into the latter of the female roles of heroine and anti-heroine, both absent from Wait's story. Kurtz, like Willems, manifests his compromise, his desertion of white standards, by a union with a native woman symbolically associated with her exotic jungle background. Kurtz' woman was savage and superb, wild-eyed and magnificent; there was something ominous and stately in her deliberate progress. And in the hush that had fallen suddenly upon the whole sorrowful land, the immense wilderness, the colossal body of the fecund and mysterious life seemed to look at her, pensive, as though it had been looking at the image of its own tenebrous and passionate soul (pp. 135–6).

Kurtz' native woman has no active part in the plot; she enters only to lament the coming of the rival, the Manager, who is to separate the hero from her, and to shout unintelligible words as the steamer departs. The rival and his party here are not themselves candidates for the heroine's affections, as are Dain and Omar in the earlier stories, but are simply hostile to her, on account of her embodiment of the hero's illicit aspirations. The hostility, manifested when the "pilgrims" open fire upon the heroine and her companions, is reminiscent of Donkin's distaste for Wait's absent lady at the comparable point in *The Nigger of the 'Narcissus'*.

More significant in *Heart of Darkness* is the anti-heroine, Kurtz' "Intended", the European woman who, with her prior claim upon the hero, stands opposed to the jungle heroine. Unlike Joanna and Aissa, these two never meet and remain each in ignorance of the other. They stand respectively for the two relevant stages of the hero's career, the "Intended" being the woman of his orthodoxy, the native girl representing his fallen, compromised activity.

The "Intended" figures in the story's conclusion when Marlow visits her, a year after Kurtz' death, in order, in effect, to lay the ghost of their "intimacy".

There remained only his memory and his Intended – and I wanted to give that up, too, to the past, in a way – to surrender personally all that remained of him with me to that oblivion which is the last word of our common fate (p. 155).

The outcome of the interview is that Marlow, confronted with this woman who still believes passionately in Kurtz' integrity, finds himself unable to tell her the truth and ends by telling her a lie, which supports her unreal, idealistic picture of the man. Marlow's position here is similar to that of Lingard in *An Outcast of the Islands* who, having brought Joanna to Sambir, decides to keep from her the knowledge of Willems' betrayal and association with Aissa.

Marlow is more fortunate than Lingard in that no one intervenes to upset his concealment of truth.

The role of the Intended in *Heart of Darkness* serves chiefly to give us a strong final sense of the contrast between the orthodox Kurtz, whom she remembers, and the compromised figure of Marlow's acquaintance. Wait, by the end of *The Nigger of the 'Narcissus'*, is buried and all but forgotten, but Kurtz, in the memories of Marlow and the Intended, dominates the conclusion of *Heart of Darkness*. The interview between these two people closes the story on the open question of truth, which in *The Nigger of the 'Narcissus'* had been settled unambiguously by Allistoun's suppression of the mutiny.

The issue between the heroine and the anti-heroine is comparable to that between the rival and the nemesis figure. In both cases one figure is an upholder of traditional moral values while the other belongs to, or operates in the domain of the jungle, where the white man's laws do not run. Marlow and the Intended belong to the European world Kurtz has abandoned, and between them, for different reasons, they perpetuate the memory of the hero as he was before his compromise with savage ways. The Manager and the native woman, on the other hand, are associated with Kurtz' jungle phase, the one as rival, the other as accomplice.

In this story we see the Conradian hero clearly flanked by a full complement of four supporting figures, grouped in two pairs of opposites, in an arragement which may be represented as follows:

	MALE	FEMALE
1st (WHITE) WORLD	Nemesis (Marlow)	Anti-heroine (Intended)
2nd (BLACK) WORLD	Rival (Manager)	Heroine (Native woman)

This is, of course, a particular schematic representation of the central part of the larger Conradian pattern, and may also be traced in *An Outcast of the Islands*, although there the male roles (Omar and Lingard) are less well-defined than in *Heart of Darkness*. Related symmetries can be found in most of the later stories.

In the fourfold arrangement of roles in *Heart of Darkness*, just as the heroine and anti-heroine are associated respectively with the conventional (or prelapsarian) and unconventional (or compromised) stages of the hero's career, so the rival and the nemesis confront each other over the moral, ideological issue of exploitation and enlightenment, excess and restraint. Both oppositions are clearly rooted in the conceptual dualism, the conflicting ideological worlds against the background of which the story is unfolded. The antagonism between the female figures clearly echoes that of Aissa and Joanna. That between the males, faintly prefigured in Omar and Lingard, is a close restatement of the relationship of Donkin and Allistoun.

Apart from the absence of female characters from the earlier story, *Heart of Darkness* is structurally very close to *The Nigger of the 'Narcissus'*. Wait and Kurtz are recognizably similar creations, both being men of great influence whose reputations are the mainsprings of their respective plots. In these novellas of comparable length each hero is flanked by a rival and a nemesis whose roles are structurally alike, the rival in both cases revealing himself ultimately as a jealous competitor in the world of the hero's compromise, while the nemesis figures, remaining faithful to tradition and restraint, succeed in both thwarting the rivals' ambitions and arresting the heroes' careers. Although widely different in setting and narrative tone, these two stories form as close a pair in the Conrad canon as do the two first novels, *Almayer's Folly* and *An Outcast of the Islands*.

The two novellas are further drawn together by their explicit concern for truth, its discovery or elusiveness, an issue which also surfaces in many of Conrad's later novels. In *The Nigger of the 'Narcissus'* Allistoun's vindication of truth, in the face of falsehoods spread among the crew as a result of Wait's influence and Donkin's activities, is the turning point of the story, the factor which restores order aboard the *Narcissus* and so brings her to a safe journey's end. *Heart of Darkness* is largely the relation of Marlow's sceptical quest for truth between the unsatisfactory opposites of facile idealism (such as is upheld by both his aunt and Kurtz' Intended) and corrupt materialism (practised by the Manager and his associates). Marlow, who "can't bear a lie" (p. 82), and who finds "in the work" his "own reality" (p. 85), discovers through the paradox of Kurtz that the idealism which attracts him is finally inseparable from the repellent "horror". The closing scene of the story, in which Marlow shies away from truth, draws dramatically the outcome of his quest.

Yet it is over the theme of truth that these two stories are most sharply divided. For whereas Allistoun, the nemesis figure of *The*

Nigger of the 'Narcissus', is self-assured and successfully expounds and imposes a view of human affairs unreservedly endorsed by his story, Marlow, his counterpart in *Heart of Darkness*, repudiates certainty in favour of scepticism and the power of deception. The difference between the two stories in attitude to truth should not be exaggerated, however; for it can also be said that from another point of view both tales conclude with a deliberate suppression of unpleasant verities. Marlow, having experienced a glimpse of the horror at the heart of darkness and having undertaken to report aright the cause of Kurtz to the unsatisfied, in the final scene denies his hero by refusing to testify to Kurtz' ultimate revelation. In a very similar way Allistoun, having outfaced Wait and the mutinous crew of the *Narcissus*, acts serenely as if nothing of note had occurred; the belaying-pin, the "fact" of the matter, which symbolizes the essence of the mutiny, the equivalent of Kurtz' "horror", once exhibited, is ritualistically returned to its normal inoffensive place, and soon after, with similar ritualistic accompaniment, the body of Wait is dropped over the side of the ship. On the face of things, neither Kurtz' adventures nor Wait's presence aboard the *Narcissus* effects any lasting change. The core of the difference between the two stories lies in the nemesis figures, for while Allistoun, who (from the hints he drops) has seen such things before, remains serenely untroubled by his encounter with Wait, Marlow emerges deeply changed by his dealings with Kurtz.

6 *Lord Jim* and the Short Stories of 1900–2

Lord Jim was the next tale Conrad completed after *Heart of Darkness*, its composition concluded in July 1900. When he began it is less certain; he was working on it in May 1898, while still writing *Youth* and before turning to *Heart of Darkness*, and he may have begun a short story akin to the "Patna" episode as early as July 1896.* The novel is closely bound up with Conrad's earlier work, to which it stands very much in the relation of a summation. *Nostromo*, the next major work, after a number of exploratory shorter tales, was to involve a radically new approach to the structural pattern.

From its immediate predecessors, *The Nigger of the 'Narcissus'* and *Heart of Darkness*, *Lord Jim* takes the figure of the hero as an embodiment of paradox; Jim belongs to the same family as Wait and Kurtz, men of deceptive promise whose truly exceptional ideals are flawed by excess in achievement. The subordinate roles of rival and nemesis in *Lord Jim* are also developments of the corresponding parts in the preceding tales. From the earlier novels, *Almayer's Folly* and *An Outcast of the Islands*, the new story borrows the Malayan setting of its long concluding section. The plot-structure of *Lord Jim* is particularly close to that of *An Outcast of the Islands*; in both novels, after criminal failings in the white world have made the hero an outcast, he is transported to the jungle of Borneo, where he finds a temporary field for his activities until arrested by a nemesis from the world he has betrayed. The greatest difference between these two novels, apart from the much more sophisticated narrative techniques of *Lord Jim*, lies in their respective heroes. Willems remains of much the same type as Almayer, a generally feeble character whose desires outrun his performance, while Jim is a deeply paradoxical figure, a detailed development of the kind introduced by Wait and Kurtz.

* Frederick R. Karl, *Joseph Conrad: the Three Lives* (New York, 1979) p. 378.

The paradox of Jim, like that of Kurtz, is reflected in his name, "Lord Jim", the juxtaposition of a common diminutive with the style of nobility. It is reflected too, like that of Wait, in his deceptive appearance as a seaman.

> This was my first view of Jim. He looked as unconcerned and unapproachable as only the young can look. There he stood, clean-limbed, clean-faced, firm on his feet, as promising a boy as the sun ever shone on; and, looking at him, knowing all he knew and a little more too, I was as angry as though I had detected him trying to get something out of me by false pretences. He had no business to look so sound (p. 40).
>
> He stood there for all the parentage of his kind, for men and women by no means clever or amusing, but whose very existence is based on honest faith, and upon the instinct of courage. . . . He was the kind of fellow you would, on the strength of his looks, leave in charge of the deck – figuratively and professionally speaking. . . . I would have trusted the deck to that youngster on the strength of a single glance, and gone to sleep with both eyes – and, by Jove! it wouldn't have been safe. There are depths of horror in that thought. He looked as genuine as a new sovereign, but there was some infernal alloy in his metal (pp. 43–5).

Like Kurtz, his close contemporary, Jim is a man from whom great things are expected by his fellows and by whom great deeds are performed within a limited context. Yet paradoxically, again as in Kurtz, the very quality which makes Jim remarkable is also an excess, a lack of restraint, which negates his achievement.

Whereas in *The Nigger of the 'Narcissus'* Conrad pays little attention to the psychological nature of the hero's flaw and paradox, and whereas he gives only a brief glance in that direction in *Heart of Darkness*, *Lord Jim* is a concentrated study of the central character and the anomaly he represents. Whereas Kurtz is seen for only a short time through the eyes of a puzzled and seemingly more naive Marlow, Jim is subjected to microscopic scrutiny by an apparently older, wiser, and quasi-paternal narrator, who also enlists the opinions and points of view of a range of more or less impartial witnesses (Brierly, Chester, the French Lieutenant, Stein). The paradox of Jim, the discrepancy between his ideals and his performance, is not only the mainspring of the novel's plot but is also its chief subject.

The scrutiny of Jim's motives and fallibilities reveals a situation similar to the case of Kurtz, in which an apparently sympathetic idealism, pursued without regard to common frailties, results in criminal failure and excess. Jim's idealism, of a more specific nature than Kurtz' vague missionary zeal, consists in what Marlow calls, somewhat too broadly, his "imagination", a faculty for transforming everyday realities through day-dream into heroic melodrama.

"How steady she goes," thought Jim with wonder, with something like gratitude for this high peace of sea and sky. At such times his thoughts would be full of valorous deeds: he loved these dreams and the success of his imaginary achievements. They were the best parts of life, its secret truth, its hidden reality. They had a gorgeous virility, the charm of vagueness, they passed before him with a heroic tread; they carried his soul away with them and made it drunk with the divine philtre of an unbounded confidence in itself. There was nothing he could not face (p. 20).

Stein's "diagnosis" of this condition is more precise: Jim is "romantic" (p. 212), romanticism in this context consisting in an idealized view of the world as a place in which pursuit of a superhuman standard of conduct is rewarded with success and recognition.

The world view which lies at the heart of Jim's paradoxical nature is interestingly very close to that which Conrad had himself adopted in his portraits of Lingard and Allistoun. *The Nigger of the 'Narcissus'*, completed about fifteen months before the composition of *Lord Jim* began in earnest, exemplifies in the figure of Captain Allistoun the notion that an inflexibly high standard of personal courage and discipline will overcome all odds, defeating not only human opposition but also the adverse contingencies of nature. Allistoun himself, of course, is no dreamer, but like Marlow and MacWhirr a decisively practical soul; yet the mood of his creator in 1896 was scarcely distinguishable from that subjected to analysis in the delineation of Jim some two years later.

In Jim's romanticism, his abnormally developed faculty for imagination, we recognize the ideal or "dream" (another of Stein's terms) of the early Conradian hero, the will to transform himself and the world about him to some more elevated level. Jim's ideal is particularly close to that of Kurtz, not only in that it adopts a high moral tone and is eventually exercised against a jungle background, but also in its dangerous requirement of a superhuman set of values. In this lies its fatality, for just as Kurtz, setting himself above human standards in pursuit of his ideals, ended in criminal excess, so Jim, living on the level of his unattainable dreams, is on several occasions found unready to meet the less strenuous but none the less immediate demands of reality, and ends his career convicted of dereliction of duty. Conrad is careful to emphasize that the same idealistic qualities which interest Marlow and account for Jim's outstanding successes in Patusan are also the cause of his failings as an officer. "It was the same mood, the same and different, like a fickle companion that to-day guiding you on the true path, with the same eyes, the same step, the same impulse, to-morrow will lead you hopelessly astray" (p. 235).

Jim's idealism so cuts him off from reality that he is unable to respond to demanding situations. He knows, of course, what should be done, and no mere want of courage prevents him from doing it, yet his elevated picture of existence is so far removed from the actuality of events that he cannot, at short notice, get himself into action.

> He had been taken unawares – and he whispered to himself a malediction upon the waters and the firmament, upon the ship, upon the men. Everything had betrayed him! He had been tricked into that sort of high-minded resignation which prevented him lifting as much as his little finger, while these others who had a very clear perception of the actual necessity were tumbling against each other and sweating desperately over that boat business (p. 95).

Aboard the *Patna* Jim is paralysed not by fear of shipwreck but by the distasteful circumstances, so out of key with his conception of the heroic mode, in which the wreck would take place, with the overload of passengers and the disreputable crew. Because the actual emergency, as it occurs, is so out of harmony with comparable situations he has faced in imagination, he is unable to play his proper part.

> He was not afraid – oh no! only he just couldn't – that's all. He was not afraid of death perhaps, but I'll tell you what, he was afraid of the emergency. His confounded imagination had evoked

for him all the horrors of panic, the trampling rush, the pitiful screams, boats swamped – all the appalling incidents of a disaster at sea he had ever heard of. He might have been resigned to die but I suspect he wanted to die without added terrors, quietly, in a sort of peaceful trance (p. 88).

Under such circumstances Jim's imagination works against him, magnifying the complex miseries of the situation and preventing his active grasp of what should be done.

Jim is therefore a typical Conradian hero, distinguished by an ideal, by pursuit of a "dream", which makes him at once potentially capable of exceptional achievement and liable to criminal excess. Like Kurtz and Wait, moreover, Jim is not only himself an anomalous figure, at once gifted and flawed, but is also portrayed to reflect the ironic paradox of the Conradian universe, wherein any unusual exertion of will is met by a negating counter movement. Jim's wish to distinguish himself through heroism leads him to a conspicuous act of cowardice, and later his creation of an autocratic state for himself in Patusan is returned to chaos through the nemesis of Gentleman Brown.

Conrad usually presents the operation of these ironies through a dualistic conflict, a dialectic between the poles of which the hero is caught, as Almayer is torn between black and white worlds, and Kurtz between the principles of enlightenment and exploitation. In most of the novels from the time of *An Outpost of Progress* the dualistic conflict manifests itself ideologically as between idealism and materialism, order and anarchy, or altruism and individualism, but *Lord Jim*, being psychological rather than ideological in its general orientation, reverts to the simpler mode of the early Malayan novels, in which the hero pursues his career between two cultures, black and white, Malay and European. The dualism of Jim's universe, like that of Almayer's, has little or no conceptual significance.

Jim, like Willems, having committed an offence against the white code, is eventually transplanted to the jungle, where he makes another attempt and meets a large measure of success, which is then curtailed at the story's climax by a nemesis in the shape of a character from the white world he has abandoned. As in the earlier Malayan novels, there is no significant ideological difference in *Lord Jim* between the white and black worlds; they are, on the contrary, close equivalents. In Patusan Jim meets much the same range of

men, from honourable leaders to unscrupulous brigands, as the
story presents in the white world; beside Stein we may place
Doramin, beside the French Lieutenant Dain Waris, beside the
Captain of the *Patna* Cornelius, and beside Brown the Rajah Allang.
As in the earlier stories, the significance of the dichotomy of the two
worlds lies not in any cultural or philosophical difference between
them but in the very fact of their separateness, by virtue of which the
hero, although a published outcast in one realm, may still find
footing in the other.

The immediate result of this cultural relativism, in *Lord Jim* as in
Almayer's Folly and *An Outcast of the Islands*, is that the white hero,
having failed in his native context, is able to take the easier option of
repeating his attempt in the black world. Jim's withdrawal to
Patusan, facilitated by the powerful father-figure of Stein in much
the same way as Lingard arranges Willems' escape to Sambir, is not
only a retreat but also a deliberate move into a non-white world, in
which the stringent conditions of the European code do not
necessarily apply. In making the transition, slightly shameful in
itself because it involves rejection of his own native heritage
(symbolized by his father, the stereotypical benevolent Anglican
country clergyman), Jim "left his earthly failings behind him and
that sort of reputation he had, and there [encountered] a totally new
set of conditions for his imaginative faculty to work upon" (p. 218).
The black world is not exactly more primitive than the white, but is
more pliable, less rigidly formed, and, of course, on a much smaller
scale, and is for all these reasons more amenable to the imposition of
Jim's ideals. Marlow remarks "how, three hundred miles beyond
the end of telegraph cables and mail-boat lines, the haggard
utilitarian lies of our civilization wither and die, to be replaced by
pure exercises of imagination, that have the futility, often the
charm, and sometimes the deep hidden truthfulness, of works of art"
(p. 282).

The issue turns upon the familiar Conradian notions of discipline
and fidelity to the common task. The white world demands these
qualities inexorably from a white man, whereas the black world
may allow him a compromise. A sound traditionalist like Marlow is
stimulated by the white world's challenge, whereas the romantic,
imaginative soul of Jim can prosper only in the more flexible black
environment. Marlow describes an illuminating occasion when Jim
accompanied him to the borderline between the two worlds, where
the river of Patusan runs out to the sea.

I breathed deeply, I revelled in the vastness of the opened horizon, in the different atmosphere that seemed to vibrate with a toil of life, with the energy of an impeccable world. This sky and this sea were open to me. The girl was right – there was a sign, a call in them – something to which I responded with every fibre of my being. I let my eyes roam through space, like a man released from bonds who stretches his cramped limbs, runs, leaps, responds to the inspiring elation of freedom. "This is glorious!" I cried, and then I looked at the sinner by my side. He sat with his head sunk on his breast and said "Yes," without raising his eyes, as if afraid to see writ large on the clear sky of the offing the reproach of his romantic conscience (pp. 331–2).

Jim, committed to the limited environment of Patusan, is cowed by the wider world outside, to which Marlow can respond as to a challenge. Jim, like Willems and Wait, for all his excellent qualities has none of "the perfect love of the work" of seamanship which, to Marlow, is the "only reward" (10). Jim seeks less immediate rewards, in pursuit of which he is prepared to compromise, to take the easy option, which he does not only in accepting Stein's offer of retreat to Patusan but also in shipping aboard the *Patna*, a local steamer run lazily under easy-going foreign management. The accident which befalls this ship is a retribution for Jim's want of character in remaining her chief mate, just as Brown's fatal raid is retribution for the subsequent leap into the anonymity of Patusan.

Jim's movement from the white world to the black, like the comparable moves of Almayer and Willems, is therefore a compromise, an expression of his essential weakness, which should be compared also to Wait's arrival aboard the *Narcissus* and to Kurtz' adoption of savage ways in the jungle. Jim's compromise, however, belongs most closely with those of Almayer and Willems in that it has no precise ideological implications. Wait stands at the centre of controversy over the question of discipline and individual rights, and Kurtz raises the problem of conventional moral restraint opposed to idiosyncratic licence, but Jim's defection to Patusan has little or no conceptual implication beyond a broad and general antithesis between the domains of duty and "imagination". We can only speculate as to why, having introduced in *The Nigger of the 'Narcissus'* and *Heart of Darkness* the ideational orientation he was to pursue in most of his later novels, Conrad reverted in *Lord Jim* to the type of framework he had used in *Almayer's Folly* and *An Outcast of the*

Islands, where the background conflict is, as it were, merely geographical and not significantly philosophical.

Although *Lord Jim* does not exhibit the ideological interest of its immediate predecessors, it does develop in other directions. It remains, for instance, Conrad's most sustained piece of character analysis and perhaps his most successful. It was also by far his most complex essay to date in narrative virtuosity, the direct precursor, in this respect, of *Nostromo* and *Chance*. It may be safe to conclude that, in this novel, Conrad devoted his energies to the narrative method and to the psychological portraiture it was designed to reveal, putting in abeyance the ideological themes to which he was shortly to return.

The direct structural consequence of the absence from *Lord Jim* of any closely examined ideological conflict is a rearrangement of the secondary characters surrounding the hero. In each of the two preceding tales, the rival and the nemesis are clearly divided in opposition over the ideological issue of the story; Donkin stands opposed to Allistoun in *The Nigger of the 'Narcissus'* and the Manager to Marlow in *Heart of Darkness*. The rival and nemesis of *Lord Jim*, Cornelius and Brown respectively, are not divided by any conceptual issue, but work in cooperation for the hero's downfall. Again, in *Heart of Darkness* the ideological conflict of the story is reflected in the disparity between the hero's two women, the idealistic European fiancée, and the exotic black woman associated with Kurtz' savage indulgences. In *Lord Jim* there is no antiheroine, and the heroine, Jewel, has no significant ideological associations. We are therefore returned to the situation of the early Malayan novels in which the secondary characters are defined chiefly by the geographical or cultural areas to which they belong.

Like most Conradian heroes, Jim marks his compromise, his easy option of removal to a less stringent world, by association with a woman belonging to the world or party he has newly chosen. Jim in Patusan finds Jewel, who is of partly white ancestry (her grandfather was "a white; a high official" (276)), but who belongs to the jungle world in much the same ways as do Nina and Aissa. When Jim arrives in Patusan, Jewel, an orphan, is under the guardianship of the despicable Cornelius, her oppressive stepfather, who is also the man Jim replaces there as Stein's agent. The situation among these three, Jim, Jewel and Cornelius, is structurally a re-creation of that among Willems, Aissa and Omar in *An Outcast of the Islands*. Jim is the white outcast who, like Willems, wins the affections of a local woman, Jewel, who is in turn, like Aissa, under the guardianship of the hero's rival, a man established in the settlement, whose position the newcomer threatens. The structural parallelism goes further; just as Omar attempts Willems' death, so Cornelius conspires, first with the natives and then with Brown, to destroy Jim; and just as Aissa becomes insanely possessive and finally kills Willems when he attempts to leave her, so Jewel ends condemning Jim for accepting the fatal responsibility in an act of self-sacrifice which she sees as desertion.

Lord Jim is manifestly a greater novel than *An Outcast of the Islands*, primarily because its hero is much more finely conceived and skilfully portrayed than Willems. Differences of this kind, which show themselves chiefly in the content and technique of the novels, can also be traced in structural terms. Willems remains a selfish and generally unsympathetic creature, whereas Jim, his undeniable misdeeds minimized through the benevolent eyes of Marlow, is probably the most appealing of Conrad's heroes. The disparity in their natures is reflected in their respective relationships to their adopted jungle homes and to the women they find there. Willems in Sambir, like Almayer, has no long-term object but escape and return to the white world. His affair with Aissa, a pure-bred native who remains largely alien to him, is a transient passion based on misunderstanding and imperfect sympathy. Jim, on the other hand, makes a life-long commitment to Patusan and gives himself totally to its people and affairs, with no thought of returning to the white world. His relationship with Jewel is correspondingly more sympathetic, she being herself part European and predisposed to share his aims. The rapport between them extends even to her acquisition of his mannerisms, as Marlow observes.

> Her mother had taught her to read and write; she had learned a good bit of English from Jim, and she spoke it most amusingly, with his own clipping, boyish intonation. Her tenderness hovered over him like a flutter of wings. She lived so completely in his contemplation that she had acquired something of his outward aspect, something that recalled him in her movements, in the way she stretched her arm, turned her head, directed her glances (p. 283).

The nobility of Jim's nature, which shows itself in his dynamic and constructive career in the world of his compromise, is thus reflected

in the strongly positive association into which he enters with Jewel.
Jewel's only important similarity to Aissa, beyond their common
structural role as heroine and representative of the black world, is
her failure to comprehend the hero's compromise, to realize that,
however great he appears in her world, he is there as a defector from
another, which has a large and damaging claim upon him. For this
reason Jim, for all his power and glory, is no less a prisoner in
Patusan than is Willems in Sambir; "he was imprisoned within the
very freedom of his power, and she, though ready to make a foot
stool of her head for his feet, guarded her conquest inflexibly – as
though he were hard to keep" (p. 283).

Jewel is the product of a combination of Aissa's role as heroine
with an expansion of the part of the hero's accomplice played
implicitly by Kurtz' native woman. In a rather similar way,
drawing on *An Outcast of the Islands* and *Heart of Darkness*, we can see
Jim's rival, Cornelius, as combining the paternal proprietary
jealousy of Omar with the materialistic competition of the
Manager, for Cornelius is both Jewel's stepfather and Jim's ousted
commercial predecessor in Patusan. Although his position in the
plot is similar to that of his counterpart in *An Outcast of the Islands*,
Cornelius is more significantly related to his immediate predecessors
in *The Nigger of the 'Narcissus'* and *Heart of Darkness*. Like Donkin and
the Manager, he stands opposed to the hero as a meaner contrasting
figure engaged in the same pursuit. Donkin is the worst type of
sailor, the Manager a paragon of mercenary acquisitiveness, and
Cornelius a failed and embittered commercial agent, each of them
confronting the hero with what his career would amount to in the
absence of what Marlow (in *Heart of Darkness*) calls "the redeeming
idea", which in Jim's case is his romantic "imagination".

With the third of the secondary characters, the nemesis Brown,
we come to the most important single innovation in plot structure
introduced in *Lord Jim*. Here again Conrad builds upon his earlier
work, giving Brown some characteristics drawn from Marlow in
Heart of Darkness, from Allistoun, and from Lingard in *An Outcast of
the Islands*. Like them, Brown comes from the white world which the
hero has abandoned, challenges the hero's achievement by confronting him with his past failures, and effectively ends his career.
Brown, however, opposes the hero not from a contrasting position of
orthodoxy, as do his predecessors, but as himself a case of failure and
dereliction of the hero's own type. The new development in the
nemesis figure, making him an *alter ego* more comparable than

antithetical to the hero, demands particular notice, especially because Conrad was frequently to use it again.

The *alter ego* relationship between Jim and Brown is established with meticulous deliberation, so as to be obvious to even the lightest of readers. Both men lay emphatic claim to the status of "gentleman" (pp. 131 and 345), although both are fugitive outcasts from the world where the style might be meaningful. Brown in flight, moreover, takes refuge in the same creek in Patusan across which Jim had made the leap which brought him to dominance in the settlement, and it is over this creek that the two men have their fatal conference (pp. 359 and 380). Brown sees himself and Jim as men of the same kind, engaged upon the same mission of robbery and extortion.

> When he asked Jim, with a sort of brusque despairing frankness, whether he himself – straight now – didn't understand that when "it came to saving one's life in the dark, one didn't care who else went – three, thirty, three hundred people" – it was as if a demon had been whispering advice in his ear. . . . He asked Jim whether he had nothing fishy in his life to remember that he was so damnedly hard upon a man trying to get out of a deadly hole by the first means that came to hand – and so on, and so on. And there ran through the rough talk a vein of subtle reference to their common blood, as assumption of common experience; a sickening suggestion of common guilt, of secret knowledge that was like a bond of their minds and of their hearts (pp. 386–7).

Brown has visions of "stealing the whole country" and is annoyed that already "some confounded fellow had apparently accomplished something of the kind" (p. 366). This view of Jim as Brown's facsimile, while incomplete, has none the less a sufficiency of truth to enable Brown to undermine with it Jim's judgment and authority.

The nemesis is the most variable element in the structural pattern at this stage in Conrad's work. We have seen that he is absent from *Almayer's Folly*, is introduced somewhat clumsily as Lingard in *An Outcast of the Islands*, appears as the sinister but faintly burlesque phantom in *Karain*, is apotheosized as Allistoun in *The Nigger of the 'Narcissus'*, and brought abruptly to earth and to the centre of the stage as Marlow in *Heart of Darkness*. Marlow in *Lord Jim* relinquishes the role; indeed, he has no part in the plot there except the purely functional one of introducing the outcast Jim to a succession of benefactors. The nemesis role is taken over, with a vengeance, by Brown, who is not merely, like his predecessors, the instrument of the hero's arrest, but is also himself a representative of the hero's moral weakness.

At first sight there appears to have been a complete reversal in Conrad's conception of this figure between Allistoun and Marlow on the one hand, who stand for European orthodoxy and the discipline of the craft, and Brown on the other, who, like the hero, is a criminal outcast. Yet the psychological confrontation and close interaction between Brown and Jim is prefigured in that between Marlow and Kurtz, for both are cases of interplay between two men whose shared nature and brief achievement of mutual understanding are crucial to the story. Moreover, all the nemesis figures – Brown, Marlow in *Heart of Darkness*, Allistoun, Old Viola, Jones, Jörgenson, and the others – no matter what their differences, are distinguished primarily by certain common characteristics: they all belong to a world the hero has deserted, and they all stand directly opposed to his career in the world he has chosen. Marlow summarizes Brown's case in words which make this role explicit:

> To me the conversation of these two [Brown and Jim] across the creek appears now as the deadliest kind of duel on which Fate looked with her cold-eyed knowledge of the end. No, he didn't turn Jim's soul inside out, but I am much mistaken if the spirit so utterly out of his reach had not been made to taste to the full the bitterness of that contest. These were the emissaries with whom the world he had renounced was pursuing him in his retreat. White men from "out there" where he did not think himself good enough to live. This was all that came to him – a menace, a shock, a danger to his work (p. 385).

There is no doubt, therefore, that despite his moral turpitude Brown is as much a nemesis as Allistoun or Viola.

What Conrad achieves in *Lord Jim*, by making this figure a rogue and by confronting the hero not with a representative of moral and disciplinary orthodoxy but with a man who exhibits the hero's own weaknesses exaggerated to the pitch of villainy, is chiefly an alteration of the moral balance of the tale in the hero's favour. Jim is a more sympathetic figure than any of his predecessors, not only because he has the scrupulously expansive Marlow as his Horatio, but also because, unlike the earlier heroes, he is clearly of much greater integrity than his final antagonist. Where the devious Willems is confronted by the straightforward Lingard, the derelict Wait by the dutiful Allistoun, and the abandoned Kurtz by the self-possessed Marlow, Jim the would-be hero and saviour is counter-poised only by the destructively unprincipled Brown.

Whereas the earlier heroes evidently meet no more than their deserts, Jim by contrast seems persecuted by an unjust fate. The irony built into the structure of Conrad's universe from the days of *Almayer's Folly* takes on a vicious new twist. At the same time, Jim is allowed a much greater and more positive achievement in his adopted world than any of the earlier heroes, making his retribution therefore the less acceptable. The severity of the nemesis principle is considerably stronger here than in any of Conrad's earlier novels. The result is a much darker over-all view of the human situation, darker even than that in *Heart of Darkness*, where the "horror" has at least been halted and repressed by the end of the story. The "horror", the disruptive principle in *Heart of Darkness*, as in *The Nigger of the 'Narcissus'*, *An Outcast of the Islands*, and even *Almayer's Folly*, lies in the machinations of the compromised hero, the cessation of whose activities is a restoration of general moral balance. In *Lord Jim*, on the other hand, although Jim is tainted with something of the mysterious inner blackness of his predecessors, a taint which causes him to abandon the many lives in his charge on the *Patna*, the career which is actually terminated by Brown's intervention is apparently sound. In other words, there is no reason to suppose that without the appearance of the nemesis figure Jim's activity in Patusan would have concluded tragically. The earlier heroes are stopped in destructive courses, but Jim's later career, had it not been for Brown, would have been blameless. Brown's intervention therefore seems a merely mechanical retribution for forgotten sins and serves no justifiable preventive purpose.

The various innovations we have noted in *Lord Jim* point collectively in this same direction. The sympathy generated for Jim through Marlow, his strong relationship with Jewel, his successes in Patusan, and above all the disreputable nature of his final opponent, all serve to heighten the reader's involvement with the hero while at the same time distancing the retributive forces which work against him. The result is a starker universe in which, it seems, even the most deserving, once compromised, are denied earthly atonement.

Jim's position as hero differs from that of his immediate

predecessors. The hero is, by definition, always the structural centre of the story, but Wait and Kurtz, in the telling of their tales, are off stage the greater part of the time. But Jim is rarely out of the centre of vision throughout his long history, being in this respect similar to the less engaging figures of Almayer and Willems. The combination of this unrelentingly close portrayal with a sympathetic character topples the Conradian universe. The irony of the hero's end is no longer fully counterbalanced by the enormity of his weakness and the flagrancy of his compromise. Jim, like Heyst and many of the later heroes, seems to rise in merit above the inscrutable system by which he is condemned.

Having completed *Lord Jim* in July 1900, Conrad began work on *Typhoon* in September and finished it in January the following year. *Typhoon* is at first sight and odd story for Conrad to have written at this stage in his work, partly because it has a comic ending and overtones, and partly because its hero, Captain MacWhirr, has none of the usual attributes; he embodies no paradox, is guilty of no compromise or desertion, and is pursued by no nemesis. The explanation seems to lie in the story's relation to *Lord Jim*. *Lord Jim* deals with an "imaginative" and "romantic" hero who is destroyed by an ultimately unbridgeable gulf between the realm of his aspirations and that of implacable facts. *Typhoon* is a study of a hero who thinks and operates on a purely factual level, and who thereby not only survives the kind of testing which Jim failed at sea but also proves himself a match for Jim in the field of colonial administration.

The story is more than a little tongue-in-cheek. The literal-minded MacWhirr is not a rounded character on the same level as Jim. His dogged and humourless conversation, pursued to the point of pedantry in his exchanges with Jukes, is caricature rather than portraiture, and his combination of utter simplicity with specta-cular competence is generally unconvincing. *Typhoon* stands to *Lord Jim* in the relation of an exercise in thematic inversion, using, as it were, the major key instead of the minor and creating an effectually opposite mood. It is as if Conrad set out, fresh from the protracted study of Jim, to create his antitype, perhaps by way of experiment or formal exercise, simply to see how such a man might fare. That the creation was more a logical possibility than a psychological verisimilitude did not deflect him from a brilliant undertaking.

MacWhirr's situation aboard the *Nan-Shan* is very similar to

Jim's aboard the *Patna*. Both ships are sailing in eastern waters under a foreign flag. Both heroes are surrounded by officers and men not themselves capable of confronting disaster. Both ships carry a large number of native passengers for whose welfare the white officers are responsible. And both vessels encounter accidents which make their survival seem, for a time, highly unlikely. The great difference between the two cases is, of course, that whereas the *Patna* is abandoned by her officers, including Jim, the *Nan-Shan*, under the captaincy of MacWhirr, is brought bravely through the crisis.

MacWhirr stays at his post and steams his ship through the storm because he is the antitype of Jim, a man of no imagination and therefore of no fear or impulse. He lives on a purely literal level, seeing only the most immediate implications of what goes on around him. "There were matters of duty, of course – directions, orders, and so on; but the past being to his mind done with, and the future not there yet, the more general actualities of the day required no comment – because facts can speak for themselves with overwhelming precision" (p. 9). Because he does not visualize the consequence of the storm MacWhirr steams into it without losing his nerve, whereas Jim, the visionary creator of the state of Patusan, abandons the *Patna* precisely because he foresees with graphic clarity the apparently inevitable results of her accident.

The relation between *Typhoon* and *Lord Jim* is cemented by the character of Jukes, who is first mate aboard the *Nan-Shan*, just as Jim was first mate of the *Patna*. Jukes, who in his own story contrasts with and counterbalances the figure of MacWhirr, is a paler version of Jim, a young, relatively inexperienced, but highly promising officer endowed with a hyperactive imagination. His inclination to inactivity as the ship is engulfed by the hurricane is closely similar to the detachment of Jim's last moments aboard the *Patna*.

Jukes remained indifferent, as if rendered irresponsible by the force of the hurricane, which made the very thought of action utterly vain. Besides, being very young, he had found the occupation of keeping his heart completely steeled against the worst so engrossing that he had come to feel an overpowering dislike towards any other form of activity whatever. He was not scared; he knew this because, firmly believing he would never see another sunrise, he remained calm in that belief.

These are the moments of do-nothing heroics to which even good men surrender at times. . . . He conceived himself to be calm – inexorably calm; but as a matter of fact he was daunted; not abjectly, but only so far as a decent man may, without becoming loathsome to himself (pp. 51–2).

Jukes is roused from this mood by the orders and encouragement of his captain, while Jim, in the absence of any such support or control, gives way and deserts his post.

Just as Jim's failure as an officer is ultimately echoed in the collapse of his administration in Patusan, so MacWhirr's foolhardy success in outriding the storm is repeated in his solution to the problem of the Chinamen's disputed property. Once again the situation has gone quite beyond Jukes, for all his assumed intellectual superiority, when the captain's dogged simplicity discovers a workable answer in the straightforward equal sharing of the money. The solution is unambitious and characteristically aimed at nothing higher than meeting the immediate problem. Unlike Jim in Patusan, MacWhirr makes no gesture towards any larger concept of law, equity, or government, and avoids any undue personal involvement with the outcome. His only object is to achieve a common-sense level of fairness with a minimum of disturbance.

Falk belongs with *Typhoon*, not only chronologically but also as Conrad's only other major story in a predominantly comic mood. As soon as he had completed *Typhoon* in January 1901, Conrad began *Falk*, which was to occupy him into the late spring. The two tales are comic not only in the Aristotelian sense that they both have happy endings, in which their respective heroes triumph over obstacles, but also in that they include a high proportion of Conrad's best humorous writing, particularly in association with MacWhirr in *Typhoon* and with Hermann and with Falk himself in the later story. Both works are in a sense the product of a single creative impulse. The light-hearted brilliance which they share contrasts with both the intense seriousness of *Lord Jim* and the sombre gloom of the tales which were to come immediately after – *Amy Foster*, *Tomorrow*, and *The End of the Tether*. Both stories, moreover, are explorations of happy alternatives to the grim fatalism of *Lord Jim*. Just as *Typhoon* portrays the success of a man who is in every significant way Jim's opposite, so in *Falk* we see a man who, like Jim, bears the guilt of a heinous but ambivalent sin, but who is able despite this to circumvent his rivals and win his lady.

Falk's story is worked out in terms of the Conradian pattern. At the root of his case lies a paradox, the absurdity that the force which provides his prime motivation, the very will to survive, in him reaches such a strength as to endanger his survival. Falk is "dominated . . . by the singleness of one instinct. He wanted to live. He had always wanted to live. So we all do – but in us the instinct serves a complex conception, and in him this instinct existed alone"(p. 223). Under the compulsion of this drive Falk kills and eats a man, purely defensively and without criminal intent, an act which, although enabling him to survive, upsets the balance of his life. The paradox becomes overt when the *same* compelling life force, abnormally strong in Falk, requires him to take a wife and attracts him to Hermann's niece. "He was hungry for the girl, terribly hungry, as he had been terribly hungry for food" (p. 224). Falk is too straightforward a man to conceal his past from his future wife, yet his misdeed makes him wholly unacceptable to Hermann, the girl's guardian, who is a model of middle-class respectability. Falk's will to survive thus cuts him off from the very goal it requires him to achieve.

Falk is therefore a Conradian hero of much the same general type as Willems or Jim, a man with a hidden, guilty past and a bad reputation who seeks to overcome these disadvantages by making a new start in a new sphere. The new sphere in Falk's case is the world of Hermann's niece, symbolized by the ship *Diana* of Bremen, which is comfortable, reputable, chaste, pure and ordinary. Falk, like Jim in Patusan, is at first totally alien to this new world. His passionate nature and slightly unsavoury reputation are anathema to the placid Hermann. He represents a world and temperament which are deliberately excluded from the *Diana*.

> There apparently no whisper of the world's iniquities had ever penetrated. And yet she lived upon the wide sea: and the sea tragic and comic, the sea with its horrors and its peculiar scandals, the sea peopled by men and ruled by iron necessity is indubitably part of the world. But that patriarchal old tub, like some saintly retreat, echoed nothing of it. She was world proof. Her venerable innocence apparently put a restraint on the roaring lusts of the sea (p. 156).

It remains for Falk to penetrate this chaste sphere "by the power of a simple and elemental desire" (p. 156). Like the other heroes, Falk in attempting to ameliorate his position seems only to make it more acute by entering a world which has the initial effect of magnifying his problems.

The hero's move towards the world of the *Diana* is typically centred upon the heroine, Hermann's niece, who embodies much of her uncle's spirit. She is placid, domestically inclined, even-tempered, modest, neat and apparently pure. At the same time, however, there is about her a power, size, and vitality which clearly provide the basis of the attraction she holds for Falk. To Falk, Hermann's niece represents the ideal of vitalism, which is his own driving force, combined with a domesticity and respectability which has hitherto been beyond his reach.

> She was the tender and voiceless siren of this appalling navigator [Falk]. He evidently wanted to live his whole conception of life. Nothing else would do. And she, too, was a servant of that life that, in the midst of death, cries aloud to our senses. She was eminently fitted to interpret for him its feminine side (p. 236).

The worthy Hermann himself is cast as Falk's rival. Like Omar and Cornelius he stands in a quasi-paternal relation to the heroine and, like Omar, resents the hero's intrusion on the grounds that he falls outside the pale of orthodoxy. Hermann is generally a comic figure, but his opposition is none the less effective, in that Falk is able to make no headway towards the niece until the uncle's hostility has been placated.

In the story of Falk Conrad also develops his favourite theme of reputation. The heroes from Willems onwards tend to be associated in their stories with a public notoriety, which may be either generally adulatory, like that of Kurtz, ambivalent like that of Wait, or infamous like that of Jim. Falk's reputation, which, like those of his predecessors, springs directly from the very qualities of his character which make him distinctive and ill-fated, is vaguely sinister and is, as we would expect, close to that of Jim – the bad odour of a solitary man concealing a guilty past. Falk is particularly sensitive about the suspicions which others have of him, his one desire beyond survival and marriage with Hermann's niece being for respectability and social acceptance. "This desire of respectability, of being like everybody else, was the only recognition he vouchsafed to the organization of mankind" (p. 198). Falk, whose disreputably passionate love of life has cut him off from humanity, wishes now to be received into the placid and proper sphere of the mundanely respectable Hermann.

Conrad employs Schomberg as the local fountainhead of the hero's bad name, a part which that unsavoury expatriot had already essayed in Lord Jim and one which he was to enlarge considerably in Victory. In Victory, indeed, Schomberg expands his role to encompass that of the rival, becoming there, like Cornelius in Lord Jim, the jealous informant who shows the agent of nemesis the way to take his victim. Conrad had already in the Manager and in Donkin established a relationship between the rival and the source of rumour concerning the hero. It is this facet of Schomberg which lies at the root of Falk's reaction to the hotel keeper: "He had for Schomberg a repulsion resembling that sort of physical fear some people experience at the sight of a toad" (p. 197).

The narrator's part in Falk resembles that of Marlow in Heart of Darkness with respect to the matter of the hero's reputation. Just as Marlow there intervenes to shield Kurtz from the Manager's malice, so here the narrator takes Falk under his protection and helps him to circumvent the effects of Schomberg's hostile gossip. In both these cases, as in that of Lord Jim, the chief narrator undertakes the role of guardian of the hero's reputation, the role of Horatio in the closing scene of Hamlet.

The difference between Marlow in Heart of Darkness and the narrator in Falk is that the former is also the hero's nemesis while the latter is the instrument of his release and rehabilitation. For Falk, like its immediate predecessor, Typhoon, has one of Conrad's rare happy endings. Instead of being confronted with his crime and made to accept its consequences, as are Willems, Kurtz, Wait and Jim, Falk is allowed to expiate it by merely revealing it, through the mediation of the narrator, to the inimical Hermann. The reason for this conclusion so uncharacteristic of Conrad's fictional world can only be that in Falk, as in Typhoon, the author was deliberately experimenting with inversions of his usual themes. In Typhoon he portrayed a man whose impossibly complete lack of imagination renders him immune to the vitiating excesses of men such as Kurtz and Jim. In Falk he creates a hero who, because his excess is precisely an unusual vitality and love of life, will not succumb to the death which overtakes his predecessors once their secrets are revealed to the world.

The happy experimental mood of Typhoon and Falk did not persist. Within a few weeks of completing the latter in June 1901,

Conrad finished the tragic tale of *Amy Foster*, which was itself followed some six months afterwards by the ironic story *Tomorrow*. These two tales are linked by their setting, which in both cases is "Colebrook" on the south coast of England. They are also linked, more significantly, by their subjects, both concerned with young men who leave their native lands to find their fortunes in the wide world. The autobiographical relevance of both stories is obvious, particularly in *Amy Foster*, where the hero is an east European who comes to England unable to speak a word of the language. This is Yanko Goorall, who leaves his own country in hope of finding a better living in America, but pines thereafter for his homeland. Goorall, whose destiny is presented as completely outside his control, is unable to return, whereas Harry Hagberd in *Tomorrow* is a more cheerful prodigal who pays his father a fleeting visit after sixteen years of absence. Both stories end sadly; Goorall dies of homesickness and neglect, while Harry, unrecognized by his father, goes blithely on his way, leaving to misery the woman his father had designed for his wife.

Perhaps because of their close reference to his own life, Conrad put little or nothing of his usual structural pattern into either of these stories. *Amy Foster* resembles *Falk* in several ways; in each story a strange man of doubtful background and character falls in love with a girl of an extremely conservative and rigorously ordinary familial origin. Amy is the heroine who, like Hermann's niece, responds to the stranger, while Hermann's opposition to Falk is echoed in the hostility of Amy's family and neighbours. Yanko Goorall himself is driven to survive and woo her despite the circumstances by an "instinctive love of life" (p. 130), comparable to Falk's compulsive vitality. Goorall's heroine, however, finally deserts him because of the very strangeness which she had at first found attractive. It is as if in this story Conrad takes a realistic look beyond the happy ending of *Falk* to ask himself how such a pair of lovers from such disparate worlds could possibly perpetuate their happiness.

7 The End of the Tether

The End of the Tether, which Conrad completed in October 1902, is the last of the works of the period dominated by The Nigger of the 'Narcissus' and Lord Jim, and with it we return from short stories to the full-blown narrative structure. The new hero, Captain Whalley, like Wait, Kurtz and Jim, is a remarkable man concealing a guilty secret for reasons which are largely honourable, and like them he finds himself drawn into a false situation where the combined machinations of a rival and an agent of nemesis bring him to his death.

Whalley, like Wait and Jim, has all the appearance of a reliable officer, but is in reality, because of his rapidly failing eyesight, a danger to the ship he commands. The paradox is heightened by Whalley's past exploits as a seaman, by his very real strength of character, and by his physical soundness, all of which belie and conceal his increasing incapacity. Blindness, however, is a symptom, not the moral root of Whalley's problem, which lies deeper and which precedes the onset of his disability. The Captain first commits himself to an anomalous situation when he enters into partnership with the uncongenial Massy, a venture about which he has serious doubts on account of Massy's character and because, in tacitly allowing his new partner to continue under the delusion that he was a wealthy man, Whalley has practised on him a small but deliberate deception.

The paradox of Whalley, the eminent explorer and sea-captain who cannot see, is a symptom and emblematic outgrowth of the bargain with Massy, which is, in turn, a classic instance of the ambivalent compromise of the Conradian hero. Whalley's taking command of the Sofala and associating himself with the disreputable Massy, particularly under a shadow of false pretence, gives the hero cause for thought.

He would now consider calmly the discretion of it before saying the final word tomorrow. . . . He seemed already to have lost

something of himself; to have given up to a hungry spectre
something of his truth and dignity in order to live. . . . What a
disagreeable impression that empty, dark, echoing steamer had
made upon him. . . . In the solitude of the avenue, all black
above and lighted below, Captain Whalley, considering the
discretion of his course, met, as it were accidentally, the thought
of death (pp. 213–14).

Whalley's end is determined from the moment of the bargain which
makes him Captain and shareholder of the steamer in which he will
drown.

On the other hand, Whalley's motives, even more than those of
Kurtz, Jim and Falk, are pure and worthy. He is, indeed, the most
selfless and least culpable of Conrad's heroes to date. His object in
associating with Massy is in no sense personal gain, for he wishes
only to support himself while preserving his capital for his
impoverished daughter. His own shortage of funds, moreover, after
a lifetime of profitable work, is the result of no fault of his, but of the
collapse of his bank. As he himself observes, while considering the
compromise into which he has been forced, he has no real choice in
the matter (p. 213).

The only morally dubious aspect of Whalley's compromise is his
passive deception of Massy as to his own financial situation, leaving
the other to suppose that a man of Whalley's age and background
must be reasonably wealthy. His reason for this does not lie in the
circumstances, for Massy would probably have accepted Whalley
for the money the old man could indeed offer, which was sufficient to
meet the need. Whalley conceals the truth largely to ease his
personal relations with Massy, which, he rightly supposes, would be
intolerable if the owner knew that his Captain had nothing more to
invest, lend, or withhold. "Clearly, with a fellow of that sort, and in
the peculiar relation they were to stand to each other, it would not
have done to blurt out everything" (p. 215). When Whalley does
come around to the truth it is too late, the deception being too far
gone, and Massy cannot believe him. This, then, is Whalley's only
flaw, his desire to preserve, in his unavoidable dealings with Massy,
a fragment of the respect and independence to which, as a ship-
owner and Captain, he had become accustomed. It is for this small
grain of human pride that Whalley suffers.

Matters take a more serious turn when Whalley begins to lose his
sight. He does not wish to withdraw from his arrangement with

Massy because in that event, under their agreement, the latter would be able to delay repayment of Whalley's investment for a year, during which time the old man would have no support. If, on the other hand, the Captain can hide the truth a little longer, the terms of their agreement will be up, and he will be able to withdraw his money and depart. This he tries to do, thus entering upon a deeper and more dangerous level of deception in his dealings with Massy. His attempt to keep going despite his failing eyes is "to set at nought the common rule of conscience and . . . to struggle against the very decree of Providence" (p. 254). He becomes "a fellow that, as it were, stood up against God Almighty Himself" (pp. 254–5). On a more literal level, Whalley is from this point onwards guilty of deliberately making his ship "unseaworthy" (p. 300).

Whalley's association with Massy is the seed of his destruction, for Massy himself eventually brings about the collision in which the Captain dies. Massy, an obvious agent of nemesis, is, like Brown in *Lord Jim*, a distorted reflection of the hero. He is, as Whalley has been, a ship-owner, and while an unforeseeable turn of fortune has deprived Whalley of his savings a comparable chance, a lucky number in a lottery, has brought Massy into unexpected wealth. While Massy runs himself into debt in hopes of another lucky number, Whalley submits himself to Providence, trusting that despite his failing eyes there will be no accident. Beyond this they are opposites. Massy, who is no true seaman, is acquisitive and lazy, while Whalley, who belongs to the fraternity of Allistoun and MacWhirr, is a paragon of discipline and selfless integrity. The association between these two men is incongruous from the first and is, as Whalley's instinct tells him, a compromise of fatal proportions.

From the time he boards the *Sofala*, therefore, Whalley is increasingly enmeshed in the consequences of an anomalous situation which he himself, albeit in justifiable desperation, has created. His objective, the ideal in pursuit of which he submits to Massy's conditions, is represented by Whalley's absent daughter, Ivy, for whose sake he wishes to preserve his remaining capital while continuing to earn his own support. Ivy has no active role in the story and can therefore hardly be called the heroine, although her position as the hero's inspiration, symbolizing Whalley's selfless devotion to what he believes to be his duty, endows her with the essential features of the Conradian hero's female partner. One is reminded of Kayerts' daughter, Melie, in *An Outpost of Progress*.

The part of the rival in this story falls to the *Sofala*'s mate, Sterne.

Because the only female in the plot is off-stage, the nature of the antagonism between Whalley and Sterne has no sexual connotation and is purely professional. Sterne, whose one object is to "get on a bit in the world" (p. 235), joins the *Sofala* in the expectation of supplanting the aging Whalley as Captain. When Whalley shows no sign of retirement Sterne begins to plot against him, looking for some failure he could use to secure the old man's dismissal, and in this way he stumbles across the fact of Whalley's encroaching blindness. Ironically Sterne's rivalry has no effect in the story, as Massy, who has already discovered Whalley's secret for himself, decides to use the Captain's disability as a means to wreck the vessel in order to obtain the insurance money.

The story continues the overall drift of *Lord Jim* by increasing the sense of a malign universe ruthlessly pursuing the hero with a fate out of all proportion to his human failings. Whalley is far less "to blame" than is Jim and, indeed, from a practical point of view commits no offence at all. His association with Massy, his compromise, is entirely forced upon him by bad luck and by his determination not to be a burden on his daughter. His only sin, his failure to disabuse Massy of the notion that he was rich, is hardly inexcusable and is without material consequences in the story. Whalley, much more than Jim, is a man of unusual ability marked out for destruction for a single small misuse of his talent.

Whalley, moreover, is hounded by fate even before he makes the fatal compromise. He is visited with two pieces of misfortune which, in combination, drive him to the partnership with Massy; his daughter makes a poor marriage and needs his financial assistance, while at the same time his personal fortune is lost in the fall of a banking house. The story draws our attention to Whalley's undeserved reversals, for the Captain himself is a believer in luck and is reflecting upon the subject just as the news of his own catastrophe reaches him. His son-in-law, he reflects, is a victim of "bad luck".

> His own [luck] had been simply marvellous, but he had seen in his life too many good men – seamen and others – go under with the sheer weight of bad luck not to recognize the fatal signs. For all that, he was cogitating on the best way of tying up very strictly every penny he had to leave, when . . . the shock of the big failure came; and, after passing through the phases of stupor, of incredulity, of indignation, he had to accept the fact that he had nothing to speak of to leave.

Upon that, as if he had only waited for this catastrophe, the unlucky man, away there in Melbourne, gave up his unprofitable game, and sat down – in an invalid's bath chair at that, too. 'He will never walk again,' wrote the wife (pp. 175–6).

Massy is also a great believer in luck. Having once won the Manila lottery, he wastes all his profits on more tickets in the conviction that he will win again. The reader cannot escape the point of the contrast between Massy's undeserved luck (even although it brings him no lasting happiness) and Whalley's misfortunes. The just are deprived and punished while the unjust thrive.

Once Whalley has made his compromise and shipped aboard the *Sofala*, the pursuit of fate becomes relentless. While he is ironically allowed to retain the bodily fitness upon which he relies, Whalley is deprived of sight, the faculty essential to his work. Even so, the Captain might have worked out his last three months and withdrawn without penalty from the agreement, had not Massy discovered his weakness and decided to turn it to this own advantage by arranging a false accident for the ship. Once the collision has occurred Whalley, faced with the choice of either taking a share of the blame for the "accident" or telling the truth about his attempts to deceive Massy, elects to go down with the ship rather than face either shame.

The very issue of the disposition of Providence is brought into the open in this tale in the conflicting views of Whalley and his friend, Van Wyk. Whalley, despite his own misfortunes, is an optimist. "Captain Whalley believed a disposition for good existed in every man. . . . They might be silly, wrongheaded, unhappy; but naturally evil – no. There was at bottom a complete harmlessness at least" (p. 289). Van Wyk, largely on the strength of having been jilted by a woman, takes the opposite view and adopts a stance of "disgust with the world" (p. 290). The story appears to bear out Van Wyk's view by its crushing destruction of the innocuous Whalley at the hands of Massy. The actual ending is more complex, however, largely because Van Wyk himself, as a result of his friendship with Whalley, revises his philosophy and returns to the world he had abandoned. Just when the world for Whalley becomes "a dark waste" (p. 333) which he is willing to relinquish, Van Wyk discovers in Whalley himself a redeeming human dignity which inspires him to take up his public life again.

The point, implicit in *Lord Jim*, is now made plain. The scale of universal justice, which exacts full punishment for the least infraction, bears no relation to the scale of human values. Jim and Whalley are flawed but worthy men whose attempts to arrive at a workable compromise between their human natures and the strict demands of honour are met by the mechanical rigour of a retribution which makes no allowance for circumstance or human weakness. In both stories the final note is the discordant contrast between the inflexibility of fate and the heroism of human endeavour.

The End of the Tether is the last story of Conrad's first mature phase. This phase is distinguished chiefly by its paradoxical heroes, men of deceptive promise, whose pursuit of high-minded but ill-judged ideals exposes their inner unsoundness. Such are Wait, Kurtz, Jim and Whalley. The most striking developmental feature of this period concerns Conrad's introduction and reconsideration of the nemesis figure. Allistoun is plainly a stronger version of Lingard in *An Outcast of the Islands*, but with Marlow in *Heart of Darkness* we meet a nemesis who is full of doubt and who makes himself something of an accomplice to the guilty hero. The next step is taken in *Lord Jim*, where Brown is drawn as Jim's *alter ego*, reflecting starkly the negative side of the hero's moral character. Massy confirms the direction taken by Brown. The result of these changes in the nemesis role is a shift in the moral perspective of Conrad's fiction. As the nemesis figure ceases to be a pillar of orthodox rectitude and becomes a sharer in an embodiment of the hero's guilt, the retributive weight of the story increases. As the agent of nemesis becomes less sympathetic, the hero's guilt is diminished proportionally; where Wait and Kurtz are evidently depraved, Jim and Whalley are presented as reluctant sinners who are more victims than villains. The last novels and stories of this phase present a cold universe in which the best of men are forced by character and circumstance to deviate from the moral path, are denied any way of atonement, and are strictly pursued to destruction by the evil powers they have aroused. The last story, *The End of the Tether*, is an essay on the very question of universal justice, of providence, in which its hero pathetically believes. For Conrad, however, the moral balance of the universe has, at this point, something of the starkness of classical tragedy. Meritorious individuals, singled out for trial, are rigorously penalized when their very virtues bring them paradoxically into disgrace. It was this view which was to be elaborated in the great novels of his next phase, the political stories of his middle period.

Part III The Second Phase

8 *Nostromo*

The phase of Conrad's writing from *The Nigger of the 'Narcissus'* to *The End of the Tether*, a period dominated by the achievement of *Heart of Darkness* and *Lord Jim*, has much in common with Greek tragedy. It presents us with men of exceptional character or vision, whose efforts, selfish or otherwise, to achieve a better world are frustrated partly by their own limitations but no less by the littleness of those around them, of men such as Donkin, the Manager, Cornelius, and Massy. The structural pattern of these stories turns upon the figure of the hero whose character embodies the paradox of flawed humanity endowed with exceptional character or ideals. In the earlier stories, principally *Almayer's Folly* and *An Outcast of the Islands*, the hero, while involved in paradoxical situations, remains himself a relatively ordinary and uncomplicated figure. The anomaly of his life lies in his external circumstances rather than in himself. From Wait to Whalley, however, the heroes are plainly microcosmic reflections of the paradoxical universe. Their stories are built around themselves, men of exceptional status but who, rather like the heroes of Sophoclean tragedy, fall foul of fate in trying to live up to their full potential.

After *The End of the Tether*, the last story in the *Typhoon* volume, Conrad began to work full-time on *Nostromo*, unquestionably his greatest technical achievement in the novel form, which occupied him until August 1904. In this work he introduced a radically new approach to the structural problem involved in his earlier fiction. That this change was to some degree deliberate is suggested by Conrad's own observations in his "Author's Note" to *Nostromo* and by the sequence of his stories in the immediately preceding period. After finishing the tale of Captain Whalley, he wrote, "it seemed somehow that there was nothing more in the world to write about" (p. vii). That such a feeling had in fact come upon him is corroborated by the decline in length and complexity of his stories since *Lord Jim*. Since completing *Jim* in mid-1900 Conrad had attempted only one serious long story, *The End of the Tether*, which, in spite of its many virtues, remains a somewhat tired and pale essay in the Conradian pattern. The author's experimental interest in the limits and variations of this pattern is evinced by such stories as *Typhoon*, *Falk*, and *Tomorrow*, which focus upon particular details of the structure. He was ripe for what he called retrospectively "a subtle change in the nature of inspiration" (ibid.), which led him to *Nostromo*.

Even so, *Nostromo*, for all its innovation in scope and structural technique, did not take Conrad into a totally new realm. The South American setting is, indeed, a novelty, but the use of a complex political scenario as the framework for a plot is embryonically present in Conrad's earliest novels. Almayer and Willems act out their destinies against a background of native political intrigue, and Jim in Patusan becomes involved in a similar struggle between three or four local parties of different racial origins. A strong political undercurrent flows through *Heart of Darkness*, while the companion work, *The Nigger of the 'Narcissus'*, is an intense study of a miniature political contest aboard a merchant ship. *Nostromo*, the first of Conrad's so-called "political" novels, is in this respect a logical continuation of the direction taken by *The Nigger of the 'Narcissus'* and the second half of *Lord Jim*.

A clear indication of the genuinely new departures taken by this novel is the fact that Nostromo is not the only central figure; he is absent from long sections of the story and stands definitely to one side of the main line of the plot, which follows the origin and growth of the Gould Concession. Structurally as central as Nostromo is Charles Gould, although he has largely faded from the story by the last of its three sections, in which Nostromo becomes more prominent. Once we admit the possibility of two heroes in this tale, moreover, two others, Decoud and Monygham, demand similar recognition, since they are both originators of independent lines of action which, rooted each in a fully developed character, have bearing upon the main course of events.

In all of Conrad's earlier novels the actions turn unambiguously upon a single central figure to whom the other characters, however prominent, are from a structural point of view clearly subordinate. Even Kurtz, whose actual presence spans only a few pages, is unquestionably the hero of *Heart of Darkness*, because it is around him, and not the locquacious Marlow, that the action turns. These earlier heroes are not only mainsprings of action but also the focal points of the Conradian structural pattern; in them, or in their actions, lies the fatal paradox; the ambivalent compromise, at once both guilty and distinguished, lies in their past; and theirs are the powerful voices and reputations by which others are variously attracted and repelled. In *Nostromo*, however, there is no such single central figure. Much of the action turns upon Gould, not Nostromo, and both Decoud and Monygham also make specific and emphatically independent contributions to its evolution. Again, Nostromo is not the sole possessor of the qualities associated with such earlier hero types as Kurtz, Wait and Jim; he is a man of widespread repute who becomes paradoxically compromised over his dealings with the silver, but the same is true (in a different way) of Gould, while Monygham re-enacts a past "crime", and Decoud pursues a heroine representative of an ideal.

Even so, there remains a sense in which Nostromo is the most important, although not the sole hero of the novel. The very fact that his name provides the book's title suggests that this is so, for it was Conrad's frequent practice to name novels for their heroes, as in *An Outcast of the Islands*, *The Nigger of the 'Narcissus'*, *Lord Jim*, *The Secret Agent*, and *The Rover*. Nostromo, although a background figure through the first half of the novel, is none the less primary in that he alone stands conspicuously maintaining a precarious balance between the ideological extremes of his world. The other heroes in the story, Gould, Decoud and Monygham, make their respective compromises through a distinct commitment to some current of the politico-ideological stream which forms the story's plot; Gould allies successively with material interests, Ribierism, and Sulacan separatism; Decoud becomes first a Ribierist and then the leading spirit of the separatist movement; while Monygham, under Emilia's protection, enters Sulacan high society and risks his dubious respectability to preserve the safety of his patroness during the rebellion. Nostromo, however, makes no such commitment, acting to the end for himself alone. In this respect he prefigures the other heroes of Conrad's "political" novels, Verloc and Razumov, men who try in vain to steer an independent course of self-interest between the conflicting polarities of political ideas.

Nostromo thus introduces a new type of hero and a new approach to the Conradian structure. The heroes of Conrad's first mature phase are embodiments of paradox, men possessed of exceptional qualities which entail vitiating weaknesses. The paradox of these central figures then extends itself into their respective plots as their characters generate situations of self-defeating endeavour. The heroes of the political novels, on the other hand, are not significantly paradoxical in character, and their plots are not generated directly by any purposive action on their part. The anomalies of their stories arise rather from the heroes' attempts to *avoid* decisive action which would commit them to either side in a dualistic conflict. The paradox now lies not so much in the character of the hero as in the dualistic conflict of his world, which ensures, first, that he cannot maintain his stance of neutrality and, secondly, that having compromised himself by action on behalf of one side the hero will be met with extreme retribution from the direction of the other. The paradox in the novels of this phase might be said to be universal rather than psychological. The heroes themselves, instead of rare and striking figures like Wait, Kurtz and Jim, are now relatively colourless, naturally passive, and temperamentally mild figures, such as Verloc and Razumov. Nostromo displays more verve than his immediate successors, but even he makes his object not to effect some change in the world around him, but simply to secure his own comfort while eschewing entanglement.

The hero who is not an ambitious idealist but rather one who seeks the easy option of neutrality in a universe of dualistic conflict is the distinguishing mark of Conrad's second mature phase, which includes *Nostromo, The Secret Agent, Under Western Eyes*, and a number of contemporaneous short stories. The change from a hero who provokes his nemesis by striving after a goal to one who desires primarily to avoid commitment further shifts the moral balance of Conrad's stories, continuing the direction of movement observed from Wait to Whalley in the first phase. The heroes of the second phase are generally forced into action against their own will and better judgment. The retribution they draw upon themselves seems therefore the less deserved. Where the heroes of the previous phase are men destroyed by their failure in some undertaking they have planned and embarked on for their own ends, the heroes of the second phase are victims of inequitable fate, punished in spite of their initial unwillingness to become involved in conflict.

Nostromo therefore marks several structural departures. It is on a much broader scale than any of the earlier novels – a broader scale, in fact, than Conrad was ever to attempt again – concerning itself not with the career of a single hero, but with the evolution of a whole society, and involving no less than four distinct characters, each of whom follows the course of a Conradian hero through compromise into paradox. At the same time, the novel abandons the hero type of

Wait, Kurtz, Jim and Whalley, to present in Nostromo himself the first of a new type, Conrad's "political" hero, who typically aims not to create a world in conformity to an ideal, but to achieve his own comfort and security without committing himself actively to either side in the struggle which rages around him.

The framework of the universe presented in *Nostromo* is the familiar Conradian dualism, now rendered in an emphatically political mode. The earliest Malayan novels are worked out against the background of a broadly racial dualism in which political concerns are secondary. In both *Heart of Darkness* and *The Nigger of the 'Narcissus'*, where the racial contrast still plays some part, the story turns towards an ethico-political dualism of licence versus control, anarchy against authority. This ideological conflict, held largely in abeyance through *Lord Jim* and *The End of the Tether*, reappears in *Nostromo*.

The history of Costaguana is a succession of revolutions, oscillating between the rule of a partly enlightened aristocracy and the tyranny of popular dictatorships. Into this situation come, initially, two men, Gould and Nostromo, Gould to take up his late father's mining concession, and Nostromo "to make his fortune" (p. 220). The Gould Concession, granted to Charles Gould's father, reflects the political state of affairs, in a typically Conradian image, as at once a source of great wealth, being a rich silver mine, and a deadly burden, because of its exposure to the rapacity of Costaguana politicians. The father dies, having spent vain years attempting to make of the mine a working concern and having warned his son in the strongest terms against becoming involved in it. "He implored his son never to return to Costaguana, never to claim any part of his inheritance there, because it was tainted by the infamous Concession; never to touch it, never to approach it, to forget that America existed, and pursue a mercantile career in Europe" (p. 57). The Concession, in short, presents a difficult and dangerous state of affairs which Charles Gould may either take up or leave alone.

Gould does not ignore his father's injunctions, but is, on the contrary, strongly influenced by the dead man and much affected by his fate. Yet he decides, none the less, upon disobedience. His father's death "filled his breast with a mournful and angry desire for action", for which action "the mine was obviously the only field" (p. 66). Like the typical Conradian hero of the earlier novels, Gould is impelled by desire for action to make some mark upon the world. His action, moreover, is directed by a vague but strong idealism.

> Mines had acquired for him a dramatic interest. He studied their peculiarities from a personal point of view, too, as one would study the varied characters of men. . . . Abandoned workings had for him a strong fascination. Their desolation appealed to him like the sight of human misery, whose causes are varied and profound. They might have been misunderstood (p. 59).

The mine is inevitably the focus for Gould's action, and Gould is a man who (in Decoud's words) "cannot act without idealizing every simple feeling, desire, or achievement" (pp. 214–15).

Gould sees the mine not simply as a material difficulty which might, if overcome, be turned to profit, but rather as a challenge to his sense of humanity. The Concession is to him a potential source of good, which has yielded so far only misery because of its entanglement with the corruption of politics in Costaguna. Gould's aim is to bring order out of this chaos by not only working the mine but also making it an instrument for the furtherance of civilization. The ravine beneath the mountain into which the mine is dug is called "the paradise of snakes" (p. 105). Gould, with a glance at the story of Eden, later remarks that his operations there have "disturbed a great many" snakes and "brought mankind into it" (p. 209), an observation revealing the extent of his idealization. He sees himself in the position of a creator bringing order and life into a world of chaos inhabited by forces of evil.

Gould's ideals are shared and reflected by Emilia, to whom, significantly, he proposes marriage at the very point when, having just learnt of his father's death, he decides to return to Costaguana. "His future wife was the first, and perhaps the only person to detect this secret mood which governed the profoundly sensible, almost voiceless attitude of this man towards the world of material things" (p. 59). She shares with him his ambitions for the mine and is conspicuously at his side from the beginning of his work. In particular, she organizes the social functions of the Gould Concession, establishing medical and spiritual care for its employees and making herself the centre of society in the nearby town of Sulaco.

Emilia is the heroine of Gould's world, the female reflection of his ideals, who lives at the heart of his sphere of operations. The sphere is the mine and, more broadly, the political situation of Costaguana, from which the mine is inseparable. Like Wait before him and Verloc and Razumov after, Gould, in pursuit of his ideal, enters a world of dualistic political conflict, a world torn by the perennial strife between licence and authority. His compromise consists originally of a reluctant alliance with "material interests". In order to open up his mine Gould needs capital, for which he turns to Holroyd, an American millionaire who is prepared to back the operation as long as it proves itself profitable. Thus Gould, although personally interested in the mine as a sphere for the active realization of his ideal, is forced from the first to consider also its purely financial returns. "Charles Gould, on his part, had been obliged to keep the idea of wealth well to the fore; but he brought it forward as a means, not as an end. Unless the mine was good business it could not be touched. He had to insist on that aspect of the enterprise" (p. 75).

Holroyd, with whom Gould makes this compromising agreement, is an acute reflection of Don Carlos himself – an aloof, autocratic, wealthy man who idealizes the monetary power he commands. Holroyd's obsessive founding of Protestant churches in South America and his vacuous talk about the "destiny" of his nation function as a gentle parody on a somewhat larger scale of the Goulds' ideals, their missionary work among their employees and their visionary conception of the mine. The subtle bond of confidence between Gould and Holroyd, which has a vital function in the plot and which goes beyond the merely financial aspects of their bargain, underlines their alliance and personal similarity.

The immediate effect of Gould's compromising alliance with material interests is the discernible beginning of a rift, which subsequent moves will widen before the end of the story, between Charles and his heroine. After Holroyd's first visit to the Goulds in Sulaco, Emilia "wondered aloud why the talk of these wealthy and enterprising men discussing the prospects, the working, and the safety of the mine rendered her so impatient and uneasy, whereas she could talk of the mine by the hour with her husband with unwearied interest and satisfaction" (p. 70). While never offering open opposition to her husband's course of action Emilia, unlike Gould, remains personally unaffected by the materialistic involvement of the mine and is even able at the end to repudiate this entirely when she allows the whereabouts of the lost silver to remain unknown. Speaking to her husband of their departed guests, she says, "But you have listened to their conversation? They don't seem to have understood anything they have seen here." To this Gould replies, with the practical outcome of the visit in mind, "They have seen the mine. They have understood that to some purpose" (p. 70). At this point neither wife nor husband is aware of the incipient divergence of their attitudes, yet by the novel's end Gould's entanglement with material interests has left Emilia a virtual widow.

The nature of Gould's compromise is further displayed in the costume he wears during this conversation with Emilia as he is on the point of departure from his house in Sulaco for the mine. The native integrity of Charles Gould is associated with his English background and education, an association which contrasts sharply with the corruption and disorder of Costaguana. The political factions of Costaguana, although manifested largely in a stark admixture of bloodshed and rhetoric, are founded upon materialistic greed. At this early stage Gould's costume still displays his English affinities; he wears "riding breeches, leather leggings (an article of apparel never before seen in Costaguana), a Norfolk coat of grey flannel, and those great flaming moustaches, [all of which] suggested an officer of cavalry turned gentleman farmer" (p. 71). Along with this, however, he also wears "a soft, grey sombrero, an article of national costume which combined unexpectedly well with his English get-up" (p. 84). The concession to local dress, although not yet incongruous, is significant of Gould's compromise. His use of material interests to gain his idealistic ends exposes him to the climate of Costaguana.

At this early stage Gould has, of course, no conscious intention of involving himself in the internal affairs of his adopted country. His aim, on the contrary, is to establish the mine as an "imperium in imperio", an autonomous, supra-national organization. The material interests of the mine, however, while providing the means to Gould's end, at the same time present the lure and temptation which ensure both that Costaguana will not leave the mine alone and that Gould will not hold forever aloof from the extension of his material powers into Costaguana.

Charles Gould was competent because he had no illusions. The Gould Concession had to fight for life with such weapons as could be found at once in the mire of a corruption that was so universal as almost to lose its significance. He was prepared to stoop for his weapons. For a moment he felt as if the silver of the mine, which had killed his father, had decoyed him further than he meant to go; and with the roundabout logic of emotions, he felt that the worthiness of his life was bound up with success. There was no going back (p. 85).

Gould's identification of his life with the mine, combined with his willingness to compromise by allying his idealism with material interests and to "stoop for his weapons", ensures his eventual participation in the very conflict from which it is his primary object to remain aloof. Such is Gould's paradox; the more the mine works as an idealistic force the greater will be its involvement with the materialistic forces to which the ideal is opposed.

The next step, the second phase of Gould's compromise with materialism and its political ramifications, comes when he lends tacit support to the enlightened dictatorship of Don Vincente Ribiera.

What was currently whispered was this – that the San Tomé Administration had, in part, at least, financed the last revolution, which had brought into a five-year dictatorship Don Vincente Ribiera, a man of culture and of unblemished character, invested with a mandate of reform by the best elements of the State. Serious, well-informed men seemed to believe the fact, to hope for better things, for the establishment of legality, of good faith and order in public life (p. 117).

Again, Gould's object is to secure in Costaguana a situation of political stability within which the mine can operate. The step is reasonable in itself and does not appear morally improper, given Gould's premise that his own ideals are worthy of universal application. The dangers of the move are made plain in the persons of the two chief men whom Gould has now brought into his alliance: Ribiera, the new head of state, and General Montero, Minister of War.

Ribiera strikes the perceptive Emilia as "more pathetic than promising, this first civilian Chief of State Costaguana had ever known, pronouncing, glass in hand, his simple watchwords of honesty, peace, respect for law, political good faith abroad and at home" (p. 119). The stated objectives are commendable, but the person, "obese to the point of infirmity" and "physically almost a cripple", does not inspire confidence. With Ribiera, moreover, comes General Montero, the material force which, together with Holroyd's money and Gould's influence, maintains this government in power.

> The white plume, the coppery tint of his broad face, the blue-black of the moustaches under the curved beak, the mass of gold on sleeves and breast, the high shining boots with enormous spurs, the working nostrils, the imbecile and domineering stare of the glorious victor of Rio Seco had in them something ominous and incredible; the exaggeration of a cruel caricature, the fatuity of solemn masquerading, the atrocious grotesqueness of some military idol of Aztec conception and European bedecking, awaiting the homage of worshippers (p. 122).

Montero's exaggerated uniform covering a sensual and unintelligent man of native origin is another image of Gould's compromise. And the alliance with Ribierism is more immediately disastrous than that with Holroyd, precisely because Holroyd is less unlike Gould than is Ribiera and is not dependent upon a Montero. The anomaly of Ribierism is that Montero necessarily comes with it.

Montero manifests indifference to the ideals of Holroyd and Ribiera when he follows the new President's fine speech with a brusque toast to the American, "to the health of the man who brings us a million and a half of pounds" (p. 120). Ribiera's government is scarcely established when Montero, aided by his literate brother Pedro, places himself at the head of popular and military revolt, before which the mild Ribiera collapses completely. Ribiera cannot stand against Montero, as the General is the actual basis of the President's power. Ribiera therefore comes in flight to Gould, who is now worse off than before, confronted with an uprising against a government with the interests of which the mine has been closely associated.

Gould's eventual response is to take yet another step into the mire of compromise by putting himself at the head of a separatist movement, using the power and influence of the mine to create an independent state out of the province of which Sulaco is the capital. The concept of separation is actually originated by Decoud in collaboration with Emilia, each of whom has his own motives: Decoud to save and remain with Antonia, and Emilia to preserve the idealistic conception of the mine. After agreeing to the plan of

Decoud, Emilia walks (significantly) *away* from her husband's room.

> The fate of the San Tomé mine was lying heavy upon her heart. It was a long time now since she had begun to fear it. It had been an idea. She had watched it with misgivings turning into a fetish, and now the fetish had grown into a monstrous and crushing weight. It was as if the inspiration of their early years had left her heart to turn into the wall of silver-bricks, erected by the silent work of evil spirits, between her and her husband. He seemed to dwell alone within a circumvallation of precious metal, leaving her outside with her school, her hospital, the sick mothers and the feeble old men, mere insignificant vestiges of the initial inspiration. 'Those poor people!' she murmured to herself (pp. 221–2).

Emilia's conspiracy with Decoud to conceal from her husband news of Montero's victory, in order to draw him into the separatist scheme, marks simultaneously a deepening of Gould's involvement with native politics and another clear stage in the breakdown of confidence between the hero and heroine. What happens here between Gould and Emilia is an instance of the usual development of the Conradian paradox; the compromises which the hero makes in order to achieve the ideals identified with the heroine have the effect of increasing his distance from her.

The well-intentioned plotting of Emilia and Decoud would probably have been unnecessary, for Gould, although disliking both Decoud himself and the separationist policy, takes up their cause without protest once he understands the situation, because, in his view, he has no alternative but to continue on the path he has already chosen. He does so with deep regret, but convinced that he must pursue his policy of using the mine's increasing influence to try to control and stabilize the political situation. The narrator's statement of Gould's thoughts at this point are worth quoting at length as the most explicit formulation of the hero's paradoxical predicament.

> To him, as to all of us, the compromises with his conscience appeared uglier than ever in the light of failure. His taciturnity, assumed with a purpose, had prevented him from tampering openly with his thoughts; but the Gould Concession had insidiously corrupted his judgment. He might have known, he

said to himself, leaning over the balustrade of the *corredor*, that Ribierism could never come to anything. The mine had corrupted his judgment by making him sick of bribing and intriguing merely to have his work left alone from day to day. Like his father, he did not like to be robbed. It exasperated him. He had persuaded himself that, apart from higher considerations, the backing up of Don José's hopes of reform was good business. He had gone forth into the senseless fray as his poor uncle, whose sword hung on the wall of his study, had gone forth – in the defence of the commonest decencies of organized society. Only his weapon was the wealth of the mine, more far-reaching and subtle than an honest blade of steel fitted into a simple brass guard.

More dangerous to the wielder, too, this weapon of wealth, double-edged with the cupidity and misery of mankind, steeped in all the vices of self-indulgence as in a concoction of poisonous roots, tainting the very cause for which it is drawn, always ready to turn awkwardly in the hand. There was nothing for it now but to go on using it (pp. 364–5).

It is evident that by this time, unlike most Conradian heroes, Gould is largely aware of the paradoxical situation into which his compromise has plunged him. He sees that in using the material and political powers of the mine against the intrigues of Costaguana politics he is being drawn into the very practices from which it is his object to maintain distance.

The pattern of Gould's career so far has followed that of the early heroes Almayer and Willems, men whose purposive action places them in a world of dualistic conflict, in which every deliberate step they take towards their goal involves deeper compromise and further entanglement in the universal struggle. Like them, Gould identifies his ideal with a heroine, with whom, after an initial period of unison, he finds himself increasingly at odds; and like them he finds himself opposed in his efforts by a man from within the world he has selected for his sphere of operations, a rival whose enmity is provoked by the hero's very successes. We would therefore expect, all other things being equal, that towards the end of the story the growing tension would snap and Gould would be confronted, probably with fatal result, by the consequences of his compromises, as are Almayer and Willems and all the heroes of the intervening novels. Yet this does not happen in *Nostromo*. Not only does Gould survive the end of the story, but he defeats his rival, Montero, and succeeds in his separatist venture.

Gould's impunity does not mean that Conrad has changed his view of the human situation to allow his hero to evade the usual nemesis. Gould is still in action at the end of the story because *Nostromo* is uniquely structured among Conrad's works and because Gould is not the sole hero of the story. The end of the book centres not upon Gould but on Nostromo, who does complete the normal cycle from compromise to destruction, while Gould, after the decision to pursue separatism, is kept all but invisible in the background. *Nostromo,* furthermore, while taking its plot from a short slice of time, is full of both allusions to the past and hints of the future. It portrays, rather like the Wagnerian story, one turn of a cycle that might be indefinitely repeated. For this reason it is impossible to select a single event with which the story "begins"; the granting of the Concession, the decision of Charles Gould to disregard his father's warning, the alliance with Holroyd, the adoption or the failure of Ribierism could all be put forward for the position with more or less equal plausibility. In a similar way, although the story stops with the death of Nostromo, it does not really "end" there, as the main political sequence of events, in which Gould has become inextricably involved, is still very much in motion.

We are told, for instance, that after the political separation and the establishment of a government consistent with Gould's ideas there grows up a democratic opposition made up chiefly from Italians and natives, former employees of the railway and of the mine itself (pp. 478–9). At the same time, some of Gould's political allies are saying that the logical and necessary conclusion of their work must be the annexation of the rest of Costaguana to the new state, and that the democratic party is lending its support to this view (pp. 509–11). Clearly, as Monygham observes, "there is no peace and no rest in the development of material interests" (p. 511). The silver of the mine is like Wagner's gold; it cannot allow the world in which it is at large to rest stable, but is always at work to keep the balance of forces swinging.

Gould will not, therefore, be allowed to enjoy for long the momentary success of his latest compromise. The new state is, by the time the story closes, already looking towards its next crisis, a choice between widespread internal discontent and a war of annexation, a selection of paths from which Gould will be unable to hold aloof.

Gould's nemesis is not avoided, but merely suspended by the end of the novel.

In yet another sense, however, Gould pays the price of his concession to material interests even within the pages of the story, for towards the end he becomes plainly the prisoner of the mine rather than its master and has lost his relationship with Emilia. Emilia herself gives us the final picture of Gould.

> She had a clear vision of the gray hairs on his temples. He was perfect – perfect. What more could she have expected? It was a colossal and lasting success; and love was only a short moment of forgetfulness, a short intoxication, whose delight one remembered with a sense of sadness, as if it had been a deep grief lived through. There was something inherent in the necessities of successful action which carried with it the moral degradation of the idea. . . . He was perfect, perfect; but she would never have him to herself. . . . [S]he saw clearly the San Tomé mine possessing, consuming, burning up the life of the last of the Costaguana Goulds; mastering the spirit of the son as it had mastered the lamentable weakness of the father. A terrible success for the last of the Goulds (pp. 521–2).

Emilia sees, as in a way she has seen from the beginning, the fate towards which Gould is heading as a logical result of his decision to return to Costaguana and his willingness to compromise.

While Gould's end remains below the horizon at the conclusion of *Nostromo*, another character, Martin Decoud, is seen to complete the full Conradian heroic cycle from initial compromise through paradox to fateful nemesis. Decoud, although he enters the story at a point after its beginning (when he returns from Europe to his native Costaguana to help support the declining Ribierist cause) and dies well before its end, is one of the novel's four focal figures. Like Gould, Nostromo and Monygham, Decoud acts independently at a crucial stage so as to affect the course of the plot and cannot therefore be viewed as a minor character subordinate to some other hero.

Decoud's character has two salient features; he is a sceptic and is also an adept in the use of words. In this lies the particular form of the paradox which engulfs him, for his fate is to become a literary propagandist, a spinner of words, while at the same time believing nothing of the doctrines he expounds.

Like the other heroes, Gould, Nostromo and Monygham, Decoud is personally an outsider, a man of European culture and racial background, although, like Gould, he has a family history of settlement in Costaguana. When we first hear of him Decoud, like Gould, is in Europe, with the option of remaining uninvolved in the affairs of the South American republic. He engages himself in these affairs, however, largely because of Antonia, the devoted daughter of José Avellanos, a noted Costaguana statesman and patriot. Antonia is for Decoud, much as Emilia is for Gould, an ideal woman under whose influence begins his involvement with Costaguana. Decoud arrives in Sulaco in connection with an arms deal he has been negotiating on his travels, but after a reunion with Antonia he abandons his intention of continuing on his way and elects to remain, allowing himself to be recruited by her father to the liberal cause.

Antonia is therefore, from Decoud's point of view, the heroine of the story. Like other Conradian heroines, from Nina and Aissa through Jewel to Emilia Gould, Antonia represents both something to which the hero aspires and something which, by his very nature, he is debarred from attaining. Emilia represents the humanitarian aspect of Gould's idealism, but is increasingly separated from him by the means he employs in pursuit of these goals. Antonia attracts Decoud by her European outlook and education, her emancipation and freedom of thought which make her his natural partner.

Antonia could hold her own in a discussion with two or three men at a time. Obviously she was not the girl to be content with peeping through a barred window at a cloaked figure of a lover ensconced in a doorway opposite – which is the correct form of Costaguana courtship. It was generally believed that with her foreign upbringing and foreign ideas the learned and proud Antonia would never marry – unless, indeed, she married a foreigner from Europe or North America, now that Sulaco seemed on the point of being invaded by all the world (p. 150).

Decoud shares her foreignness, something of her pride, and much of the European orientation cultivated by her father. Yet he is barred from her by his scepticism which prevents him from sharing unreservedly in her Costaguana patriotism and devotion to the Ribierist cause. The situation which therefore develops between them is comparable to that between Willems and Aissa; each finds much to admire in the other, but the woman is bound to a country and people where the man finds himself threatened in body and stifled in spirit.

Decoud compromises at first by deciding to remain with Antonia in Costaguana and by adopting her family's politics, currently expressed in fanatical support of the Ribierist cause. To this end he becomes "the Journalist of Sulaco" (p. 159) by Don José's appointment, taking control of a newspaper christened the *Porvenir*. The irony of this undertaking lies not in the mere journalism (which Decoud had practised occasionally in Europe) but in the fact that the *Porvenir* is a political organ committed unreservedly to the liberal doctrines backed by Avellanos and Gould, in which doctrines, by and large, Decoud has no faith.

Having compromised and involved himself in local affairs for the heroine's sake, Decoud, like Willems, finds that his own survival is threatened by his adopted environment. As an intelligent and sensitive man, although unable to accept Costaguana politics at face value, he is disturbed by the strife and suffering it generates.

> The reality of the political action, such as it was, seemed closer, and acquired poignancy by Antonia's belief in the cause. Its crudeness hurt his feelings. He was surprised at his own sensitiveness.
>
> "I suppose I am more of a Costaguanero than I could have believed possible," he thought to himself.
>
> His disdain grew like a reaction of his scepticism against the action into which he was forced by his infatuation for Antonia (p. 176).

At the same time, again like Willems, he is placing himself in physical danger of reprisal by his action on behalf of the heroine's party. The paradox is clear; he is unable to live without Antonia, but in remaining with her he endangers his mental and bodily survival.

Decoud's solution would be to take Antonia away from Costaguana, which is just what he wishes to do. "He also had his aspirations, he aspired to carry her away out of these deadly futilities of pronunciamentos and reforms" (p. 183). He is prevented by her ties to the country and by her liberal patriotism, both imaged in her devotion to her father, who is himself the focal point of the "pronunciamentos and reforms" which Decoud sees as "utterly wrong" (p. 183). Avellanos therefore appears, with respect to

Decoud, in the role of the rival, the figure who opposes the resolution of the hero's difficulties with the heroine, much as Montero, the enemy of Ribierism, becomes the rival of Gould.

Although there is no personal animosity in this particular rivalry, Avellanos, the effective force binding Antonia to Costaguana, is in several significant ways the very antithesis of Decoud. Where Decoud is a sceptic without allegiances, Avellanos is a patriot and a passionate believer in "the doctrine of political rectitude" (p. 137); and whereas Decoud becomes a writer only under protest, Avellanos is already the author of a large exposition of his ideas in the light of the history of his country. Avellanos, moreover, is a professional diplomat, while Decoud exhibits the artistic intellectual's contempt for political machinations.

Don José Avellanos desired passionately for his country: peace, prosperity, and (as the end of the preface to "Fifty Years of Misrule" has it) 'an honourable place in the comity of civilized nations.' In this last phrase the Minister Plenipotentiary, cruelly humiliated by the bad faith of his government towards the foreign bondholders, stands disclosed in the patriot (p. 140).

Structurally, therefore, Avellanos stands opposed to Decoud much as does Omar to Willems, being the heroine's father, representing an orthodox spirit alien to the hero, and preventing, by his very existence, the satisfactory union of the lovers.

Decoud's response is the Conradian hero's characteristic decision to immerse in the "destructive element" of his compromise. Since he can neither take Antonia out of Costaguana nor remain contentedly with her under the existing conditions, he resolves to alter the conditions by committing himself further and taking a directive part in local affairs. He devises and promulgates the idea of separatism, the political movement which will dissociate the western province from the rest of the country and thereby, he hopes, end Antonia's involvement in the degradation of Costaguana politics. He explains his idea to Emilia with particular lucidity: "She [Antonia] won't leave Sulaco for my sake, therefore Sulaco must leave the rest of the Republic to its fate. . . . I cannot part with Antonia, therefore the one and indivisible Republic of Costaguana must be made to part with its western province. Fortunately it happens to be also a sound policy" (p. 215).

The idea of separation is directly "contrary to the doctrine laid down in the 'History of Fifty Years' Misrule'" (p. 185). The Avellanos patriotism encompasses the whole country and cannot easily contemplate the dismemberment of Costaguana. Just as Omar in *An Outcast of the Islands* dies at the point of Willems' triumphant introduction of the Arabs to Sambir, so Avellanos is effectively killed by the adoption and success of Decoud's separatist doctrine. His unwilling expression from his deathbed of consent to this move is his last action (p. 239).

Despite the collapse of his rival, however, Decoud is still enmeshed in a paradoxical situation. The first essential to the preservation of the western province as a political entity is the removal of the latest consignment of silver from the mine, which will otherwise fall into the hands of the Monterists. As the originator of the separatist policy, it is right that Decoud himself should oversee this operation, while at the same time his own safety dictates his temporary departure from Sulaco, threatened as it is by Montero's oncoming forces. Decoud therefore accompanies Nostromo, taking the lighter of silver out into the Gulf under cover of darkness, and finds himself once again separated from Antonia.

The lighter is struck in the darkness by Sotillo's troopship. Nostromo manages to bring it safely to the Great Isabel (an island in the Gulf), where he hides the treasure and leaves Decoud, intending to return when he has made contact with his friends in Sulaco. But for various reasons Nostromo does not return, and Decoud, unable to bear the solitude, commits suicide by jumping into the sea weighted with bars of silver. There is therefore no nemesis character involved in Decoud's end, which is self-inflicted in an isolation caused by a sequence of accidents, but the imagery surrounding the event is precisely sculpted to the pattern of the usual Conradian heroic catastrophe. Decoud, as a sceptic who has compromised by becoming involved in Costaguana politics, is cast adrift in the Gulf when he is struck by a native troopship on a political errand. The drifting in the Gulf reflects the former aimlessness of his existence, while the collision is an obvious representation of the liabilities entailed by his compromise. His solitude on the island is emblematic of his deliberate intellectual aloofness from human affairs, the logical conclusion of his sceptical disavowal of all commitment. Decoud's nemesis, the solitude of the Costaguana Gulf, is therefore a typical Conradian end, in which the hero is fatally confronted with the extreme implications of his own conduct. As Brown is to Jim, Jones to Heyst, so is the solitude of the Gulf to Decoud.

> Solitude from mere outward condition of existence becomes very swiftly a state of soul in which the affectations of irony and scepticism have no place. It takes possession of the mind, and drives forth the thought into the exile of utter unbelief. After three days of waiting for the sight of some human face, Decoud caught himself entertaining a doubt of his own individuality. . . . On the fifth day an immense melancholy descended upon him palpably. . . . His sadness was the sadness of a sceptical mind. He beheld the universe as a succession of incomprehensible images (pp. 497–8).

In this frame of mind, driven to ultimate disbelief, Decoud shoots himself and drops into the Gulf.

The solitude of the Gulf which kills Decoud is an image also of the separationist policy, for on the Great Isabel Decoud himself experiences the extreme of separation. The marooning and death of Decoud show that separatism, although genuinely beneficial to the western province, is tainted with immoral selfishness and therefore ultimately moribund, both in that it is conceived by Decoud for a selfish reason (to secure the company of Antonia) and in that (as Antonia herself later realizes) it involves the casting off of a larger and poorer part of the country. Typically Decoud dies from an excessive application of the principles involved in his own compromise. The silver ingots which weigh down his body signify the material, selfish aspect of the separatist policy, of which the treasure was to have been a key instrument.

The treasure is also instrumental in the scheme of Dr Monygham, whose career similarly exhibits aspects of the Conradian heroic pattern. His nature is itself paradoxical, in that he is at once both a confirmed pessimist, taking an exceedingly cynical view of humanity, and a dedicated humanitarian, deeply sensitive to the sufferings and misfortunes of others. His cynicism evidently rests upon his own past experience of political persecution, captivity and torture, in the course of which, it is said, he made extorted confessions implicating many of his fellows.

> His confessions, when they came at last, were very complete, too. Sometimes on the nights when he walked the floor, he wondered,

grinding his teeth with shame and rage, at the fertility of his imagination when stimulated by a sort of pain which makes truth, honour, self-respect, and life itself matters of little moment (p. 373).

This grim confrontation with his own weakness makes of the Doctor a severe judge of the motives of others, and in the grossly acquisitive and unprincipled context of Costaguana politics he finds himself at odds with every other major character in the story, excepting only Emilia, whose unaffected and selfless charity he idealizes.

Monygham's obsession with his disgrace drives him, after another political revolution has brought about his abrupt release, to a self-imposed isolation from European society. Like the other heroes of the story, he is not a native Costaguanero but is of European family, and for him, as for the others, loss of European characteristics under the exigencies of the local situation is generally significant of moral decline. When released from prison Monygham is physically decrepit and dressed in a comical parody of native costume.

And these conditions seemed to bind him indissolubly to the land of Costaguana like an awful procedure of naturalization, involving him deep in the national life, far deeper than any amount of success and honour could have done. They did away with his Europeanism; for Dr. Monygham had made himself an ideal conception of his disgrace (p. 375).

Thus "bound" to native evils Monygham becomes, to a large extent by his own choice, an "outcast" (p. 310) from European society in Sulaco.

Monygham is, none the less, a man of great compassion, as is shown generally by his performance of medical duties and, in particular, by his care of such individuals as the Violas. His rough cynicism is, in fact, the product of his insight into suffering and an expression of contempt for those who ignore it. It is therefore natural that he should turn to Emilia, the only character of uncompromising humanity in the story, and one who shares his concern for the basic welfare of the common people. Emilia therefore becomes his heroine. "He believed her worthy of every devotion" (p. 376). And by the same token Gould, who appears to Monygham to have sacrificed Emilia's happiness and to have imperilled the safety of the workers for the sake of material interests, is his hated rival.

In pursuit of his ideal Monygham effects a compromise. In order to win Emilia's friendship and, through her, the post of medical officer, he makes a partial re-entry into the European society he had previously abandoned, and from any true sympathy with which he is still debarred by his outlook. As with Gould and Nostromo, the state of Monygham's dress again illuminates the compromise.

> Had it not been for the immaculate cleanliness of his apparel he might have been taken for one of those shiftless Europeans that are a moral eyesore to the respectability of a foreign colony in almost every exotic part of the world. The young ladies of Sulaco, adorning with clusters of pretty faces the balconies along the Street of the Constitution, when they saw him pass, with his limping gait and bowed head, a short linen jacket drawn on carelessly over the flannel check shirt, would remark to each other, "Here is the Señor doctor going to call on Doña Emilia. He has got his little coat on." The inference was true. Its deeper meaning was hidden from their simple intelligence. . . . The little white jacket was in reality a concession to Mrs. Gould's humanizing influence. The doctor, with his habit of sceptical, bitter speech, had no other means of showing his profound respect for the character of the woman who was known in the country as the English Señora (p. 45).

The abandonment of the ragged native costume in which he had been liberated, in favour of clean clothes of European style indicates Monygham's desire to return, for Emilia's sake, to the world from which his past and his experience have cut him off.

The course of Monygham's career is not unlike Jim's. Both men are initially gifted and idealistically disposed, but both are trapped by circumstances into commission of a great betrayal, the guilt of which sets them apart from their own people. Just as Jim then compromises by taking the limited world of Patusan as the scene for the exercise of his talents, so Monygham, in order to practise medicine under Emilia's patronage, enters the faintly hostile social world of Sulaco, from which he has been long estranged. Each man enjoys the society of his heroine in his new environment, but each is threatened there by a rival (Cornelius and Gould respectively) who introduces a more serious and potentially fatal threat in the guise of a nemesis, a figure who confronts the hero with his past crimes.

Jim's nemesis is Brown who, on information supplied by

Cornelius, is able to engineer the situation which results in Jim's defeat and death. Brown represents Jim's past failure to meet the standards of his own people and forces Jim into a re-enactment of the *Patna* episode, into another betrayal of a group under his care, a betrayal which this time results in the hero's death. Monygham's nemesis is Señor Hirsch who, although in no way abetted by Gould, none the less comes to Sulaco to consult Gould and is first introduced to Monygham in Gould's drawing-room. Monygham encounters Hirsch for the second time when he finds the dead, tortured body hanging from the beams of the upper room in the Custom House. Hirsch has been captured and tormented by Sotillo, who is determined to extort from him some story which will place the lost silver within his reach. In much the same way Monygham was himself years before tortured by one Father Beron for information about a non-existent Costaguana conspiracy. On that occasion the doctor had "confessed", betraying his fellows and bringing upon himself a lasting sense of shame. In the hanging body of Hirsch, he is brought face to face with the nightmare that still haunts him.

Hirsch is the very personification of fear, the "man of fear" (p. 461), as Nostromo calls him, whose unsuspected presence in the lighter reveals to Sotillo the plot to remove the silver from Sulaco. There is, indeed, nothing more that Hirsch could have told Sotillo that the latter could not very quickly have deduced for himself, since the unfortunate prisoner had no idea of the treasure's real whereabouts. He belongs to no political party and subscribes to no particular ideal, but represents simply the human capacity for fear which, as Nostromo on the lighter with Hirsch is well aware, constitutes an unpredictable threat to any purposeful undertaking. "'His being here is a miracle of fear –' Nostromo paused. 'There is no room for fear in this lighter,' he added through his teeth" (p. 274).

Monygham, like Jim, has in his past failed catastrophically to subdue his fear of hurt. His compromise consists in a superficial reconciliation with a society in which he has no faith, for the purpose of becoming once again a practising physician, a task which allows him to heal, or at least to ameliorate, the pains of others. His own pain, however, previously evaded by means of a false confession and betrayal, remains to be faced. In Hirsch Monygham is symbolically confronted with the fate he had once managed dishonourably to escape.

From this point the patterns of the careers of Jim and Monygham diverge, for whereas Jim fails to deal adequately with Brown and is consequently overcome, the doctor rises to the occasion symbolically presented by Hirsch and, rare among Conradian heroes, successfully expiates his old guilt. In the presence of Hirsch's body Monygham announces to Nostromo his plan, which consists, in effect, of a re-enactment, in opposite moral circumstances, of his past crime. Formerly Monygham had been held prisoner by a political fanatic, tortured, and forced to betray others; now he proposes to place himself in the hands of Sotillo, another such fanatic, to risk torture and death by pretending to a secret knowledge of the whereabouts of the silver, and to make Sotillo think that he is willing to betray Gould and the pro-European party.

His object in all of this is to protect Emilia (and, coincidentally, the other Europeans and the mine workers) by causing Sotillo to think that the treasure is not lost but has been deliberately concealed by Gould. As long as Sotillo believes that the treasure may still be recovered, the doctor reasons, he will not waste time persecuting his political enemies. Yet Monygham, who himself believes the treasure lost in the Gulf and has no knowledge of its true location, clearly faces torture and death when Sotillo loses patience in the fruitless search.

In knowingly placing himself under such danger and in carrying out his plan to the last minute without wavering, the doctor does in fact achieve his purpose and save from Sotillo's vengeance Emilia and the other supporters of Gould's policies. Having long withstood Sotillo's threats, Monygham was on the very point of being hanged when the forces of rescue arrived. Having thus confronted and faced down the recrudescence of his past terror, he is free to enjoy his reward.

'I've made my career – as you see,' said the Inspector-General of State Hospitals [Monygham], taking up lightly the lapels of his superfine black coat. The doctor's self-respect marked inwardly by the almost complete disappearance from his dreams of Father Beron, appeared visibly in what, by contrast with former carelessness, seemed an immoderate cult of personal appearance. Carried out within severe limits of form and colour, and in perpetual freshness, this change of apparel gave to Dr. Monygham an air at the same time professional and festive (p. 508).

His expiation is marked by the departure of Father Beron, his old tormentor, from his thoughts, and his fuller acceptance into Emilia's circle is shown by his more deliberately formal style of dress. Moreover, with the increasing absorption of Gould in the affairs of the mine towards the end of the story Monygham finds his rival virtually removed from the field and himself in free possession of Emilia's companionship.

Monygham's bliss is not complete, of course, for he remains bitterly cynical in outward expression and is made miserable by Emilia's unhappiness. None the less Conrad leaves us in no doubt that the doctor is a happier man, rewarded both materially and spiritually for his final victory over fear. Very few other major Conradian figures are allowed to pass triumphantly through the cycle of failure, compromise, and nemesis. Why, then, is Monygham permitted to do so? The answer may be that Monygham is a special case, in that he is rendered, by his past experience, a man totally without illusion. Thereafter, much like MacWhirr (another triumphant hero, but one who is never guilty of moral failure), he becomes incapable of any great reach of imaginative self-deception such as leads the other heroes into untenable positions. His strength lies in that his view of the world is close to that of the author. Whether Conrad was himself as extremely prone to cynicism built upon a bedrock of sentimental sympathy is not quite the point; what is relevant is that the anonymous first narrator of *Nostromo* has a capacity for penetrating human pretensions and comprehending the feelings of others to a degree elsewhere approached in the story only in the character of Monygham. Intellectual perspicacity and human understanding are not qualities notably present in the usual Conradian hero; Heyst, the only other one who might claim to be significantly endowed with them, still falls behind Monygham in this respect. By means of these qualities Monygham arrives at a position of self-effacement and an estimation of the real value of human actions that makes him prepared to risk pain, death, and moral degradation, and in so doing to effect his own redemption.

At the same time Conrad portrays Monygham as a limited character, whose reward is circumscribed and whose success is not allowed to overshadow the falls, actual or imminent, of the surviving central figures of the story, Gould and Nostromo. The doctor remains a lonely and isolated figure, whose love for Emilia is not "the most splendid of illusions, but like an enlightening and priceless misfortune" (p. 513). His self-sacrifice for the good of the European community achieves its immediate end, but effects no lasting redemption beyond his own. Monygham is really no less cut off from the world around him at the conclusion of the story than he was at the beginning.

There remains Nostromo himself, the first of a new line of heroes, which also includes Verloc and Razumov. The earlier heroes, including Gould and Decoud, are placed in situations of self-defeating endeavour. They are men of unusual abilities which are generally directed outwards in attempts to improve the world along the lines of the heroes' ideals. They fail because flaws in their own natures render the ideals impossible of achievement without vitiating compromise. The new line of heroes, which begins here with Nostromo, presents us with a man whose object is no longer to pursue any ideal beyond the bounds of self-interest, but rather to attain the largely negative goal of surviving in passive comfort without compromising involvement in the conflicts of the world around him. Such men are Verloc, playing off anarchists against reactionaries for his own profit; and Razumov, seeking only to pursue his studies and lead a quiet life without political entanglements.

Such, too, is Nostromo, the first of the line, who appears in the same story as Gould, the last and perhaps the most magnificient of Conrad's idealistic supermen. The combination shows us that *Nostromo* is not only the second chronological turning point in Conrad's literary career but also a brilliant piece of structural composition creating between two characters a contrapuntal relation which forms the chief axis of the novel. Decoud and Monygham, important as they are, figure only episodically in the story, which turns upon the antithesis of Nostromo and Gould, "the two racially and socially contrasted men, both captured by the silver of the San Tomé mine" (p. xi). Gould is aristocratic, Anglo-Saxon, reserved and idealistic, while Nostromo is "a Man of the People" (ibid.), Italian, flamboyant and fundamentally self-centred. While Gould follows the established path of the early Conradian hero from idealism through compromise towards destruction, Nostromo, manifestly unidealistic and unconcerned with the state of the world at large, endeavours unsuccessfully to avoid precisely the kind of purposive action and moral commitment which is essential to Gould.

Nostromo, as he himself tells Decoud, has come to Costaguana "to make his fortune" (p. 220). Here he finds himself in a land of violent political tensions between two extremes, with both of which he develops loose affiliations. On the one hand he is a man of plebeian origin with deep roots in the common people, among whom he has a high reputation and a large following. On the other hand his wish to make his fortune, combined with his initial political neutrality, leads him to place his abilities at the disposal of the Sulaco oligarchy, represented by Captain Mitchell and ultimately by Gould himself. At the beginning of the events of the novel, therefore, Nostromo stands between the opposing forces of popular discontent and authoritarian government and is, moreover, a vital factor in the precarious balance between them; it is through his agency that the European party controls an effective work-force in Sulaco and keeps a semblance of order among the factions of the populace.

Giorgio and Teresa Viola are particularly important to the thematic structure of the story because they span the gulf between the Goulds' idealism and the popular movements by which Gould is opposed. The Violas, Giorgio as a former follower of Garibaldi and Teresa as a deeply religious woman and the story's mouthpiece of traditional demotic moral and domestic values, are at once of the people and at the same time committed to the highest of selfless goals, resolving what would otherwise remain a discord in the story between democracy and idealism. Giorgio Viola, "the Garibaldino", is an ardent republican who has fought for his cause both in Italy and South America. At the same time, however, he is "full of scorn for the populace, as your austere republican so often is" (p. 16), because, as himself a strict political idealist, he has no sympathy with the mercenary motives behind the popular movements in Costaguana. In this way he is naturally allied with both Charles Gould, as one who has striven after a vision of an improved world, and, as a democrat, with the people, including Nostromo. In a rather similar way Teresa is representative of basic moral and religious standards of personal integrity, which makes her at once the friend and protegée of Emilia and a strong-voiced advocate of proletarian values.

The Violas together represent a steady and uncompromising standard which contrasts, in the course of the story, with the respective moral disintegrations of both Nostromo and Gould. They succeed, in a sense, in preserving something of what both the chief heroes gradually lose. They do so, however, at considerable cost.

They remain secondary and ineffective characters, variously protected or attacked by others but themselves initiating nothing. Teresa from the beginning suffers from an illness, a pain which, significantly, "had come to her first a few years after they had left Italy to emigrate to America and settle at last in Sulaco" (p. 25), and which finally kills her, not by mere coincidence, at the very moment when the town is taken over by revolutionaries. Giorgio survives, but becomes increasingly removed from the reality of things. From the beginning the inn which he keeps, named "Albergo d'Italia Una", signifies (so far as the story is concerned) an impossible dream, and towards the end Giorgio himself becomes a withdrawn, Bible-reading patriarch, whose ineffective attempts to apply traditional moral precepts to the upbringing of his daughters results in Nostromo's accidental death.

Nostromo's relations with the Violas reveal the tensions of his initial situation. On the one hand they are his adopted family, to whom he is both a son and something of a protector, and he has tacitly committed himself to eventually marrying their elder daughter, Linda. On the other hand, he has large personal ambitions which hinder him from settling into a life of hard-working orthodox domesticity, and in pursuit of these vague ends he labours for the rich European party, exerting himself to win the praise and attention of powerful men like Mitchell and Gould. Essentially Nostromo is seeking personal profit while avoiding commitment. The difficulties of this position are expressed in Teresa's criticisms of Nostromo's conduct. When we first hear her she is complaining that he has deserted the family in a time of danger in order to "run at the heels of his English" (p. 19). The fullest exchange between them takes place as she lies dying during the Monterist revolution.

Nostromo said nothing, and the sick woman with an upward glance insisted. "Look, this one [the revolution] has killed me, while you were away fighting for what did not concern you, foolish man."

"Why talk like this?" mumbled the Capataz between his teeth. "Will you never believe in my good sense? It concerns me to keep on being what I am: every day alike."

"You never change, indeed," she said, bitterly. "Always thinking of yourself and taking your pay out in fine words from those who care nothing for you."

There was between them an intimacy of antagonism as close in

its way as the intimacy of accord and affection. He had not
walked along the way of Teresa's expectations. It was who
had encouraged him to leave his ship, in the hope of securing a
friend and defender for the girls (p. 253).

As Teresa perceives, Nostromo's selfishness is holding him back
from either making his fortune by commitment to the European
party or settling into the regular life-pattern of the common people.
Nostromo keeps his options open by cultivating both the good
opinion of his employers and popularity among the working classes.
To commit himself to the democratic party or to adopt a normal
plebeian level of existence would lose him the esteem of Mitchell
and the Europeans, while to become an open supporter of the
policies of Ribiera and Gould would deprive him of his popular
support. Balanced between two worlds he occupies a unique
position, on account of which he exercises considerable powers; his
following among the people makes him an effective leader of the
harbour work force, which in turn, as long as he steers clear of
involvement in politics, makes him a valuable employee to
Mitchell. Nostromo is thus the linch-pin upon which the cohesion of
local economy depends, the channel of command between the
European capitalists and the local workers. Yet he can function in
this way only as long as he avoids open espousal of either popular or
patrician values, and as long as he holds aloof from both wealth and
domestic obscurity.
Nostromo at the beginning of the story is living on his reputation
his popularity with the people, which makes him an effective leader
and his good name with the Europeans as an efficient foreman. His
reputation depends upon his avoidance of commitment, and he is
therefore an essentially vague character, without defined motives or
long-range plans. The thin sketching of his personality in the first
half of the story, far from being a weakness of the novel, is integral to
its purpose. Nostromo, at the beginning, is indeed little more than a
name. "The only thing he seems to care for, as far as I have been
able to discover," observes Decoud, "is to be well spoken of" (p.
246). He is "a man for whom the value of life seems to consist in
personal prestige" (p. 248). The number and variety of his names is
in keeping with the nebulosity of his character. He is known
variously as Nostromo, the Capataz, Gian' Battista, Juan, Giovanni
and, later, Captain Fidanza.
The crisis of Nostromo's career comes when he accepts the job of

removing the consignment of silver from Sulaco by sea in order to keep the Monterists from capturing it and, if possible, to deliver it to pro-separatist forces outside. This undertaking is not of his choosing, but is pressed upon him. To the Europeans he appears the only man for the job, and his vanity, when the matter is so put to him, causes him to accept it, yet Teresa sees at once the implicit dangers of the venture.

> "They have turned your head with their praises," gasped the sick woman. "They have been paying you with words. Your folly shall betray you into poverty, misery, and starvation. The very leperos shall laugh at you – the great Capataz" (p. 257).

After a little thought Nostromo begins to see that to take charge of the treasure is like "taking up a curse" upon himself (p. 259), and that, without seeing quite what he was doing, he has given up the neutrality and good name which was the basis of his eminent position.

The point, as he soon realizes, is that for as long as he has charge of the treasure he is a marked man, whom anyone would kill to take it from him. The silver therefore exiles him. Once he has put out to sea with it he cannot come back; to return without it would be to admit publicly to failure or worse, and to return with it would be courting death. He sums up these conclusions in the lighter to Decoud.

> "Señor," he said, "we must catch the steamer at sea. We must keep out in the open looking for her till we have drunk all that has been put on board here. And if we miss her by some mischance, we must keep away from the land till we grow weak, and perhaps mad, and die, and drift dead, until one or another of the steamers of the Compania comes upon the boat with the two dead men who have saved the treasure. That, señor, is the only way to save it; for, don't you see? for us to come to the land anywhere in a hundred miles along this coast with this silver in our possession is to run the naked breast against the point of a knife. This thing has been given to me like a deadly disease" (p. 264).

As Decoud perceives, Nostromo has "his own peculiar view of this enterprise".

His only course, having accepted charge of the treasure, is to deliver it as required to Barrios. Delivery of the treasure to Barrios, however, will virtually ensure the ultimate success of the separatists and, inevitably, make Nostromo one of the foremost heroes of their victory. From that point he will be largely identified with the governing party and will forfeit to that extent the following he has had among the poeple. Nostromo's acceptance of the job of delivering the silver occupies a point in his career exactly corresponding to the appearance of Haldin in Razumov's rooms and to the order Verloc receives to blow up the Observatory. From this moment the hero finds himself in the position of having to either take sides or go to the wall. He has, against his will, accepted compromise and commitment.

There follow the unforeseen collision with Sotillo's troopship and the concealment of the silver on the Great Isabel. When Nostromo returns he learns from Monygham that, through Hirsch, Sulaco now believes the silver to have been lost in the Gulf and Decoud drowned. At this point, other things being equal, Nostromo might simply have confided the real whereabouts of the treasure to Gould and returned to his normal duties. What deflects him from this path is his meeting with Monygham who, unintentionally, upsets Nostromo greatly by showing him how little the supposed loss of the treasure really means to the European party, who were concerned chiefly to remove it from the rebels' clutches. Nostromo begins to take the view that his own interests, and quite possibly his life, have been put at risk very lightly by people who now show no concern for the outcome of his adventure.

> "Was it for an unconsidered and foolish whim that they came to me, then?" he interrupted suddenly. "Had I not done enough for them to be of some account, *por Dios*? Is it that the *hombres finos* – the gentlemen – need not think as long as there is a man of the people ready to risk his body and soul? Or, perhaps, we have no souls – like dogs?" (p. 435).

In this frame of mind he returns to the home of the Violas to decide what he should do.

Teresa had died shortly after Nostromo's departure with the silver, killed by the sound of a shot fired by one of the rebels "as surely as if the bullet had struck her oppressed heart" (p. 470). Nostromo feels particularly guilty on this score, because he had refused to fetch her a priest, as she had requested, in order to keep his appointment with the lighter of silver. By the time he gets back to shore, disgusted at the dangers to which he has been so lightly exposed by the Europeans, he is strongly inclined to accept both Giorgio's republicanism and Teresa's advice. "They keep us and encourage us as if we were dogs born to fight and hunt for them," he says of the rich. "The vecchio [Giorgio] is right. . . . Teresa was right too" (p. 418).

At the inn after his return Nostromo meets Giorgio, who advises him, for purely idealistic reasons, to do as Monygham has suggested and depart at once by train with a vital message for Barrios. Nostromo does so, having no time to pass on to anyone he trusts (he does not trust Monygham) the truth about Decoud and the silver. When he returns to the scene some time later, events have taken the decision out of his hands. With Decoud dead and four bars of silver gone with him to the bottom of the Gulf, Nostromo cannot tell the truth without incurring suspicion of theft and even murder. Yet Nostromo, like Gould, having compromised and taken risks, appears to have been successful. He has made his fortune.

His success, however, like Gould's, plunges him into a network of typical Conradian ironies. Although he now possess a far greater personal fortune than he can ever have hoped for, he can reap only fractional benefit from it for fear of discovery. On him, as on Gould, material wealth has a deleterious psychological effect. A man accustomed to living openly and rejoicing in popular acclaim, Nostromo now becomes furtive and cut off from those around him.

And to become the slave of a treasure with full self-knowledge is an occurrence rare and mentally disturbing. But it was also in great part because of the difficulty of converting it into a form in which it could become available. . . . The crew of his own schooner were to be feared as if they had been spies upon their dreaded captain. He did not dare stay too long in port. . . . To do things by stealth humiliated him. And he suffered most from the concentration of his thoughts upon the treasure.

A transgression, a crime entering a man's existence, eats it up like a malignant growth, consumes it like a fever. Nostromo had lost his peace; the genuineness of all his qualities was destroyed (p. 523).

Once again Conrad uses dress to accentuate a change in the inner man. In his days of innocence Nostromo dressed naturally "in the checked shirt and red sash of a Mediterranean sailor" (p. 96), but after he obtains the treasure we see "the vigour and symmetry of his powerful limbs lost in the vulgarity of a brown tweed suit" (p. 527). The unsuitable clothing is the outward sign of the paradox of Nostromo's new situation as a rich man who must pretend relative poverty, a man of the people who must hide from public view, a sailor who dresses like a shopkeeper.

At a deeper level, however, Nostromo's situation remains much the same as it was. His object is still to "make his fortune", to use and enjoy the treasure which has now come into his possession. Against this object are the demands that he should enter into society, abandon his solitary, uncommitted way of life and undertake a proper measure of responsibility and public purpose. These demands, formerly voiced by Teresa Viola, are in the closing stages of the story represented by her elder daughter, Linda, the woman whom Nostromo is generally expected to marry. "Linda, with her mother's voice, had taken . . . her mother's place" (p. 529). Nostromo has no particular desire to marry Linda, for he is attracted to her younger sister, Giselle, yet he cannot marry Giselle, because Giorgio would not permit the elder daughter to be so passed over, and neither can Nostromo carry her off, for fear of losing the silver.

The connection between the Viola girls and the treasure is established when a lighthouse is built on the Great Isabel where Nostromo has concealed the silver. He secures the appointment of Giorgio as keeper of the light, knowing that he himself will then be able to visit the island publicly as Linda's suitor. The silver thus prevents him from offending Giorgio by either repudiating Linda or running off with Giselle. To continue his visits to the treasure he is obliged to accept open betrothal to the elder daughter.

The two girls represent the paradoxical tension between Nostromo's goal, the satisfaction of his appetites, and the gravitational pull of social norms. The orthodox Linda, like Teresa, stands for public and approved domestic stability, whereas Giselle is licentious, passionate and thoroughly desirable in a definitely unconventional fashion.

> As time went on, Nostromo discovered his preference for the younger of the two. . . . His wife would have to know his secret or else life would be impossible. He was attracted by Giselle, with her candid gaze and white throat, pliable, silent, fond of excitement under her quiet indolence; whereas Linda, with her

intense, passionately pale face, energetic, all fire and words, touched with gloom and scorn, a chip of the old block, true daughter of the austere republican, but with Teresa's voice, inspired him with a deep-seated mistrust (p. 524).

The treasure itself dictates that Nostromo should prefer Giselle, for he could not reveal its secret to the "austere" Linda, who has inherited her parents' high and idealistic standards. Giselle, who embodies his desire for freedom and luxury, is quite compatible with his possession of the silver and is even entrusted with knowledge of its existence. The irony lies in the fact that, precisely because of the treasure, Nostromo cannot make his preference for Giselle publicly known.

We can recognize here a familiar Conradian theme and pattern. In the tension between Nostromo's desires and what is generally expected of him we see the old opposition of selfish freedom and social responsibility, of licence and control, previously explored in the stories of Wait and Kurtz. Each of the Viola sisters stands at one pole of this dichotomy, Giselle symbolizing the hero's personal will and desire, Linda his moral duties in the public domain. They therefore take on the roles of heroine and anti-heroine respectively in relation to Nostromo. Giselle is the heroine, the woman who stands at the centre of the world the hero desires to enter. Linda is the anti-heroine, the rival for the hero's affections who comes from the orthodox world he has deserted through his compromise. It is no accident that Linda becomes keeper of the lamp "that would kindle a far-reaching light upon the only secret spot of his life" (p. 525).

The ending of Nostromo's story is worked out in terms of the familiar pattern employed earlier for Willems and Kurtz. In pursuing his personal goals the hero turns his back on the world of moral orthodoxy and commits a crime. The new life he wishes to shape for himself is directed towards a heroine, a young and desirable woman, but the hero is still tied to the anti-heroine, who belongs essentially to the respectable, authoritarian world he has abandoned. His position is threatened by a rival, who advances a competing claim to the heroine's affections, and he is finally confronted with fatal consequences by a male figure, the nemesis of an offended orthodoxy, who exacts punishment for the original crime.

Nostromo's rival is a pale and insubstantial figure, put into the story, one suspects, merely to complete the pattern. This is Ramirez,

who has succeeded Nostromo as captain of the Sulaco cargadors
and who, like him, has fallen violently in love with Giselle. Ramirez
watches Nostromo jealously, discovers his nightly visits to the island
and, thinking that Giselle is the reason, reports these to Linda.
Nostromo is not shot because of Ramirez' information, for Giorgio
thinks he is shooting at Ramirez himself, but the threat of eventual
discovery through the rival's jealousy is present in the story's closing
pages.

The nemesis is Giorgio, an Italian of republican sympathies like
Nostromo, but separated from him by a strict idealism which looks
down upon material motives, an "austere contempt for all personal
advantage" (p. 31). Giorgio, who "had all his life despised money"
(p. 31), stands opposed to Nostromo, the thief of the silver. The
albeit accidental shooting of Nostromo is therefore a retribution for
the theft and for the motive of personal gain, which had all along
prevented Nostromo's final entry into the Viola family.

The patterning of characters in the final phase of Nostromo's
story is virtually identical to that in *Heart of Darkness* and therefore
bears close similarity also to those of *An Outcast of the Islands* and
(apart from the female figures) *The Nigger of the 'Narcissus'*. The
situation may be represented in a diagram of the same type as that
used for the figures surrounding Kurtz.

	MALE	FEMALE
1st (ORTHODOX) WORLD	Nemesis (Giorgio)	Anti-heroine (Linda)
2nd (UNORTHODOX) WORLD	Rival (Ramirez)	Heroine (Giselle)

Here, as in the earlier story, the central theme is a contrast between
duty and personal desires—respectively the first and second
"worlds" of the diagram—with the nemesis figure and the anti-
heroine belonging to the realm of the former and standing opposed
to the rival and the heroine. Again strong personal animosities
develop between the nemesis figure and the rival (Giorgio thinks he
is shooting at Ramirez) and between the anti-heroine and the
heroine (Linda knows Giselle is flirting with her betrothed and at
one point attacks her physically).

We have seen that Nostromo first appears as a hero of a different
kind from Kurtz. Kurtz is one of the line of Conradian central

figures, running from Wait to Whalley and Gould, who are embodiments of paradox, and whose careers are therefore models of self-defeating endeavour. Nostromo is the first of those whose object is not to achieve a positive ideal but to secure their own comfortable independence in worlds of conflicting extremes. His immediate successors are Verloc and Razumov, both of whom wish only to steer non-commital courses of safety between warring parties. The outstanding problem is why Conrad reverted, for his conclusion of *Nostromo*, to the structural pattern of the earlier stories, introducing several new characters in order to do so (for both Linda and Giselle, as well as Ramirez, are effectively new in the last two chapters of the book), returning to the highly-charged symbolic manner of the tales of Wait and Kurtz.

The result suggests a possible degree of uncertainty in handling the new heroic style or, more probably, a wish to keep the novel from growing disproportionately long. *Nostromo* is the only novel in which Conrad attempted to deal simultaneously with a plurality of heroes, and their careers within it are not entirely coterminous. As Gould's affairs are approaching what promises to be a cataclysmic resolution, Nostromo is still setting out on his attempt to balance a compromise between opposing forces. His act in appropriating the silver corresponds structurally to Verloc's attempt on the Observatory and to Razumov's betrayal of Haldin, both deeds which take place relatively early in their respective stories. Had Nostromo been accorded a development of plot proportionate to those of his successors, it seems fair to assume that his story would have been prolonged to something like twice its present length. It may be that, foreseeing this, Conrad opted for a quick ending, to achieve which he drew upon the fictional mechanisms he had already evolved for dealing more rapidly with the heroes of shorter stories.

9 *The Secret Agent* and the Short Stories of 1904–7

Conrad's three great political novels, *Nostromo*, *The Secret Agent*, and *Under Western Eyes*, share a common basic pattern in which the key figure is the hero who, in his very effort to avoid commitment to either side in a dualistic conflict, builds himself a high reputation with both, as a result of which he is forced ironically into a compromising action, which in turn results in the death of another party. The two latter stories have the further complication that the person sacrificed to the preservation of the hero's position is the idolized brother of the heroine. This intensification of the hero's paradoxical position is absent from *Nostromo*, where the heroine, Giselle, has little integral importance and remains something of an afterthought to the main story.

Nostromo was completed in the summer of 1904. Between that time and the completion of the first (serial) version of *The Secret Agent* in November 1906, Conrad wrote four short stories, three of which bear closely upon the chief elements of the political novels. (The fourth, *The Brute*, like a number of Conrad's later short stories, is an inconsequential piece with little or no relation to the mainstream of his work.) The first of these, *Gaspar Ruiz*, in spite of Conrad's disclaimer in his 'Author's Note', is clearly an offshoot of *Nostromo*. Not only does it deal with the world of South American revolutions, but it also takes as its central figure a very Nostromo-like man of the people, taciturn, powerfully-built, a natural leader, who is drawn against his own wishes into the revolutionary wars and is exploited, first by military officials and later by his vengeful royalist wife. It is clearly a study of the absorption and destruction of a naively innocent man through his unwilling involvement in a political conflict.

The remaining two short stories of this time, *An Anarchist* and *The Informer*, both look forward to the world of secret societies and double agents glanced at in the final section of *Nostromo* and given detailed portrayal in *The Secret Agent* and *Under Western Eyes*. *The Informer* concerns a man who, like both Verloc and Razumov, joins a revolutionary group in order to pass on its secrets to the police. The informer here, as in the novels, is presented as the lover of a woman whose brother is among those whom he betrays. *An Anarchist*, which again portrays an innocent and unconcerned individual caught up in political conflict, turns upon the matter of personal reputation. The central character of this slight but ironic tale, like Razumov, acquires by chance a name for revolutionary sympathies which he is quite unable to shake off, and which eventually places him in a deadly situation.

The Secret Agent was begun late in 1905 at about the same time as Conrad was writing *An Anarchist* and *The Informer*. The central character, Verloc, is a typical Conradian hero of the second phase, self-interested, seeking safety and security, indolent and avaricious. He is also, recognizably, a mature revision of Almayer.

> His eyes were naturally heavy; he had an air of having wallowed, fully dressed, all day on an unmade bed (p. 4). . . . His idleness was not hygienic, but it suited him very well. He was in a manner devoted to it with a sort of inert fanaticism, or perhaps with a fanatical inertness. Born of industrious parents for a life of toil, he had embraced indolence from an impulse as profound, as inexplicable, and as imperious as the impulse which directs a man's preference for one particular woman in a given thousand (p. 12).

He is unlike Almayer, however, and close to Nostromo, in the manner of his pursuit of "what is dearest to him – his repose and his security" (p. 52), which consists in an attempt to move neutrally but profitably between two antagonistic political worlds. For Verloc is a secret agent, a man at once trusted among anarchist revolutionaries and yet paid and protected by police officers and foreign ambassadors.

Verloc is personally committed to neither side. He sees his work, it is true, in terms of the "vocation of a protector of society" (p. 5), but he does it not from any affection for the concept of social order, but because "protection is the first necessity of opulence and luxury" (p. 12). He does not even believe that the dissidents upon whose activities he reports present any real threat to the status quo; "at the notion of a menaced social order he would perhaps have

winked to himself if there had not been an effort to make in that sign
of scepticism" (p. 12). He is a secret agent because he finds he can
make an easy and apparently secure living by playing the two sides
against each other, fostering radical activities while encouraging
reactionary fears.

There is, however, a paradox inherent in this position. Verloc
desires the protection of social order as the condition of his own
security, but this can be maintained only for so long as his activities
in both spheres, with both the radicals and reactionaries, stop short
of achievement. That is, he must maintain a balance, without either
provoking strict measures by his employers that might effectively
suppress the actually feeble dissent upon which he spies, or allowing
his radical friends to carry out any plan which might succeed in
disrupting the order upon which he depends. His work for both sides
must remain ineffective. The paradox, the precarious nature of
Verloc's position, is reflected, as Mr Vladimir observes, in his
appearance of well-fed middle-class comfort. For all his anarchist
connections, Verloc "looked uncommonly like a master plumber
come to present his bill" (p. 27). He is, in addition, married, a
manifestation of conventional stability which surprises the Assistant
Commissioner.

Yet Verloc, like Nostromo, has a reputation, both with the
anarchists who use his shop as a meeting place and with Heat, the
detective who uses him as a source of information. He is "the famous
and trusty secret agent, so secret that he was never designated
otherwise but by the symbol Δ in the late Baron Stott-
Wartenheim's official, semi-official, and confidential correspondence; the celebrated agent Δ, whose warnings had the power to
change the schemes and the dates of royal, imperial, or grand-ducal
journeys, and sometimes cause them to be put off altogether"
(p. 27). Verloc's reputation, which, like Nostromo's, is mysterious
as to its original acquisition, is the mainstay of his livelihood.

As a man of wide repute Verloc stands in line with Wait, Kurtz,
Jim, Whalley and Nostromo. Like several of these he is also
endowed with an abnormally penetrating voice, symbolic of his
persuasive powers, which Verloc demonstrates for Mr Vladimir's
benefit (pp. 23–4). The voice, as in the cases of Wait and Kurtz,
shows the hero's ability to propagate his name abroad and his
tendency to do so by means of rhetoric, the mouthing of plausible
ideologies.

Verloc's goal in life, his own personal comfort and security, is embodied in the story's heroine, his wife Winnie, described as an easy-going, domestic woman of strong sexual attraction. What Verloc does not appreciate is that Winnie has married him primarily in order to secure a home for her retarded brother, Stevie. He therefore misjudges entirely her reaction to Stevie's death, assuming that this will make no difference to his marital position. It is part of Verloc's paradox that in sacrificing Stevie in an attempt to preserve his domestic comforts he unwittingly alienates his wife to the point of murder.

In the role of Stevie, Conrad expands his structural pattern in a new direction. Like certain other celebrated fictional idiots (Dostoevsky's Myshkin, for instance, and Faulkner's Benjy), Stevie serves to make a strongly ironic comment on the "normal" characters around him. In contrast with the mindless posturings of Verloc's anarchist friends, Michaelis, Yundt and Ossipon, Stevie alone shows a genuine social conscience and true sympathy for the poor and oppressed. He sees the evil of the world (evil which, for all its mockery of the anarchists, the novel does not for a moment deny) and responds sympathetically to the limit of his ability, immediately giving whatever he has to those whom he believes to be in need. His role is very close to that of Decoud in *Nostromo*, who has a similar perceptive faculty, is similarly oppressed by the political and social evils he sees, and who also dies accidentally in the course of a supposedly ameliorating action in which he has been persuaded to cooperate. Decoud's undertaking the editorship of the *Porvenir* corresponds precisely to Stevie's assistance of Verloc in the bomb episode. Both Stevie and Decoud are motivated generally by an appreciation of social injustice, although neither can be said to be in full agreement with the specific undertaking to which he has been persuaded through the pressure of those close to him.

Both Stevie and Decoud die as a direct result of becoming involved in the hero's dealings, Decoud because Nostromo neglects to return for him, and Stevie because of an accident with Verloc's bomb. There is therefore a sense in which, although unintentionally, the self-seeking hero sacrifices the more sincere, altruistic character in an effort to preserve his personal security. This pattern is repeated in Haldin's betrayal by Razumov in *Under Western Eyes*.

It is at first tempting to see this sacrificial male figure in the political novels, the sincere and self-denying counterpart of the egocentric hero, as the successor to the rivals, such as Omar, Donkin, the Manager and Cornelius, of the earlier stories. They are, like some of these rivals, effectually eliminated as a result of the hero's actions, and in the cases of Stevie and Haldin they possess the affection of the woman to whom the hero aspires. There is, however, no actual rivalry between these characters and the heroes, and their relations with the heroines, if any, are merely fraternal. The true rivals in the first two political novels, Ramirez in *Nostromo* and Ossipon in *The Secret Agent*, are insignificant figures. The sacrificial male is a new creation peculiar to the political novels, who has no real counterpart in the earlier stories – unless we might count Dain Waris in *Lord Jim*, Arsat's brother in *The Lagoon*, and Makara in *Karain*, each of whom dies as a result of the hero's effort to achieve his object.

The man who dies is clearly present in the story to underline the enormity of the hero's self-interest, which he does both by presenting a more sincere and altruistic counterpart and by dying because of the hero's machinations. The presence of such a figure alerts us to a shift in Conrad's attitude towards the hero, a change that takes place between Jim and Whalley on the one hand and Nostromo, Verloc and Razumov on the other, and which in some ways counteracts the moral amelioration which the heroes achieve when they cease active pursuit of their ideals. The political heroes make their respective compromises solely in order to preserve or more easily achieve their personal ambition of ease and security. The innocent sacrifices of Decoud and Stevie, along with the only slightly less innocent sacrifice of Haldin, all serve to emphasize the danger to others of the heroes' unrestrained pursuit of what at first sight might appear to be relatively modest, harmless goals. It is true that in no case is the hero driven primarily by malice towards the man whose death he brings about, but the point lies precisely in his preparedness to risk the life of another simply to preserve himself from danger.

The political heroes, for all their taciturnity, uninvolvement and inwardness, are a dangerous strain of the Conradian heroic breed. Not only are they directly responsible for the deaths of their quasi-accomplices, but they must also take indirect responsibility for the passing of certain women, the mothers of the heroines and also, in two cases, of the sacrificed males. Teresa Viola dies of an old illness at the point when revolutionaries enter Sulaco, but she dies unconfessed, lamenting the fact that Nostromo, in order to be able to take charge of the silver, has deserted her and refused to fetch her a priest. Nostromo later experiences guilt on this account, acknowledging that he has, in effect, allowed Teresa to die in exchange for his possession of the treasure. Razumov similarly causes the decline and decay of Mrs Haldin, when he betrays her son to execution, a fact of which he is constantly reminded when he subsequently seeks her daughter's company. In *The Secret Agent* Winnie's mother voluntarily leaves the Verloc household in order to avoid putting a strain upon the goodwill of Verloc towards Stevie. We do not hear of the old lady's fate after the deaths of her family in the course of the story, but her ride from the shop to the small almshouse lodging she has obtained for herself is presented as a symbolic departure from life. It is true that Verloc does not seek this sacrifice from his mother-in-law, nor does he know of it until after its accomplishment, but he is responsible to the extent that the move was made in order to preserve his goodwill towards Stevie, whom he subsequently sends to his death.

As with the sacrificial male, antecedents of the sacrificial female are hard to find in the earlier stories. Dead or discarded mothers of previous heroines, such as Mrs Almayer, Jewel's mother, and the long-departed Mrs Whalley, do not meet the case, since their deaths are not tied in any specific way to the advancement of the heroes' interests. The sacrificial females in the political novels reinforce the point that the heroes' selfish struggles present real dangers not only to those, like Decoud, Stevie and Haldin, who allow themselves to become involved in perilous undertakings, but also to those who, by age, sex and circumstances, are debarred from any positive intervention whatsoever.

The placement of Winnie's mother in the sequence of dying women which runs from Teresa Viola to Mrs Haldin is important not only to illustrate one of several ways in which the political novels form a well-defined structural group, but also to show that the long section describing her ride to the almshouse is not a brilliant but gratuitous aside, but an integral feature of the novel. It belongs to *The Secret Agent* no less integrally than the death of Teresa belongs to *Nostromo* or the passages showing the decay of Mrs Haldin belong to *Under Western Eyes*. The point needs emphasis because the narrative construction of the novel seems at first glance to be very patchy, a difficulty compounded by the fact that the story exists in two versions, the original serialized version published between October 1906 and January 1907, and the book, with which we are familiar, published later in 1907.

We are here concerned only with the final version, which differs in construction from Conrad's earlier novels in that it consists essentially of a number of protracted interviews or conversations between assorted pairs of characters, joined by relatively short stretches of narrative. Of course, any novel seriously concerned with the interaction of characters is likely to exhibit a high proportion of dialogue, but *The Secret Agent* proceeds to an unusually high degree through a series of carefully staged interchanges, which not only reveal the personalities involved but also carry the burden of the plot, at least up to the point of Verloc's murder. We have the interview between Verloc and Mr Vladimir, that between Chief Inspector Heat and the Assistant Commissioner, the first between the Assistant Commissioner and Sir Ethelred, that of Winnie and her mother in the cab, that between Heat and Verloc (overheard by Winnie), the second of the Assistant Commissioner and Sir Ethelred, and the final conversation of Verloc and Winnie leading up to her murder of her husband. Like a chorus at the ends of the first and last acts of a tragedy, we have also the Professor and Comrade Ossipon twice meeting and conversing in the Silenus.

This way of proceeding in a novel was new to Conrad. There are occasional lengthy interviews in the earlier works, notably those between Lingard and a succession of other characters in the later stages of *An Outcast of the Islands* and that between Marlow and Jim after the trial in *Lord Jim*, but in no other novel had Conrad relied so heavily upon the device. Hitherto he had used either impersonal narration or subnarrators, like Marlow and Mitchell, or some combination of the two. The two-party dialogue is an appropriate vehicle for the plot of *The Secret Agent*, however, because it shows, in a much more direct way than would be possible in plain narrative, the irony of a world in which characters constantly talk and work at cross-purposes or with the object of concealing rather than revealing their thoughts.

The novels of Conrad's second phase differ from his earlier work, not only in their presentation of the hero as attempting neutrality between conflicting worlds rather than striving openly for mastery in one sphere, but also in their depiction of a generally fragmented society. The earlier novels focus almost exclusively on their heroes, giving only incidental glimpses of the wider scene against which they move. The politico-social environments of Sambir and Patusan, graphic and engaging as is their portrayal, are only backgrounds against which the courses of the respective heroes are run. In *Nostromo*, on the other hand, the political world of

Costaguana is the real focus of a story which has no single predominant character. Much the same is true of the London of *The Secret Agent*. The fragmentation of society in *Nostromo* is conveyed by the very proliferation of characters and interested groups within the story: the miners, the railwaymen, the OSN, the church, the western province, the plain, the cargadors, the soldiers, the engineers, Gould, Avellanos, Montero, Ribiera, and so forth. *The Secret Agent*, created on a much more restricted canvas, achieves much the same end by means of its interviews, in which the novel evolves through an elaboration of misunderstandings. The device is used to a similar degree in *Under Western Eyes*, where the same fragmentation is again presented, although in this somewhat longer story Conrad also employs a subnarrator, the teacher of languages.

The ironies of *The Secret Agent* interlock in a plot of the familiar Conradian type, in which the hero, in pursuit of his own ends, is forced into a compromise which has the ultimate result of frustrating the purpose for which he made it. Verloc, attempting to live his life of indolence in the enticing company of his wife, is threatened by Mr Vladimir. Vladimir upsets the balance of forces upon which Verloc's existence depends by insisting that the British police be provoked into severe reprisals against the anarchists. Verloc's anarchists are more verbal than active; the three with whom he is most closely associated are collectively responsible for propaganda and are intellectuals rather than activists. Verloc knows that these men will never carry out the kind of outrage Mr Vladimir demands and is therefore obliged to organize it himself. This he does, with Stevie's help, in the hope of satisfying Vladimir and so preserving his own income and security. Yet the deed is a severe compromise of his principles, both because his formulated purpose is to protect society, not to throw bombs at it, and because he rightly foresees that a disturbance in the balance of forces will work ultimately to his disadvantage.

Verloc's compromise lies in his giving way to Vladimir's demand. It can be compared to Nostromo's appropriation of the silver, an act which similarly results in the loss of the hero's independence of action, while only temporarily satisfying his wish for personal security. In both cases the hero acts with the immediate object of preserving his uncommitted position, but does so by means of a deed which in the event entails the frustration of that purpose. Verloc's act can also be compared to the compromises of the earlier heroes, the retreats to black worlds of Jim, Willems and Almayer, for instance. Like them, Verloc is forced, by the inherent paradox of his position, to accept an undesirable course of action which promises to bring him to his goal, but he finds that the consequences of this capitulation in the end deprive him of what he seeks. By his compromise Verloc, like the earlier heroes, finds himself uncomfortably exposed by his active participation in the conflict of political forces.

Mr Vladimir wants to stimulate repressive action against the anarchists and coerces the hitherto passive Verloc to fabricate an anarchist outrage. It appears at first that the plan will work and that the desired reaction will vent itself on Michaelis, one of Verloc's radicals, although, as his portrayal makes clear, a man harmless to the point of imbecility. Chief Inspector Heat, whose attitude to the political situation, like Verloc's, consists in the desire to preserve a quiescent equilibrium, is inclined to overlook the clue which links Verloc to the bombing and to arrest Michaelis, the obvious suspect, upon circumstantial evidence.

Heat's relation to Verloc is much like that of Lakamba to Almayer in *Almayer's Folly*. They are, as it were, inverted images of each other, counterparts on opposite sides of the dividing line between two worlds. They resemble each other both physically, as heavy, ponderous men approaching middle age, and in their temperaments and attitudes. Heat, like Verloc, is a "protector" of the public (p. 101), who fulfils his role by underhanded methods. Verloc associates with revolutionaries in order to sell information about them to the authorities, while Heat refrains from action against Verloc in order to profit from such information. There is evidently some truth in the assistant Commissioner's observation that "the reputation of Chief Inspector Heat might possibly have been made in a great part by the Secret Agent Verloc" (p. 131). The two are, in a sense, mutually sustaining; Verloc creates Heat's reputation by supplying him with information, while Heat affords Verloc protection so that he may continue to operate.

This arrangement, which is an aspect of the initial paradoxical balance of hostile forces, is broken by Verloc's compromise. In order to satisfy Mr Vladimir he has to arrange an effective outrage without giving Heat prior notice. This in turn, however, imperils Heat's reputation with his superiors and causes the Assistant Commissioner to take over the case. The arrangement between the two men is thus broken; Heat loses Verloc's information and, as a direct result, Verloc loses Heat's protection.

The intervention of the Assistant Commissioner prevents the bombing from having its intended effect and, at the same time, completes the breakdown of Verloc's balance of forces by withdrawing police protection from secret agents. The Commissioner steps in partly because Heat himself has obviously failed in this instance to predict and prevent the crime, but primarily in order to placate his wife, whose society friends would be offended at the arrest of Michaelis. The Assistant Commissioner takes the case out of Heat's hands and, instead of pursuing Michaelis, follows the clue which points to Verloc.

His action in disturbing the established pattern of interchange between Verloc and Heat corresponds structurally to Mr Vladimir's demand that Verloc arrange the bombing. In both cases the principal interferes with the balance of forces operated by his agent. In the architecture of the story, Heat's interview with the Assistant Commissioner is the counterpart, on the opposite side of the fence, of Verloc's meeting with Mr Vladimir. Both the Assistant Commissioner and Vladimir are high officials, normally removed behind desks from the immediate scene of action, into which they none the less make incursions during the story by suspending the normal routine of understanding between their respective agents. The resolution of this antithesis comes in the scene in which the Assistant Commissioner confronts Vladimir with the truth (pp. 225–8).

In the relations just set out among these four characters, Verloc, Heat, Vladimir and the Assistant Commissioner, we see Conrad developing a form of patterning which he had not used systematically since *Almayer's Folly*, the ranging of characters in equivalent but contrasting pairs across the ideological dualism which provides the framework of the story. The dualism in this case is political and lies specifically between the powers of law enforcement and the seekers of disruption. On the one side stand Heat and his superior, the Assistant Commissioner; on the other stand Verloc and his employer, Mr Vladimir. Heat is the inverted image of Verloc, while Vladimir is similarly paired with the Assistant Commissioner.

Two other characters, Sir Ethelred and the Professor, may also be placed within this pattern. Sir Ethelred is the Home Secretary, to whom the Assistant Commissioner reports. Massive, aristocratic and patriarchal, he is the embodiment of social stability. The Professor, who avoids arrest by carrying a bomb upon his person and who devotes his life to the discovery of a perfect detonator to be used for the destruction of the established order, is his opposite. The two are also completely contrasting bodily types, Sir Ethelred being huge to the point of virtual immobility, while the Professor is puny, undersized and physically insignificant. It is the Professor who gives Verloc the explosive for his attempt on the Observatory, while it is Sir Ethelred who authorizes the Assistant Commissioner to proceed in his intention to get the truth out of Verloc after the explosion. They thus provide respectively the material means for the Secret Agent's compromise, and the impetus for its retribution.

Sir Ethelred and the Professor represent the logical ultimates of their respective parties. The Home Secretary is described in terms of English tradition and solidarity. "The Assistant Commissioner's figure before this big and rustic Presence had the frail slenderness of a reed addressing an oak. And indeed the unbroken record of that man's descent surpassed in the number of centuries the age of the oldest oak in the country" (p. 136). The Professor, on the other hand, aims to "destroy public faith in legality" (p. 81) primarily by means of violent explosions. He draws the contrast between himself and the upholders of law and order in these terms:

> Their character is built upon conventional morality. It leans on the social order. Mine stands free from everything artificial. They are bound in all sorts of conventions. They depend on life, which, in this connection, is a historical fact surrounded by all sorts of restraints and considerations, a complex, organized fact open to attack at every point; whereas I depend on death, which knows no restraint and cannot be attacked (p. 68).

The Professor is "the perfect anarchist" (p. 95). If we therefore include the Professor and Sir Ethelred as the patrons of their respective parties, the alignment of characters in *The Secret Agent* looks like this:

ORDER	ANARCHY
Sir Ethelred	The Professor
The Assistant Commissioner	Mr Vladimir
Chief Inspector Heat	Verloc

We shall see that Conrad develops some comparable bipolar symmetries in *Chance* and *Victory*.

The two poles or parties to the dualism in *The Secret Agent* are clearly related to those in the earlier novels. Not only does this contrast of order and anarchy reflect the wider political conflict of stability and revolution in *Nostromo*, but it also recalls the psychological and social antitheses of control and licence explored in *The Nigger of the 'Narcissus'* and *Heart of Darkness*.

Within the dualistic framework, despite the innovations introduced into the political novels, the usual Conradian fictional pattern can still be traced clearly. The hero, in striving towards an ideal, effects a compromise or takes a moral short-cut which, although bringing him closer to his object, sets in motion the forces which will bring about his defeat. In *The Secret Agent*, Verloc's attempt to blow up the Observatory has two immediate effects: the death of Stevie and the investigation of this by Chief Inspector Heat. Heat's investigation is taken over by the Assistant Commissioner, an intervention which, in the structure of the story, comes as the ironically fated reaction from the other side meeting and frustrating the hero's move. Through the Assistant Commissioner's unforeseeable but structurally appropriate interference the bombing is brought swiftly home to Verloc, who now, in a desperate effort to save himself, abandons secrecy and reveals to the police his dealings with the embassy. This in itself means the end of his career, and accordingly he begins preparations to leave the country. His death, however, is the result not of anarchist vengeance for this betrayal, but of Winnie's anger on learning of the demise of her brother. Verloc, who had not desired or even expected Stevie's death, had believed that the boy risked no more than possible arrest and imprisonment. The fatality, although accidental, arose none the less directly from Verloc's compromise, and Winnie's response, which he also failed to anticipate, is the ultimate outcome.

Verloc's death is therefore the result of his compromise in much the same way as the deaths of Wait, Kurtz, Jim and Nostromo are each consequences of their respective easy options. There is no separate nemesis figure in *The Secret Agent*, no single character corresponding structurally to Allistoun, to Marlow in *Heart of Darkness*, or to Gentleman Brown. Verloc, like Willems, is killed by his heroine, but his death is brought about by a combination of people: Heat, the Assistant Commissioner and Vladimir, as well as Winnie herself.

The story has no specific character in the nemesis role, and the only identifiable rival, Comrade Ossipon, comes on to the scene in

that capacity only after Verloc is dead, when he approaches Winnie
with the hope of seducing her and taking money from her. Once he
has obtained the money and found out that she has killed Verloc he
abandons her, and she, alone and afraid of being hanged for what
she has done, commits suicide. The rival figure is similarly
diminished in the other two political novels.

Conrad's relative loss of interest in the rival and nemesis figures in
the political novels is compensated by the greater intensity of the
heroine's part. Earlier stories either lacked a heroine completely
like *The Nigger of the 'Narcissus'*, or had perfunctory and somewhat
stereotypical characters in that role, such as Jewel, Nina and the
native woman of *Heart of Darkness*. Before *Nostromo*, Conrad's most
developed female portrait was Aissa, credible enough for her own
story, but clearly too exotic and contrived a figure for the maturer
novels. Emilia Gould may therefore be said to be Conrad's first
serious heroine. Although her part in the story is relatively small,
her moral influence is immense; she does as much as, if not more
than her husband to effect their common ideals, and it is she who
pronounces the final word on the silver and the mine. Successive
heroines, Winnie Verloc, Natalia Haldin, Flora de Barral, Lena,
Rita and Mrs Travers, have similarly central roles, not only
affecting the courses of events but also providing the moral focus for
their respective stories in ways that even the most prominent of the
earlier heroines, Jewel and Aissa, could not have managed.

The heroines of the political novels embody their respective
heroes' several ideals of luxury, indolence, and personal fame, but
more generally they represent the principle of neutrality which the
heroes abandon in their act of compromise. Emilia remains
disinterested in local politics, Winnie has no concern for her
husband's political dealings, and Natalia refrains from joining any
group or party. The women remain committed to non-political
humanitarian ideals, particularly Emilia and Natalia, both of
whom engage actively in work for the poor and the sick, but also
Winnie, whose humanity shows itself chiefly in her selfless care for
Stevie. The heroines' neutrality, however, is altruistic, while the
uninvolvement sought by the heroes tends to be selfish and
materialistic. The major stories of the second phase are distinguished not only by the heroes' attempts to remain uninvolved but
also by the heroines' assertions of humanity. The relation between
hero and heroine in these novels changes accordingly. She is still the
embodiment of his desires, in that she both remains uncommitted

politically (as he would like to do) and represents to him an easy and desirable way of life, but she is also contrasted with the selfishness which the hero displays in pursuit of his goals, and for this reason is cut off from him by the end of the tale.

A literary reason for Conrad's new interest in female characters may be found in the movement we have already observed in *Nostromo*, away from plots which turn exclusively upon a single male hero, towards a kind of novel which looks more widely into the world and deals with situations involving a number of characters of more or less equal weight. The worlds of the political novels do not turn solely upon individual fates, nor are they entirely dominated by male figures. *Nostromo* is in this respect a transitional work, in that Emilia, although an important and fully rounded character, is overshadowed by the males and allowed little direct involvement in the action. With Winnie Verloc we come to the first of Conrad's heroines to claim almost equal status with the hero. Winnie, who is herself the perpetrator of Verloc's death, is the first of a line of heroines which includes notably Flora de Barral and the heroines of the novels of the last phase.

Winnie herself passes through the Conradian cycle of ideal, compromise, paradox and retribution, a movement hitherto reserved for the heroes. Her goal in life, her ideal, is security, not so much for herself as for her retarded brother, Stevie. Her determination to achieve this causes her to reject the attentions of a tradesman's son, for whom she feels affection and who would doubtless have made her a good husband. Her choice falls instead upon Verloc, for the simple reason that he, unlike her other admirer, is willing to accept Stevie into his household. Winnie's motives are of the highest, but in allying herself to Verloc, of whose nature and character she chooses to know very little, she is, in the manner typical of the Conradian hero, lowering her personal standards to achieve an easy solution. From this point her life follows the usual Conradian pattern, as she discovers that the means she has adopted in order to achieve her goal ultimately deprives her of success. Verloc, whom she married to secure Stevie's livelihood, involves the boy in an episode which causes his death.

When Winnie is seen as the central figure of her own tragic pattern, certain other aspects of the novel fall into place about her. Stevie is clearly her hero, in the sense that it is for his sake that she makes the compromise, much as the Conradian hero usually makes his fateful move for an ideal in which the heroine is involved. (The story is not, in this respect, symmetrical; Winnie is Verloc's heroine, but Winnie's hero is Stevie, not Verloc.) Her nemesis appears in the form of Comrade Ossipon, who treats her as she has treated Verloc, although their motives differ considerably. Just as Winnie had married Verloc for financial security, so Ossipon now comes to Winnie with the real object, concealed under an offer of sympathy, of taking her money. This he succeeds in doing, and with his defection nothing stands between Winnie and suicide.

The Secret Agent displays the salient structural features of Conrad's second mature phase. Its hero is not so much a flawed idealist as a selfish materialist, not a man of action but one inclined to withdrawal and passivity. Its heroine is more fully developed than the heroines of the first phase, and figures chiefly as a representative of humane considerations, which representation keeps her neutral with respect to the political conflict that provides the story's dualistic setting. The hero's compromise involves his own loss of this neutrality and his consequent alienation from the heroine. At the same time this story has certain special characteristics linking it structurally to works both earlier and later in Conrad's canon. The device of pairing characters across the dualism of the story, palely adumbrated in *Almayer's Folly*, is strongly apparent in *The Secret Agent*, and was to be revived in some of the later works. The depiction of the heroine as a character with her own pattern of compromise, paradox, and nemesis, looks forward to the novels of the last phase, where the heroine's independent role becomes a distinctive structural feature.

The theme of unwilling involvement, which runs from *Nostromo* through *The Secret Agent* and *Under Western Eyes* into Conrad's later work, is studied also in the two shorter pieces written between the completion of *The Secret Agent* and the inception of *Under Western Eyes*. *Il Conde*, written in the last months of 1906, is about an elderly gentleman who has enjoyed a completely calm, private and untroubled life. When suddenly forced to confront violence and lawlessness from a member of his own social class, he is shattered by the shock and goes into decline. D'Hubert, the hero of *The Duel*, written in the winter of 1906–7, is a very similar case. An inoffensive but unremarkable soldier, he is drawn into a pointless quarrel with a fellow officer which, through no fault of his, becomes a lasting and widely-known feud. He wishes only to forget the affair, but is allowed no honourable way of doing so. Unlike the Count, however, d'Hubert finally faces and defeats his antagonist, a victory which also brings him the love of his heroine. Both these stories look, albeit in relatively superficial ways, at the plight of the new Conradian hero, the man who seeks to follow a quiet life unobtrusively but who is prevented by ironic fate from doing so.

10 *Under Western Eyes* and *The Secret Sharer*

Under Western Eyes was begun in December 1907, and completed over the next two years. It continues several of the structural characteristics we have observed in its immediate predecessor, namely, a political theme which is larger than the career of the individual hero, a strong and significant part for the heroine, a tendency to place characters in pairs of opposites, and heavy reliance upon extended dialogues in the form of set pieces or interviews as a means of furthering the plot. It also shares the central theme of this phase, the reluctant hero unwillingly dragged into an undertaking he would rather have avoided, and thereby committed against his wishes to one side of the conflict.

The hero is Razumov, whose personal aim in life, closely comparable to the respective goals of Nostromo and Verloc, is avoidance of involvement in the political struggle between reaction and revolution which rages around him. His essentially noncommittal nature is reflected in his behaviour and appearance.

> His good looks would have been unquestionable if it had not been for a peculiar lack of fineness in the features. It was as if a face modelled vigorously in wax (with some approach even to a classical correctness of type) had been held close to a fire until all sharpness of line had been lost in the softening of the material. . . . In discussion he was easily swayed by argument and authority. With his younger compatriots he took the attitude of an inscrutable listener, a listener of the kind that hears you out intelligently and then – just changes the subject (p. 5).

His neutrality is reflected also in his origins, his illegitimacy, which leaves him with no inherited allegiance to class or creed. He is in fact the natural son of Prince K. by the daughter of an archpriest, a parentage which cannot be openly acknowledged. Razumov therefore comes into the world with no particular social or political affiliations, but identifies himself more widely with the Russian people as a whole.

> His closest parentage was defined in the statement that he was a Russian. Whatever good he expected from life would be given to or withheld from his hopes by that connexion alone. This immense parentage suffered from the throes of internal dissensions, and he shrank mentally from the fray as a good-natured man may shrink from taking definite sides in a violent family quarrel (p. 11).

At the same time, however, like Nostromo, Razumov is desirous of maintaining a certain figure in the world, which in his case is to be achieved through academic work and progress. Such a wish, the narrator points out, is natural. "There was nothing strange in the student Razumov's wish for distinction. A man's real life is that accorded to him in the thoughts of other men by reason of respect or natural love" (p. 14).

Razumov wants "safety", "an ordered life", so as to pursue his studies and thereby win a reputation and "conquer a name" (p. 71), an ambition which depends upon his keeping up a neutral attitude towards political strife. Like Nostromo and, in a slightly different way, Verloc, Razumov needs to preserve his independence; but the paradoxical nature of his position and the compromise in which this involves him bring him ultimately to admit, "I am independent – and therefore perdition is my lot" (p. 362). The paradox arises from the fact that Razumov's very conduct in seeking to avoid notice and the formulation of political opinions earns him a reputation as a deep political thinker.

> Amongst a lot of exuberant talkers, in the habit of exhausting themselves daily by ardent discussion, a comparatively taciturn personality is naturally credited with reserve power. By his comrades at the St. Petersburg University, Kirylo Sidorovitch Razumov, third year's student in philosophy, was looked upon as a strong nature – an altogether trustworthy man. This, in a country where an opinion may be a legal crime visited by death or sometimes by a fate worse than mere death, meant that he was worthy of being trusted with forbidden opinions (p. 6).

Razumov's very avoidance of political discussion thus draws him ironically to the attention of revolutionary plotters. At the same time the fact that he has no acknowledged family, the symbolic reflection of his absence of commitment in the class struggle, makes him the obvious confidant for Haldin, the fugitive revolutionary assassin, who says to him, "It occurred to me that you – you have no one belonging to you – no ties, no one to suffer for it if this came out by some means. There have been enough ruined Russian homes as it is" (p. 19).

The arrival of Haldin in Razumov's rooms is therefore a great irony, an outcome of the hero's cultivated neutrality, which he could hardly have foreseen, but which in fact follows inevitably from his position. Razumov himself thinks of Haldin's appearance in terms of "three years of good work gone . . . turned from hope to terror, because events started by human folly link themselves into a sequence which no sagacity can foresee and no courage break through. Fatality enters your room while your landlady's back is turned . . ." (p. 83). The moment corresponds to Mr Vladimir's demand that Verloc blow up the Observatory, and to the entrusting of Nostromo with the silver, both happenings which place the hero in the position of being able to achieve his goal only by means of a serious compromise. In each case the hero succumbs to temptation.

Once Haldin is in his room, Razumov can only either ensure that he escape or give him up. Merely to turn him out would be to risk his being seen and his visit, with its incriminating implications, being discovered. In the event he attempts at first to do as Haldin asks and deliver a message to Ziemianitch, by whose means Haldin expects to escape; but when Ziemianitch is found to be too drunk to move, Razumov despairs and, in great anger against Haldin, experiences an access of conservative sentiment. In this mood he consults Prince K., who refers him to General T., on whose orders Haldin is then arrested.

Razumov thus makes his compromise. In order to maintain his position of independence he momentarily takes one side and, in so doing, betrays a member of the other. Haldin, duly executed shortly afterwards, is sacrificed by Razumov in much the same way that Decoud is sacrificed by Nostromo and Stevie by Verloc. Razumov, like Nostromo and Verloc, now finds that, contrary to his expectations, the matter does not rest here. He is handed over to Councillor Mikulin, who presses him to serve the conservative cause. Razumov is of particular interest to Mikulin precisely because he is trusted by the revolutionaries and by them generally believed to have been associated in Haldin's plot. To make him a successful double agent, Mikulin counts on "the revolutionary self-delusion which credited Razumov with a mysterious complicity in the Haldin affair. To be compromised in it was credit enough – and it was their own doing. It was precisely *that* which stamped Mr Razumov as a providential man . . ." (p. 309). Razumov, of course, does not want to become involved in this work, but under political pressures his protests were vain. "Mr. Razumov was led to defend his attitude of detachment. But Councillor Mikulin would have none of his arguments. 'For a man like you,' were his last weighty words in the discussion, 'such a position is impossible'" (p. 294). In much the same way as Verloc, having unwillingly made his attempt on the Observatory, is then forced to give evidence against Mr Vladimir, so Razumov, having been virtually obliged to betray Haldin, is then made to become a government spy against the radical camp in Geneva (to which, through a chain of Haldin's associates, he has an introduction).

The plot structure of *Under Western Eyes* is a slightly more elaborate version of that of *The Secret Agent*. The hero, to maintain his own profitable detachment, engages in a compromising action which results in the death of a sincere, unselfish male character, with whom he himself is implicitly contrasted. In both cases the dead man leaves a devoted sister, who is the story's heroine, an embodiment of the hero's ideal, and in both cases the brother and sister have a mother whose dedication to her son causes her to fade visibly and pathetically, again underlining the hero's unwitting brutality. Later, in both novels, the hero's betrayal of the brother becomes known, as a result of which revelation his own career is brought to a violent and abrupt conclusion.

There are, of course, many differences within the larger similarity of framework. Natalia Haldin is a different person from Winnie Verloc. She does not make the hero's acquaintance until after his compromise and the consequent death of her brother, and it is not she who is the agent of his downfall after his confession to the betrayal. Her role, more like Emilia's than Winnie's, is largely passive. She is, none the less, unambiguously Razumov's heroine, for although he clearly cannot be said to sacrifice Haldin in order to win her, she represents the path of reconciliation which is the selfless equivalent of Razumov's somewhat egocentric detachment. Although she is the sister of the fanatically committed assassin, her own position looks beyond revolution to the end of the dualistic conflict.

> I must own to you [she says to the narrator] that I shall never give up looking forward to the day when all discord shall be silenced. Try to imagine its dawn! The tempest of blows and of execrations is over; all is still; the new sun is rising, and the weary men united at last, taking count in their conscience of the ended contest, feel saddened by their victory, because so many ideas have perished for the triumph of one, so many beliefs have abandoned them without support. They feel alone on earth and gather close together. Yes, there must be many bitter hours! But at last the anguish of hearts shall be extinguished in love (pp. 376–7).

While Razumov wishes only to live his own life without the risks and costs of involvement in the political struggle, Natalia Haldin sets her eyes on its cessation. Both, in a sense, therefore repudiate the conflict, although Natalia works meanwhile for the good of the victims, "sharing her compassionate labours between the horrors of overcrowded jails, and the heart rending misery of bereaved homes" (p. 378), while Razumov seeks only to preserve himself. Natalia is a typical heroine of Conrad's second phase, an altruistic woman whose compassion holds her aloof from the political conflict in which the hero becomes embroiled.

Miss Haldin is like Emilia and Winnie in that she is herself largely free, at least by the end of the novel, from the vain or hypocritical motives which activate those around her. Like Emilia, she finds a solution in withdrawal from political action and dedication to basic humanitarian concerns. The chief tonal differences between *The Secret Agent* and *Under Western Eyes* stem from the divergence of their heroines. Whereas the former novel concludes with Winnie's murder of Verloc and eventual suicide, the latter ends on a note of resolution with Natalia's promise of forgiveness (p. 353) and her return to Russia to help the sick and the prisoners. Razumov himself, rather like both Gould and Verloc, virtually disappears from the last pages of his story, when the stage is occupied by the heroine and several of the secondary characters.

Under Western Eyes is rich in portraits of Razumov's revolutionary associates, some of whom also occupy places in the structural dynamics of the plot. Peter Ivanovitch, the radical feminist, is perhaps Conrad's most expanded creation of the hero's rival. He is

Razumov's rival in the world of Russian exiles in Geneva, the world in which the hero finds himself as a result of his compromise, much as Omar is Willems' rival in Sambir and Cornelius Jim's in Patusan. When Razumov arrives he finds Peter Ivanovitch established as prominent among the revolutionaries, whose society he is to infiltrate. He takes an immediate dislike to the man and sees through the hypocrisy of his feminist doctrines, which are in reality a cover for his exploitation of women like Tekla and Madame de S. Peter Ivanovitch, moreover, is in the process of attempting to gain control over Natalia Haldin, which makes him Razumov's rival in a sexual triangle. In the outcome Razumov thwarts his rival by placing Natalia beyond his reach, but Peter Ivanovitch is an active survivor of the story's end, by which point the hero has been defeated and removed from the conflict.

With Peter Ivanovitch, Conrad introduces what is in effect the second theme of the novel. The first theme is the political struggle and Razumov's unwilling involvement in it. The second is the question of feminism, the woman's role in the larger conflict, a theme which grows naturally at this point in Conrad's career from his newly developed interest in the place of the heroine in his novels. After the creation of Emilia Gould, to whom Natalia Haldin is very close in temperament, and of Winnie Verloc, the author turns explicit attention to the nature of female influence, its place in politics, and related male attitudes. It is clear from *Under Western Eyes* that, although Conrad allowed central importance to the humanitarian values represented by Natalia Haldin and Tekla, he has no time for political feminism which, in the person of Peter Ivanovitch, he associated with the cant and deception of radicalism. The presence of the theme here remains none the less the middle stage between the creation of a heroine like Emilia Gould and the concentrated study of "sexual politics" presented in *Chance* and further examined in the stories of the last phase.

Several other female roles in the story are tied in with this feminist theme. Besides Peter Ivanovitch's victims, Tekla and Madame de S., there are also other revolutionary females, Sophia Antonovna and the daughters of Julius Laspara, as well as Mrs Haldin and her daughter. The most important of these, after the Haldin ladies, is Sophia Antonovna, in whose character we can trace elements of the anti-heroine role. In the "Little Russia" of Geneva she is the other woman, besides Natalia, who competes for Razumov's attention, although, as she is considerably older, her competition is doctrinal rather than sexual. She is a dedicated revolutionary, committed through a lifetime's involvement with the cause, and is apparently free from the fanaticism and hypocrisy which undercuts most of Conrad's anarchists and radicals. "Stripped of rhetoric, mysticism, and theories, she was the true spirit of destructive revolution" (p. 261).

In Razumov's new world Sophia Antonovna is the representative of the world he has betrayed. She is in touch with Haldin's associates in Russia and embodies the best spirit of Haldin's revolutionary principles. It is she who takes the task of reconciling Razumov to the Geneva group and she who tests and finally accepts his claims. She therefore stands, with respect to the hero, in opposition to Miss Haldin, who stands for a neutral or middle way between the two extremes. Like earlier anti-heroines, such as Willems' Joanna and Nostromo's Linda, she stands to the hero much as a guilty conscience, a reminder of his concealed betrayal and his unmet obligations. The heroine, on the other hand, represents what he desires, which is in this case a way of non-involvement between opposing forces. It is no doubt significant that Sophia Antonovna is fortuitously absent from the revolutionary gathering at which, under the influence of Natalia Haldin, Razumov confesses to the betrayal. Later, when Miss Haldin has gone, Razumov becomes once again acceptable to the revolutionaries and is visited again by Sophia Antonovna. Although no personal rivalry develops between the two women, they are, for Razumov, exclusive alternatives.

The agent of Razumov's nemesis is a male figure from the revolutionary brotherhood which the hero has betrayed. This is Nikita, nicknamed Necator, the practised killer of the movement, who is passionately jealous of Razumov from the first, and who, when the hero's betrayal is confessed, inflicts deafness upon him by bursting his eardrums. Like Conrad's other nemesis figures, such as Gentleman Brown and Mr Jones, Nikita reflects in himself perversions of the chief characteristics of the hero upon whom he inflicts punishment. His many killings of "gendarmes and police agents" (p. 266) correspond to Razumov's work in bringing about the execution of Haldin and the anticipated arrest and liquidation of other revolutionaries. His "burlesque of professional jealousy" (p. 267), manifested in reaction to the high esteem in which Razumov is held by most of the Geneva group, is the counterpart to Razumov's concern for his own reputation. Most important, it turns out that Nikita too, like Razumov, is a double agent, a police informer masquerading as a revolutionary, "a scoundrel of the worst kind – a traitor himself, a betrayer – a spy" (p. 380). Razumov, therefore, like Jim and Heyst, meets his fate at the hands of an exaggerated embodiment of his own sins.

Apart from this elaboration of the usual Conradian fictional pattern which centres upon the hero, his aspiration, compromise and downfall, *Under Western Eyes* also develops a partial antithetical pairing of characters across its dualistic framework in much the same way as does *The Secret Agent*. Most obvious is the focal pair, the hero and heroine, who have in common their unwilling involvement in a political conflict in which neither wishes to take part. Both look for ways of neutrality, Razumov selfishly by attempting to remain secure and isolated, Natalia in a more genuine spirit of detachment by working for reconciliation. The two are none the less pulled towards opposing parties; Razumov, through his connection with Prince K., begins to aid the powers of reaction, while Natalia, through her relationship to Haldin, is in danger of being drawn into revolutionary circles.

A further structural balance occurs between Razumov's natural father, Prince K., and Natalia's mother, Mrs Haldin. Neither parent is significantly engaged in political activity, for they are both largely passive and ineffectual figures, but whereas Mrs Haldin tends to lament the oppressiveness of the Russian authorities, Prince K. is to some extent identified with this establishment. Each parent has considerable influence upon the fate of the respective children. It is through Prince K., retired but still identified with conservatism, that Razumov is first introduced to the ministers of reaction. Mrs Haldin's excessive devotion to her son's memory keeps Natalia in touch with the revolutionary circles in which Haldin had moved.

Another antithesis is formed between Mikulin and Peter Ivanovitch, the leading representatives within the scope of the story of the two parties. Each is fanatically devoted to his cause, but with a highly suspect private morality. Peter Ivanovitch obviously exploits and lives upon the women whom he brings under his personal fascination. Very similarly, Mikulin is "a bachelor with a love of comfort, living alone in an apartment of five rooms luxuriously furnished; and . . . known by his intimates to be an enlightened patron of the art of female dancing" (p. 305). Their careers are complementary; Peter Ivanovitch rises from the status of a convict to become a revolutionary leader, whereas Mikulin, born into the ranks of the governing class (he is the "confidant and right-

hand man of his former schoolfellow and lifelong friend, General
T." (p. 306)), is first seen as a leader, but finally meets political ruin
and becomes "something very much like a common convict"
(p. 306). In the very last pages of the novel these two men are seen,
with supreme irony, to meet accidentally in a railway carriage and
to converse amicably for "half the night" (p. 381).

A final and most interesting pair, although in no definite way
related to the novel's political dualism, is that of Ziemianitch and
Tekla, two representatives for the common people, associated
respectively with Razumov and Miss Haldin. Razumov beats
Ziemianitch in a rage of frustration at finding him drunk and
therefore unable to arrange Haldin's departure. This action
establishes a connection between himself and the peasant; "the
fearful thrashing he had given the inanimate Ziemianitch seemed to
him a sign of intimate union, a pathetically severe necessity of
brotherly love" (p. 35). The Ziemianitch episode, however, is
potentially most dangerous to Razumov's position, for its discovery
would show the reactionaries that he had at one point been working
with Haldin as an accessory and would reveal to the radicals that
Razumov had been in some way involved in Haldin's failure to
escape. He is therefore most relieved when Sophia Antonovna tells
him that Ziemianitch, by committing suicide, has confirmed
suspicions that it was he (Ziemianitch) who had betrayed Haldin,
from which point Razumov feels himself safe from discovery. The
mystic bond which the hero feels with this common man, whose
path fatefully crosses his own, is strengthened by a number of
meaningful parallels between the two men. Both are identified with
the Russian people, Ziemianitch by his background and conduct,
Razumov through intellectual choice. Both are under suspicion of
being police spies involved in Haldin's betrayal. Ziemianitch's
suicide, supposedly in "remorse", is the thematic counterpart to
Razumov's confession.

A similar thematic relationship exists between Tekla and Natalia
Haldin. Both subject their lives to the interests of the male figures
around them, and it is Tekla who takes over the care of Razumov
when Natalia, after his confession, has to turn away from him.
Natalia is designed by Peter Ivanovitch to succeed Tekla as his
personal servant and secretary. Both women later return to Russia,
Natalia to work for the sick and imprisoned, Tekla to look after the
special case of Razumov. Tekla's career thus mirrors Natalia's in
much the same way as Ziemianitch's does that of Razumov.

Under Western Eyes is structurally very close to *The Secret Agent*. Its hero and heroine are of the same general types, both of which can be identified as characteristic of Conrad's second mature phase. It makes use of the sacrificial, or victimized male and female figures, also found in *The Secret Agent* and *Nostromo*. It also employs the device of pairing characters across the conceptual dualism of the story. The two stories are also close in content, both dealing with political radicalism and repression from a stance of sympathy for the victims.

The focal point remains the hero, a man of abilities who seeks to develop and profit from his talents by keeping free from political involvement, but who is drawn by circumstances into compromise and destruction. Both men incur their fate directly because their compromise involves the sacrifice of a more or less innocent victim. The Conradian hero of the second phase, much more specifically than even Jim or Whalley, is guilty of a lethal betrayal. It was to this issue of betrayal, to the question of the hero's duty to his fellow man, that Conrad turned in what was to be the last story of this phase.

The Secret Sharer, written as Conrad was putting the final touches to Razumov's story in the last months of 1909, stands in much the same relation to *Under Western Eyes* as does *Typhoon* to *Lord Jim*. It tells, in essence, the same story as the longer tale, but allows the hero to avoid the mistake, the compromise, which he makes in the novel, and so to bring his affairs to a satisfactory conclusion. In *Typhoon* MacWhirr, free from Jim's "imagination", doggedly takes his ship without panic through a storm situation comparable to that in which Jim abandons the *Patna*. In *The Secret Sharer* the Captain (he has no personal name) is confronted, like Razumov, with a murderer who pleads extenuating circumstances, and is then faced with the question of whether to hand him over to the law or assist him in his escape. Where Razumov hesitates and finally betrays his visitor, the Captain accepts his duty to protect the fugitive at all costs.

The Secret Sharer is therefore a re-examination in miniature of the moral problem of the hero in the novel which immediately precedes it, and is of particular interest for the light which the relative sharpness of its lines may shed upon the much larger and sometimes shadowy canvas of *Under Western Eyes*. The short story offers only three central figures, the Captain, Leggatt and Captain Archbold, who correspond structurally to Razumov, Haldin and General T. respectively. There are no female characters, no rival and (because the hero avoids compromise) no nemesis. The tale should also remind us closely of the situation at the crucial point of *Nostromo*, where the hero, having agreed to take the lighter of silver to sea for safety, finds his voyage encumbered with the unwelcome person of Decoud, a fugitive under virtual sentence of death from the revolutionaries on account of his propagandist activities for the Sulaco Europeans. Nostromo thus finds himself in command of a boat with an outlaw as his unexpected passenger, much as does the Captain in *The Secret Sharer*.

The Captain, like Nostromo and Razumov, is one of Conrad's "political" heroes, whose object is to secure his own independence against the encroachments of opposing parties in a struggle with which he does not wish to be involved. For the Captain, who is a newcomer to his ship and crew, this means in practice that he must establish his command on a firm basis, an undertaking which is severely threatened by his shelter of Leggatt. The Captain, like Razumov and, to an extent, Nostromo, is a lone and solitary figure without footing or contacts, and is therefore obliged to make his own way. As he himself tells Leggatt,

> I had been appointed to take charge while I least expected anything of the sort, not quite a fortnight ago. I didn't know either the ship or the people. Hadn't the time in port to look about me or size anybody up. As to the crew, all they knew was that I was appointed to take the ship home. For the rest, I was almost as much a stranger on board as himself [Leggatt] (p. 110).

As a result he has, like Razumov, to be particularly circumspect in order to avoid the suspicion with which the untried newcomer is usually met. "I felt," he says, "that it would take very little to make me a suspect person in the eyes of the ship's company" (p. 110). The Captain is therefore placed in the position of the major political heroes, seeking to maintain his independence (in this case the authority of unhindered command at sea) in a world of strangers all too likely to take sides against him. Like Nostromo, Verloc and Razumov, he is obliged to resort to dangerous duplicity in pursuit of his end.

Leggatt resembles Haldin and Decoud as the fugitive, already vitally committed to the "political" struggle, who places himself in the hero's care. He is the sacrificial male of the political novels, except that in this short story, because of the hero's strength of character, the sacrifice is avoided, and Leggatt is allowed to make good his escape. He is closest to Haldin, his immediate predecessor, in that the crime for which he is pursued is murder, but a murder committed under mitigating circumstances of which the hero is asked to take cognisance. Like the other sacrificial males, including Stevie, Leggatt is also presented as being significantly comparable to the hero and, indeed, as offering a standard which the hero should emulate. Where Stevie is the sincerely compassionate witness to social injustice which Verloc so widely fails to be, Leggatt is an exemplary officer who has, in a crisis, enforced discipline and saved his ship. Such men, however, pay a price for their excellence; Stevie is mentally retarded, Haldin an outlaw, Decoud a fugitive, and Leggatt himself an inadvertent killer. The heroes confronting these men are therefore faced with a version of the Conradian paradox that effective action involves its own negation, a paradox which Nostromo, Verloc and Razumov successively fail to circumnavigate. Only the Captain in *The Secret Sharer* is able to both accept the value of Leggatt's action while at the same time purging its associated guilt.

In *The Secret Sharer* Conrad emphasizes particularly the *alter ego* aspect of this potentially sacrificial figure. Leggatt is not only (apart from his crime) an exemplary officer, such as the Captain aims to be, but also resembles the Captain physically, shares his clothing and accommodation, and is openly regarded by him as an "other self". The relationship between the Captain and Leggatt in this story therefore shows clearly something which is also true of the relationships between Nostromo and Decoud, Verloc and Stevie, and Razumov and Haldin. The political heroes themselves are no longer, like the heroes from Wait to Whalley, embodiments of the Conradian paradox, men who exhibit both unusual abilities or powers and vitiating weaknesses. They are relatively colourless figures whose aims are not to alter the world but rather to secure their own independent place within it. The paradox, which lies in their situations rather than in themselves, is represented externally in the sacrificial male, a character who has an exceptional vision but who is also cut off from society (in the cases of Decoud, Haldin and Leggatt by an alleged crime, in Stevie's case by imbecility) and is therefore prevented from effective action. The neutral hero, confronted by this *alter ego*, whose utter dependence upon him is stressed in each story, is then required to deal with the paradox in his disposal of his dependent fellow man.

As in most of Conrad's stories, the hero's handling of the paradox is worked out across the framework of a conflicting duality of forces, forces which, in the novels from 1902 to 1909, are expressly political in nature. Nostromo, Verloc and Razumov are placed in situations of acute tension between conservative and radical powers. *The Secret Sharer*, looking back to *The Nigger of the 'Narcissus'*, transposes the conflict to the world of a ship at sea, where it appears as the contrariety of authoritarian discipline and the individual desires and feelings of the crew. Leggatt's arrival places the Captain on the horns of this dilemma. He must either betray the fugitive and hand him over to the lawfully constituted officer, Captain Archbold, who comes to claim him, or else risk the breakdown of discipline on his own ship when its crew discover that their commander is himself accessory to a serious disciplinary infraction. The Captain therefore stands between Archbold and the crew, the latter represented chiefly by the mate, much as Razumov stands between Mikulin and Peter Ivanovitch, or Nostromo between the Gould Concession and the Sulaco democratic movement.

To give up Leggatt is the obvious and tempting thing to do and would correspond to the betrayals of the earlier political heroes. Unlike them, however, the Captain at once recognizes as paramount the bond between himself and his dependent and has no thought of surrendering him to authority. None the less, it is not "right" for him simply to accept and identify with Leggatt, any more than it would be "right" for Razumov to join Haldin unreservedly, for Verloc to become an anarchist in earnest, or for Nostromo to give himself to popular insurrection. The hero's task is not to engage in the conflict, for both sides of which Conrad shows a roughly balanced mixture of contempt and respect, but to steer a way through it to a satisfactory and guiltless independence, such as is to some degree achieved by Emilia Gould and Natalia Haldin. The Captain, in particular, cannot accept as permanent and final his identification with Leggatt, for the obvious reason that to do so would be to condone indiscipline and to run the perpetual risk of the breakdown of his command.

The Captain must steer a middle way, asserting his individuality against both Archbold and his own crew. Here, as usual with Conrad, there are deep ambiguities on both sides. Archbold represents law and authority, the near-divine right of captains formerly expounded in the persons of Allistoun and MacWhirr, yet he is also shown to be a liar and an incompetent who fails to measure up to the higher standards of seamanship represented by Leggatt. The crew, while strongly inclined to be critical of their new Captain's unorthodox methods, are themselves given to indiscipline, particularly the first and second mates, who are both brought into line by the Captain as the story progresses.

To complete his course without compromise the Captain must avoid both extremes. He must neither surrender Leggatt to Archbold nor allow Leggatt to remain as a threat to his own authority. There are, therefore, two movements to the tale. In the first, the fugitive is taken on board by the Captain and successfully concealed from Archbold. In the second, the disruptive influence of Leggatt not only causes the Captain to act in a manner which brings him to ridicule and disrepute among the crew, but also has a phychological effect upon him adverse to the exercise of his new command.

> There are to a seaman certain words, gestures, that should in given conditions come as naturally, as instinctively as the winking of a menaced eye. A certain order should spring on to his lips without thinking; a certain sign should get itself made, so to speak, without reflection. But all unconscious alertness had abandoned me. I had to make an effort of will to recall myself back (from the cabin) to the conditions of the moment. I felt that I was appearing an irresolute commander to those people who were watching me more or less critically (p. 126).

Having been brought aboard, therefore, Leggatt must be removed. The hero's own success requires that he not only save Leggatt from Archbold but also dismiss him, which he does in the second movement of the story.

This is accomplished when, with exaggerated risk, the Captain takes his ship at night dangerously close to land so that Leggatt may swim unnoticed to safety. The risk is psychologically and logically necessary, for the Captain, having accepted his responsibility for Leggatt in the first movement of the tale, must complete the second movement without renouncing or going back upon what he has done. He cannot therefore simply abandon his protegé, but must go as far as he can to ensure the fugitive's safety. He has his reward, the sign of his success, when the floating hat left by the escaped swimmer becomes the "saving mark", which enables the Captain to bring his ship out of the danger he has taken her into. The hat, he says, "was saving the ship, by serving me for a mark to help out the ignorance of my strangeness" (p. 142). Thus Leggatt departs leaving the Captain, who has come through the trial of their association, in "the perfect communion of a seaman with his first command" (p. 143).

The two-part movement of this story, the acceptance of the "sharer" followed by his reconsignment to the sea from which he came, is reminiscent of *The Nigger of the 'Narcissus'*, where Wait is first received by the crew and later repudiated. The comparison displays both the essential continuity between Conrad's first mature phase and the period of the political novels, and the structural difference between these two phases, which results from the new type of hero introduced by Nostromo. The earlier heroes are enbodiments of paradox who find themselves frustrated in action by their inherent limitations, whereas those of the political phase are men, not themselves particularly distinguished, who seek to avoid the perils of decisive action but find themselves in paradoxical situations represented by other characters, the sacrificial males, for whom they are in some way responsible. In *The Nigger of the 'Narcissus'* the central figure is Wait, the embodiment of paradox, whose wish to secure an easy passage causes him to become the figurehead of a near mutiny, which fails because of the crew's reaction against Donkin, the rival, the inevitable mouthpiece of the discontents Wait inspires. In *The Secret Sharer*, however, the hero is not Leggatt, the figure of paradox, the man at once excellent and tainted who in this respect corresponds to Wait, but the Captain who, confronted by the paradox Leggatt represents, must make the right decisions.

The structural change noted here between *The Nigger of the 'Narcissus'* and *The Secret Sharer* is generally true of the two phases in the Conrad canon which they respectively represent. The novels from the period between *The Nigger of the 'Narcissus'* and *The End of the Tether* tend to take the figure of paradox as their hero. The novels after *Nostromo*, which is itself a special case exhibiting features of both phases, place a neutral and relatively colourless figure in the focal role, while introducing the embodiment of the Conradian paradox as a new character type, the sacrificial males, Decoud, Stevie and Haldin. The over-all result might be said to be a general shift of perspective, an externalization of the paradox which, in the later phase, ceases to be primarily a function of character and becomes more a feature of the universe.

The earlier heroes generate their own paradoxes by undertaking purposive activity, pursuing specific outward-looking ambitions which are frustrated, in the event, by the heroes' own limitations. Nostromo and his successors, on the other hand, take a wholly different attitude to the world. While they are no more egocentric than men like Wait, Kurtz and Jim, their object is not to affect the world in which they find themselves, but rather to secure purely personal goals and their own independence. Their confrontations with the Conradian paradox therefore come about not in reaction to their positive exertions but rather as a trial imposed upon their stance of neutrality. The single general feature which most distinguishes the stories of this phase is their examination of the hero's desire to avoid commitment.

The stories of the first mature phase display a relatively simple universe in which purposive activity is regularly frustrated by the hero's failure to avoid catastrophic entanglement in the dualistic conflict of his environment. Kurtz' attempt to implement his ideals provokes a restraining visit from the Manager and Marlow, while Wait's efforts to affect the discipline of the *Narcissus* involve him in the struggle between Donkin and Allistoun. The next phase arises in response to the natural question of what would happen should the hero deliberately avoid the kind of activity liable to provoke a fateful reaction. Some approaches to the question are apparent in characters like MacWhirr, who is devoid of personal ambition, and Whalley, whose aim is merely to stave off disaster, both men who are sought out for trial despite their lack of provocative action. In the heroes who follow Nostromo, however, we see that avoidance of positive action is certainly not Conrad's answer. Men like Verloc and Razumov, who try to live inconspicuous lives, aiming at modest personal profit secured unobtrusively and without commitment to controversial activity, are ironically confronted with paradoxical situations which demand their open adherence to one or other of the conflicting parties. The political novels show that neutrality is not the solution. *The Secret Sharer*, which is the concluding tale of Conrad's political phase, adds the qualification that a viable neutrality must be won through trial, that the paradox must be confronted before it can be avoided.

Part IV   The Third Phase

11 *Chance* and the Short Stories of 1910–11

Conrad's third phase comprises *Chance*, *Victory*, *The Shadow-Line* and a number of contemporary short stories. In this phase the hero becomes a man who, like the heroes of the second phase, seeks non-involvement in the conflicts of life, but one who does so selflessly and harmlessly by simply withdrawing into isolation. There are no victims to this neutrality, no Decouds, Haldins, Teresas, or elderly widows. On the contrary, the new heroes, far from sacrificing others to their need for security, compromise themselves from motives of humanity in order to alleviate sufferings which they might, without risk to themselves, have left behind them. The heroes of the second phase compromised their neutrality against their will under pressure of circumstances, but the new heroes, Anthony, Heyst and Renouard, deviate from their policy of isolation in order to effect the "rescue" of a fellow creature, who is usually the heroine.

The essential feature of the third phase is the hero's tendency to retreat into isolation or inactivity and his compromise of this withdrawal in undertaking a purposive course of action, consisting usually in the actual or attempted rescue of the heroine. The rescue motif is not essential to these stories, for the hero's compromising undertaking may, as in *The Shadow-Line*, be altogether of another kind. It does occur in most of them, however, and is no less prominent in the novels of the fourth and final phase.

The development of the rescue motif in Conrad's fiction has its roots in the heroines of the political stories. Conrad's interest in his heroines grew steadily from his first attempt at a plausible and morally significant female character in Emilia Gould. Winnie Verloc and Natalia Haldin, different as they are, continue a rising theme, that of the innocent and generally well-intentioned woman entrapped and to some extent victimized in a world dominated variously by husbands, brothers and lovers. Between the completion of *Under Western Eyes* and *The Secret Sharer* at the end of 1909, and

that of *Chance* in March 1912, Conrad wrote four shorter pieces.
Two of these, *Prince Roman* and *The Partner*, are brief and casual tales
with no bearing on the major works, but the others, *A Smile of Fortune*
and *Freya of the Seven Isles*, longer and more careful stories, both take
up the theme of the beleaguered female, which was to dominate
Chance and *Victory*. Both are concerned with marriageable daughters
who are in the care of morally weak and socially isolated fathers and
are sought after by passing sea-captains, who in the end fail them –
an outline which, apart from the final failure, might also be
abstracted from *Chance*.

The earlier of these two stories, *A Smile of Fortune*, completed in
September 1910, is a more hesitant, less assured handling of the
theme. Alice, the "heroine" (the term seems hardly appropriate),
remains passive, and her attitude to the hero, a mixture of fear and
fascination, is unclear and perhaps unimportant. The hero, who is
similarly uncertain of his feelings for her, loses interest in her before
she shows any response, and what might have been a romantic
encounter becomes a source of acute social embarrassment. The
point of the story, which leaves the heroine precisely where it found
her, lies in the ironic consequences for the hero who, to salve his
conscience, buys a shipment of potatoes from her father. He
unexpectedly makes a great profit from the sale of these, but is none
the less forced to resign his command in order to avoid having to
return to the small island where Alice and her father are awaiting
him.

Freya of the Seven Isles also presents a heroine victimized, in this
case unintentionally, by a father and a lover. From loyalty to the
weak and demanding father, she postpones her departure with her
lover, who meanwhile, partly through his own recklessness, falls
victim to his despised and ousted rival. Freya herself, who dies as a
result of her lover's loss, is not entirely free from blame, but it was
strength of mind, not weakness, which caused her to defer her
elopement to what she thought would have been the proper
moment. Freya is the central figure in her story, whereas the central
figure in *A Smile of Fortune* is not Alice but the narrator, the hesitant
lover. After Winnie Verloc, therefore, Freya Nelson (or Nielson) is
the first woman to approximate to the hero's focal role as chief agent
in Conrad's fictional pattern. She formulates an objective, her
elopement with Jasper, and brings this to the point of accomplishment because of her strength of character; yet this same quality,
paradoxically, also causes her to delay, missing earlier opportuni-

ties, in order to fulfil what she takes to be her duty to her father and
before the world. The hero is lost during this period of waiting
imposed by Freya herself.

Common to both these stories and to *Chance* is the pivotal triangle
of heroine, lover, and father, with the father as a dangerously selfish
figure largely responsible for the heroine's difficulties. The theme of
Chance, however, is a new departure for Conrad, arising from the
increasing importance of his heroines since Emilia. Here he turns for
his conceptual framework from politics to sexuality. The dualistic
conflict in *Chance* arises not from the struggle of conservative and
radical ideologies but from the encounter of masculine and feminine
principles. The structural backbone of the novel is an elaboration of
that foreshadowed in *The Secret Agent*, where two characters, a
counterbalanced male-female pair, each progress through the
Conradian cycle of purposive action, compromise and paradoxical
self-frustration.

The hero and heroine of *Chance* are Captain Roderick Anthony
and Flora de Barral, but a logical account of the structure of its plot
begins not with them but with their respective fathers, Carleon
Anthony and De Barral the financier, for it is these two men who
establish the conceptual polarity in terms of which the story is
conducted. Carleon Anthony, dead before the tale begins, had two
children, both of whom ran away and deserted him as soon as they
were old enough to do so, namely Roderick, the hero, and Zoe,
known in the story as the feminist, Mrs Fyne. The father is
remembered as a poet, author of a quantity of sentimentally erotic
verse.

> The late Carleon Anthony, the poet, sang in his time, of the
> domestic and social amenities of our age with a most felicitous
> versification, his object being, in his own words "to glorify the
> result of six thousand years' evolution towards refinement of
> thought, manners, and feelings." Why he fixed the term at six
> thousand years I don't know. His poems read like sentimental
> novels told in verse of a really superior quality (p. 38).

De Barral, the heroine's father, was famous in his day as a great
financier, a once unknown man who, by the simple expedient of
advertising an offer of ten per cent returns, attracted heavy
investment and rapidly established a great financial empire. Just as
Carleon Anthony's fame rested upon his poetry, so did De Barral's

upon his advertisements. The financial empire had its beginning
when one day, for no apparent reason, De Barral

> went out into the street and began advertising. That's absolutely
> all that there was to it. He caught in the street the word of the time
> and harnessed it to his preposterous chariot.
>
> One remembers his first modest advertisements headed with
> the magic word Thrift, Thrift, Thrift, thrice repeated; promising
> ten per cent on all deposits and giving the address of the Thrift
> and Independence Aid Association in Vauxhall Bridge Road.
> Apparently nothing more was necessary (p. 78).

Both fathers have therefore enjoyed high repute which has had
strong influence upon their respective offspring. Both are also men
whose fame is insubstantial, hollow (the name "De Barral" being an
obvious pun), and misleading as to their true natures. Carleon
Anthony, whose verse glorifies civility and sentimentalizes domestic
love, was himself autocratically demanding of his family.

> [I]n his domestic life that same Carleon Anthony showed traces
> of the primitive cave-dweller's temperament. He was massive,
> implacable man with a handsome face, arbitrary and exacting
> with his dependents, but marvellously suave in his manner to
> admiring strangers. These contrasted displays must have been
> particularly exasperating to his long-suffering family (pp. 38–9).

Carleon's son, the hero, runs away to sea in reaction against his
father, and the daughter becomes a feminist and marries a mild and
unpoetic man, the "pedestrian" John Fyne, of whom her father
disapproves. De Barral is similarly exposed as a fraud, in a more
technically legal sense of the term, when his financial empire
collapses, involving many people in extensive losses. De Barral
himself is prosecuted, convicted and sentenced to imprisonment for
his conduct, a process which draws his daughter, Flora, through a
sequence of traumatic experiences.

The two fathers are structural counterparts in the story, both in
their respective relationships to the hero and heroine and in their
cultivation of deceptive public reputations. De Barral's advertising,
which is at worst fraudulent and at best naively vacuous, corresponds as a piece of deceptive rhetoric to Anthony's insincere
domestic poetry. The men are none the less respectively representa-

tive of principles which the story presents as opposites, and which, through the fathers' influence upon the children, become the conceptual duality upon which the plot is woven. Both are basically egocentric men, yet their self-centred natures manifest themselves in different ways. Anthony camouflages his own character, which is "savage" (p. 38), "erotic", and "autocratic" (p. 309), under a false front of sentimental idealism, which disguises the primitive urges under the forms of civility, chivalry and domesticity. De Barral, on the other hand, takes the way of materialism, accumulating phenomenal wealth by playing upon the greed of others and proving extremely possessive himself in his relationship with Flora.

The opposition between idealism and material acquisition, displayed in a somewhat caricature fashion in the persons of Carleon Anthony and De Barral, is prominent in much of Conrad's earlier work. The contradictory heroes of the first mature phase frequently exhibit both idealistic and materialistic impulses. Thus Kurtz, perhaps the plainest case, is both the source of the highest ideals of colonial policy and guilty of the grossest forms of exploitation. In *Nostromo* Gould, who sets out with grand ideals, is obliged to involve himself with "material interests", while the revolutionary characters include not only the greedy Sotillo but also the idealistic freedom fighter Viola.

In *Chance*, for the first time, the opposition of materialism and idealism is applied directly to the field of human sexual relations. Flora de Barral and Roderick Anthony come together under the shadows of their fathers. As a result, their relationship is initially based upon compromises which come very close to bringing about its eventual destruction. Captain Anthony "was the son of a poet with a considerable gift of individualizing, of etherializing the common-place; of making touching, delicate, fascinating the most hopeless conventions of the so-called, refined existence" (p. 193). The inheritance manifests itself in a deliberate cultivation of high-minded rectitude in Anthony's relations with Flora, an unworldly attitude which in him, as in his father, is an outgrowth of eccentricity.

He certainly resembled his father, who, by the way, wore out two women without any satisfaction to himself, because they did not come up to his supra-refined standard of delicacy which is so perceptible in his verses. That's your poet. He demands too much from others. The inarticulate son had set up a standard for himself

with that need for embodying in his conduct the dreams, the
passions, the impulses the poet puts into arrangements of verses,
which are dearer to him than his own self – and may make his
own self appear sublime in the eyes of other people, and even in
his own eyes (p. 328).

The outcome is that, when Anthony takes action in pursuit of his
heroine, his inherited idealism drives him into a stand of artificial
and strained magnanimity, the arrangement whereby Flora is to be
his wife in name only.

In a very similar way Flora, who believes that De Barral is "the
only human being that really cared for her" (p. 380), enters into this
arrangement for her father's sake and marries Anthony initially in
order to secure shelter and protection for De Barral on his release
from prison. In Mr Fyne's slightly exaggerated account she

> led him on, or accepted him, if you like, simply because she was
> thinking of her father. She doesn't care a bit about Anthony, I
> believe. She cares for no one. . . . She loves no one except that
> preposterous advertising shark (pp. 243–4).

This version is exaggerated because, as Flora later admits, she is not
devoid of feeling for Anthony even from the first; yet it remains true
that her father's well-being is the primary reason for her entering
into the arrangement. Flora, therefore, makes a compromise
answering to Anthony's. He offers her a pseudo-marriage for reasons
of false idealism, which she accepts in order to secure the material
position of her father. Her action is a clear echo of Winnie's
marriage to Verloc for the sake of Stevie.

The hero and heroine are the central pair of counterbalanced
characters in the story. There are a number of parallels between
their situations: both lost their family life in early youth and were
brought up by distant relations; both are friendless, solitary persons
("You told me you had no friends," says Anthony to Flora.
"Neither have I" (p. 224)); and both are "outside all conventions"
(p. 210) because of their isolation. It is this last quality of being
independent and unconstrained by norms of conduct that makes
their joint compromise feasible, for the agreement between them is a
violation of nature, as Marlow points out in a passage which
provides the moral keystone of the story.

Of all the forms offered to us by life it is the one demanding a couple to realize it fully, which is the most imperative. Pairing off is the fate of mankind. And if two beings thrown together, mutually attracted, resist the necessity, fail in understanding and voluntarily stop short of the – the embrace, in the noblest meaning of the word, then they are committing a sin against life, the call of which is simple. Perhaps sacred. And the punishment of it is an invasion of complexity, a tormenting, forcibly tortuous involution of feelings, the deepest form of suffering from which indeed something significant may come at last. . . (pp. 426–7).

Flora and Anthony are two solitaries seeking love. In agreeing to the ostensibly loveless arrangement they are each guilty of a compromise which, while it does indeed secure them mutual companionship, condemns them to a false situation and strains them to the very brink of separation.

The respective compromises are undertaken in the spirits of the respective fathers. Flora initially sees marriage as a commercial transaction, in which she effectively sells herself to Anthony in order to purchase shelter and a living for herself and her destitute father. Anthony sees himself as a "knight" (the subtitle of Part II) and, impelled by an exaggerated chivalric idealism, refuses to take any advantage of Flora, imposing upon them both the magnanimous renunciation of conjugal rights. The result, as Marlow observes, is a "tortuous involution of feelings", in which Anthony is restrained by his high code of conduct from any display of love for Flora, and she is held back from any explicit attempt to release him from his hastily given word because she is "afraid to add to the exasperation of her father" (p. 395) and is offended at Anthony's acceptance of her own ill-considered evaluation of the relationship as merely an arrangement of convenience. (The undertones of commercial bargaining between Anthony and Flora are a thematic echo of *A Smile of Fortune*, where the hero, led to the heroine out of commercial concerns, fails to woo her and buys his way out with a mercantile transaction.)

The situation is complicated by what can only be called the "interference" (the term is Marlow's) of several secondary characters. The most important of these are young Flora's Governess and Mrs Fyne, Captain Anthony's sister and Flora's "best friend" during the period of De Barral's imprisonment. Each of these women interferes with the development of the relationship between

Flora and Anthony by instilling a false conviction at a crucial point.
The Governess, at the moment of deserting the De Barral household
after the financier's fall, takes the opportunity to abuse Flora, then
still a child, and to tell her that she is unlovable. Mrs Fyne, through
the unwilling mouthpiece of her husband, conveys to Anthony, in a
vain attempt to prevent his marriage with Flora, the information
that Flora has no love for him; it is thus that Anthony learns of the
materialistic view that Flora takes of the relationship. These two
pieces of misleading untruth combine with the paternal influences
already operating upon the hero and heroine to drive them into the
false situation of mutual renunciation.

The crucial moment comes in Anthony's London hotel room
when Flora arrives, shortly after Fyne has told the Captain that his
prospective bride has no love for him and has further accused
Anthony of taking advantage of her position to lure her into a
marriage she does not desire. Anthony, convinced but shocked that
Flora feels no love for him, reacts strongly against the accusation.
His idealistic sense of honour propels him to the extreme of
renunciation of conjugal rights, while leaving open to Flora the
material advantages of a legal marriage.

> If Anthony's love had been as egoistic as love generally is, it
> would have been greater than the egoism of his vanity – or of his
> generosity, if you like – and all this could not have happened. He
> would not have hit upon that renunciation at which one does not
> know whether to grin or shudder. . . . And his vanity was
> immense. It had been touched to the quick by that muscular little
> feminist, Fyne. 'I! I! Take advantage of her helplessness. I! Unfair
> to that creature – that wisp of mist, that white shadow homeless in
> an ugly dirty world. I could blow her away with a breath,' he was
> saying to himself with horror. 'Never!' All the supremely refined
> delicacy of tenderness, expressed in so many fine lines by Carleon
> Anthony, grew to the size of a passion filling with inward sobs the
> big frame of the man who had never in his life read a single one of
> those famous sonnets singing of the most highly civilized,
> chivalrous love. . . (pp. 331–2).

Anthony's "vanity" is his inheritance from the "aristocrat" (p. 72),
his father, an exaggerated sense of chivalric dignity which drives
him to make his "magnanimous" offer to Flora.

The reaction of Flora, who has up to this time believed in and enjoyed Anthony's love, is one of bitter chill. Anthony's offer appears to her as coldness, as a rejection of her person, confirming the words of the Governess which she had never been able to forget.

> And you may be sure that a girl so bruised all over would feel the slightest touch of anything resembling coldness. She was mistrustful; she could not be otherwise; for the energy of evil is so much more forcible than the energy of good that she could not help looking still upon her abominable governess as an authority. How could one have expected her to throw off the unholy prestige of that long domination? She could not help believing what she had been told; that she was in some mysterious way odious and unlovable. It was cruelly true – *to her*. The oracle of so many years had spoken finally (p. 263).

Flora therefore believes from this moment that Anthony has no real love for her and is driven to accept his renunciation, entering the marriage in a purely commercial spirit to become his wife in name and his companion in return for his shelter and support for herself and her father.

The reciprocal compromises of Anthony and Flora are thus the products of influences exerted by two pairs of secondary characters, one member of each pair affecting the hero, the other member affecting the heroine. It is tempting to see these characters in terms of the rival-type which appears in most of the earlier stories. De Barral, in particular, has a number of the requisite qualities, being someone whom Anthony must accept along with his heroine, someone who has a conflicting personal claim upon the heroine and who therefore pits himself against the hero even to the point of death. De Barral's part is, moreover, clearly analogous to those of Omar and Cornelius, who also appear as restrictive father-figures resisting the heroine's union with the hero.

There is not much profit, however, in construing any of these characters in the nemesis role. In a manner which looks back to the domestic situation of *The Secret Agent*, the hero and heroine of *Chance* are each the nemesis of the other. Anthony's vanity, which realizes itself as an artificial chivalry, presupposes that woman is weak and passionless, needing male protection but antipathetic to a full sexual relationship. This is not Flora's natural condition, but such she becomes, for Anthony, as a result of their bargain. Similarly Flora, believing herself unlovable, sees man as motivated towards herself only by possessive rapacity. In her eyes Anthony's magnanimity makes her his prisoner. Each is therefore met in the other by the false character their compromise has created. Anthony's idealism is confronted by a passionless woman who needs his protection but spurns his love, while Flora's materialism is met by a man who possesses her and carries her off but who has no love for her.

Chance therefore presents us with a highly concentrated version of the Conradian fictional pattern. For the first time, apart from *The Secret Agent* (which, in this respect, stands to *Chance* as an experimental piece), Conrad places hero and heroine on an equal footing, involves them both in a conceptual dualism, brings them together in an act which is for each of them a compromise, and makes each then work as the nemesis, the ironically appropriate visitation of punishment upon the other. The secondary characters of the story, the fathers, the Fynes, the Governess, and others, have no special role in the pattern beyond their influences from one or other side of the conceptual dualism upon the hero or heroine.

The structural symmetry of *Chance* does not stop with these three pairs of counterbalanced characters we have so far observed. Each of the third pair (both women) is connected to a male, who exercises a faintly ameliorating influence upon his partner's actions. The Governess is associated with the young man Charley, whom she hoped to marry, for mercenary reasons, to Flora, and who shows some sympathy for the girl by cutting short the Governess' parting verbal attack. Very similarly, Mrs Fyne's husband, John, is only reluctantly his wife's agent in her interference between Anthony and Flora.

A final pair of characters emerges in the last phase of the story aboard the *Ferndale*. An alignment is established here in which the first mate, Franklin, takes the Captain's side against Flora and her father, while Powell, the second mate, befriends the newcomers and finds himself out of sympathy with Franklin's attitude. The remainder of the crew share Franklin's view; he is their spokesman and the only one of them to appear as a named character. Franklin idolizes Anthony and jealously resents the unhappiness which, not knowing the full story, he believes that Flora has brought upon the Captain. Powell takes Flora's part. This does not involve him in opposition to Anthony, to whom he is completely loyal, but it is none the less true that Powell later replaces, first, Franklin as chief mate and, later, Anthony himself as Flora's husband.

The characters of *Chance* may therefore be grouped in pairs beside the central pair of hero and heroine as follows:

Flora (heroine)	Anthony (hero)
De Barral (heroine's father)	Carleon Anthony (hero's father)
Governess (influence upon heroine)	Mrs Fyne (influence upon hero)
Charley (associated with Governess)	Mr Fyne (associated with Mrs Fyne)
Powell (supports the heroine)	Franklin (supports the hero)

Among the important characters this leaves out only Marlow who, as the principal subnarrator, is neutral with respect to the conflict in which hero and heroine are engaged.

The central paradox of *Chance* manifests itself in the way in which an overdeveloped sense of chivalry in the male makes him incapable of a proper sexual approach to the female, imposing upon her a similar restraint, while an exaggerated sense of her material dependence upon the male prevents the female from responding naturally to him and reinforces his own chivalric inhibition. The conceptual dualism of idealism and materialism thus devolves in the story upon a vicious psychological circle. The tension created by this problem is resolved in the second Part of the story, the voyage of the *Ferndale* recounted by Powell through Marlow. This is the focal section of the novel, narrated sequentially with relatively little subnarrative interference and presenting the "catastrophe", the climactic consequences of the crucial compromise. The voyage of the *Ferndale* in *Chance* thus corresponds structurally to the Patusan episode in *Lord Jim* and to the Geneva phase of Razumov's career in *Under Western Eyes*. In the case of *Chance* we know that it was this climactic episode with which Conrad began, working as early as 1898 on a tale provisionally called *Dynamite*.

The dynamite cargo of the *Ferndale* is emblematic of the potentially explosive state of tension created by the joint compromise of Anthony and Flora. The ship is the world to which they have withdrawn in pursuit of their ideal, a normal marital relationship, much as Jim withdraws to Patusan, Whalley to the *Sofala*, and Razumov to Geneva. Like the earlier heroes, Flora and Anthony find that the world of their compromised withdrawl is vitiated by paradox. Anthony now has the woman of his choice as his wife and constant companion, but under a condition which debars him from consummation. Flora has a husband and a home, but the husband shows her no affection and the home is made a prison. In this section of the story old De Barral becomes the embodiment of the paradox which the central pair have invoked. Flora, as a normal woman, desires Anthony as a husband, but the aspect of her nature, represented by De Barral, which has accepted the marriage as a bargain for material ends, now rejects Anthony and reacts to life aboard the ship as a constraint, an imprisonment, the penalty to be paid as her part of the contract. Anthony, by his renunciation, has opened the way for De Barral's opposition by allowing Flora to believe that her father is the only one who really cares for her and by fostering De Barral's illusion that Flora has no real feeling for Anthony.

The situation aboard the *Ferndale* seems all set to conclude with a bang, as do the comparable situations in most of Conrad's other works – *An Outcast of the Islands, Lord Jim, The End of the Tether, Under Western Eyes*, and *Victory*, for instance, in all of which the hero perishes in some kind of detonation, collision, or combustion. Yet in *Chance* the apocalypse is largely averted; Anthony, indeed, is drowned, but not until some years after his achievement of a full and happy union with Flora. Remembering that *Chance* was Conrad's first novel to win anything approaching popular success in his own lifetime, and bearing in mind the starkly tragic ending of *Victory*, his next full-length work and closely related to *Chance*, we may be tempted to think that Conrad here softened his usual gloomy view of the world as a concession to his public. While there may be truth in this, however, it must also be said that Heyst and Lena in *Victory* are different in kind from Anthony and Flora, and that the happy ending in *Chance* is carefully prepared and qualified within the story.

Anthony himself, having made his tragic renunciation, becomes a largely passive figure who initiates no further significant action. When a collision at night in "half a gale" (p. 315) threatens to explode the dynamite and destroy the *Ferndale*, it is Flora and Powell who between them light the flare which prevents the accident. The cooperation of the Captain's wife and the second mate at this point is crucial to the outcome of the story. Anthony aboard the *Ferndale* is flanked by his two officers, one of whom, Franklin, represents the vain, unrealistically honourable side of Anthony which rejects Flora, while the other, Powell, embodies the normal male response to Flora's femininity. It is Powell, Flora's sympathizer, who defuses the tension of the situation by observing and reporting De Barral's attempt to poison the Captain. Anthony's response is persistence in his idealistic course of renunciation, an offer of release from the bargain to Flora, with an admission that he cannot outface her father's opposition (p. 429). It is only at this point, when De Barral and Anthony have together brought the relationship to the verge of termination, that Flora can make the vital acknowledgement of her love. This done, significantly under the observant eyes of Powell, Anthony responds in kind, and De Barral obligingly takes the poison he had intended for the Captain.

The victory is largely Flora's, testifying to her youth and resolution, her ability to break free from the bonds of her compromise. Anthony moves only after she had done so. The paradoxes of the situation disappear with De Barral, and Flora and Anthony achieve their goal. The story does not end here, however, for Anthony's errors have still to be paid for and Powell's part in Flora's triumph acknowledged. Some years after De Barral's death the collision episode is repeated, when the *Ferndale* is once again run down by another ship at sea. This time there is no dynamite aboard, but neither is the crash averted. Anthony succeeds in sending Flora to safety on the other ship, the *Westland*, but is himself left behind to perish when Powell is taken aboard the *Westland* in mistake for the Captain. The mistake of identity is highly significant and prefigures Powell's ultimate replacement of Anthony as Flora's husband. It is, in a sense, Anthony's idealism, his insistence upon acting out the heroic role of "the knight", which costs him his life, for having saved Flora he is determined to be the last man off the sinking ship (p. 439) and so misses his opportunity of escape. In the end, therefore, Anthony, like Kurtz, Jim and Gould, pays a price for his high ideals.

Anthony is the hero of *Chance*, and is a typical hero of the third phase. He is initially, like Heyst and Renouard, a recluse who has withdrawn from a troubled world, in his case to a placid but successful life at sea. He compromises this retreat, very much as does Heyst, in order to effect the "rescue" of the heroine, who, like Lena, is being victimized by the world. The rescue of the heroine, which in *Chance* involves her becoming Anthony's companion at sea, is a departure from the hero's adopted course, an abandoning of his principle of isolation, which has disastrous consequences. Just as Jones and company pursue Lena to Samburan in *Victory*, so Flora is joined at sea by her father, who represents the world Anthony had rejected and whose antagonism to the hero reaches its climax in an attempt on his life.

The most obvious technical features of *Chance* are the symmetrical patterning of its characters around the dualism of idealism and materialism, and the immense complexity of its narrative method. Conrad had used subnarrators in several earlier novels – Marlow himself appears in this capacity in *Lord Jim* – and he had also employed the protracted interview between two or three characters as a means of advancing the story, as in *The Secret Agent*. In *Chance* he pushes both devices to the hilt, using Marlow and Powell as subnarrators and covering almost half the book in the form of interviews, such as those between Marlow and the Fynes and between Marlow and Flora. One reason for his reversion to these techniques in the novels of this period is to lend dramatic immediacy to long sections of the stories, which would inevitably read dully if narrated impersonally. In *Chance* the inherently dramatic parts are presented with little subnarrative interference, the sections narrated by Powell concerning his finding of a berth aboard the *Ferndale* and the events he witnessed on De Barral's last voyage. The other parts, which fill in the background to Powell's narration, are told by Marlow more or less in the order he discovered them through occasional personal intervention and through his conversations with Flora and the Fynes.

A second, but closely related reason for the technical complexity of *Chance* is the need to unify what would otherwise be a broad and far-ranging story. To give the information necessary to a proper understanding of the climactic events aboard the *Ferndale*, Conrad must include not only the circumstances of Anthony's meeting and marriage with Flora but also a detailed account of crucial phases of Flora's childhood, some views of Anthony's background, and the history of De Barral, a collection of events spread over many years and involving several diverse careers. The inclusion of Marlow as collector and narrator of most of this information within the frame of Powell's two-part story of his own association with Anthony's ship results in a well-polished formal unity. Marlow is, in addition, allowed to play an integral part in Flora's life within the story as, first, her saviour from attempted suicide and, later, the agent who negotiates her marriage to Powell.

The narrative technique of *Chance*, which is a matter of the presentation of the story rather than of the structure of its plot, is not itself our concern. It is, however, to be observed that Conrad's use of involved narrative devices does not seem to be tied in any particular way to the structural patterning of his plots. *Chance* is, indeed, among his most carefully crafted structural symmetries, but the turn towards symmetry which Conrad takes in this novel does not itself dictate the narrative method. *Victory*, the next full-length novel, exhibits a comparable degree of structural patterning, but is narrated straightforwardly and in the third person.

12 *Victory* and the Short Stories of 1912–14

Victory was begun very soon after the completion of *Chance*, probably several months before the date Conrad gave, October 1912. It was completed in May 1914, and published the following year. The resemblance of its plot to that of *Chance* is immediately striking. In both stories a withdrawn, idealistic, wandering man is impelled by motives of pure chivalry to rescue and unite to himself a young, defenceless, victimized woman. In both cases the union provokes an extreme jealousy, which results in attack upon the hero, and both heroes, Anthony and Heyst, act under the constraining influence of deceased fathers. The two stories are none the less far from identical. The main theme in *Chance* is the psychological strain upon the marriage of Flora and Anthony, which results from the combination of his exaggerated chivalry with her attempt to use the marriage as a refuge for herself and her father. Although there is something of a comparable tension between Lena and Heyst in *Victory*, the main theme here is not Heyst's match with Lena but his withdrawal from the world, his compromise, and the retribution. Anthony's personal compromise is almost overshadowed by the career of Flora, but with *Victory* we return to an unambiguous focus upon the hero.

Axel Heyst stands in the main line of Conradian heroes. The early heroes of the period from Wait to Whalley embody the paradox that purposive action is self-defeating. Their successors in the second phase, the "political" heroes, Nostromo, Verloc and Razumov, study the case of the man who, for largely selfish reasons, attempts to avoid purposive action by steering a neutral but ultimately untenable course between the conflicts which occupy his fellow men. The heroes of the third phase, amongst whom Heyst is pre-eminent, are men who withdraw from the world, not for reasons of self-aggrandisement or self-preservation, but in a spirit of idealistic, philosophical detachment and rejection.

At the end of his first phase Conrad appears to have embarked on the political novels in response to the question, "What happens if the hero is not, like Kurtz or Jim, an ambitious man who seeks to bend the world to his will, but one who tries to avoid catastrophe by keeping clear of commitment in worldly affairs?" At the end of this second phase he appears to have confronted the further question, "What happens if the neutrality of the hero is unselfish and takes the form, not of deriving personal profit from the quarrels of others, but of a complete and rationally executed withdrawal from the world?" The answer which emerges in the careers of Anthony and Heyst is that such a man, precisely because his withdrawal is idealistic and unselfish, will be unable to ignore the cries for help from the world's victims, will therefore compromise his withdrawal by submitting to alliances and entanglements, and will thereby bring retribution upon his head.

Axel Heyst becomes a "man of universal detachment" ("Author's Note", p. x) under the influence of his father, a pessimistic moral philosopher who concluded the unbringing of his son with the dying words, "Look on – make no sound" (p. 175). Under his father's tutelage,

> The young man learned to reflect, which is a destructive process, a reckoning of the cost. It is not the clear-sighted who lead the world. Great achievements are accomplished in a blessed, warm mental fog, which the pitiless cold blasts of the father's analysis had blown away from the son.
> "I'll drift," Heyst had said to himself deliberately.
> He did not mean intellectually or sentimentally or morally. He meant to drift altogether and literally, body and soul, like a detached leaf drifting in the wind currents under the immovable trees of a forest glade; to drift without ever catching on to anything (pp. 91–2).

Heyst's rejection of the world is therefore made on a remotely Schopenhauerian philosophical principle of pessimism, and contrasts strongly with the noncommittal neutralities of the political heroes, cultivated for the sake of personal gain and security.

Heyst's withdrawal from the world initially takes the form of mere wandering in remote places, an activity analogous to the sea-going careers of those other Conradian hermits, Anthony and Lingard. Eventually, however, as a result of his association with

Morrison, Heyst settles on the virtually uninhabited island of Samburan, the name itself reminiscent of Sambir and Patusan, the places of withdrawal of Almayer, Willems and Jim. His motive is not simply escape but, more specifically, adherence to two particular philosophical precepts derived from his father: avoidance of action and abstention from personal ties. Heyst sees action, "the first thought, or perhaps the first impulse, on earth," as the "barbed hook, baited with the illusion of progress, to bring out of the lightless void the shoals of unnumbered generations" (p. 174). Of ties, referring to his own association with Morrison, he says, "I only know that he who forms a tie is lost. The germ of corruption has entered his soul" (pp. 199–200). By abstaining from action and ties Heyst hopes to avoid the evils of the world, which his father's outlook has led him to expect.

Yet Heyst is not an uncritical or complete disciple of his father. He is unable to maintain an attitude of sweeping contempt towards humanity and, failing in this, he adopts, on his father's recommendation, "that form of contempt which is called pity" (p. 174). The younger Heyst, as his actions show, does not despise mankind, but feels sorry for those who are caught in the world's grip. If the elder Heyst, therefore, stands roughly in the place of Schopenhauer (divested of his metaphysics and epistemology), the son is placed closer to the teachings of Christ, to whom he is broadly assimilated by the story. Heyst, who pities the world, is seen by Morrison as an "agent of Providence" (p. 16), and associates himself with a woman of low origin called Magdalen. (An early Gnostic tradition held that Jesus and Mary Magdalen were lovers.) Like Christ in the mediaeval story of the Harrowing of Hell, moreover, Heyst is appointed to confront and defeat the Devil, in the plausible person of Mr Jones, in what that worthy himself regards as "a sort of test" (p. 335).

Heyst's ideal, therefore, is not merely one of withdrawal from the world, nor does his philosophy consist solely in rejection. He does not, like his father, deny his own humanity or turn his back completely upon his own kind. This failure to pursue the principle to its logical end renders Heyst's position contradictory, at once cynical and humanitarian, and therefore exposed to the nemesis, which awaits all Conradian heroes whose ideal deviates from pure simplicity.

The sight of his kind was not invincibly odious to him. We must believe this, since for some reason or other he did come out from his retreat for a while. Perhaps it was only to see whether there were any letters for him at the Tesmans. I don't know. No one knows. But this reappearance shows that his detachment from the world was not complete. And incompleteness of any sort leads to trouble. Axel Heyst ought not to have cared for his letters – or whatever it was that brought him out after something more than a year and a half in Samburan. But it was of no use. He had not the hermit's vocation! That was the trouble, it seems (p. 31).

Heyst's "failing" here can best be compared to Jim's. Just as Jim in Patusan dies because he is unable to do as Stein advises and follow "usque ad finem" his decision to cut himself off from sympathy with the white world, so Heyst, leaving his island retreat, becomes involved in action and forms ties which eventually bring about his death. The ideal of isolation is incapable of consistent application – or at least the hero is incapable of so applying it – and the results are fatal. The only Conradian heroes to avoid the nemesis of inconsistency are those like MacWhirr, the Captain in *The Secret Sharer*, and (to an extent) Anthony, who combine great courage with a simple and almost absurdly rigorous application of principle. Heyst and most of the other heroes are too deeply reflective to enjoy the luxury of consistent conduct. "The habit of profound reflection", Conrad observes, "is the most pernicious of all the habits formed by the civilized man" ("Author's Note," pp. x–xi).

Just as Nostromo is driven by vanity to accept charge of the lighter of silver, so Heyst, through what his father would regard as the weakness of human sympathy, returns to the inhabited world and answers Morrison's cry for help. This is Heyst's first compromise, his selfless willingness to intervene in the affairs of the world in order to "rescue" (p. 51) others and in so doing to abandon his father's principles by taking action and forming ties. Having aided Morrison with a loan of money which amounts to a gift, Heyst cannot escape the other's gratitude and, too gentlemanly to make an abrupt departure, is forced into first company and then partnership.

The partnership with Morrison in the Tropical Belt Coal Company touches upon the old Conradian theme of "progress", for the Company is described as "a great stride forward" (p. 21), although Heyst himself subscribes to this illusion only out of "loyalty" (pp. 203) to Morrison. They are, none the less, jointly engaged in an idealistic undertaking which has, as its immediate object, the creation of a material reward for Heyst, Morrison's way of repaying the debt. In pursuit of this undertaking Morrison dies, and Heyst, although the death is in fact natural, is generally supposed to have brought it about in order to increase his own profits from the Company. Morrison thus occupies vestigially the place of the sacrificial male associate of the heroes of the political novels and belongs structurally to the line of Decoud, Stevie and Haldin. Like them, he contrasts sympathetically with the hero beside whom he stands, for Morrison's journeys about the islands are made not in order to avoid mankind but rather to seek out and care for the poorer, more isolated native settlements. Like the political heroes, Heyst bears the guilt for his comrade's death, which is an apparent result of his own compromise, although, in Heyst's case, there is no actual responsibility.

A further outcome of Heyst's compromise, of his inconsistency in returning to civilization and associating with Morrison, is that he acquires thereafter an ill reputation, chiefly, but not entirely, as a result of what happens to Morrison. The agent of this notoriety is Schomberg, the same who figures also in *Lord Jim* and *Falk*, whose jealous hatred of the hero is ignited by Heyst's conduct in Sourabaya and given fuel by the unfortunate demise of Morrison. Schomberg's jealousy is originally baseless and irrational, resting on nothing more than the fact that Heyst does not frequent his hotel (pp. 26–7). It is precisely the kind of unpredictable worldy aggravation that Heyst's principle of withdrawal was conceived to avoid. In compromising his principle and involving himself with mankind, Heyst inevitably provokes Schomberg, who takes on the role of the Conradian rival, the successor to the Manager and Peter Ivanovitch.

Heyst's response to the failure, with Morrison's death and the collapse of the Company, of his first venture into action and human society, is a yet more rigorous withdrawal. In this phase of his existence, as the only white man left on the small remote island of Samburan, living alone among the decaying effects of the Tropical Belt Coal Company, he is the archetypical Conradian hero, the defeated solitary withdrawn into hiding from the world. Like earlier heroes, however, Heyst is driven by the paradox inherent in his position to swing ever more widely between the conceptual poles of his universe. Just as pity forced him out of the jungle into association with Morrison, so an even stronger feeling of pity, reinforced by a growing sexual love, drives him to break the solitude of Samburan by rescuing Lena.

The removal of Lena from Schomberg's hotel is "in its essence the rescue of a distressed human being" (p. 51). Conrad's novels of the last phases are preoccupied with chivalric rescues; besides Heyst's of Lena there is also Anthony's of Flora, Renouard's of Arthur, Lingard's of the Travers, George's of Rita, and Peyrol's of Arlette. In *Victory* Heyst's intervention on Lena's behalf is openly compared to his earlier salvation of Morrison. He approached her with "the same sort of impulse which years ago had made him cross the sandy street of the abominable town of Delli in the island of Timor and accost Morrison. . ." (p. 71). The orchestra from which he removes her is an emblem of the world of human ties and actions which Heyst dislikes as a matter of taste and which his father held in contempt. His rescue of Lena from the group dominated by the abhorrent Zangiacomo is a repetition of his release of Morrison from the clutches of local officialdom. The comparison is ominous, since we already know that the association with Morrison ended in failure and intensified withdrawal. Heyst himself recognizes that he has again infringed his own principles: "I suppose I have done a certain amount of harm, since I allowed myself to be tempted into action. It seemed innocent enough, but all action is bound to be harmful" (p. 54).

The immediate effect of this rescue is a bitter intensification of Schomberg's rivalry, which has now become specifically sexual. Schomberg had hoped to seduce Lena and regards Heyst's removal of her as a theft. His attitude here reminds us of the similar reactions of Omar and Cornelius of similar "thefts" of women by earlier heroes. Schomberg's revenge is to direct the agent of nemesis against the hero, much as Cornelius and the Manager had directed similar agents against Jim and Kurtz respectively. Heyst's second and more serious irruption into action and human ties thus provokes a more extreme reaction from the forces of the world which his father's philosophy held in such contempt.

Like most of the other heroes, Heyst acquires a reputation which is instrumental in shaping his career and downfall. Wait's influence aboard the *Narcissus* depends upon his charismatic attraction; Marlow's interest in Kurtz is fostered by the many tales he hears about him; Jim's notoriety after the trial drives him into the retreat to Patusan, and the acclaim he wins there is one of the factors which brings Brown after him. Nostromo's position in Sulaco rests upon his reputation among both the Europeans and the common people, and Razumov's cultivated taciturnity ironically makes him known and trusted in revolutionary circles. Heyst's reputation, augmented and perverted by Schomberg, presents him as a successful but probably spineless trickster who, having accumulated a fortune from his victims, has retired with it in temporary hiding to Samburan. It is this false picture, painted by Schomberg and supported by circumstantial details, that determines Jones to set off in Heyst's pursuit.

Jones' departure from Sourabaya in chase of Heyst is the turning point of the novel which, like most of Conrad's longer works, comprises two main sections or movements: a setting out of the background situation, which usually takes well over half the story; and the enactment of the hero's last conflict, ending in his death or defeat. The first movement often requires narrative convolutions or the employment of subnarrators, while the second is usually told straightforwardly and relatively rapidly. Heyst's background, his relationship with his father, the Morrison affair, and the events leading up to the rescue of Lena, are covered in the first movement of *Victory*. The second movement, set on the island and, a little like a classical tragedy, confined to a short span of time, relates the hero's union with his heroine and encounter with his nemesis. Closely comparable in this respect is the Patusan section of *Lord Jim*. Other clearly distinguishable "second movements" are Willems' life and death in Sambir, Whalley's time aboard the *Sofala*, Razumov's period in Geneva, and the voyage of the *Ferndale* in *Chance*. *Nostromo*, perhaps Conrad's greatest novel, is structurally atypical because its second movement, Nostromo's wooing of Giselle and his death at the hands of her father, is very brief and apparently truncated.

Between the point in the story where Jones leaves Sourabaya and his arrival on Samburan occurs a brief interlude during which we see Heyst alone on his island with Lena. The situation should be idyllic, but it is not, because, like most of Conrad's hero–heroine relationships, it is disturbed by unresolved difficulties, which stem ultimately from the paradoxical conduct of the hero. Willems is attracted to Aissa, but despises himself for the repudiation of his white heritage, while she, seeing his dissatisfaction, becomes jealous and eventually kills him to prevent his departure. Jim is happy with Jewel, but his white background catches up with him and takes him from her. Gould and Emilia drift apart as Gould's efforts to realize his ideals involve him with material interests. Verloc and Winnie, united by mutual convenience, are set at odds by Stevie's death. In a very similar way Razumov's betrayal of Haldin keeps him from marrying Natalia. Flora and Anthony are kept apart, even after marriage, by the influences of their respective fathers. Heyst and Lena are no exception, for although physically united they are still troubled by Heyst's paternal philosophy of isolation. Heyst himself is aware of a "physical and moral sense of the imperfection of their relations" (p. 222).

Although no doubt in love with Lena, he still cannot avoid seeing his association with her through his father's eyes – the paternal portrait hangs prominently in their bungalow – as a "loss of his bitter liberty" (p. 213). Since the rescue Heyst had "no longer belonged to himself" (p. 245). Through Lena, "Life had him fairly by the throat" (p. 221). The result is that, being obliged to consider her safety, he cannot treat Jones with the utter indifference which might, had Jones sought him out before the rescue, have rendered Heyst immune from harm.

The closing movement of *Victory* is one of Conrad's most highly structured pieces of story-telling. The action is worked out among six characters on the island, grouped into two parties of three, paired against each other in much the same way as are the chief characters in *The Secret Agent* and in the *Ferndale* episode of *Chance*. The pattern here is as follows:

$$
\begin{array}{ccc}
\text{Heyst} & \longleftrightarrow & \text{Jones} \\
+ & & + \\
\text{Lena} & \longleftrightarrow & \text{Ricardo} \\
+ & & + \\
\text{Wang} & \longleftrightarrow & \text{Pedro}
\end{array}
$$

The story is not one of simple confrontation, however, but shows rather the breakdown of each of the two opposing parties, the dissolution of the bonds that bind their members, as the stress of contact with the other party reveals and enlarges inner tensions.

Jones is at first sight the antithesis of Heyst. Where the Swede is robust, manly, and open, Jones is cadaverous, effeminate (by implication homosexual), and secretive. Where Heyst has a broadly Christian mantle thrown over him by the symbolism of the story, Jones is cast as the Devil. He tells Heyst that, "Having been ejected . . . from his proper social sphere because he had refused to conform to certain usual conventions, he was a rebel now, and was coming and going up and down the earth" (p. 317–8). Beneath the obvious contrast, however, as with Jim and Brown, Marlow and Kurtz, and Razumov and Nikita, lies a deeper bond of similarity. Jones, like Heyst, is a wanderer with pretensions (how valid is never established) to gentility who has put aside the conventions of human society. Ricardo tells Heyst that "you and the governor [Jones] ought to understand each other" (p. 364), and Jones himself says to Heyst, "You and I have much more in common than you think" (p. 321). Jones' frequent "boredom" with life is the counterpart of Heyst's detached apathy. The meaning is that Jones is Heyst's distorted mirror image, much as Brown is Jim's, the product of the hero's policies pursued without his own restraining, compromising, spark of humanity. Heyst's isolation, divorced from his compassion, becomes Jones' predatory existence on means extorted from others. Jones is Heyst seen in terms of Schomberg's slanders.

Jones himself is Heyst's nemesis, pursuing the hero in a manner recognizably similar to that of Brown, Massy and Nikita, a demonic exaggeration of the hero's own moral failing come on behalf of an offended or rejected world to exact poetic justice. Jones, however, unlike his predecessors, carries out his task as one of a team, which comprises, beside himself, Ricardo and Pedro. The three of them are characterized by Heyst as embodiments of "evil intelligence" (Jones), "instinctive savagery" (Ricardo), and "brute force" (Pedro) (p. 329).

Much as Jones reflects Heyst, so Ricardo reflects Lena. Ricardo compares himself to Lena in that they have both chosen to follow "gentlemen" rather than become "wage-slaves" (p. 296), and in that they were "born alike, bred alike" (p. 297). The narrator mentions "the similarity of their miserable origin in the dregs of mankind" (p. 308) as the probable source of their mutual understanding. Just as Jones represents the outside world breaking vengefully in upon Heyst's seclusion, so Ricardo appears to Lena as "an unavoidable presence, which had attended her all her life. He was the embodied evil of the world" (p. 298) from which, in following Heyst, she had tried to escape.

Whereas Heyst meets Jones in a number of cat-and-mouse conversations, Lena is met by Ricardo. Jones does not know of her existence until the last few pages, but Ricardo, whose knowledge of her presence on the island was one reason for his enthusiasm in the venture, seeks her out privately soon after his arrival. While Heyst combats the "evil intelligence" of Jones with the sole power of his own unarmed intellect, Lena fends off the "instinctive savagery" of Ricardo through the strength and guidance of her own sexual intuitions.

The remaining pair, Wang and Pedro, at first appear to have nothing in common, Wang being a simple but cultivated and civilized Chinese peasant, while Pedro is a mentally sub-normal South American bandit, whose only features are unusual strength and a dog-like devotion to Jones. The parallel between them emerges from the events of the story. Wang, the sole employee of the Tropical Belt Coal Company who elects to remain on Samburan, becomes Heyst's follower, his personal servant, much as Pedro enslaves himself to Jones. While Heyst and Lena confront Jones and Ricardo respectively, Wang is particularly impressed by Pedro, at the sight of whom he is prompted to steal Heyst's revolver and, soon after, to desert his master (p. 311). When Jones and Ricardo hear that Heyst's servant has deserted him, they take the opportunity to send Pedro as Wang's replacement (p. 324), but Pedro himself is later dismissed by Ricardo (pp. 369–70), with the result that, when the shooting starts, both "teams" are without their henchmen. Wang and Pedro meanwhile meet by accident, and Pedro is shot by the Chinaman.

It is clear that the grouping of characters in parties of three in the second phase of *Victory* involves an allegory loosely based upon the Platonic threefold division of the soul, with Jones and Heyst representing reason or intellect, Ricardo and Lena standing for passion or instinct, and Pedro and Wang as embodiments of the active or effective faculty. Writing of this kind is radically new in Conrad, for although occasional patches of allegory might, no doubt, be extrapolated from his earlier stories, no sustained piece of psychomachy can be found there remotely comparable to that in *Victory*. It might be argued that the Conradian fictional pattern itself, with its central notion of the paradox inherent in the active pursuit of ideals, and its ancillary figures of heroine, rival and nemesis, is an elaborate allegory of the human condition, in which the variously conflicting forces are given personal roles; but the term allegory, taken at its broadest in this way, might be applied to any meaningful fictional writing. The fact remains that there is a strong difference in kind between the allegorical disposition of the six main characters in the second movement of *Victory* and the arrangement of characters in the variations of the Conradian fictional pattern we have examined hitherto.

Conrad's usual fictional structure, which forms the backbone of all his major novels and stories, including *Victory*, has its roots in the nineteenth century, in Schopenhauer and Wagner and, more generally, in the poets and philosophers of the Romantic Movement. It consists essentially of the placement of the individual, the hero, at the centre of a universe in which a metaphysical irony is then demonstrated as the hero's efforts are systematically negated by characters embodying the forces which he brings into being by his acts. The concept of the hero whose frustrations come from within, the idea that the exercise of will is inherently productive of evil, and the view of the universe as an impersonally indifferent mechanism geared to the final negation of human aspirations, together stamp this structure as post-Romantic. Literary appraisals of Conrad have reached compatible conclusions, finding his ancestry in the Romantic novelists of England, France and Poland, and in the French symbolist poets of the later nineteenth century.

The allegorizing of the Samburan episode, on the other hand, looks back to a much older tradition of mediaeval and classical allegory, with its origins in Platonic thought. Here, instead of the usual one-to-one confrontation of the hero with his nemesis, each figure is split into three personalities, each recognizably representative of one of the three divisions in the ancient picture of the soul. The heroine is recruited to play the hero's instinctive or appetitive part, while the hero and his nemesis become the respective embodiments of reason and its perverted antitype. Extra characters, Wang, Ricardo and Pedro, are created to take the other roles.

How did Conrad arrive at the use of what was for him a new technique of plot structure in the second movement of *Victory*? It did not come completely out of the blue, for looking back over the two or three longer works immediately foregoing we can see an approach to this formal allegorizing in the tendency to group characters in "teams" of opposing pairs. This device, in turn, is a natural extension of the dualistic framework across which almost all of Conrad's longer plots are woven. In the very first novel, *Almayer's Folly*, there is a tendency to counterbalance characters across the opposition of black and white worlds, where Lakamba faces Almayer, Babalatchi faces Lingard, and Dain faces the half-white Nina. Patterning of this kind draws little attention to itself in the works of Conrad's first mature phase, but reappears inescapably in *The Secret Agent*, where the six most significant male characters (apart from Stevie, who is neutral with respect to the political dualism of the plot) arrange themselves obviously into three contrasting pairs. A similar arrangement occurs across the sexually based dualism of *Chance*.

The patterning of characters in pairs of opposites in these earlier novels has no function beyond its relation to the dualistic framework of the plot in any given case. In *Victory*, however, Conrad takes the device a stage further by representing in each team or party an allegorical breakdown of the psyche, choosing – deliberately or not – the Platonic analysis as his model. This was a natural move for him to make at the stage at which he had arrived in the evolution of the hero-type. From being a selfish seeker of secure and profitable neutrality in the political novels, the Conradian hero becomes, in the novels of the third phase, a man who shuns society for philosophical and temperamental reasons, reasons which carry no taint of self-interest but which owe something to Stoicism, something to Byronism, and something to the Christian eremitical tradition. Once the hero becomes a figure of rational withdrawal from society and not a self-seeker, once he becomes Anthony, Heyst, or Renouard, instead of Nostromo, Verloc, or Razumov, then he ceases to be representative, as most of the earlier heroes are, of the full range of common humanity, and becomes a rare specimen, almost an abstraction. Heyst, for example, is by himself an unusual, perhaps unique individual, whose personal fate, all other things being equal, would have limited significance; he meets his end because he attempts and fails to implement an inhuman and necessarily exclusive philosophical position, which few readers are likely to treat with sympathy, much less to adopt. The encounter between Heyst and Jones, therefore, would lack universality, to which the novel as it stands undoubtedly aspires, were it not for the presences of Lena, Ricardo, Wang and Pedro. These additional figures are attached to the principals primarily in order to make the situation of the hero and his antagonist into one which reflects the common human condition, and not merely the logical outcome of a rational eccentricity.

Each of the two parties in the second part of *Victory* is directed by its "intelligent" member, who is the ostensible leader; but both leaders have placed themselves to a large extent under the control of the second, instinctive or appetitive member. Jones comes to Samburan at Ricardo's urging and allows him to dictate the pace of their dealings with Heyst; Heyst, meanwhile, finds his action constrained by the necessity of protecting Lena. The third member of each team embodies the group's effective power; the brute strength of Pedro backs the veiled threat of Jones' presence, and the services of Wang, which include the growing of food, do so much to make civilized life on Samburan possible for his master. Pedro and Wang, like Ricardo and Lena, are initially under the control of their respective leaders, Jones and Heyst, but soon begin to act independently. The long second movement of *Victory*, the protracted confrontation of the hero and his nemesis upon the secluded island, is worked out in terms of the internal dissolution of both groups under the pressures of their collective strife.

The third member of each group bears a close symbolic relation to his principal, revealing in his own person implications hidden beneath his leader's rational and cultivated manner. Pedro exhibits the mindless brutality which is the reality underlying the false gentility of Mr Jones. Wang's relationship to Heyst is of a similar nature, but is much more complex. Like Heyst, Wang deserts his own people to live alone with a woman on a remote island. His most pronounced characteristic, in a story where his active role is small, is his ability to appear and disappear unexpectedly, his motives and locomotion remaining inscrutable, a characteristic which surely parodies on a domestic scale Heyst's adopted mode of life as a solitary wanderer who occasionally turns up unpredictably. The comparison emphasizes what is manifest elsewhere in Lena's apprehensions, namely that Heyst, for all his humanity and integrity, is unreliable, because he has put himself outside the common network of social and behavioural bonds. Wang's abrupt comings and goings, harmless under normal circumstances, become critical under pressure, when the Chinaman silently removes Heyst's revolver, his only means of physical defence, and withdraws to the other side of the island. Like Heyst, Wang takes himself out of a world which threatens him with tasteless and potentially dangerous encounters. The logical end of this line of conduct, an end which Heyst himself, to his own undoing, does not pursue, is to close the door in an attempt to secure one's retreat. This Wang does when, in response for Heyst's request for sanctuary for himself and Lena, he tells Heyst,

> with horrible Chinese reasonableness that he could not let us pass the barrier, because we should be pursued. He doesn't like fights. He gave me to understand that he would shoot me with my own revolver without any sort of compunction, rather than risk a rude

and distasteful contest with the stranger barbarians for my sake (p. 347).

Wang is the only survivor of the six characters on the island.

Lena's apparently irrational fear of Wang (pp. 182, 223, 315) now becomes clear; she is instinctively responding to the spirit of self-preservation in the Chinaman and fearing the same in Heyst. Lena fears that her rescuer will abandon her, just as Wang abandons Heyst, and as Heyst himself is reputed to have sacrificed Morrison. Heyst, because he does not hold consistently to his father's principles, does not in fact abandon either Morrison or Lena, and it is for this reason, essentially, that he loses Wang's support in the face of Jones. Wang symbolizes an extreme policy of which Heyst himself is incapable. Heyst is not prepared to save himself at all costs from the world personified by Jones, and therefore forfeits the material aid of Wang, who, with the revolver, might have enabled him to do so.

The remaining pair of characters, Lena and Ricardo, are also initially dominated by the "gentlemen" they respectively serve. Just as Wang and Pedro represent the efficient, forceful power which complements the rationality of Heyst and Jones, so Lena and Ricardo stand for the instinctive or appetitive principle lacking or subdued in the characters of their respective masters. Once again, as the crisis looms, the subordinate figures begin to disregard their principals and to act independently. Ricardo keeps the existence of Lena a secret from Jones, holds clandestine meetings with her, and ends by plotting to do away with both Heyst and Jones if he can secure Lena's cooperation. Lena, for her part, conceals from Heyst her meetings with Ricardo, partly to protect Heyst and partly because she hopes, by trapping and disarming Ricardo, to show her devotion to her rescuer. The disobedience is fatal to both camps; in ignoring Heyst's instructions and remaining in the bungalow to meet Ricardo, Lena is mortally wounded by Jones, and Ricardo himself is later shot by his master for the attempted treachery.

The "conspiracy" between Lena and Ricardo, which involves both of them in a form of revolt against their respective masters, is symbolic of the rebellion of passion against the government of reason. Neither Jones nor Heyst is comfortable with the natural range of human emotions. Heyst has in the past cut himself off from emotional relationships, and even with Lena he suffers from a degree of habitual constraint. Jones, like most of Conrad's nemesis

figures a perverted image of his victim, is a homosexual whose
revulsion for women is pathological. In the allegory, however,
Jones' panic-stricken reaction to the female presence symbolizes the
confrontation of rational cunning with a vital force beyond its
control. It is in fact the force of sexual love, to which Heyst has
surrendered himself, that frustrates Jones' designs, for it is in order
to pursue Lena that Ricardo both turns against Jones and dismisses
Pedro from his post as watchdog over Heyst's bungalow.

The allegory worked out in the second movement of *Victory*
through the dissolution of the two opposed groups of characters is
shot through with the characteristically Conradian spirit of paradox. On the one hand it is true that Heyst's compromise, his
desertion of the principle of absolute aloofness preached by his late
father and his consequent involvement through Lena with human
passion, is his salvation from Jones, in that it is Lena's presence
which draws off Ricardo, disarms him, causes Pedro's dismissal, and
so renders Jones himself vulnerable. On the other hand, it is Heyst's
association with Lena which, through Schomberg, causes Jones to
visit him in the first place, and it is her death, from a bullet
apparently meant by Jones for Ricardo, which drives Heyst to
suicide.

Victory shows the same over-all pattern of action as most of
Conrad's longer novels; the hero makes a compromise or offends
against a principle and finds himself as a result in a situation of
conflicting demands. His attempts to resolve the paradox involve
him only in movement between wider and wider extremes across
the ideological dualism of his universe. In the end he meets his
nemesis, a figure in whom he sees reflected the stark logical
ultimates of the course upon which he was embarked, a meeting
which terminates the hero's career, usually with his death. Heyst's
principle, or ideal, is withdrawal from the world. His compromise is
his tendency to return and to rescue unfortunates who cross his path,
first Morrison and then Lena. Each rescue provokes a reaction.
After Morrison's death and the collapse of their joint venture, Heyst
stops wandering among primitive men and takes to isolation on
Samburan. The outcome of his subsequent closer association with
Lena is death.

There is no final answer. We are not meant to conclude that
Heyst was "wrong" in rescuing Morrison or in loving Lena, even
although, had he not done so, had he not compromised and
abandoned his principle of withdrawal, he would presumably have

survived. Yet this mere survival would have made Heyst, like MacWhirr, a semi-human colossus who beats the world by being less than human. As it is, he is more like Jim and Nostromo, men whom the world defeats because they excel in humanity. The title, after all, is *Victory*. Heyst, like Kurtz, Jim and Nostromo, shows in his life and dying that he is greater than those who destroy him.

Between the beginning of *Victory* in the spring of 1912 and the beginning of *The Shadow-Line* in January of 1915 Conrad completed three shorters stories: *The Inn of the Two Witches*, *Because of the Dollars*, and *The Planter of Malata*. The first of these bears no significant relation to Conrad's major work and is simply a retelling of a "gothic" tale which had appeared in print more than half a century before. The other two stories, however, are miniature restructurings of the basic plot of *Victory*, involving a recluse living remote from civilization who becomes involved with a woman and, as a result, receives a generally unwelcome and fatal visit from the outside.

The continuity between *Victory* and *Because of the Dollars* is indicated by the character of Davidson, who appears in both as the benevolent steamboat captain arriving on the scene of the hero's retreat at the climactic moment. In the shorter story, however, Davidson, who occupies a very minor place in *Victory*, is brought to the foreground, where he re-enacts the point, made concerning Heyst in *Victory*, that kindly intervention in the affairs of men is liable to be disastrously misrepresented. The story is a compact and somewhat burlesque version of the novel. Davidson befriends Laughing Ann, who is then, in a roundabout way, killed in helping to save him from bandits. When he takes responsibility for her orphaned child his unsympathetic wife refuses to believe his explanation of the infant, assumes it to be his own, and makes this her excuse for returning to her family in Europe.

Yet it is not Davidson who corresponds structurally to Heyst, but a seedy drifter named Bamtz. It is Bamtz who actually rescues Laughing Ann by taking her with him, after a succession of other men have deserted her, to the jungle. There the world follows them in the persons of three grotesque villains, Fector, Niclaus, and a brutal Frenchman without hands. These men are actually following Davidson, who is paying Bamtz a charitable visit on account of Ann. Bamtz, therefore, like Heyst, is unearthed by a trio of rascals indirectly as a result of his rescue of a woman. Yet Bamtz is otherwise very different from Heyst, being a morally weak character who throws in his lot with the bandits in an abortive conspiracy to rob Davidson. This tragi-comical little tale stands in roughly the same sort of relation to *Victory* as does *The Informer* to *The Secret Agent* or *Gaspar Ruiz* to *Nostromo*—a simplified and somewhat exaggerated miniature.

The Planter of Malata is a more serious piece and forms a closer parallel to *Victory*, with which it was contemporaneous. The hero, Renouard, is a paler version of Heyst, a man who chooses to withdraw from the corruption and superficiality of society to a virtually solitary life on a small island. Like Heyst, Renouard already has a dubious reputation, in his case spread largely by the newspaper editor, whose job includes the purveyance of gossip. Like Heyst, he makes periodic reappearances in the world, and on one such occasion rescues the man whom he calls Walter, but whose real name turns out to be Arthur. This Arthur, after a financial scandal for which he was unjustly blamed, had taken to wandering, drink and drugs, and was close to collapse when noticed by Renouard who, out of kindness, takes Arthur to be his assistant on Malata.

Arthur, whose position is very like that of Morrison, dies soon afterwards, through no fault of his rescuer. Renouard's next step, like Heyst's, is the more extreme one of falling in love, with the additional complication that the woman he chooses, as he later discovers, is the remorseful fiancée of Arthur. The situation among Renouard, Arthur and Felicia Moorsom (the fiancée) echoes that of Heyst, Morrison and Lena in *Victory*, which is in turn a reflection of the relationship of hero, heroine and sacrificial male in the political novels. In each case the hero is held responsible for the death of a former associate, and this death, in each case, particularly upsets the heroine in her relations with the hero. Lena is the only one of these heroines who has no tie of blood or affection with the deceased male, and even she feels great concern over Morrison's story.

Although Morrison and Arthur continue the line of Decoud, Stevie, and Haldin as more or less innocuous victims of the world who die in the course of a common enterprise with the hero, there is a difference between the role of this figure in the political novels and the part he plays in *Victory* and *The Planter of Malata*. In the political novels Decoud, Stevie and Haldin are deliberately sacrificed by their respective heroes in pursuit of their own ends, but Morrison and Arthur die of natural causes despite the care which their respective heroes lavish upon them. The heroes' responsibility for the deaths of Morrison and Arthur exists only in the minds of others. The stories show the heroes, Heyst and Renouard, as clearly innocent and, indeed, commendable in their conduct towards the departed comrades. Although the pattern of characters remains much the same, the heroes of the third phase are again different from their political predecessors in their innocence of actual harm and evident goodness of intention towards others.

Whereas Lena in *Victory* has no prior connection with Morrison, Renouard's heroine turns out to have been Arthur's fiancée. In spite of this ironic twist, *The Planter of Malata* continues to follow much the same course as *Victory*. Felicia discovers that her Arthur is the same man whom Renouard took to Malata. Renouard, through mere reticence, has concealed Arthur's death, and now continues to hide it in order to prolong his enjoyment of Miss Moorsom's company. The result is a repetition of the pivotal event in *Victory*, in which the recluse on his island is visited by a trio of worldly emissaries, for with Felicia come her father and her aunt.

The world which Renouard rejects and which the Moorsoms represent is more narrowly conceived than the world of fallen humanity condemned by Heyst's father and epitomized in Jones. The Moorsoms come from the world of what the story calls "Fashion and Finance", and it is this world which has victimized Arthur and from which, by implication, Renouard is a fugitive. Felicia's father is an extremely fashionable writer and lecturer on philosophical subjects. For all his philosophy, the story reveals him as a selfish and ineffective man, dominated by his daughter and overly concerned about his financial investments. The aunt is a snobbish lady to whom Renouard is acceptable only when in evening dress.

Felicia herself is completely envelloped in her sentimentalized concept of remorse for her treatment of Arthur, whose injured reputation she is determined to restore by marrying him. This makes her incapable of responding to Renouard, to whom she says of Arthur,

Don't you know that reparation was due to him from me? A sacred debt – a fine duty! To redeem him would not have been in my power – I know it. But he was blameless, and it was for me to come forward. Don't you see that in the eyes of the world nothing could have rehabilitated him after I had given him my hand. As to giving myself up to anything less than the shaping of a man's destiny – if I thought I could do it I would abhor myself (p. 76).

Felicia is therefore another of those Conradian women who are destructively obsessed with the notion of self-sacrifice. Among her various predecessors in this respect are Winnie Verloc, Freya, Flora and Lena, all of whom, different as they are from one another in many ways, pursue an ideal of self-sacrifice to the point where it prevents natural love and causes death. Felicia, preoccupied with her mission for Arthur, cannot see the truth of Renouard's love and leaves him to a suicide, in which, once again, he emulates Axel Heyst.

The paradox of *Victory*, rooted in the inconsistency of Heyst's attitude to the world, is that in finding love he finds also destruction. The same is true in the more restricted context of *The Planter of Malata*, where Felicia is both the "happiness' her name suggests, what Renouard calls "the eternal love itself", and "one of these aristocrats . . . the mere froth and bubble on the inscrutable depths which some day will toss [her] out of existence" (pp. 76–7). Renouard, like Heyst, abandons his policy of detachment to fall in love, only to find that with love comes the world of which he had, all too justly, been originally afraid.

The paradox of the story is woven across a dualism which is, once again, recognizably similar to that of *Victory*. Renouard, like Heyst, oscillates between the poles of rejection of worldly values and involvement in human affairs. In this story the heroine herself symbolizes the world, whereas Lena in *Victory* is one of its victims; the paradoxical nature of Renouard's personality is shown simply in his selection of Felicia as the embodiment of his ideal. The two of them, hero and heroine, themselves stand for mutually repellent poles: the fallen world and its rejection, high society and "plebeian" industry (p. 75), Felicia's theatrical idea of self-sacrifice and Renouard's consuming love.

13 *The Shadow-Line*

The Shadow-Line, written mostly in 1915, continues Conrad's exploration of the hero who is temperamentally averse to action and inclined to detachment, the theme of *Victory* and *The Planter of Malata*. It is, none the less, a backward-looking novel in that it does this in terms of a background and central metaphor taken from his earlier writings. The voyage recounted in *The Shadow-Line* has a common autobiographical root with that of *The Secret Sharer*, written in 1909, a voyage in which the narrator takes a ship to which he is a stranger out of the Gulf of Siam and experiences difficulty in getting past the island of Koh-ring. The theme of the story is worked out in terms of the metaphor of command at sea, involving such images as the violent storm and the healthy-looking seaman with a mortal illness, all of which return us to the world of *The Nigger of the 'Narcissus'* of 1896–7. More generally, *The Shadow-Line* reverts to the sea-story genre in which, apart from *The Secret Sharer*, Conrad had not indulged since *Falk* and *The End of the Tether* more than a decade before.

In theme and structure, however, *The Shadow-Line* is a logical continuation of Conrad's work in *Victory* and belongs to that group of stories, initiated by *Chance*, in which the hero's object is not so much to achieve anything through action as to attain an ideal of detachment by deliberate abstention from action. The hero of *The Shadow-Line*, who has no name and to whom we shall therefore refer simply as the Captain, is a man who decides to withdraw from his work and profession. He gives up his job as mate aboard a steamer without explanation and resides idly in a hostel while thinking inconclusively of booking a passage home. What had in Heyst been a philosophically based policy and in Renouard a rather vague reaction becomes in the Captain a psychological state associated with his transition from youth to manhood, the crossing of the "shadow-line". He alludes to this state of mind frequently in the story.

I had never in my life felt more detached from all earthly goings on. Freed from the sea for a time, I preserved the sailor's consciousness of complete independence from all land affairs. How could they concern me? (p. 19).

He felt at that time that "There was nothing original, nothing new, startling, informing to expect from the world: no opportunities to find out something about oneself, no wisdom to acquire, no fun to enjoy" (p. 23). He talks of his "deep detachment from the forms and colours of this world" (p. 35), a feeling of withdrawal which persists well after he has put to sea and which is vanquished only at the successful conclusion of the first voyage.

Like Anthony, Heyst and Renouard, the Captain is unable to maintain his chosen course of isolation. At the sailors' home he meets Captain Giles, an experienced older man widely recognized as "an expert in . . . intricate navigation" (p. 12). Giles' expertise sees through the hero's malaise, discovers a vacant post as commander of a sailing ship, and penetrates a plot to prevent the hero obtaining it. The extreme slowness with which the hero responds to Giles' promptings emphasizes the Captain's inertial condition. Yet he is in the end persuaded to take the offered command.

This is his compromise, corresponding to Heyst's rescues of Morrison and Lena, to Renouard's engagement of Arthur, and to Anthony's involvement with Flora. The compromise does not, in this case, include a rescue, except in the rather tenuous sense that the hero's acceptance of the command "rescues" the stranded ship after its previous master's demise, and there is no heroine in *The Shadow-Line*. The hero's detachment is compromised in this story simply in order to gain the coveted post of captain of a sailing vessel once the possibility of doing so has been pointed out to him. The effect, however, is closely comparable to the results of the similar inconsistencies of conduct manifested in the rescues carried out respectively by Anthony, Heyst and Renouard. The Captain, having rejoined the world and resumed professional activity, is faced with a nemesis in the general form of an ironic image of his old self, in much the same way as Heyst, for example, is confronted by Jones after the rescue of Lena.

The Captain, persuaded back into participation in life, follows a course generally similar to that of Heyst. He first provokes a rival, in this case the supercilious Hamilton, who attempts to snatch the command from under his nose. Hamilton, however, is easily defeated and plays only a small part in the story. The similarity to *Victory* is continued in the subsequent isolation of the hero from the world, in this instance aboard a ship at sea, and in the way in which he is then joined by two flanking figures who act out with him, as if a team, the second movement of the story. Just as, in the second movement of *Victory*, Heyst on his island faces his nemesis along with Lena and Wang, so in the second part of *The Shadow-Line* the Captain confronts his destiny on a ship at sea with the particular assistance of two of his officers.

The nemesis is in both cases a perverted reflection of the hero in a figure which rejects and negates the common values of human society. The equivalent in *The Shadow-Line* to *Victory*'s Mr Jones is the Captain's late predecessor, whose malicious spirit is responsible for the great difficulties of the voyage from which Captain and crew are lucky to emerge with their lives. The link between the Captain and his predecessor is established when the newcomer arrives aboard his ship, seats himself in the cabin and stares at his reflection in a mirror.

> It struck me that this quietly staring man whom I was watching, both as if he were myself and somebody else, was not exactly a lonely figure. He had his place in a line of men whom he did not know, of whom he had never heard; but who were fashioned by the same influences, whose souls in relation to their humble life's work had no secrets for him (p. 53).

The imagery is particularly clear; the new Captain seats himself in his predecessor's chair, looks at his own reflection in a mirror and thinks about the similarity between himself and those who have occupied the place before him. He sees himself thereafter as "a member of a dynasty, feeling a semi-mystical bond" with the previous captain (p. 62), whose eccentricities are exaggerated equivalents of his own failings. The detachment and inactivity to which the Captain is liable are reflected in the former master's behaviour, his keeping the ship "loafing at sea for inscrutable reasons" (p. 58), his not seeming "to want to make use of his luck" (p. 56), his decision to "cut adrift from everything" (p. 62), all of which add up to delay, decay and eventual death.

The problems of the voyage are largely a legacy of the late captain. The disease which weakens and incapacitates all the crew, excepting only the Captain and Ransome, is kept under control by quinine, but after the ship has put to sea it is discovered that a useless mixture had been substituted by the old captain for the reserve supply of quinine, which he presumably sold for his own profit. This much, within the story, is fact. There is also the suggestion, from the deranged mind of the mate, Mr Burns, that the spirit of the late captain is responsible for the calm and unpredictable weather which holds the ship idling for days along the east coast of the Gulf, that his ghost haunts the latitude 8° 20′ which the ship has to pass. The late captain is therefore seen as chiefly responsible for delaying the ship and weakening the crew, delay and weakness being the outcome of his eccentricities in life.

The new Captain is himself liable to bouts of inactivity, as the first movement of the story shows, and the problems of the voyage, which arise from the very similar failings of his predecessor, are the difficulties he has to face as a result of his compromise. The hero has not abandoned his tendency to apathy and detachment on taking his command; on the contrary, he succumbs to Mr Burns' doctrine of bewitchment (p. 84) and shows a tendency to sit idle in his cabin when he should be on deck (p. 107). He is therefore right in taking upon himself the responsibility for the problems of the ship. He blames himself for not spotting the absence of the quinine before the ship left port (p. 95) and expects the men to reproach him violently for their predicament (p. 96). Symbolically the deeds of the old captain, the consequences of which the hero now faces, are the logical end of his own initial line of conduct.

The nemesis in the ghostly person of the late captain is therefore confronting his successor with the extreme implications of detachment, in much the same way as Jones confronts Heyst with the consequences of life outside the restraints of human society. The climax comes when the weather breaks and threatens, in the weakened condition of the crew, to swamp the ship. The Captain then faces his nemesis successfully and joins the very few Conradian heroes to emerge enlarged but undamaged from their experiences.

The Captain is flanked by two men who assist him considerably in this confrontation: Mr Burns, the chief mate, and Ransome, the ship's cook. Burns and Ransome represent aspects of the Captain himself, much as Lena and Wang represent aspects of Heyst in *Victory*, except that in *The Shadow-Line* the three persons of the hero's party are not so delineated as to stand for the three divisions of the Platonic soul. Burns and Ransome, in each of whom are reflected both the strength and weakness of the central figure, belong to the line of paradoxical characters, such as Wait, Kurtz and Jim, who were themselves central figures in earlier novels.

The Captain is a man whose high professional competence, attested in the story by such authoritative figures as Kent, Giles and Ellis, is undermined by the state of detachment which causes him to abandon his job with no immediate intention of finding another. In Mr Burns this odd condition is represented as fierce energy and determination vitiated by the debilitating weakness of fever. Burns is the first man aboard struck down by sickness, even before the ship leaves port, and is kept on board only at his own earnest request. He is obliged to keep to his bed until the climax of the confrontation with the spirit of the old captain, in which he takes a leading part. His energy is manifested in his fiery whiskers, his vehement manner, his determination not to abandon his post, and above all by his insistence that the malice of the old captain, in which he has a literal belief, must be faced and cannot otherwise be circumvented.

Ransome is strongly reminiscent of Wait, a man who appears to be an excellent seaman, but who is not so in reality because of an invisible illness.

> Even at a distance his well-proportioned figure, something thoroughly sailor-like in his poise, made him noticeable. On nearer view the intelligent, quiet eyes, a well-bred face, the disciplined independence of his manner made up an attractive personality. When, in addition, Mr. Burns told me that he was the best seaman in the ship, I expressed my surprise that in his earliest prime and of such appearance he should sign on as cook on board a ship.
>
> "It's his heart," Mr. Burns had said. "There's something wrong with it. He mustn't exert himself too much or he may drop dead suddenly" (pp. 67–8).

Ransome, "carrying a deadly enemy in his breast" (p. 68), also reflects the Captain's weakness of character. Ransome fears that he will die if he acts strenuously, and his consequent wish to live quietly and without physical effort is an image of the Captain's less justifiable tendency to indolence. Yet Ransome, like Burns, rises to the crisis and, being paradoxically the only strong man left aboard beside the Captain, is instrumental in getting the ship through the storm. The anomalous combination of weakness and strength in the

Captain's character is imaged in Ransome's physical condition.

Both Ransome and Burns emblemize not only the weakness of the Captain's tendency towards detachment but also the strength which enables him, in the event, to overcome it. Burns, although bedridden, insists on being taken on the voyage and, once under way, becomes the chief exponent of the doctrine that the malice of the dead captain must be faced. "Skulking's no good, sir," he says to the Captain. "You can't slink past the old murderous ruffian. It isn't the way. You must go for him boldly – as I did. Boldness is what you want. Show him that you don't care for any of his damned tricks. Kick up a jolly old row" (p. 116). At the climactic moment Burns leaves his bed to come on deck and confront the spirit of his old enemy, which he does by laughing deliriously at the weather before he faints and has to be carried down again. His efforts are successful, as the Captain himself acknowledges: "By the exorcising virtue of Mr. Burns' awful laugh, the malicious spectre had been laid, the evil spell broken, the curse removed. We were now in the hands of a kind and energetic Providence. It was rushing us on. . ." (p. 125).

The ship now has the wind she needs in order to make port, but to take advantage of this the Captain requires men to handle the sails. Beside himself and Ransome, all the men, including Burns, are too weak to do more than lend sporadic assistance in these operations. It is at this point that Ransome risks death from heart attack to save the ship. Ransome's heroism here reflects the innate professionalism and sense of duty in the Captain himself. Yet it comes into play only at the risk of death; and, indeed, Ransome does die in a sense, for the result of his experience on this voyage is that he decides he must give up his career as a seaman.

The name Ransome clearly implies a kind of sacrifice, and the man does risk his life and give up his work in the course of saving the ship. As in *Victory*, Conrad here uses a specifically Christian reference; the cook is called upon as if "to give his life a ransom for many" (Matthew 20 : 28). The implication for the central figure is clear. The inactivity which the Captain initially displays, like Heyst's detachment, is a sure path to personal safety if followed to the limit and without deviation. In a similar way Ransome's quiet and effortless mode of life as a cook keeps him safe from the threat of his weak heart. In action and participation, on the other hand, lie danger and possible death. Ransome's relinquishing of his secure detachment in order to resume the full responsibility of a seaman is a sacrifice which the story requires the Captain also to make.

Ransome's sacrifice is emblematic of that which the Captain makes in coming to terms with his responsibilities.

Both Ransome and Burns represent the conflict in the Captain between detachment or inactivity and professional involvement, a conflict which has been decided by the end of the voyage with the crossing of the "shadow-line". Both men have therefore completed their tasks by the end of the story. Mr Burns, who stands for the confronting and outfacing of the spirit of detachment, remains in possession of the deck.

I left for the shore in the steam-pinnace, and on looking back beheld Mr. Burns actually standing up by the taffrail, still in his enormous woolly overcoat. The bright sunlight brought out his wierdness amazingly. He looked like a frightful and elaborate scarecrow set up on the poop of a death-striken ship, to keep the seabirds from the corpses (p. 130).

Ransome, on the other hand, takes his departure. He represents the fear of activity which has now been overcome, and his removal from the ship, symbolically significant of the Captain's victory over his own psychological paralysis, occupies the closing paragraph of the story.

He exclaimed, flushed up dusky red, gave my hand a hard wrench – and next moment, left alone in the cabin, I listened to him going up the companion stairs cautiously, step by step, in mortal fear of starting into sudden anger our common enemy it was his hard fate to carry consciously within his faithful breast (p. 133).

The event has many of the same connotations as Leggatt's leaving the ship at the end of *The Secret Sharer*.

The Captain's reluctant parting with Ransome is significant of his own conquest of the impulse to withdraw fearfully from life. Ransome, like Heyst and Renouard, is so strongly aware of the inherent evils of the world that he is unable to accept any place in it. In his farewell to Ransome the Captain dissociates himself from this withdrawal and accepts the necessity for active involvement in life. This he has already made explicit in his last interview with Giles.

"I am going on board directly," I said. "I shall pick up one of my

anchors and heave in to half-cable on the other as soon as my new
crew comes on board and I shall be off at daylight tomorrow."

"You will?" grunted Captain Giles approvingly. "That's the
way. You'll do."

"What did you expect? That I would want to take a week
ashore for a rest?" I said, irritated by his tone. "There's no rest for
me till she's out in the Indian Ocean and not much of it even
then."

He puffed at the cigar moodily, as if transformed.

"Yes, that's what it amounts to," he said in a musing tone. It
was as if a ponderous curtain had rolled up disclosing an
unexpected Captain Giles. But it was only for a moment, merely
the time to let him add: "Precious little rest in life for anybody.
Better not think of it" (p. 132).

In this conversation, which counterbalances the long interchange
with Giles in the first movement of the story, lies the point of the tale.
The Captain has abandoned his initial pose of inexplicable
detachment and inactivity and has engaged himself fully in the
demands of his calling.

The Shadow-Line exhibits the fundamentals of the Conradian
fictional pattern. The hero, the Captain, adopts an ideal, in this case
the pursuit of indolent detachment, but compromises by accepting a
command and thereafter oscillates between the poles of the novel's
dualistic conceptual framework. The dualism in this story, closely
related to those of *Chance, Victory*, and *The Planter of Malata*, is
between detachment and involvement, withdrawal and responsibility, rest and activity. The Captain compromises under Giles'
pressure and under the temptation of commanding a sailing ship
and having thus, like Heyst, re-entered the world finds himself as a
result confronting a nemesis in the spirit of the old captain, a nemesis
whose attributes of obstruction, dereliction of duty, and delay, are
perversions of his own ideal of inaction. The dualism and paradox of
the story are embodied in both Burns and Ransome, each of whom
manifests both a strong will to perform his duty and at the same time
a paralysing and inhibiting sickness. The Captain is unusual among
Conradian heroes in that he triumphs in the end, presumably
because, unlike Anthony, Heyst and Renouard, he finally abandons
his withdrawal from the world and resumes his career in the
mainstream of life.

The Shadow-Line belongs to Conrad's third phase because it studies a hero who attempts to retreat from involvement and responsibility. It is a fitting conclusion to this phase in that it permits the hero to revoke his decision by shouldering responsibility and taking up the commitment of command. The association in this story of the Captain's change of heart with the process of growing up, of crossing the "shadow-line" between youth and manhood, suggests that in retrospect Conrad found traces of immaturity in the stance of heroes like Anthony and Heyst who, less willing to give up their isolation, are more typical of this phase and meet more rigorous ends.

Part V The Final Phase

14 Distinctive Features of the Later Novels

After *The Shadow-Line* Conrad wrote two short stories, *The Warrior's Soul* and *The Tale*, neither of which has any great bearing upon the mainstream of his work. In August 1917, however, he began *The Arrow of Gold*, which was completed in rather less than a year. In the autumn of 1918 he returned in earnest to the unfinished manuscript of *The Rescue*, which he had begun over twenty years before in 1896. This was finished by the following spring, after which time he commenced work on *Suspense*. *Suspense* was to occupy Conrad until his death, when it was still incomplete, but it was put aside from December 1921, to the following June, while he wrote *The Rover*, the last novel he was to finish.

Although a majority of Conrad's critics have seen a marked decline in his work of this final phase, it is important to remember that Conrad himself thought highly both of the completed *Rescue*, which he seriously hoped might win him a Nobel Prize, and of *Suspense*, which was "planned as the chef-d'oeuvre of his later years".*

The suspicion that Conrad had reached the end of his creative potential by the time of *The Arrow of Gold* has been fostered in part by the amount of reworking of earlier material involved in the novels of the final phase. *The Arrow of Gold* borrows names, situations and family groupings of characters from the unfinished work *The Sisters*, of which seven short chapters had been written at the end of 1895 and in the early months of 1896. *The Rescue*, begun under the title *The Rescuer* in the spring of 1896, was a revision and completion of a story with which Conrad had struggled sporadically for almost a decade, carrying it from the period of *An Outpost of Progress* well into the years of *Nostromo*. Both *The Rover* and *Suspense*, on the other hand, are drawn from largely new material, both being essays in the

* Karl, p. 813.

historical novel of the Napoleonic period, a new venture which Conrad had been researching and preparing for some time and which shows that he was far from "written out" towards the end of his life.

The earlier material embedded in the final versions of *The Arrow of Gold* and *The Rescue* is confined to matters of verbal style and to relatively superficial aspects of plot. The structures of both these novels follow a general pattern which is also apparent in *The Rover* and which is in several respects a development of the plot pattern of *Chance*. Whatever the judgment of the overall merits of these novels, therefore, it is neither sufficient nor correct to say that Conrad was not capable of conceiving a fresh plot in these years, or that he had ceased to develop as a novelist.

The plot structure common to *The Arrow of Gold*, *The Rescue* and *The Rover* is a further development of the pattern we have followed through Conrad's major writings to this time. The focal point is still the matter of the hero's commitment to a cause, race, or party, of his compromise, and of the paradoxical conflict of loyalties or interests in which he becomes enmeshed as soon as he engages in action. The conceptual framework of the novel remains dualistic, as the hero is pulled between the poles of his voluntary commitment and his instinctive desire for freedom from ties and responsibilities. The main characters of the story still occupy structural positions akin to those in the earlier tales; we still have, besides the hero himself, caught in a dilemma of his own creation, a heroine with whom he desires union, a rival for her attention whom the hero must face and expel, and a figure of nemesis who in the end confronts the hero with the falsity of his position and contrives to bring about his downfall.

The novels of the last phase continue the main structural trend of *Chance* and *Victory*. The heroes, George, Lingard and Peyrol, are men like Anthony and Heyst, who adopt a wandering, detached form of life from which they depart, for largely selfless motives, in order to assist someone else. The heroines, Rita, Mrs Travers and Arlette, are given prominent roles in the stories, not as mere embodiments of the heroes' ideals, but as female figures with a degree of independent significance in their plots who are themselves subjected to a conflict of forces similar to, but different from, those facing their respective heroes. The later heroines are closest to Flora in *Chance*. Like Flora they have each a prior commitment to another man who becomes the hero's rival. Corresponding in this position to Flora's father are Ortega, Mr Travers and Scevola in the later novels. The situation in the latter part of *Chance*, where the heroine is torn between Anthony and De Barral, is repeated with minor variations in each of *The Arrow of Gold*, *The Rescue* and *The Rover*.

In terms of Conrad's development as a creator and shaper of fiction the most striking feature of the pattern of the later novels is the strong place given to these heroines. Rita and Mrs Travers are perhaps not as successful characters as are Emila Gould and Natalia Haldin, but they are given much more prominence in their respective stories. They are, along with Flora, the only heroines of Conrad's full-length novels whose weight counterbalances that of the heroes.

The later heroines are distinguished from their predecessors in that they do not themselves embody the cause or ideal which prompts the hero to action. Nina is the figure upon whom Almayer projects his hopes of opulent living in Europe; Jewel is acquired by Jim along with his new life in Patusan; Emilia, whom Gould marries as he takes over the Concession in Costaguana, represents the ideals of humanity and civilized progress with which he approaches the task; Winnie embodies Verloc's desire for domestic comfort; Natalia Haldin stands for the kind of humanitarian political neutrality which Razumov wished vainly to attain. In the later novels, however, the heroines are indifferent with respect to the causes for which the heroes act. Rita is, indeed, active in the Carlist cause, but she is so only because of her past association with the Prince and not through any political tradition or conviction. Mrs Travers meets Lingard only after he has engaged in the affairs of Hassim and Immada. She becomes personally sympathetic to this undertaking, but it remains true that the safety of her own party is jeopardized by Lingard's loyalty to his black friends. Arlette has both royalism and revolution in her background, but has no personal interest in, or even knowledge of the mission upon which Peyrol meets his end.

In the major novels up to and including *Under Western Eyes* the hero's compromising action is taken in pursuit of a cause or ideal with which, whether before or after the fact, the heroine may be identified. In the later novels, including *Chance* and *Victory*, the hero rescues, or attempts to rescue the heroine in the course of pursuing some ideal or cause with which she has no inherent association. The Conradian hero first becomes noticeably an actual or potential rescuer of the heroine in two of the stories belonging to the years 1910–11, *A Smile of Fortune* and *Freya of the Seven Isles*, in both of which the attempted rescue fails. The seal is set upon the rescue motif in *Chance*, the next full-length novel, where Anthony eventually succeeds in detaching Flora from her predatory father. Thereafter, wherever a heroine is involved in the story, the matter of her rescue from some man or situation becomes a focal issue of the plot. Earlier heroes, on the other hand, cannot be said significantly to save or rescue their heroines. Willems does not rescue Aissa, nor does Kurtz rescue his native woman, nor Gould Emila, nor Verloc Winnie, nor Razumov Natalia Haldin. Jim might be said to have accomplished the release of Jewel from Cornelius in the course of his take-over in Patusan, but this rescue is effected behind the scenes and is not a crucial feature of the story's plot.

There appears therefore to have been a major change in Conrad's conception of the heroine's role between *Under Western Eyes*, the last of the great political novels, and *Chance*. The heroine ceases to be in any important way an embodiment or projection of the ideal the hero is pursuing and becomes instead an actual or potential victim whom the hero attempts to release. Symptomatic of this change is the tendency in the later novels for the heroine to have a prior commitment to another man, who is in some sense her persecutor but from whom she cannot, for moral or personal reasons, completely divorce herself. Of this kind is Flora's connection with De Barral, Rita's with Ortega, Mrs Travers' with her husband, and Arlette's with Scevola. These men, who become the heroes' rivals as the stories develop, have claims on the heroines, ties of blood, marriage or obligation which cannot be ignored. They are similar to such earlier rivals as Omar and Cornelius, but they differ both in the heroine's acknowledgement of the bond which holds her and in the central importance which the story attaches to this bond and to the hero's efforts to dissolve it.

There remain wide divergences among the heroines on either side of this general division. Mrs Gould, for instance, is a far cry from the early exotic heroines of *Almayer's Folly*, *An Outcast of the Islands*, and *Heart of Darkness*. Equally, Rita is a rather more complex portrait than Flora de Barral. The general division stands, none the less, as a crucial turning point in Conrad's development.

The change in viewpoint introduced by the post-1910 heroines is in the direction of a clearer recognition of the claim of humanity, a theme which is rooted in the novels of the political phase. The heroines of *Nostromo*, *The Secret Agent*, and *Under Western Eyes* all undertake championship of the poor and disadvantaged, who are the chief sufferers in the conflicts which form the backgrounds of their stories. Emilia takes care of the mine workers and their families; Winnie avenges the murdered Stevie, the inarticulate spokesman of the downtrodden working class; and Natalia turns her back on the political struggle in order to comfort its victims. The heroines of the next phase, beginning with Alice Jacobus, Freya and Flora, are themselves victims whom the heroes must try to save. Their sufferings at the hands of such men as De Barral, Schomberg, Ortega, Travers and Scevola, become emblematic of a pitiful human condition which it is the hero's task to remedy.

The later heroines' problems centre upon the men who have prior claims on them. These rivals are sinister, sometimes even demonic figures, whom the heroes are required in some way to confront and vanquish in episodes which (except in *Victory*) are the dramatic climaxes of their stories. The heroes have varying degrees of success. Peyrol, at the price of his own life, succeeds in destroying Scevola, and George manages the elimination of Ortega. Anthony removes De Barral only with a great deal of help from Powell and Flora, while Lingard fails to resolve the problem which Travers' presence has set him. Heyst is unable to defeat the emissaries of the vengeful Schomberg. As in the earlier stories, the rival is brought into play as a direct result of the hero's action, specifically by his pursuit of the heroine, but whereas the earlier rival, such as Omar and Cornelius, remains a relatively minor figure in his story, the later rival assumes larger proportions and is generally involved in the climax of his plot. The climactic scene of *Chance* is the final confrontation of Anthony and De Barral, much as that of *The Arrow of Gold* is the struggle of George and Ortega over Rita.

All of this suggests that an important structural development took place in Conrad's work around the early months of 1910, with the emergence of his heroine from a place of subordination to a more central position and with the new use of the rescue motif as the mainspring of the plot. The novels immediately preceding this date, the three great political works, *Nostromo*, *The Secret Agent* and *Under Western Eyes*, are devised on the older model. Their heroines, Emilia, Winnie and Natalia, although unquestionably Conrad's most successful female portraits up to that time, still figure primarily as representative of the heroes' ideals, the heroes' failures of achievement being symbolized in their ultimate divorces from their respective heroines. These three woman have each a certain amount of independent significance, particularly Winnie, whose circumstances of compromise and retribution are set forth as a miniature reflection of her husband's career; but it is none the less true that, by their place in the structural pattern of their stories, they belong with the earlier heroines, such as Nina, Aissa and Jewel, and not with those of the later period, whose enlarged role they merely anticipate.

In the major works after 1909 the heroine emerges as engaged in a conflict between two antagonistic male figures, one of whom is the hero, the resolution of her conflict being the point upon which the whole story turns. From the hero's point of view the chief task imposed by the plot now becomes the rescue of the heroine from the situation in which she is in some way held by the rival. The rescue theme is announced in the two main works of 1910–11, *A Smile of Fortune* and *Freya of the Seven Isles*, in both of which the central character is a woman placed between two rival men. All the longer novels completed after this time have the rescue-motif at their heart.

Only *Victory* stands a little to one side, for although it does turn upon a rescue, Heyst's rescue of Lena, it does not, as do these other novels, place the heroine quite between the hero and a rival to whom she has a prior commitment; Lena is not significantly committed to Schomberg in the way in which Flora is committed to her father, Mrs Travers to her husband, or Rita to Ortega. In this respect *Victory* looks back to the pre-1910 structure, and accordingly gives more weight to the nemesis figure than to the rival. Schomberg fades from the story once he has set Jones on Heyst's trail. The climax of the story is acted out between Heyst and Jones, the nemesis, whereas in the other novels of this period it is the rival whom the hero faces at the dramatic crisis of the plot.

In spite of the partial exception of *Victory*, and leaving aside *The Shadow-Line*, which has no heroine and therefore no rescue motif, the dividing point between Conrad's pre-1910 work and that which followed is generally clear. We can, moreover, subdivide the later writings on grounds of more detailed structural considerations, just as we have already subdivided the pre-1910 works into those of the preliminary phase, those of a more mature and complex phase (introduced by *The Nigger of the 'Narcissus'*), and those of the "political" phase (introduced by *Nostromo*). The development which distinguishes the last three complete novels from those of the phase dominated by *Chance* and *Victory* is the clear placement of the hero between two male figures, one representing his independence, the other his commitment. The issue of commitment as opposed to self-indulgence, neutrality, or detachment is central to Conrad's work and apparent in all his major stories, but it is not until we come to *The Arrow of Gold* that Conrad hit upon the idea of creating a character to stand for the hero's independence and of setting this figure in structural opposition to the nemesis which the hero faces as a result of his active commitment to a cause.

The heroes, George, Lingard and Peyrol, are all seamen, wanderers and unattached; the words "rover" and "adventurer" are frequently applied to them, and none of them could be wholly exonerated from the charge of piracy. One of the figures associated with each of these heroes is another free-spirited sailor, who represents this uncommitted, independent, and slightly disreputable way of life. George thus stands with Dominic, Lingard with Carter, and Peyrol with Symons. Dominic and Carter actually work with their respective heroes aboard ships which symbolize the heroes' freedom; and Symons, who like Peyrol is a former Brother of the Coast, comes briefly aboard Peyrol's tartane as a captive before being allowed, in an important symbolic gesture, to go free.

The second male character in each case is associated with the cause or ideal which the hero, when persuaded to commit himself in action, takes up. George joins the Carlist cause and meets Blunt, an officer in the pretender's army engaged to fight for the movement; Lingard very similarly commits himself to the restoration of an exiled prince and to this end enlists the aid of Jörgenson, a man who has dabbled before in native politics; Peyrol takes over Réal's assignment from the French Navy to deceive the English as a move in the Revolutionary War. This second figure is, in each case, something of an *alter ego* to the hero and, like such earlier *alter ego* figures as Gentleman Brown, serves also as the agent of nemesis whose intervention is the immediate cause of the hero's downfall. Blunt wounds George in the duel which results in his final separation from the heroine; Jörgenson blows up the ship, which action destroys Lingard's chances of helping Hassim and, again, results in the hero's having to part from his heroine; Réal unwittingly persuades Peyrol to leave Arlette and Escampobar and to go to his death on the naval mission.

These pairs of figures, one on each side of the hero, represent the opposing principles of freedom from involvement and commitment to a cause. Within the stories the two figures are strikingly contrasted. While Blunt is very much an officer and an aristocrat, Dominic is a freebooter and a man of the people, much like Nostromo, from whose original Conrad drew him; Carter knows nothing of Lingard's native schemes, but is a capable and aggressive sailor, while Jörgenson, an expert in local politics, is passive and a destroyer of ships; Réal is a patriotic French officer, while Symons is a former pirate now enlisted in the hostile British navy. The hero stands between them, with something of himself reflected in each, and the course of his story is plotted in his movements from one to the other.

The general disposition of the central characters in all of these three novels may be represented thus:

At the centre are the hero and heroine, each caught between two contrary influences. Unity of plot arises from the interaction of hero and heroine in the course of the story and from the fact that the hero is himself one of the two conflicting influences acting upon the heroine.

The final stories are also distinguished by their dramatic construction. We have noticed that most of Conrad's earlier full-length novels are written in two "movements", the first slow and generally the longer, in which the plot is wound up and the hero entangled in a dualistic conflict as a result of his initial action and compromise, and the second, more quickly paced and shorter, in which the hero confronts the consequences of the situation he has created. Such two-part schemes can be traced most clearly in *An Outcast of the Islands*, *The Nigger of the 'Narcissus'*, *Nostromo*, *Under Western Eyes*, *Chance*, *Victory* and *The Shadow-Line*. The last novels, however, are composed on a definite three-part plan. The first part still covers the hero's involvement in a dualistic conflict, but the conflict here is between the call of his free-roaming sea-life and the demands of the cause to which he has committed himself. The first movement of the story ends with a split or separation between the hero and the figure which symbolizes his independence. This occurs in *The Arrow of Gold* when George sinks his ship and loses contact thereafter with Dominic; in *The Rescue* when Carter upsets Lingard's plans by attacking the native boats; and in *The Rover* when Symons "escapes" from captivity aboard Peyrol's tartane. At about the same point the hero also parts temporarily with the nemesis figure. Blunt returns to Spain, Jörgenson remains aboard the *Emma* while Lingard leaves with the prisoners, and Réal is sent off to Toulon. In the second part of the story the hero confronts and disposes of the rival and – except in *The Rover* where, for good reasons, this does not occur – achieves as a result a period of union with the heroine. Thus George drives Ortega to attempted suicide and goes away with Rita, and Lingard hands Travers over as a prisoner to the natives and spends a night alone with Mrs Travers. (Peyrol, in a rather similar way, captures and immobilizes Scevola, so freeing Arlette to marry Réal.) In the final phase the hero faces the nemesis, who here re-enters the story, and suffers separation from the heroine. Blunt returns and wounds George, causing Rita to leave him; Jörgenson blows up the *Emma*, bringing about Travers' release and the departure of Mrs Travers with her husband; and Réal comes back, takes Arlette, and prompts Peyrol to depart on the fatal mission. These three stages, well marked in each of the plots, distinguish the novels of the last phase no less sharply than does the realignment of characters around the hero and heroine.

The novels of the last phase thus present the Conradian pattern in a new way. The hero is still, like his closer predecessors, a man who desires a free and uncommitted life, a wish associated with his choice of career as a sailor. Like earlier heroes he compromises this way of life by becoming entangled in affairs on dry land, affairs such as George's Carlism, Lingard's plan for assisting Hassim, and Peyrol's desire to strike a blow for France. The last novels present the hero's compromised and paradoxical situation by placing him between two other male characters, one a fellow seaman, the other standing for his line of compromised commitment. The latter figure is the hero's nemesis, for in these stories, as in those which come before, the tensions arising from the hero's attempt to resolve his dilemma by compromise end in an inescapable and drastic confrontation with the extreme implications of the course to which he has committed himself. In each of these three stories, therefore, the hero has to deal successively with two difficult antagonists, first disposing of his rival to achieve a union with the heroine, and then facing his nemesis. The three-part structure of these stories is largely dictated by the presence of these two antagonists, for after the initial stage in which the grounding is laid and the plot wound up, there remain two further stages, one for the disposal of the rival, and the last for the satisfaction of the nemesis.

15 *The Arrow of Gold*

The Arrow of Gold begins with the hero, George, in a situation typical of a Conradian protagonist at the outset of his adventures. He is a wanderer at a loose end, a seaman ashore after a long voyage with no clear plans for the future. The disengaged hero is known as "Young Ulysses", a name which reflects his isolated wanderings and indicates ironically his relative inexperience. In this he is very like Jim before he joined the *Patna*, and like Heyst before his encounter with Morrison, but he is most like his immediate predecessor, the Captain in *The Shadow-Line*, who gives up his job as a ship's officer and idles in port talking vaguely about going home. George speaks of his own idleness at this time (p. 11) and points out that he was then still very much a young man without attachments or definite purposes.

> I had just returned from my second West Indies voyage. My eyes were still full of tropical splendour, my memory of my experiences, lawful and lawless, which had their charm and their thrill; for they had startled me a little and amused me considerably. But they had left me untouched. Indeed they were other men's adventures, not mine. Except for a little habit of responsibility which I had acquired they had not matured me. I was as young as before. Inconceivably young – still beautifully unthinking – infinitely receptive (p. 8).

Conrad connects this story with *The Shadow-Line* by calling it a tale of "initiation (through an ordeal which required some resolution to face) into the life of passion" ("Author's Note", p. ix), for the preceding story is also one of initiation across the shadow-line between the independence of youth and the responsibilities of full manhood.

George is fascinated by an Englishman called Mills, whose role corresponds closely to that of Captain Giles in *The Shadow-Line*. Mills is a somewhat older man, worldly and well-connected, whom the hero respects and admires. Just as Giles in *The Shadow-Line* is responsible for prodding the subject of the story into purposive activity, being instrumental in his leaving an idle life and taking up a difficult command, so Mills in *The Arrow of Gold* is the deliberate means of George's association with the dangerous Carlist cause. On his hearing of George before their first meeting, "at once it occurred to Mills that this eccentric youngster was the very person for what the legitimist sympathisers had very much at heart just then: to organize a supply by sea of arms and ammunition to the Carlist detachments in the South" (p. 5). It is Mills who introduces George to Blunt, together with whom he has decided that George "should be drawn into the affair if it could be done" (p. 5); Blunt and Mills together then take George to meet Rita. Giles reappears at the conclusion of *The Shadow-Line* to confirm and approve the hero's successful passage from youth to maturity, and in a very similar way Mills returns at the end of *The Arrow of Gold*, after George has won and lost his heroine, to break to him the news of her departure and to encourage his going back to the sea (pp. 349–51).

The cause to which George commits himself, in a context which looks back to the political novels of Conrad's middle period, is Carlism, the movement to restore the Bourbon Don Carlos to the throne of Spain. The cause itself, with its aura of romance and its political circumstances, has much in common with the ideals of Conrad's earlier heroes, but George, like most of the heroes from *Nostromo* onwards, is not unreserved in his commitment to action. Like Nostromo, George is torn between, on the one hand, the various inducements which attract him to political enterprises and, on the other, his wish to remain his own man, to live a free and independent existence which, in his case, is exemplified in the life of a wandering sailor. The balance for George is swung in favour of action in the cause by the heroine, Rita.

After his initial meeting with Rita, George left her house "committed to an enterprise that could not be talked about; which would have appeared to many senseless and perhaps ridiculous, but was certainly full of risks, and, apart from that, commanded discretion on the ground of simple loyalty. It would not only close my lips but it would to a certain extent cut me off from my usual haunts and from the society of my friends; especially of the light-hearted, young, harum-scarum kind. This was unavoidable" (p. 87). As a result of his involvement with the cause George thus feels himself "thrown back" upon his "own thoughts and forbidden to

seek relief amongst other lives" (pp. 87–8). The antagonism
between his new life and his old, between his commitment to the
Carlist cause and his existence as a rover of the seas, is clearly drawn.
His meeting with Rita and consequent enlistment entails a
distancing from George's former ties. Only when Rita has finally left
him at the end of the story does he return freely to his "other love",
the sea (p. 351).

Rita, unlike such early heroines as Jewel, cannot be identified
with the goal of the hero's action, because the heroine herself here
has a dual relation to the cause. Rita is a Carlist in that she comes of
royalist peasant stock and is a former lover of the legitimist
pretender, yet she does not, any more than does George, surrender
herself intellectually to the doctrines of legitimacy. She is widely
regarded as "the guardian angel" of the movement on account of
the financial backing she gives it, but as "a pupil of Henry Allègre"
she has "no illusions of that sort about any man" (p. 72), even about
the Prince, whom she now supports not out of political conviction
but from loyalty to a friend (p. 101).

George joins the Carlist movement simply from devotion to Rita;
he has no real concern for the principle of legitimacy. The point is
made explicit in his conversation with Dominic as they are out
together one night on a gun-running expedition.

> "I suppose Alphonso and Carlos, Carlos and Alphonso, they are
> nothing to you, together or separately?"
> I said: "Dominic, if they were both to vanish from the earth
> together or separately it would make no difference to my feelings"
> (p. 126).

George's enlistment is therefore an ambivalent act, structurally
comparable to Nostromo's undertaking to convey the silver of the
mine to safety, or to Verloc's agreement to arrange an attack on
Greenwich Observatory; in each case the hero adopts a course of
action, which is not wholly congenial to his temperament, in order
to achieve a relatively selfish ulterior end. The action itself, like
Nostromo's taking charge of the lighter or Razumov's becoming a
counter-revolutionary spy, might in other circumstances have been
considered blameless, or even bravely noble, but is rendered
dubious by the hero's secret motives.

The crucial matter of motive is raised in George's interview with
the Carlist agent, the Marquis of Villarel.

"I am afraid, Señor, that you are affected by the spirit of scoffing and irreverence which pervades this unhappy country of France in which both you and I are strangers, I believe. Are you a young man of that sort?"

"I am a very good gun-runner, your Excellency," I answered quietly.

He bowed his head gravely. "We are aware. But I was looking for the motives which ought to have their pure source in religion."

"I must confess frankly that I have not reflected on my motives," I said. "It is enough for me to know that they are not dishonourable and that anybody can see they are not the motives of an adventurer seeking some sordid advantage."

He had listened patiently and when he saw that there was nothing more to come he ended the discussion.

"Señor, we should reflect upon our motives" (p. 251).

George does reflect upon his motives after the failure of his gun-running operation, when he decides to stay in Europe none the less, instead of returning to his sea-adventures in the West Indies. He persists in his "Royalist affairs" despite the loss of his ship, because they provide what he calls his

excuse for remaining in Europe, which somehow I had not the strength of mind to leave for the West Indies, or elsewhere. On the other hand, my adventurous pursuit kept me in contact with the sea where I found occupation, protection, consolation, the mental relief of grappling with concrete problems, the sanity one acquires from close contact with simple mankind, a little self-confidence born from the dealings with the elemental powers of nature. I couldn't give all that up. And besides all this was related to Doña Rita. I had, as it were, received it from her own hand, from that hand the clasp of which was as frank as a man's and yet conveyed a unique sensation. The very memory of it would go through me like a wave of heat (p. 242).

This passage shows the persisting conflict in George's mind between his involvement with the Carlist cause and the attraction of the sea. His actual course, remaining in Europe and continuing his contact with the legitimist movement, is an attempted compromise dictated chiefly by his desire to keep in touch with Rita. This ambivalent arrangement, which satisfies his irresolution, both allows his dealings, as a gun-runner, with the sea and with seamen, and gives him a sense of continuing communion with the heroine.

George's action in working for the Carlist cause is therefore a compromise comparable to those of other Conradian heroes. Just as Verloc, for example, in order to maintain his comfortable existence with Winnie, agrees to perpetrate a blow for the radical movement, so George becomes involved on the Carlists' behalf in order to be associated with Rita. The act is a compromise because, just as Verloc is antipathetic to radicalism and anxious to preserve only his own ease and independence, so George has no deep doctrinal or personal concern for legitimacy but acts primarily out of interest in the heroine. Like the compromises of earlier heroes, this involves a certain dishonesty, in this case the kind of intellectual blindness criticized by the Marquis of Villarel, and consequently provokes reprisal.

George's compromise and association with the heroine bring him, like most of the earlier heroes, into dealings with two other male characters, one of whom is his rival for the heroine's attention while the other is the agent of reprisal and the immediate cause of his downfall. The rival in this case is Ortega, and the nemesis figure is Captain Blunt. The issue is confused in *The Arrow of Gold* by the fact that both Ortega and Blunt stand openly as George's competitors for Rita's love. Comparison with the other novels of this period, as well as the outcome of events in the story, show none the less that it is Ortega who occupies the structural place corresponding to the rivals of other novels, while Blunt is the agent of nemesis.

Blunt, the nemesis whom George's compromise provokes, eventually wounds the hero in a duel, bringing about his final separation from Rita and return to his former way of life as a wandering sailor. Blunt is angered partly by straightforward sexual jealousy, since George interferes with his chances of marrying Rita, but also by his sense that George, whom he considers "a young adventurer", is not truly committed to the Carlist cause but is merely "exploiting" Rita, and therefore the Carlists, for his own profit (p. 344).

Like many of the earlier nemesis figures, Blunt is in some respects an *alter ego* to the hero, presenting him with a distorted mirror-image of his own chief failing. Brown the pirate thus confronts Jim the adventurer, attempting to repeat Jim's takeover in Patusan, although with very different motives. Jones the "gentleman" and traveller confronts the aristocratic, wandering Heyst in an attempt to steal the treasure which he believes Heyst to have stolen and concealed. Razumov, who handed Haldin over to his death and then became a spy, is confronted by Nikita, an assassin who is himself a traitor to his friends. George, who joins a romantic lost cause for personal reasons, is confronted in Blunt by a man who has a tradition of adherence to archaic, dying and reactionary movements. Blunt is described as:

> Educated in the most aristocratic college in Paris . . . at eighteen . . . call of duty . . . with General Lee to the very last cruel minute . . . after that catastrophe – end of the world – return to France – to old friendships, infinite kindness – but a life hollow, without occupation. . . . Then 1870 – and chivalrous response to adopted country's call and again emptiness, the chafing of a proud spirit without aim and handicapped not exactly by poverty but by lack of fortune (p. 182).

After fighting on the losing side in the American Civil War and in the Franco–Prussian War, Blunt has committed himself to the legitimist side in the Carlist War, which was, as Conrad lets us know at the end (p. 341), to be another failure. The parallels with George's condition are striking, especially in Blunt's desire for adventure, his tendency to listless inactivity when not so engaged, and his wandering from place to place.

George is fascinated by this man, who appears to be in reality the kind of soldier of fortune upon whom he might model himself, a man who can say of himself, "Je suis Américain, catholique et gentil-homme" (p. 18). Blunt, the urbane exile fighting selflessly for romantic causes, appeals to a strong element in George's nature. The hero's first reaction to Blunt displays the excited admiration which affects their relationship to the end.

> I became suddenly extremely delighted with my company. A man who "lived by his sword," before my eyes, close at my elbow! So such people did exist in the world yet! I had not been born too late! (p. 15).

Blunt, who is also, when George first meets him, a suitor for Rita's hand, is therefore George's temperamental parallel in his mode of life, loyalties and bearing. Their fundamental similarity of outlook is observed by Mrs Blunt (the Captain's mother) when she says to

George, "I am aware that you are very much younger, but the similitudes of opinions, origins and perhaps at bottom, faintly, of character, of chivalrous devotion – no, you must be able to understand him in a measure" (p. 175).

While Blunt in these respects confronts George with a slightly exaggerated self-image, there are other no less vital ways in which the two men differ. The same can be said of earlier nemesis figures and their respective heroes. Although Brown is in some ways uncomfortably close to Jim, the two are totally different in the motives which bring them to Patusan and in the principles governing their lives. The same is true, in their several stories, of Razumov and Nikita, of Heyst and Jones, and of Kurtz and Marlow. The outstanding difference between George and Blunt is that George is not fully committed to the ideals which activate and govern the American. George is attracted by the manner and life-style of the soldier of fortune, but cannot give himself wholly to the somewhat extravagant causes for which the other fights. He has deliberately – like many of Conrad's heroes, and to some extent like Conrad himself – cut adrift from the traditions of race, nationality and family upon which a man such as Blunt bases his career. George himself makes the point in his conversation with Mrs Blunt.

> "A chivalrous young American may offer his life for a remote ideal which may yet belong to his familial tradition. We, in our great country, have every sort of tradition. But a young man of good connections and distinguished relations must settle down some day, dispose of his life."
>
> "No doubt, Madame," I said, raising my eyes to the figure outside – '*Américain, catholique et gentilhomme*' – walking up and down the path with a cigar which he was not smoking. "For myself, I don't know anything about those necessities. I have broken away for ever from those things" (p. 175).

George's sceptical, and perhaps even cynical attitude towards the romantic ideals which the Blunts take very seriously is the reason why Blunt cannot believe in the sincerity of George's relationship with Rita and therefore criticizes the hero openly as an "ad-venturer." Blunt is such a rigid idealist that he cannot give his love unreservedly to Rita for fear that he might be, or be thought to be, influenced by the attraction of her vast material fortune, the wealth she has inherited from Allègre (pp. 189–190). George, although the fortune means nothing to him, is less absurdly fastidious than Blunt and does become, for a time, Rita's lover. Blunt naturally assumes George is a fortune-hunter and accuses him accordingly.

Blunt, Rita and George are three of the chief characters of the first section of *The Arrow of Gold*, the section in which they meet and begin to work together in the Carlist cause, while George and Blunt at the same time develop a mutual jealousy over Rita. The section ends with the failure of their enterprise and the breaking of their circle; George loses his ship, Rita returns to Paris, and Blunt rejoins the legitimist army in Spain. The fourth character of this phase of the story, who also disappears from the scene immediately after the failure of George's gun-running operation, is Dominic.

Dominic and Blunt stand here for the two opposing poles of George's world. Blunt, himself a man of complete dedication and scrupulous ideals, represents complete commitment. Dominic, on the other hand, stands for disengagement, the life of a sea adventurer. He has no real interest in the political situation, but joins the gun-running operation from a sense of challenge and adventure. "Dominic's general scorn for the beliefs, and activities, and abilities of upper-class people covered the Principle of Legitimacy amply; but he could not resist the opportunity to exercise his special faculties in a field he knew of old. He had been a desperate smuggler in his younger days" (p. 90).

In this first phase of the story Blunt and Dominic are George's fellow conspirators. They both serve the cause because they share a boldness and love of adventure, which also characterizes George himself, although we never see Blunt and Dominic together. They differ fundamentally in attitude, Blunt being a committed idealist while Dominic is primarily a seaman with no interest in the cause beyond the love of the challenge and the chase.

The first phase of the story ends with the collapse of the gun-running enterprise, shortly after Rita has left for Paris and Blunt returned to the army. The climax of this general dispersal is George's loss of his ship when, in order to avoid capture, he sinks her in an act which, he says, "left in me the memory of a suicide" (p. 256). In destroying his ship in the Carlist cause George is taking another step away from his sea-life into the false situation of his legitimist activity. The loss of the ship, he writes, "took away all that there was in me of independent life" (p. 256). The disappearance of Dominic from the story at this point follows logically; Dominic and George were bound together only by the love of sea adventure, which the loss of the ship has now rendered impossible. "Even Dominic failed me," says George, "his moral entity destroyed by what to him was a most tragic ending of our common enterprise" (p. 256). Dominic is seen no more, and when George tries to trace him towards the end of the tale he is told only that the man has gone into hiding, presumably as a result of the catastrophe in which George had involved him. "It looked uncommonly", George concludes, "as if Dominic's heart were broken" (p. 340).

At this point, when George returns to Marseilles after the sinking of his ship, his involvement in the Carlist cause prompted by his love for Rita has resulted in his loss of contact with the sea.

> I had nearly lost my liberty and even my life, I had lost my ship, a money-belt full of gold, I had lost my companion, had parted from my friend; my occupation, my only link with life, my touch with the sea, my cap and jacket were gone – but a small penknife and a latchkey had never parted company with me. With the latchkey I opened the door of refuge (p. 257).

All he has left at this point is his Carlist connection, the key which opens the door of Rita's house where he, as a Carlist agent, has been given lodging. This is the first major turning-point in the story where, having cut his connections with the sea and lost the comradeship of Dominic while retaining his latchkey and Carlist associations, George is spiritually prepared for his encounter with Ortega.

The second, climactic phase of *The Arrow of Gold* begins immediately. On his return to Marseilles George reports to the resident Carlist agent, who asks him to help by meeting and accommodating the fellow-agent who turns out to be none other than Rita's feared and fanatical lover. Conrad reinforces the structuring and pace of his story by emphasizing that exactly a year has passed since George first met Mills and was introduced by him to Blunt (p. 263). The carnival setting, which formed the background to that first meeting, now recurs as the context in which George recognizes his rival.

Ortega has the chief characteristics of most of the Conradian rival figures. He is at once a misogynist (like Donkin) and at the same time extremely possessive of the heroine (like Omar). Most important is the fact that he has an association with the heroine which antedates her meeting with the hero and which gives him a kind of claim upon her. Ortega, a distant relative (p. 110), first knew Rita when she, as a girl, worked as a goatherd in the mountains, where he pursued and persecuted her, extorting from her a promise that she would marry him. It is therefore a precondition of their union that George and Rita confront and get rid of Ortega, much as Jim and Jewel have to deal with Cornelius, as Willems and Aissa have to face Omar, and as Lingard and Mrs Travers have to acknowledge the rights of her husband.

The rival in Conrad's later novels occupies a more significant and central position than most of his earlier counterparts. Rivals in the early stories are often secondary characters with limited roles, figures such as Cornelius, the Manager and Sterne, although there are exceptions, rivals with more expanded and focal roles, such as Dain in *Almayer's Folly* and Donkin. The rival has no very noticeable part in any of the three great political novels or in the shorter stories of that period. He reappears with renewed strength as De Barral in *Chance* where, as in the three last complete novels, he engages the hero in a confrontation which is the dramatic climax of the story.

The rivals in the last novels have a dual function. On the one hand they are tied to the heroines, whom they remind uncomfortably of past failures and present encumbrances. On the other hand, they come into the story as a result of the hero's compromise, his involvement with a cause which is not really his own, and present an overt threat to his endeavours. Ortega enters *The Arrow of Gold* as a Carlist agent whom George, as another agent, is given the task of looking after for a night in Marseilles, but Ortega is not a believer in legitimacy, for he declares himself "a free-thinker" (p. 269) and in favour of "a red revolution everywhere" (p. 278). He is therefore brought into association with George through the Carlist movement, but soon proves, in George's opinion, "no proper person" for employment in the cause (p. 270).

For Rita, Ortega is "a danger", "something ugly" in her past which she is unwilling that others, especially George, should know about (p. 103). Ortega came early into Rita's life as a member of her family and a close neighbour. He is part of her background, and retains the strong approval of her elder sister, Theresa. In the lyric pastoral setting of Lastaola, from which Rita choses to take her surname (p. 108), Ortega appeared, much like the serpent in Eden, as an inevitable complication in the garden of innocence. Rita herself first describes him to George in these terms.

He was the only son from a rich farmhouse two miles down the slope. In winter they used to send him to school at Tolosa. He had an enormous opinion of himself; he was going to keep a shop in a town by and by and he was about the most dissatisfied creature I have ever seen. He had an unhappy mouth and unhappy eyes and he was always wretched about being kept in the country and chained to work. He was moaning and complaining and threatening all the world, including his father and mother. He used to curse God, yes, that boy, sitting there on a piece of rock like a wretched little Prometheus with a sparrow pecking at his miserable little liver. And the grand scenery of mountains all round, ha, ha, ha! (p. 111).

Although raised by Rita's family in the same part of the world, from the first Ortega is diametrically opposed to her in temperament and outlook. Her open nature contrasts with his egocentric malevolence, much as his urban, commercial leanings later separate him from the life of maritime adventure which she approves in George.

A common feature of Conrad's later writing is the placement of major characters, the heroes and heroines, between pairs of secondary figures who together represent conflicting choices, impulses, or characteristics of the central figure. The Captain in *The Shadow-Line* is thus placed between Burns and Ransome. George, in *The Arrow of Gold*, finds himself in the first phase of the story between Dominic and Blunt. The last three complete novels are distinguished structurally by the fact that the heroine, as well as the hero, is treated in this way. In the second phase of *The Arrow of Gold* Rita stands torn between George and Ortega, much as Mrs Travers in *The Rescue* stands between Lingard and her husband, and Arlette in *The Rover* between Peyrol and Scevola.

As early as *The Secret Agent* Conrad had experimented with the idea of placing the heroine in a situation of conflict parallel to and reflecting that of the hero. This he did again in *Chance*, and repeated more emphatically in *The Arrow of Gold*. Rita's choice between Ortega and George, between her antipathetic childhood suitor and the new lover whom she desires, has much in common with George's dilemma expressed in the flanking characters of Blunt and Dominic. George has to decide between the attractive but irresponsible life of a sea-adventurer (represented by Dominic) and commitment to a cause (represented by Blunt); Rita must decide between the attraction of George, with his appearance of freedom and sincerity, and the familial and traditional moral pressures which Ortega can enlist against her.

In George Rita is fascinated by his way of life at sea and is thrilled by the suggestion that she might join him in it.

"You should come out with me to sea then [says George]. There may be some danger there but there's nothing ugly to fear."

She gave me a startled glance quite unusual with her, more than wonderful to me. . . .

We were all standing up now. She kept her eyes on me and repeated with a sort of whimsical enviousness:

"The sea! The violet sea – and he is longing to rejoin it! . . . At night! Under the stars!" (pp. 103-4).

Surrounded by Therese, Blunt, her other Carlist associates, and the ever-present threat of Ortega, Rita feels oppressively confined and thinks of the sea as a place of comparative simplicity. "More space. More air. Give me air, air," she says. "I envy you, Monsieur George. If I am to go under I should prefer to be drowned in the sea with the wind on my face" (p. 148).

There is something in George's sea background which answers to the state of idyllic innocence to which Rita looks back regretfully in her childhood at Lastaola. There she, like George at sea, was free from constraints, responsibilities, and conflicts, and in such a state she feels easy and at home. Now it is only in the company of George, the open, disinterested man from the sea, that she is able to be herself.

"You don't know what a relief of mental ease and intimacy you have been to me in the frankness of gestures and speeches and thoughts, sane or insane, that we have been throwing at each other [she says to him]. I have known nothing of this in my life but with you. There had always been some fear, some constraint, lurking in the background behind everybody, everybody – except you, my friend."

"An unmannerly, Arcadian state of affairs. I am glad you like it. Perhaps it's because you were intelligent enough to perceive that I was not in love with you in any sort of style."

"No, you were always your own self, unwise and reckless and with something in it kindred to mine, if I may say so without offence" (p. 217).

Rita is very like George in her search for freedom and sincerity, and is like him also in her discovery that the active pursuit of this goal is, in practice, self-defeating.

Against George, who represents to Rita honesty, simplicity and ease, stands Ortega, to whom she is bound by ties of background, family and religion. Her pious sister, Ortega's advocate, constantly reinforces the bond. Ortega is in many ways George's opposite. He is identified with orthodox commerce, where George is something of a pirate and a smuggler; he is personally spiteful and hypocritical, where George is relatively generous and transparently sincere; and he is rigid in his adherence to a vague but fanatically strict code of moral and social conduct, which makes him, like Therese, thoroughly intolerant, while George remains generally liberal and unconcerned. Ortega therefore represents a life of traditional rigidity, from which Rita wishes to be free, and to which in her eyes George stands opposed.

The dilemma Rita faces, caught between George and Ortega, is broadly similar to that which George himself experiences between the ways represented by Dominic and Blunt. On the one hand is the open life, symbolized most readily for Conrad by the sea, and on the other is the call of a duty, either inherited or invoked, which involves acceptance of responsibilities and of a strict moral code. George, like the Captain in *The Shadow-Line* and such other devotees of personal independence as Nostromo, Anthony and Heyst, has adopted a life-style free of permanent connections and responsibilities; his story is one of initiation, through his passion for Rita, into the other world in which heavy demands are made upon him, limiting his independent action. Rita, through Ortega and Therese already very much embroiled with the limits and demands of life ashore, seeks through George to regain the unconstrained innocence of her youth.

Rita's conflict is imaged, in the second section of the novel, by the active opposition between Ortega and George. It is further set out in the antithesis between the two "father" figures involved in her upbringing, her uncle, the simple but strict peasant priest, and the wealthy artist and sceptic, Henry Allègre. The uncle, associated like Ortega with Rita's rustic origins, disapproves thoroughly of what she has become. He stands for the set of established beliefs and codes of behaviour into which she, as a Spanish Catholic of poor but ancient family, was born. Allègre, on the other hand, represents, as an artist, innovation and, as an extremely wealthy man, practical independence. He is also a thorough sceptic, inherently opposed to established views, and in his care Rita was "steeped for nearly five years in the talk of Allègre's studio, where every hard truth had been cracked and every belief had been worried into shreds" (p. 56).

The result of Allègre's influence is that Rita becomes dissatisfied with the beliefs and values of her earlier background, and having inherited the artist's fortune she finds herself in a position to follow her inclinations. In particular, this makes her perceptive and critical of human pretensions. "Often when we were alone [she says] Henry Allègre used to pour it [his "scorn of the world"] into my ears. If ever anybody saw mankind stripped of its clothes as the child sees the king in the German fairy tale, it's I!" (pp. 95–6). It is therefore as a result of Allègre's influence that Rita turns away from men of fixed beliefs, attitudes and ideals, men such as Ortega and Blunt, to a man such as George, who is without pretence or hypocrisy.

Both George and Rita, therefore, stand as protagonists in the story, each flanked by one or more pairs of opposing characters, whose contrary tendencies indicate conflicts of choice and moral dilemmas. The skeletal structure of *The Arrow of Gold* might be represented thus:

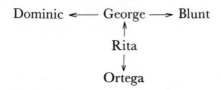

Dominic ⟵ George ⟶ Blunt

↑

Rita

↓

Ortega

Over this framework is spread a version of the familiar Conradian pattern, but with an important amplification of the heroine's part. Two of the flanking characters take on the established roles of nemesis (Blunt) and rival (Ortega). The role of Dominic, the figure embodying the hero's independence, is new in the novels of the last phase, although it has something in common with that of the sacrificial male of the political stories.

Another established role, that of the anti-heroine, also reappears in *The Arrow of Gold*, although the character, Therese, is not paired in any obvious way with an opposite or contrary figure. Therese occupies a position in *The Arrow of Gold* close to that of the anti-heroine of the early stories, characters such as Joanna in *An Outcast of the Islands* and Kurtz' Intended in *Heart of Darkness*. Like them, she belongs to the world and set of values being abandoned by the hero and heroine, whom she therefore opposes. Her case is particularly close to that of Linda Viola in *Nostromo*, who is also the older and more traditionally oriented sister of an errant heroine. Therese, with her strict upbringing in the uncle's household, disapproves of Rita's life with Allègre and of her later association with George. At the same time she is an ardent supporter of Ortega in his efforts to make Rita marry him, and she helps and abets him in the second section of the novel during the climactic confrontation. When George has held the field and driven off his rival, Therese eventually "elopes" with Ortega (pp. 341–2).

The pattern of action in *The Arrow of Gold* is basically an enlargement of that of the earlier novels. The hero, George, makes the moral compromise of joining the Carlist movement, with which he has no real sympathy, in order to associate with Rita while still enjoying a life of adventure. As a result of his action he finds himself caught in a situation of conflict. His relationship with the heroine provokes the hostility of a rival, whom he succeeds in dimissing. In the end, however, a nemesis appears, confronting him with a strongly unfavourable criticism of his compromise and its consequences, and as a result the hero is finally separated from the heroine and effectively vanquished.

In *The Arrow of Gold* George's initial compromise places him, in the first movement of the story, in a dilemma, the horns of which are represented respectively by Dominic and Blunt. In order to pursue Rita he must keep in balance these two conflicting forces, the freedom and adventure of his sea life on the one hand and the demands of duty and tradition on the other. Upon this balance depends the continuation of his association with Rita, for whom he must be both a capable and daring sailor and a man prepared to serve the Carlist cause. The attempt to reconcile in himself these contrary impulses is productive of disaster. George has proved inadequate, by the end of this phase of the story, both as a Carlist and as a gun-runner, because his first preoccupation is with neither the sea nor the cause but with Rita. At this stage of the story the hero has quarrelled and parted with both Blunt, who sees him as a personal enemy and threatens to shoot him, and Dominic, who regards the sinking of their ship in Rita's cause as something of a betrayal of their common seamanship.

In spite of the unresolved and deepening conflict in his life George, like most of the earlier heroes, persists in pursuit of his goal and his heroine. Like Willems, Jim and Heyst, he is successful in outfacing his rival and winning a temporary union with the heroine, but this success in turn brings on the final catastrophe. George's disappearance with Rita so provokes Blunt's jealousy that he makes public accusations which oblige George to fight the duel in which he is seriously wounded. Blunt's accusation that George is an adventurer exploiting Rita and the Carlist cause is the logical and appropriate outcome of the hero's compromise. Blunt, the idealist whose cause George had joined for ulterior motives, is a fitting agent of the hero's downfall, confronting him with reaction from the traditionalist world against which he has offended.

In *The Arrow of Gold*, as in *The Secret Agent* and *Chance* but more deliberately, the heroine is also at the centre of a pattern of this kind. Rita, in her involvement in the Carlist cause, is herself attempting a compromise between the conflicting principles of her upbringing. The rigidity of Carlism, its adherence to the principles of legitimacy and catholicism, reflect the attitudes of her uncle, the priest; but the freedom of her own activity, culminating in her reputed affair with the pretender and the scandal associated with her name, derives from the influence of her free-thinking, aristocratic patron, Henry Allègre. Carlism for Rita is as much a compromise as it is for George, since she neither believes in its principles nor has now anything more than a sentimental regard for the prince. She is, at the beginning of the story, neither truly free (in spite of her wealth) nor fully committed to the cause in which she acts, and on this account she is unhappy and discontented with her life.

Her friendship with George is an expression of her longing for the freedom and honesty which she finds in this man from the sea. At the same time, however, she intensifies her dilemma, for she is unable to leave her Carlist connections and go to sea with George, and instead involves him in an idealistic struggle which is alien to his nature. The result is the confrontation between George and Ortega, the two contraries whom she had vainly tried to keep apart. She is unable to accept the view of herself taken by Ortega and Therese from the rigid provincial standpoint of her ascetic uncle, yet neither can she cut herself free and go away with George. At the end of the second part of the story, after Ortega has been heard and eliminated, Rita realizes her intense dislike of Therese's morality and is willing to try living with George. Blunt's attack on George, however, is as much her nemesis as it is the hero's, for it is a reaction from the world she has deserted and one which strikes at the heart of her new purpose.

Although George recovers, and although there seems on the face of things no reason why she should not go on living with him in secrecy, Rita is defeated by the attack. Mills suggests that she left more on George's account than her own, "sacrificing" her chance of happiness for the "integrity" of his life so that he may be released from his conflict of interests and returned to the simple world of his "other love", the sea (pp. 350–1).

Rita's course through the novel is not set out in so much detail as is George's. The story is told by George himself, who does not always understand her, and although she may be said to face with George a common nemesis in Blunt she does not, like George, have to confront a sexual rival as well. A number of the story's central symbols, nonetheless, are particularly associated with her. The fortune she inherits from Allègre corresponds closely to other Conradian treasures: Kurtz' ivory, Nostromo's silver, and Peyrol's gold. It gives her the means to exercise her choice, once she becomes her own mistress, and makes her, like Nostromo, an object of power and interest. The house in the Street of the Consuls in Marseilles, which comes to Rita with the Allègre fortune, becomes emblematic of the paradoxical situation surrounding her, for when George, out of love for her, joins the Carlist cause he is given rooms here, but finds the house run and actually claimed by Rita's sister. George is therefore accepted and sheltered in the heroine's house, but at the same time confronted there by the anti-heroine, who is constantly critical of Rita and who does what she can to assist George's rival. The uncertainty as to whether the house really belongs to Rita or Therese further conveys the ambivalence of George's position with respect to Rita and the Carlist cause.

The arrow of gold, a dart-shaped ornament which Rita uses to pin back her hair, is symbolic of the anomaly with which Rita confronts George, the arrow being at once a decoration and a weapon, an object both precious and dangerous.

> That jewelled ornament, which I remembered often telling Rita was of a very Philistinish conception (it was in some way connected with a tortoishell comb) occupied an undue place in my memory, tried to come into some sort of significance even in my sleep. Often I dreamed of her with white limbs shimmering in the gloom like a nymph haunting a riot of foliage and raising a perfect round arm to take an arrow of gold out of her hair to throw it at me by hand, like a dart. It came on, a whizzing trail of

light, but I always woke up before it struck. Always (pp. 255–6).

Rita becomes the prime object of George's desire, in pursuit of which he embarks upon the impossible exercise of balancing the conflicting demands of sea and land, Dominic and Blunt, independence and commitment. The prize is great, but none the less deadly. George wins Rita for a time, but is struck down by Blunt in retaliation. The heroine draws the hero's mind away from concentration upon his personal problem of reconciling the conflict within his own nature and thus leaves him open to decisive attack. This relationship between Rita and George is closely echoed in that between Mrs Travers and Lingard in *The Rescue*.

16 *The Rescue*

Conrad began work on the novel which he eventually called *The Rescue* in the spring of 1896, after completing *An Outcast of the Islands* and at about the same time as writing *An Outpost of Progress* and *The Lagoon*. The novel was interrupted by a succession of short stories, among which are some of his best: *The Nigger of the 'Narcissus'*, *Youth*, and *Heart of Darkness*. Another short story, *Lord Jim*, rapidly grew to novel length and pushed *The Rescue* yet further aside. Conrad continued to toy with the unfinished manuscript for several years and did not stop work on it until he was well embarked upon *Nostromo*. He took it up again in earnest after *The Arrow of Gold* and brought it to completion in the spring of 1919.

The roots of the story are deep in Conrad's first mature phase. The tale of a white man who cuts himself off from and is mistrusted by his own people, who forms a binding alliance with a group of Malays, and whose plans are then upset by the unexpected intervention of other whites, has salient features in common with both *An Outcast of the Islands* and *Lord Jim*, the two full-length novels which flank the inception of *The Rescue*. The similarity to *Lord Jim* is particularly striking. In both stories a white man, of little account among his own people, establishes himself as the dominating figure in a remote Malay settlement. In both cases the white man's influence rests on a delicate balance of mutual trust and obligation between himself and the peaceful party among the natives, and in both cases this balance is destroyed when the hero is unable to leave disruptive white newcomers to be dealt with by the blacks. Just as Jim's refusal to have Brown killed results in the death of Dain Waris, so Lingard's efforts to save Mr Travers and D'Alcacer lead to the death of Hassim, and in both cases the outcome is the loss of the white man's prestige and position in the Malay settlement.

Yet *The Rescue* is not written to the same structural pattern as *Lord Jim* and the other stories of Conrad's Malayan phase, primarily because it is dominated by the relation between Lingard, the hero, and Mrs Travers, a white woman, a relationship which has no place in the earlier novels. The only early figures remotely corresponding to Mrs Travers are the anti-heroines, Joanna in *An Outcast of the Islands*, and the intended wife of Mr Kurtz in *Heart of Darkness*, white women who act like reproachful consciences to recall the heroes from involvement in the easy, delightful Malay world. Mrs Travers works in this way upon Lingard in *The Rescue*, where her presence distracts him effectively from his commitment to Hassim and Immada. From this point it is tempting to pursue the structural comparison with *Lord Jim* and to see Mr Travers as the quivalent of Brown, the leader of the party of white men which arrives unexpectedly by sea to upset the hero's relations with the natives, but the consequences of such a view will not bear scrutiny. Immada, the black woman attracted to Lingard and identified with Hassim's cause, would then become the heroine, equivalent to Aissa and Jewel, while Hassim himself, Immada's brother and protector, would be left as an incipient rival.

Such a view of *The Rescue*, although useful in that it exposes the novel's roots in the period which also gave birth to *Lord Jim*, is not tenable, because it involves too much distortion of the novel Conrad finally produced. The relationship between Lingard and Immada has neither the quality nor the significance of that between the heroes and heroines of the early stories, and there is no true rivalry between Lingard and Hassim. Most important, Mrs Travers is clearly the heroine of the novel, both as the object of the hero's sexual interest and as in her own right, after the hero himself, the second major character of the story.

The pattern of *Lord Jim* lies buried beneath the final version of *The Rescue*, much like the foundations of a mediaeval monastery concealed beneath a Tudor mansion, having something in common with the later structure but being very different from it in concept and purpose. The final story of *The Rescue* belongs structurally with the other novels of the last phase, *The Arrow of Gold* and *The Rover*, whose pattern of character and action it shares. Mrs Travers has her equivalent not in the earlier anti-heroines such as Joanna, nor even in early heroines such as Jewel, but in her close contemporaries, Rita and Arlette, women who are, like the heroes, cut off from both worlds and identified with neither a hero's present commitments nor with his neglected past responsibilities.

The analogy with the concealed foundations of an older structure may be misleading in this case, however, since Conrad did not begin *The Rescue* as a novel altogether like *Lord Jim* and then, when he completed it some twenty years later, turn it into a very different novel more like *The Arrow of Gold*. In fact the outline of *The Rescue* was clear in his mind from the beginning, as is shown by the sketch he gave of it in a letter to William Blackwood, dated 6 September 1897.

> The human interest of the tale is in the contact of Lingard the simple, masterful, imaginative adventurer with a type of civilized woman – a complex type. He is a man tenacious of purpose, enthusiastic in undertaking, faithful in friendship. He jeopardizes the success of his plans first to assure her safety and then absolutely sacrifices them to what he believes the necessary condition of her happiness. He is throughout mistrusted by the whites whom he wishes to save; he is unwittingly forced into a contest with his Malay friends. Then when the rescue, for which he had sacrificed all the interests of his life, is accomplished he has to face his reward – an inevitable separation. This episode of his life lifts him out of himself; I want to convey in the action of the story the stress and exaltation of the man under the influence of a sentiment which he hardly understands and yet which is real enough to make him as he goes on reckless of consequences.*

As early as 1897, therefore, Conrad had conceived the relation of Lingard and the white heroine, Mrs Travers, as the central feature of the novel and had designed the collapse of Lingard's Malayan plans and his final loss of the heroine as the conclusion of the story. He had devised a story in which the heroine is not, like Aissa and Jewel, identified with the world of the hero's compromise, but is a complex, imaginative, uncommitted figure, like the hero himself, who distracts him from the course he has adopted, with disastrous results. In short, Conrad had thought out, in the middle of his first mature period, the scheme for a plot the type of which he was not to realize until his last phase two decades later.

The Rescue has always been something of an anomaly. Its composition, from conception to publication, spans nearly a quarter of a century and almost the whole of its author's literary career. It is among Conrad's longest works, and was the one which he hoped would crown his achievement by bringing him a Nobel Prize, yet

---

* Quoted in Karl, p. 402.

neither popular nor critical opinion has ever ranked this among his best productions. Students of Conrad are uncomfortable with the novel's history, with the author's inability, after Herculean efforts, to make anything of it in the early years, and with its relatively rapid and easy completion so many years afterwards, giving rise to the suspicion that Conrad himself, tired and failing, was compromising in his last years by using material which, in his more obviously brilliant early period, he had rejected as unsuitable or indigestible.

A measure of explanation arises from our examination of Conrad's development as an architect of plot structures, from which it appears that the novel he had planned to write, the story which he outlined to Blackwood in 1897, was one which he was not yet equipped, not sufficiently experienced as a novelist, to construct in his early years. A plot featuring a heroine who does not entice the hero to compromising commitment, but who distracts him from the effort to balance the paradoxical conflict of his own nature, is of a type which Conrad could create only after the successful production of *Chance* and *Victory*, both of which have heroines whose "rescue" draws the hero out of, not into, the world of his retreat. These two novels in turn, along with most of the short stories of the years 1910–14, involve the type of hero whose personal aim, before he becomes entangled with the heroine, is not to build a new world for himself, but simply to avoid commitment in the existing world by becoming a sailor, a wanderer, or a hermit, a type of hero which Conrad first realized in the political novels of 1903–9. Conrad could not, therefore, have completed *The Rescue* much before *The Arrow of Gold*, because it was not until that time that he had evolved the instruments, techniques, and characters which he needed to construct that type of plot.

We reach the same conclusion if we turn to examine Conrad's treatment of his heroines. During the years of experimentation which followed the completion of *An Outcast of the Islands* Conrad evidently made an artistic decision which involved the relegation of the heroine to a secondary position for some time to come. Jewel and the other sketchy heroines of the years 1897–1902 are much simpler and less obtrusive figures than Nina and Aissa. The decision was not made without serious thought and hesitation, as the experimental works of 1896–7 clearly show; women have central roles in several of these, specifically in *The Idiots*, *The Sisters*, *The Rescuer* and *The Return*. Not until the political novels, however, beginning with *Nostromo* in 1902–4, did Conrad take a new look at the heroine and, in Emilia Gould, commence the line which leads through Flora de Barral to Rita and Mrs Travers.

The Return, completed during the "experimental" period in September 1897, is particularly interesting here, because it shows that one of the avenues down which Conrad glanced, at this turning-point in his career, involved the development of a complex, independent heroine type, which was not to reappear in his novels until the last phase. The tale presents, in a rather heavy-handed miniature, a study of lady's conventional marriage to a man with whom she has little real sympathy, her move towards leaving him for a more exciting partner, and her eventual return. Mrs Hervey, the society lady bored with the artificialities of her existence and desiring truth, openness and sincerity in a relationship, is a prototype for Rita and Mrs Travers. That Conrad was considering at this time the type of heroine who was to figure in his post-war novels is further borne out by *The Sisters*. The text of this unfinished tale is so short as to allow its heroine, Rita, little chance of development, but the direction in which she was to grow is strongly suggested by the way in which Conrad re-shaped her twenty years later as Rita de Lastaola. Both Ritas have childhoods which span two worlds, one that of peasant strictness and austerity, the other a world of relative opulence, luxury and moral vagueness. It is reasonable to suppose that the Rita of *The Sisters*, like Mrs Hervey, Mrs Travers and the later Rita, was to grow up to a life governed by middle-class conventions and by material wealth, against both of which a deeper, simpler side of her nature conducts an unsuccessful revolt.

Why Conrad chose in 1897 to put aside his complex heroine, exemplified in Mrs Hervey, in favour of the complex hero, such as Wait and Kurtz, cannot be determined. All that can be said is that he appears to have been unready to write a full-length novel, or even a good short story, around such a heroine at this stage, as is shown by his abandonment of *The Sisters*, his prolonged postponement of *The Rescue*, and his own (and almost everyone's) dissatisfaction with *The Return*. It is also clear that the course which Conrad did take as a novelist, developing his stories around their heroes in the manner we have traced, brought him eventually to a point where he was able to take up the complex heroine again. Having approached this point by way of the political heroines and Flora de Barral, he made a deliberate return, after 1917, to the material of his experimental work of 1896–7, developing Rita of *The Sisters* as the heroine of *The Arrow of Gold* and completing the novel *The Rescue* which centred upon the relationship between Lingard and Mrs Travers, a heroine with strong echoes of the unhappy wife in *The Return*.

The Rescue is a version of the Conradian fictional pattern closely similar to that of *The Arrow of Gold*. In both tales the hero is an adventurous seaman caught between the call of his quasi-piratical life and the demands of responsibility towards people from the world he has abandoned. In both, the heroine, although originally herself of the landsmen's party, is a rebel against the conventions of life ashore and finds herself strongly attracted to the hero. In their pursuit of the heroines both heroes then lose control of the equipoise of conflicting interests which, in their own lives, they had been trying to maintain, the balanced compromise between the demands of sea and land, the life of the will and the admission of responsibilities. In both cases the heroine is caught in a situation of conflict similar to that of the hero, in her case between the demands of a prior betrothal to one of her own people and the more exciting, less artificially conventionalized prospects of a union with the man of the sea.

The detailed mechanisms of the two tales differ considerably, largely because *The Rescue* employs the paraphernalia of the Malayan tales of twenty years before, whereas *The Arrow of Gold* shares the French background of Conrad's other late stories, yet the outcome is much the same in both. The hero pushes aside his rival and enjoys a temporary union with the heroine, but in so doing he loses his grasp of events and is destroyed by the snapping of the tensions he has created. Both plots employ the device characteristic of Conrad's latest novels, the use of opposing pairs of characters to embody a conceptual conflict. Just as Rita stands between George and Ortega, so Mrs Travers stands between Lingard and her husband, and just as George is flanked by Dominic and Blunt, so is Lingard flanked by Carter and Jörgenson.

Lingard's initial compromise, sketched lightly and retrospectively in *The Rescue*, is closely akin to those of the early heroes. It seems that he, like Willems, tired of lowly status and drudgery among his own people, took to slightly dishonest means (in his case some form of smuggling or piracy) as an easy way to independence, and found himself, as a result, cast out from the white world and obliged to find a new arena for his activities among blacks. The framework of this compromise, with its hint at crime and its

antithesis of black and white worlds, comes from the early Malayan
tales, but the character which emerges, a free-roving seaman with
piratical associations, is typical of the late period, the natural
companion of George and Peyrol. The hero is an "adventurer", a
term which Blunt had applied opprobriously to George and which is
now given to Lingard by both the narrator (p. 87) and Mrs Travers
(p. 134).

The result of Lingard's life as an adventurer is his involvement
with Malay natives, both because he is no longer acceptable among
whites and because, in a moment of danger on a strange shore, he
falls under obligation to the Rajah Hassim, who saves his life. His
debt to Hassim in turn embroils Lingard in native politics, for when
the Rajah is deposed and exiled the hero undertakes to organize a
military alliance for the accomplishment of his restoration. (The
imagery here is closely reminiscent of *The Arrow of Gold*, where the
hero similarly joins a campaign to restore an exiled prince.)
Lingard's motives in engaging in this struggle, apart from his
friendship for Hassim, are largely egocentric.

> That adventurer had only a confused notion of being on the
> threshold of a big adventure. There was something to be done,
> and he felt he would have to do it. It was expected of him. The
> seas expected it; the land expected it. Men also. The story of war
> and of suffering; Jaffir's display of fidelity, the sight of Hassim and
> his sister, the night, the tempest, the coast under streams of fire –
> all this made one inspiring manifestation of a life calling to him
> distinctly for interference. But what appealed to him most was the
> silent, the complete, unquestioning, and apparently uncurious,
> trust of these people (pp. 87–8).

Lingard's involvement in Hassim's cause is therefore a continuation
of his love of adventure, of his romantic idea of himself as one who
can alter the world to satisfy his own sense of right. Although
morally sympathetic, this intervention is the logical outcome and
continuation of Lingard's piracy.

The symbol of Lingard's wilful freedom is his brig.

> She represented a run of luck on the Victorian goldfields; his
> sagacious modration; long days of planning, of loving care in
> building; the great joy of his youth, the incomparable freedom of
> the seas; a perfect because a wandering home; his independence,

his love – and his anxiety. . . . His will was its will, his thought was its impulse, his breath was the breath of its existence. He felt all this confusedly, without ever shaping this feeling into the soundless formula of thought. To him she was unique and dear, this brig of three hundred and fourteen tons register – a kingdom (pp. 10–11).

The brig is the means whereby Lingard lives his life as an adventurer, taking him where he wishes, making his living, obeying his commands, and allowing him, through its weaponry, to impose his will on others.

The drift of Lingard's compromise, symbolized in his brig, takes him through piracy to involvement with the Malays which, in turn, obliges him to associate himself with Jörgenson. Jörgenson stands, first and foremost, for the white man's involvement with native affairs and its fatal effects. He is an older version of Lingard, a clear *alter ego* figure, a former sea captain who himself became entangled in native politics, married a native woman, and remained among the black people. "I was like you once," he says to Lingard. "Five and thirty years – never dropped anything. And what you can do is only child's play to some jobs I have had on my hands" (p. 100). They share a tenacity of purpose, a will to interfere and, most of all, a morality which has cut adrift from the white world. In his younger days Jörgenson had been involved in a native cause very similar to that upon which Lingard is engaged upon Hassim's behalf (pp. 102, 112). Lingard admits to Mrs Travers that Jörgenson is a man "just like" himself (p. 157).

Jörgenson embodies the fatality inherent in Lingard's compromise. He had long ago been obliged to destroy his own ship in order to avoid arrest by the Dutch authorities (pp. 100–1), a move very similar to George's in *The Arrow of Gold* and presaging the loss of the *Emma* in *The Rescue*. The man is described as a phantom, a gaunt, skeletal figure of living death, a man who has long been dead as far as the white world is concerned. His condition is a warning to Lingard of the fate which awaits the white adventurer in Malay affairs, and the knowledge which Jörgenson can give of these dealings is generally regarded as dangerous (p. 91). Jörgenson does in fact bring Lingard to the point of death, blowing up another ship as he has already destroyed his own, thereby causing the collapse of Lingard's Malayan schemes and the death of Hassim, the Captain's native comrade.

Lingard needs Jörgenson, who attaches himself to the Captain as soon as the alliance to restore Hassim is instituted. It is, indeed, from him that Lingard learns of the "Shore of Refuge" where he attempts to repeat Jörgenson's escapades of a generation before (pp. 91–2). Jörgenson comes into the story, therefore, as a direct result of the hero's compromise and involvement in a cause, much as Blunt comes into *The Arrow of Gold* when George becomes a gun-runner for the Carlists. Like Blunt, Jörgenson stands for one of the two conflicting tendencies of the hero's life, is an *alter ego* reflecting the evils of the hero's compromise, and is the eventual agent of his nemesis.

The opposite pole in the hero's dual world is imaged in the last novels in the somewhat romanticized ideal of seamanship to which the hero must remain faithful. Dominic embodies this concept in *The Arrow of Gold*, much as does Symons in *The Rover*. In *The Rescue* it centres upon a sailor who belongs to the party of whites which intrudes and upsets Lingard's adventure. This is Carter, an officer aboard Mr Travers' yacht, who has himself been something of a pirate in the past (pp. 34–5), but whose primary characteristic is his strict devotion to a seaman's duty. "I am a sailorman," he writes to Lingard. "My first duty was to the ships. . . . I fancy I have acted as a seaman and as a seaman I intend to go on acting" (p. 327). Lingard appreciates this aspect of Carter and is forced to admit that he "would trust him sooner than any man in that yacht" (p. 188). Yet Carter, associated with both the white man's code and the strict discipline of the sea, is a standing reproach to Lingard, whose doings on the Shore of Refuge do not square with Carter's idea of duty.

Carter and Jörgenson are the two conflicting poles of Lingard's world, corresponding to Dominic and Blunt respectively in *The Arrow of Gold*, Carter representing the call of seamanship, Jörgenson the temptations and perils of involvement in romantic causes. The setting of *The Rescue*, derived from its roots in Conrad's first mature phase, lends racial overtones to this dualism, so that the disciplined sea world is associated with the white standards Lingard has abandoned while the romantic, idealistic world of Jörgenson is also that of the blacks of the Shore of Refuge. The dynamism of the first part of the story (up to the point of Carter's attack on the native boats) consists primarily in the tension between the two poles which these two characters respectively embody, between Lingard's obligation to save the whites and his commitment to the blacks. The tension begins to break, and the first phase of the story ends, when

Carter acts on his own initiative against the natives, a move which corresponds structurally to Dominic's desertion of George after the loss of their vessel in *The Arrow of Gold*.

The coming of Mr Travers and his white party, which includes Mrs Travers and Carter, disturbs Lingard's plan of campaign to reinstate Hassim. When a group of Hassim's mistrustful allies takes prisoner Mr Travers and his companion, D'Alcacer, Lingard is caught in a neat conflict of loyalties. Loyalty to Hassim requires him to abandon the whites to their fate, preserve the alliance, and begin the campaign, while a sense of duty obliges him to do all he can to rescue the prisoners, who are his own people.

Lingard's alliance with Hassim has caused him to turn increasingly away from his remaining white contacts.

> He felt nowhere so much at home as when his brig was anchored on the inner side of the great stretch of shoals. The centre of his life had shifted about four hundred miles – from the Straits of Malacca to the Shore of Refuge – and when there he felt himself within the circle of another existence, governed by his impulse, nearer his desire (p. 99).

By the time the yacht appears, Lingard has "wandered beyond that circle which race, memories, early associations, all the essential conditions of one's origin, trace round every man's life" (pp. 121–2). As a result he appears strange to Mrs Travers. "He has", she says, "nothing in common with the mankind I know" (p. 149). Lingard says of himself that he has "had the time to forget where [he] began" (p. 158). The coming of the whites to the Shore of Refuge is a shock which revives old memories and, because of his current involvement, arouses antipathies. When he first set eyes on the yacht, he says,

> I could fancy she hadn't been more than an hour from home. Nothing but the look of her spars made me think of old times. And then the faces of the chaps on board. I seemed to know them all. It was like home coming to me when I wasn't thinking of it. And I hated the sight of you all (p. 155).

A part of Lingard, represented by his association with Jörgenson, has no interest in the whites beyond their removal, by any means whatever, from the possibility of interference with his plans; another part, imaged in his immediate liking for, and eventual employment of Carter, wishes to do everything in his power to preserve their safety.

The coming of the yacht and the capture of two of its passengers places Lingard in a dilemma, which is the direct result of his compromise, of his desertion of the white world in favour of Malay adventures. He expresses this conflict to Carter in a discussion of the tensions between his racial heritage and his local engagements.

> I am a white man inside and out; I won't let inoffensive people – and a woman, too – come to harm if I can help it. And if I can't nobody can. You understand – nobody! There's no time for it. But I am like any other man that is worth his salt: I won't let the end of an undertaking go by the board while there is a chance to hold on. . . . I have other lives to consider – and friends – and promises – and – and myself, too (p. 39).

The dilemma manifests itself in the way that Lingard's course of action obliges him to adopt as his agents first Jorgenson and then Carter. Jorgenson he engages to help him manage the native alliance; Carter he accepts as his lieutenant when he is obliged by Mr Travers' abduction to go ashore and consequently needs a competent officer to leave aboard the brig.

The plot unfolds as Lingard attempts to follow a middle course, one which will both save the prisoners and preserve the alliance. Not wishing to abandon his native ambitions, Lingard cannot effect the rescue by threats or force, and as a result he is only partially successful. The prisoners are returned on trust to his keeping pending a decision as to the fate of the yacht and its party.

The balance is first upset, and the problem further complicated, when Carter, left in charge of the brig during Lingard's absence ashore, on his own initiative attacks and destroys a number of native boats. Carter, the conscientious seaman, has been appointed Lingard's agent, but the trust between agent and principal is not complete. As a white man of Mr Travers' party, Carter neither understands for sympathizes with Lingard's Malayan involvements. Lingard, for his part, refuses to confide the full extent of his plans to Carter. In Carter's clear and simple view Lingard is "not straight" (p. 187). He knows that Lingard is up to something, but cannot guess what. When Lingard leaves him in command of the brig Carter asks for more detailed instructions, and Mrs Travers urges the Captain to tell him the whole story, but Lingard is unwilling to give Carter more than a vague direction to wait two or three days (pp. 232–3). Carter's unilateral action against the natives is a result of the lack of complete understanding between himself and Lingard. Not knowing the Captain's plans ashore, Carter acts as a seaman. "Perhaps you would have done better by telling me everything," he says afterwards to Lingard, "but you left me behind on my own to be your man here. I put my hand to the work I could see before me. I am a sailor. There were two ships to look after. And here they are both for you, fit to go or to stay, to fight or to run, as you choose" (p. 424). Carter's singleminded object is to save the ships, the brig and the yacht, along with their passengers if possible.

Mrs Travers, the story's heroine, belongs to neither side of Lingard's conflict. She is a white woman aboard the yacht and the wife of its owner, but much like Rita in *The Arrow of Gold* she retains a strongly independent attitude. She is initially characterized by a scornful abstraction from the world and the people around her; "an immense indifference stretched between her and all men, between her heart and the meaning of events, between her eyes and the shallow sea which, like her gaze, appeared profound, forever stilled, and seemed, far off in the distance of a faint horizon, beyond the reach of eye, beyond the power of hand or voice, to lose itself in the sky" (p. 125). Of herself she says: "I have been living since my childhood in front of a show and . . . I never have been taken in for a moment by its tinsel and its noise or by anything that went on on the stage" (p. 305). Her state of mind is closely akin to that at which Rita arrives under the influence of Henry Allègre. She sees the world around her as tedious, artificial, and barren of the truth and sincerity which she desires. "As a young girl, often reproved for her romantic ideas, she had dreams where the sincerity of a great passion appeared like the ideal fulfilment and the only truth of life. Entering the world she discovered that ideal to be unattainable because the world is too prudent to be sincere" (p. 151).

In this state of mind Mrs Travers is to a large degree isolated from her husband, who lives, like Alvan Hervey in *The Return*, very much within the conventions of society. Mr Travers is "permanently grieved by her disloyalty to his respectable ideals" (p. 152), and makes open criticism prompted by her show of sympathy for Lingard, whom Travers regards as an unprincipled adventurer and social outcast. "As a matter of fact, as a matter of experience," he says to her,

> I can't credit you with the possession of feelings appropriate to your origin, social position, and the ideas of the class to which you belong. . . . You have never taken a serious interest in the activities of my life which of course are its distinction and its value. . . . It's my belief, Edith, that if you had been a man you would have led a most irregular life. You would have been a frank adventurer. I mean morally. . . . Your conduct was above reproach; but you made for yourself a detestable reputation of mental superiority, expressed ironically (pp. 267–9).

The exchange within which these passages occur takes place in the second section of the story and corresponds closely to Ortega's verbal attack upon Rita through the closed doors of her room. In both cases the man, to whom the heroine has an actual or implicit tie, issues criticism of the lady's moral freedom of conduct from the point of view of strict social conventions.

Spiritually alienated from her husband, despising the social artificialities of the white world, and seeking human truth and sincerity, Mrs Travers is immediately attracted by Lingard and the Malayan adventure, whose history and progress he soon confides to her. Her reaction to the sight of Immada, Hassim's sister who embodies the romance and sentiment of Lingard's black world, corresponds closely to Rita's vain desire to be at sea with George. Mrs Travers

> envied, for a moment, the lot of that humble and obscure sister [Immada]. Nothing stood between that girl and the truth of her sensations. She could be sincerely courageous, and tender and passionate and – well – ferocious. Why not ferocious? She could know the truth of terror – and of affection, absolutely, without artificial trammels, without the pain of restraint.
>
> Thinking of what such life could be Mrs Travers felt invaded by that inexplicable exaltation which the consciousness of their physical capacities so often gives to intellectual beings. She glowed with a sudden persuasion that she also could be equal to such an existence; and her heart was dilated with a momentary longing to know the naked truth of things; the naked truth of life and passion buried under the growth of centuries (p. 153).

She responds favourably to Lingard, seeing in him a figure free from the social artificialities in which she is enmeshed. "She considered him apart from social organisation. She discovered he had no place in it. How delightful! Here was a human being and the naked truth of things was not so very far from her notwithstanding the growth of centuries" (p. 167). They arrive at a close mutual understanding. "There is not, I verily believe," she says, "a single thought or act of his life that I don't know" (p. 236).

Mrs Travers, alone of the whites, is taken into the secret of Lingard's Malayan plan, and she at once appreciates and accepts the claim which the blacks have upon him. She realizes that what is involved in a matter of "honour". "This is something that is your very own," she says to Lingard. "You have a right to it. And I repeat I do care for it" (p. 339). She is prepared to acknowledge his obligation to Hassim even although it conflicts with the interests of the prisoners, her husband and D'Alcacer. Yet Mrs Travers is not, like the early heroines Aissa and Jewel, or like the political heroines, identifiable with the cause pursued by her hero, and neither does she become his abettor. Although she sympathizes with Lingard's Malayan involvement, and although she does not share her husband's point of view, she never surrenders herself to Jörgenson's feeling that Lingard should sacrifice the prisoners to the exigencies of his plan. She remains, like the hero himself, caught between the polarities of the story.

Mrs Travers' ambivalence, which she shares with the other late heroines, Rita and Arlette, is illustrated in her relationship to Immada, who is herself a vestige of the early heroines and, like Aissa, a native woman identified with the world in which the hero has placed himself as a result of his compromise. On the one hand, as we have seen, Mrs Travers envies Immada's life in the romantic, open, unrestricted world of Lingard's adventure (p. 153), and later in the story she enjoys the experience of dressing in a rich native costume which Lingard had intended for the Malay princess. On the other hand, the two women are in reality very far apart. "Immense spaces and countless centuries stretched between them" (p. 140). They represent "the beginning and the end, the flower and the leaf, the phrase and the cry" (p. 148). In the event, despite Mrs Travers' romantic attempts to put herself in Immada's place, the gap is unbridgeable. Mrs Travers suppresses Hassim's message to Lingard and, perhaps as a result, the native plan is ruined.

Mrs Travers is thus placed between Lingard and her husband,

the hero and his rival, between the attraction of a free and simple life and the constraints of society and established commitments. Her dilemma, the poles of which are represented by these two men, are broadly the female equivalent of the conflict in which the hero finds himself as a result of his compromise. The plot therefore has the same basic structure as that of *The Arrow of Gold*, where both hero and heroine are placed between pairs of characters representing the poles of conflicts, the hero himself being one of the characters acting upon the heroine. The pattern in *The Rescue* may be set out thus:

$$\text{Carter} \longleftarrow \text{Lingard} \longrightarrow \text{Jörgenson}$$
$$\uparrow$$
$$\text{Mrs Travers}$$
$$\downarrow$$
$$\text{Mr Travers}$$

Mr Travers is the rival figure in *The Rescue*, the male with a prior claim to the heroine, whom the hero must outface if he is to win her. His course is remarkably close to that of Ortega, his immediate predecessor. Both men are initially antagonistic towards the heroes on a purely personal level, both stand for orthodoxy and a strict marital bond, and both are strongly critical of the heroine's moral character. Unlike the rivals of the previous phase, chiefly De Barral and Schomberg, both of whom move against the heroes in vigorous and lethal ways, the rivals of the final phase are surprisingly passive figures; both Ortega and Travers are content with merely verbal protests, and much the same is true of Scevola in *The Rover*. Ortega, outwitted by George, attempts suicide and fades from the story, while Travers, content with repeating his opinion that Lingard is an unscrupulous adventurer, allows himself to be handed back to his black captors. Yet although, in the novels of the last phase, the rival's general opposition to the hero is largely passive, it is by no means ineffective. The rivals emerge victorous as often as not; Schomberg destroys Heyst, and Mr Travers retains his wife, leaving Lingard's world in ruins; neither George nor Anthony wins a permanent victory, and Scevola takes the hero with him when he dies.

Conrad's rivals are usually, after the first two novels, transparently unsympathetic characters, potentially dangerous, but morally weak and unattractive. Such are Donkin, Cornelius, Sterne, De Barral and Schomberg. Their importance in their stories is to exhibit the Conradian paradox that purposive action is self-negating, the rivals embodying the negative counteraction to the heroes' efforts. In the novels of the first phase the rival's jealousy is aroused directly by the hero's pursuit of his ideal, which usually (but not always) involves at the same time pursuit of a heroine. In the novels of the political phase, where the hero's object is to avoid purposive action, there is no strong rival. The figure reappears in the next phase, with the introduction of the "rescue" motif; the hero rescues the heroine from a situation in which the rival has an established interest, and so provokes his fury. Here, and in the final phase, where the same pattern with respect to the rival is followed, the hostile male represents not only a merely sexual jealousy but, more widely, the orthodox, conventional world's opposition to the hero's freedom of action. The heroes are wanderers, adventurers who have cut themselves adrift from the ways of shore society; the rivals are now representatives of the values which the heroes have abandoned, and hence their tendency (especially clear in the cases of De Barral, Ortega, and Mr Travers) to criticize the heroines from the point of view of a strict moral code.

The antagonism of hero and rival in the later novels is therefore not confined to mutual jealousy over the heroine. Of Lingard and Mr Travers, before the hero and heroine have met, the narrator says: "these men who, two hours before had never seen each other, stood for a moment close together, antagonistic, as if they had been life-long enemies, one short, dapper and glaring upward, the other towering heavily, and looking down in contempt and anger" (p. 129).

Perhaps the most interesting feature of these later rivals is their doctrinal diversity. Just as in Conrad's earlier political stories (apart from the conservative *The Nigger of the 'Narcissus'*), the two parties, reactionaries and revolutionaries, establishment and radicals, are more or less equally exposed to criticism, so in the novels of the final phase the hostile orthodoxies represented by the rivals span a wide spectrum of political and social beliefs. Ortega is a bourgeois with radical, free-thinking tendencies; Mr Travers is of the patrician class and subscribes to a highly conventionalized patriotism and code of social conduct; and Scevola is a farmer with fanatical Jacobin tendencies. Common to all three is no particular dogma, class, religion, or philosophy, but the simple fact that they are all rigid in their adherence to some code or other. It is against this rigidity, against the constraint of *any* rules or conventions, that the heroes and heroines of these last novels are striving. The function of the rival is to convey the difficulty of escape from the bonds of one's social and moral background. Conrad himself neither attacks nor supports any particular code, his concern here, as generally, being to explore men's attitudes to their beliefs rather than the beliefs themselves.

In the pattern of the novels of the last phase there are three principal men besides the hero. There are the two contrasting characters who stand respectively for the poles of the hero's dilemma. The dualism represented in these two continues that between independence and commitment explored in the novels of the political phase. The third figure, the rival, belongs to neither pole of this dualism but represents the disapproving reaction and recrudescence of the shore world which the hero has already abandoned, before the story begins, in order to pursue his sea life.

The heroine is another would-be free spirit and, like the hero, finds herself caught in the Conradian paradox as her efforts towards freedom are effectively countered by an agent of restraint. The poles of the heroine's dilemma, which is somewhat simpler than the hero's since she has not already cut herself adrift from the world of her origin, are represented by the hero himself and the rival. The rival, for her as for the hero, images the conventions and manners of the world to which, by birth or marriage, she belongs. The hero, whose freedom from this world is already established, offers her an appealing alternative.

The heroine presents the hero with a distracting challenge, a call for "rescue" and human sympathy, which squares with neither the isolationism of the sea world nor the romantic egoism of the heroic ideal. She lifts him above the conflict in which he is engaged, expands his horizons, and takes him out of himself; yet the end, in each of the three last novels, is the hero's death or near destruction and the heroine's departure. The addition of the independent heroine to Conrad's fictional pattern does not entail the belief that love can transcend the problems of the human condition. The hero's moment of sympathy with the heroine is brief and costly, for in the end he falls victim to the conflict of forces he has created, and does so largely as a result of his attempted "rescue".

The unwinding of the plot is achieved in three stages. First the balance of the hero's world is upset by the figure of seamanship. Next the hero manages to dispose of the rival and achieve the rescue of the heroine. Finally he faces the nemesis, which repays his compromise with an event which separates him from the heroine and brings him to death or downfall. (This scheme needs a little adjustment to fit the rather special case of *The Rover*.)

The action of the contrasting male figures polarizing the hero's world is clearly symbolic of a force which emanates originally from within the hero himself. Conrad had used secondary characters in this way from quite early on, many of his nemesis figures, such as Marlow in *Heart of Darkness* and Brown in *Lord Jim*, being obvious *alter ego* figures whose appearance signifies the reaction of an element of the hero's own nature. In *The Rescue* Lingard vaguely recognizes that Carter's attack on the native boats, however inconvenient, is fundamentally something for which he, Lingard, is responsible.

> He was not angry with Carter. The fellow had acted like a seaman. Carter's concern was for the ships. In this fatality Carter was a mere incident. The real cause of the disaster was somewhere else, was other, and more remote. And at the same time Lingard could not defend himself from a feeling that it was in himself, too, somewhere in the unexplored depths of his nature, something fatal and unavoidable (p. 329).

Carter's seamanlike response to the situation is emblematic of the sailor side of Lingard and of what might be called Lingard's subconscious desire to adopt the line of direct action which Carter takes.

The other side of Lingard, the romantic, egoistic, heroic aspect, is embodied in Jörgenson, another *alter ego*, whose final destructive act in blowing up the *Emma* is similarly a reaction of Lingard's own nature. Just as Carter acted with the principal object of clearing the way towards the liberation of the whites, so Jörgenson is motivated by the overriding desire to sacrifice the whites to the success of Lingard's black alliance. "Beyond the simple wish to guide Lingard's thought in the direction of Hassim and Immada, to help him to make up his mind at last to a ruthless fidelity to his purpose Jörgenson had no other aim. The existence of those whites had no meaning on earth" (p. 384). When Lingard does not respond to the call for help Jörgenson has sent by Mrs Travers, the old man assumes that Lingard has been somehow entrapped by the blacks and that the plan has failed. He therefore blows up the *Emma*, killing himself and Lingard's black opponents, along with Hassim and Immada.

The dynamic conflict upon which the plot turns, like that of most of Conrad's longer stories, is an externalization of a dichotomy within the hero's character. Lingard himself realizes this after Carter has acted against the natives. He begins to see that his situation, although no longer under his direction, is in close correlation with his inner struggles.

> His natural impulse was to grapple with the circumstances and that was what he was trying to do; but he missed now that sense of mastery which is half the battle. Conflict of some sort was the very essence of his life. But this was something he had never known before. This was a conflict within himself. He had to face unsuspected powers, foes that he could not go out to meet at the gate. They were within, as though he had been betrayed by somebody, by some secret enemy. He was ready to look round for that subtle traitor. A sort of blankness fell on his mind and he suddenly thought: "Why! It's myself" (p. 329).

Whether left to himself Lingard would have resolved the conflict remains an open question. In the event, like George with Rita after the retreat of Ortega, he falls into a kind of paralysis under the influence of the heroine, with the result that the situation runs fatally out of control.

The part played by Mrs Travers is very dubious, for it is not clear whether, by suppressing Jörgenson's message, she prevents Lingard from taking measures he would otherwise have adopted to preserve the balance of events. Lingard himself assures her that her silence made no difference to his actions (p. 465), but she thinks that in so saying he is simply being "magnanimous" for her peace of mind (p. 467). The reader remains unsure, but it seems likely that Lingard is telling the truth. Even if he had known of the threat to Hassim and Immada he would not have left Mrs Travers' side that night to contact Jörgenson or otherwise to secure his position. Like George and Peyrol, he gives up, under the influence of the heroine, the effort to balance the conflict of forces and surrenders himself to the outcome.

The primary significance of Mrs Travers' withholding of the message is not that it brings about Lingard's downfall but that it shows her final unwillingness, or inability, to desert her husband and background in a complete surrender to the world of Lingard's adventure. Despite her longing for a free and romantic life, she cannot in the event leave the conventional world she despises. D'Alcacer says of people such as Mrs Travers that they "lead a sort of ritual dance, that most of us have agreed to take seriously. It is a very binding agreement with which sincerity and good faith and honour have nothing to do. Very binding. Woe to him or her who breaks it. Directly they leave the pageant they get lost" (p. 412). Aware of this, Mrs Travers suppresses Jörgenson's message because she is afraid that its effect will be to "call off" Lingard from his efforts to rescue the whites (p. 406).

In a very similar way Lingard proves unable to escape from his dilemma by simply cutting free from the call of his first world and plunging regardlessly into the Malayan adventure. D'Alcacer is also accurate in his assessment when he points out to Mrs Travers that her presence is not the only factor preventing Lingard from abandoning the white prisoners.

> For if you were not here cool reason would step in and would make Lingard pause in his passion to make a king out of an exile. If we were murdered it would certainly make some stir in the world in time and he would fall under the suspicion of complicity with those wild and inhuman Moors. Who would regard the greatness of his day-dreams, his engaged honour, his chivalrous feelings? Nothing could save him from that suspicion. And being what he is, you understand me, Mrs Travers (but you know him much better than I do), it would morally kill him (pp. 405-6).

The truth of D'Alcacer's estimation of his character is supported by Lingard's avowal to Mrs Travers that her suppression of Jörgenson's message was not responsible for his failure to act on Hassim's behalf.

The Rescue, like *The Arrow of Gold*, is a deeply pessimistic story in that it shows both hero and heroine defeated in their aspirations. In the outcome both are thrown back to the situations from which they set out, having gained little beyond the experience of what Conrad, in his Note to the earlier story, calls "passion". Both heroines return to the social world, the conventions and artificialities of which they despise, and both heroes, after the collapse of their plans and the desertion of their heroines, return to the simple life of the sea. The third novel of the trio, *The Rover*, exhibits a closely similar structural pattern but has an altogether different ending.

17 *The Rover*

The Rover, which Conrad wrote between December 1921 and June 1922, was the last story he was to complete. The core of its plot is a situation closely similar to that of *The Rescue*, which in turn has much in common with the closing section of *Lord Jim*. In all three cases a wandering seaman becomes involved with affairs on a remote coast which is, to him, a place of retreat or retirement, a "shore of refuge", as it is called in *The Rescue*. In each case the hero's existence on this shore is disturbed by the arrival from the sea of a group of potentially hostile strangers: Brown and his pirates, Travers and his white companions, and the English sailors. Yet in each case the hero is also obliged to accept responsibility for the safe withdrawal of these intruders, even at great risk to himself and his local schemes. Just as Jim guarantees Brown's retreat and Lingard undertakes to negotiate the release of Travers and D'Alcacer, so Peyrol conceals the captive Symons from those ashore and abets his secret escape back to the British ship.

The larger pattern of *The Rover* is also the same as that of the two preceding novels, with the significant difference that there is no sexual relationship between the hero and heroine, Peyrol being considerably older than Arlette and adopting from the start a fatherly (or even grandfatherly) attitude towards her. Perhaps as a result of this distancing of hero and heroine, Conrad was able to give this last novel a relatively happy ending, contrasting strongly with those of *The Arrow of Gold* and *The Rescue*. Despite this divergence, however, the disposition of the main characters is the same in *The Rover* as in the other late novels: a hero flanked by two conflicting men representing respectively his sea-life of adventure and his duties or commitments ashore, and a heroine torn between two men, one the hero, standing for freedom, the other, the rival, standing for the restrictive ties of her origin. In *The Rover*, as we shall see, the characters are disposed thus:

$$\text{Symons} \longleftarrow \text{Peyrol} \longrightarrow \text{Réal}$$
$$\uparrow$$
$$\text{Arlette}$$
$$\downarrow$$
$$\text{Scevola}$$

Peyrol, the hero, like George and Lingard before him, is a sympathetic pirate, a sea adventurer. His character was "formed under the sun of the Indian Seas in lawless contests with his kind for a little loot that vanished as soon as grasped, but mainly for bare life almost as precarious to hold through its ups and downs" (p. 1). His sea life, as a member of the notorious Brotherhood of the Coast, establishes one pole of his existence, his freedom and his association with the sea. The other pole, which becomes prominent as the story develops, is his patriotism, his commitment to the land, in his case to France, the country of his birth.

The story opens with Peyrol's compromise, his attempt to balance together these two conflicting impulses by retiring to the place of his origin to live quietly on the proceeds of his piracy. "Loot big or little was a natural fact of his freebooter's life" (p. 13), and Peyrol had suddenly and unexpectedly found himself in possession of a considerable treasure in gold. To enjoy this in peace he decides to live ashore and, at the same time, to satisfy his "instinct of rest" by settling in the place where he had been born. The indecisive, ambivalent nature of his retreat is imaged in the place he choses, for although it is a farmhouse on land it is also situated on a peninsula and is therefore surrounded on three sides by the sea. His room gives him the sense of "being in a lighthouse. . . . Not a bad place for a seaman to live in" (p. 30). The compromise is further represented in Peyrol's purchase of a boat, a tartane, which he keeps in a nearby cove ready for sea, although he never takes it any distance.

The fact was that he had discovered in himself a distinct reluctance to go away from the Escampobar farm. His desire to have something of his own that could float was no longer associated with any desire to wander (p. 97). . . . After he had made everything fast on board and had furled the sails neatly, a matter of some time for one man, Peyrol contemplated his arrangements which savoured of rest much more than of

wandering, and found them good. Though he never meant to
abandon his room at the farmhouse he felt that his true home was
in the tartane. . . . Often waking up at night he would get up to
look at the starry sky out of all his three windows in succession,
and think: 'Now there is nothing in the world to prevent me
getting out to sea in less than an hour'. . . . It was a fine thought
which somehow made it quite easy for Peyrol to go back to his
four-poster and resume his slumbers (pp. 99–100).

Peyrol's tartane reflects the old man's hovering between two lives,
yet committed to neither. He has left the sea, but has not yet fully
surrendered to the claims of the land.

The old sea life which Peyrol has largely abandoned is represented
by Symons, a former fellow pirate who had once saved his life in a
brawl. The old life of adventure asserts its claim when Symons, now
a sailor in the British Navy, accidentally becomes Peyrol's prisoner.
The conflicting pull of life ashore takes the form of patriotism, love
for the native land, and is embodied in Lieutenant Réal, an officer
in the French Navy who seeks Peyrol's help on a mission. In
addition, Peyrol, like George and Lingard, is also confronted in the
course of his story with the world from which his life as an
adventurer was an escape. Much as Lingard had left England to get
away from a society dominated by men like Mr Travers, so Peyrol,
as a young boy, by going away to sea had unwittingly escaped the
horrors of the French Revolution. Corresponding to Mr Travers as
the hero's rival is Scevola Bron, an ardent and bloodthirsty
revolutionary who confronts Peyrol with the state of affairs ashore
which, by being at sea, the hero has hitherto avoided.

The relation between the hero and the rival's world is more
closely explored in *The Rover*, where the fact of Peyrol's absence
during the Revolution, and the suspicion under which he consequently falls, are before the reader from the start. Peyrol's attitude
to French politics, much like that of George to Carlism and of
Lingard to the English social hierarchy, is one of indifference.

As to this upset [the Revolution], he took no side. It was too far –
too big – also not distinct enough. But he acquired the revolutionary jargon quickly enough and used it on occasion, with
secret contempt. What he had gone through, from a spell of crazy
love for a yellow girl to the experience of treachery from a bosom
friend and shipmate (and both of those things Peyrol confessed to

himself he could never hope to understand), with all the graduations of varied experience of men and passions between, had put a drop of universal scorn, a wonderful sedative, into the strange mixture which might have been called the soul of the returned Peyrol (p. 25).

As he says to Scevola, "I have nothing to do with your politics. I was at the other side of the world" (p. 27). Yet Peyrol is also aware, not without a trace of guilt, of the great suffering and upheaval which the landsmen around him have all come through but which he himself has escaped. He sees in Arlette the effects of the experience, and he sees in his friend the cripple an image of how miserable his own life might have been had he not run off to sea.

> Peyrol, without looking at the cripple, tried to imagine what sort of child he might have been – what sort of youth? The rover had seen staggering deformities, dreadful mutilations which were the cruel work of man; but it was amongst people with dusky skins. And that made a great difference. But what he had heard and seen since he had come back to his native land, the tales, the facts, and also the faces, reached his sensibility with a particular force, because of that feeling that came to him so suddenly after a whole lifetime spent amongst Indians, Malagashes, Arabs, blackamoors of all sorts, that he belonged there, to this land, and had escaped all those things by a mere hair's breadth. . . . Peyrol had a slight shudder at the thought: "Suppose I had been born like that." Ever since he had put his foot on his native land such thoughts had haunted him. They would have been impossible anywhere else. He could not have been like any blackamoor, good, bad, or indifferent, hale or crippled, king or, slave; but here on this Southern shore that had called to him irresistibly as he had approached the Straits of Gibraltar on what he had felt to be his last voyage, any woman, lean and old enough, might have been his mother; he might have been any Frenchman of them all, even one of those he pitied, even one of those he despised. He felt the grip of his origins from the crown of his head to the soles of his feet. . . . (pp. 96–8).

From the moment of his return to the shore Peyrol is aware of his good fortune in having avoided the afflictions of landsmen, particularly the effects of the Revolution. In dealing with Scevola, therefore, Peyrol is in a way making good his previous dereliction, facing up, as Conrad's heroes must, to the problems of life around which he has dodged in his earlier course.

Scevola, who has a prior claim on the heroine and whom it is Peyrol's task to dislodge, represents the most mindlessly ferocious aspect of the Revolution. Like his predecessors, Ortega and – to a lesser extent – Mr Travers, Scevola is a fanatic in his dedication to his dogma, and is presented as both extreme in his doctrines and unsympathetic in his personality. He has the salient characteristics of Conradian rivals back to Cornelius and Donkin, a tendency to violent rhetoric, a meanness of appearance masquerading as austerity, pronounced egoism and selfishness, and a vindictive grip on those within his power.

Scevola has a claim on the heroine, Arlette, whom he rescued from the violence of the Revolution in Toulon and brought back to the farm of which she was heiress after her parents' death in the fighting. They are apparently neither lovers nor bound by any legal tie, but it is Scevola's continuing intention eventually to "claim" Arlette as his wife. Arlette is indifferent, even hostile to Scevola, and her new love for Réal makes it necessary for her to break away from him. Peyrol's task as her rescuer is therefore to clear the dangerous Scevola from her path, which means freeing her from the clutches of the Revolution in which she was traumatically involved.

Arlette is a heroine typical of the late novels. Her background is one of opposite extremes. Just as Rita passed from peasant austerity to opulence, so Arlette is first brought up as the child of royalist landowners and then carried off by the radical Scevola to be exposed to the full fury of the Revolution. Her experience produces in her an abstraction from reality comparable to the more philosophical withdrawals of Rita and Mrs Travers. This is brought out not so much in anything she says, for Arlette is the most taciturn of heroines, as in her manner. "Nothing could hold her attention for long amongst her familiar surroundings. Right and left and far away beyond you, she seemed to be looking for something while you were talking to her, so that you doubted whether she could follow what you said" (p. 34).

In *The Arrow of Gold* and *The Rescue* the heroes personally awaken the heroines from their disinterest, but in *The Rover* Arlette falls in love, not with the hero, Peyrol, but with Lieutenant Réal. It is Réal who recalls her to life, but it is Peyrol who, in the end, achieves her rescue by carrying off Scevola and saving the Lieutenant from imprisonment or death.

As in the two preceding novels, the hero attempts (and in this case effects) the rescue of the heroine while at the same time balancing the dualism of conflicting forces which his initial compromising action has precipitated. Peyrol's compromise is his coming to live ashore in hopes of enjoying his treasure, and the paradoxical nature of this act is reflected in his situation at Escampobar, caught between land and water, owner of a ship forever ready but never actually putting to sea. The poles of his life, sea adventure and shore commitment, are represented respectively by Symons and Réal, who come into action more or less simultaneously. Symons comes ashore as a member of a secret spying party from an English ship and is captured by Peyrol, who subsequently recognizes him as a former shipmate and fellow pirate, while at the same time Réal seeks Peyrol's help in a plot to deceive the British fleet. Peyrol's situation here, in this much more condensed story, corresponds closely to Lingard's in *The Rescue*, when he is urged in one direction by Carter and in another by Jörgenson over the matter of the white prisoners.

Symons, as a former comrade, has a strong claim on Peyrol's interest. The English seaman seems to him to be "something belonging to him, not a man but a part of his own life, the sensation of a regained touch with the far-off days in the Indian Ocean" (p. 201). Of Réal, as a naval officer, Peyrol is instinctively suspicious (pp. 103–4), but he has some sympathy with him as a good seaman and is obliged to admit to himself that there was "something in the fellow" (p. 121). Réal represents duty, commitment to causes, and is in this closely comparable to Blunt, his counterpart in *The Arrow of Gold*. He is a son of royalist parents executed by the Revolution, who runs away to sea and, through rigid adherence to this calling, rises to rank in the French Navy. Réal and Peyrol are alike in that they both avoid the Revolution by taking to the sea and in their contempt for the rhetorical dogmatism of the Revolutionary movement. Réal comes to admire in Peyrol this sincerity untainted by political ideologies. "He had developed a liking for old Peyrol, the only man who had nothing to do with the revolution – who had not even seen it at work. The sincere lawlessness of the ex-Brother of the Coast was refreshing" (p. 209). Between Peyrol and Réal there is much of the *alter ego* relationship which is also to be found between Lingard and Jörgenson, between George and Blunt, and generally between Conrad's heroes and their nemeses.

Peyrol's dilemma, closely comparable to Lingard's, is acute. He could, of course, simply let Symons go, but to do so would jeopardize Réal's plan, which involves use of the tartane, news of which Symons will bear back to the English ship. To keep Symons a prisoner on board the tartane (and Peyrol has nowhere else to put him) would result, on the other hand, in his discovery by the conscientious Réal, who would doubtless turn the Englishman over to the authorities. The choice lies therefore between prolonged captivity as a prisoner of war, and possibly death, for either Symons or Réal. Réal has no very strong personal claim upon Peyrol, but the officer represents a patriotic commitment to which the Rover, now settled ashore, is sturdily responsive. "The disinherited soul of that rover ranging for so many years a lawless ocean with the coasts of two continents for a raiding ground, had come back to its crag, circling like a sea-bird in the dusk and longing for a great sea victory for its people" (p. 142). Neither man, the fellow-pirate nor the naval officer, can be sacrificed.

Where George and Lingard each pursue the dilemma to a breaking point, Peyrol finds a solution. He is able to resolve the contradiction, allowing both Symons and Réal to survive. Peyrol releases Symons, thus permitting news of the tartane to reach the English, and turns this to advantage as a means of drawing their attention misleadingly to the ship when it sails bearing Réal's false papers, which it is now hoped the English will capture and take at face value. Peyrol has primed Symons with notions about the tartane, which cause the English captain to give chase. Réal is saved from capture when, against his will, Peyrol sails without him, sacrificing his own life for the Lieutenant's.

The situation at this point is strongly reminiscent of that in *The Secret Sharer*, written over ten years before. The captain of a ship, finding himself unexpectedly visited by another sailor, one for whom he has a strong fellow feeling but who is in imminent danger of captivity by lawful authority, decides to set him free at the cost of considerable personal risk. The Captain's risk in *The Secret Sharer* lies in his close approach to the island to which Leggatt must escape by swimming; in *The Rover* Peyrol's risk is that Symons' return to the English ship will draw the enemy's attention to the tartane – as, indeed, it does. Peyrol's risk, however, is part of his larger intention to assist Réal's mission, for the British ship must chase the tartane, and be deceived by her apparent flight, if the plan is to work.

If we ask why Peyrol succeeds in resolving the tension of his situation, while Lingard fails to balance Carter and Jörgenson, and

George is unable to deal with both Dominic and Blunt, a possible answer lies in this comparison with *The Secret Sharer*. *The Secret Sharer* is itself a re-enactment of the opening situation of *Under Western Eyes*, with the crucial difference that the Captain, unlike Razumov, maintains a scrupulous loyalty to his fugitive visitor. In this way the Captain, through his own successful risk on the other's behalf, achieves the security of his first command. There is a bond between Peyrol and Symons very similar to that between the Captain and Leggatt, such that Peyrol's effort to secure the freedom of his fellow rover justly results in his own subsequent freedom to manoeuvre. After Symons' departure Peyrol is free to give the tartane over to Réal's plan, which he could not do with the English sailor aboard, and through the false information Symons carries back to his ship Peyrol is able to make the plan work.

Having resolved his dilemma and placed himself in a position to help Réal without hurting Symons, Peyrol can now proceed to rescue his heroine. The restoration of Symons to liberty and Peyrol's substitution of himself for Réal on the fatal mission does nothing to remove Scevola from the path of Arlette. Like Lingard and George, Peyrol must also confront and defeat his rival before the heroine can be free. Arlette will be no better off unless her way is cleared of Scevola to permit her marriage to Réal. The scrupulous Lieutenant himself is not up to the problem; his own best answer is the suicidal mission he has voluntarily undertaken after finding himself shamefully in love. In this situation Arlette turns to Peyrol.

The most striking difference between *The Rover* and its two immediate predecessors on the list of Conrad's novels is that here the hero is not the heroine's lover but, being very much older than she, stands in a protective, fatherly relation to her. The pattern common to all three works is somewhat obscured as a result, because Réal, who is actually Peyrol's nemesis, the agent of his fatal involvement in the cause of the country he had abandoned as a boy, survives the story to life happily ever after with the heroine. It is plausible to speculate, at this point, that Conrad was unable to write a full-length novel in which the hero and heroine achieve a full and lasting union; at any rate, he did not do so, and when, in *The Rover*, he allowed the hero to effect a successful rescue of the heroine, he also required the hero's death and substituted another man as her lover. Something very similar happens in *Chance*, where Anthony, although eventually Flora's successful rescuer, is after an interval replaced as her husband by Powell.

Something of the usual relationship between Peyrol and Arlette as hero and heroine is none the less present in *The Rover*, as is evident from this exchange between Payrol and Arlette's Aunt Catherine.

"Don't you know that the first time Arlette saw you she spoke to you and that it was the first time I heard her speak of her own accord since she had been brought back by that man [Scevola], and I had to wash her from head to foot before I put her into her mother's bed."

"The first time," repeated Peyrol.

"It was like a miracle happening," said Catherine, "and it was you that had done it."

"Then it must be some Indian witch has given me the power," muttered Peyrol, so low that Catherine could not hear the words. But she did not seem to care, and presently went on again:

"And the child took to you wonderfully. Some sentiment was aroused in her at last."

"Yes," assented Peyrol grimly. "She did take to me. She learned to talk to – the old man."

"It's something in you that seems to have opened her mind and unloosed her tongue," said Catherine, speaking with a sort of regal composure down at Peyrol, like a chieftainess of a tribe (p. 169).

Catherine, as a person of great experience who also needs the hero's aid, corresponds closely in *The Rover* to D'Alcacer in *The Rescue*. Both are forlorn lovers, disenchanted with their own lives and concerned chiefly with the well-being of the respective heroines. Catherine, in her youth, fell in love vainly with a priest, while D'Alcacer was engaged to marry a young girl who died tragically. Both, as figures of wisdom and experience, are reminiscent of Jim's Stein, another sage figure abruptly deprived of his lover long ago.

What Catherine tells Peyrol is the truth. It was he who had shaken Arlette out of the traumatic somnambulant state induced by her witnessing the bloodbath at Toulon. "Peyrol, unforeseen, unexpected, inexplicable, had given by his mere appearance at Escampobar a moral and even a physical jolt to all her being. . . . He was to her an immense figure, like a messenger from the unknown entering the solitude of Escampobar; something immensely strong, with inexhaustible power, unaffected by familiarity and remaining invincible" (p. 219). This arousal to awareness of her surroundings is a necessary precondition for Arlette's later response to Réal, much as the strength and reliability she senses in Peyrol are to be the means of her rescue. Thus, although Peyrol neither aspires to be Arlette's lover nor survives with her at the end of the story, he is plainly her hero in the sense that it is he, and not Réal, who brings her back to life and removes the obstacle of Scevola from her path to happiness.

Peyrol's rescue of Arlette is singularly effective. Anthony, Heyst, George and Lingard all carry out rescues whose successes are limited or temporary, but Peyrol makes Arlette's release permanent and complete. Again we may ask why Peyrol should be successful where almost all others fail, and again the answer takes us back to the episode of Symons' escape from the tartane, an episode which at first perhaps appears to be a detail of the plot, but which is in truth its pivotal feature. Symons' escape not only resolves the dilemma of Peyrol's universe, allowing him to keep faith at once with both sides of his nature, but also provides symbolically the means whereby Peyrol rescues Arlette. In the course of his escape Symons contrives to lock Scevola in the cabin of the tartane, where he had himself been confined by Peyrol, thus as it were leaving Scevola as a prisoner in his place. Peyrol, finding his rival placed at his mercy as a more or less direct result of his lenience towards Symons, takes full advantage of the turn of events. Scevola is taken unwillingly to sea on the tartane's last voyage and killed, along with Peyrol, when the English ship attacks. Peyrol's liberation of Symons is therefore morally central to the story. Like the Captain's loyalty to Leggatt in *The Secret Sharer*, it is the key to his success. Both George and Lingard fall short of this standard in their relations with the equivalent figures in their own stories; George and Dominic part company after George has disappointed his comrade by abandoning their ship, and Lingard's failure to trust Carter with the details of his plans results in the latter's dangerous attack on the native ships against Lingard's interests. Peyrol releases Symons to full freedom, and as a result finds his rival delivered cleanly into his hands.

The dramatic structure of this tale, despite its differences from the other two, is broadly the same three-part arrangement that is to be seen in *The Arrow of Gold* and *The Rescue*. The longish opening section of the story lays out the circumstances of the plot and is primarily concerned to introduce the two conflicting poles of the hero's life. It concludes with the departure of Symons, much as the corresponding movement in *The Arrow of Gold* ends with Dominic's disappearance, and that in *The Rescue* with Carter's independent action against Lingard's allies. In each case the hero parts ways at this point with the figure who represents his adopted life of sea adventure, the difference being that Peyrol's parting is voluntary and morally satisfactory, whereas both the other two separations are the result of accidents or misunderstandings and reflect the heroes' lack of control.

In the shorter second movement the hero confronts his rival and wins his heroine. Peyrol's case here is particularly close to that of Lingard, for each man has his rival at one point a prisoner on his ship. The confrontation in all three novels concludes when the heroine falls into the hero's arms. In Peyrol's case this occurs very briefly, and he literally hands Arlette over to Réal a page later (pp. 248–9).

The final movement features the action of the nemesis, represented in *The Rover* by Réal, the French officer whose place Peyrol takes on the fatal mission. Just as George is seriously wounded by Blunt and Lingard has his plans nullified by Jörgenson, so Peyrol is induced to die by Réal. In each case the disaster derives from the hero's commitment to a cause and is brought about by an agent of that cause, the difference being that in Peyrol's case the catastrophe is planned and accepted. Peyrol, like Wagner's Wotan, foresees and desires his end, knowing that it rounds off his life to a full close. At the end of his story, with Arlette safe and Symons free, Peyrol, the former pirate, is admitted to have been "not a bad Frenchman" after all (p. 286).

It is perhaps no more than coincidental that Conrad's career as a novelist closes in a major key with the ending of *The Rover*, one of his few stories and his only full-length novel apart from *The Shadow-Line*, in which the hero both succeeds in his object and balances satisfactorily his own account with fate. Peyrol dies in the process, but he does so willingly, under no compulsion beyond his feeling for Arlette and his patriotism, and he is, besides, an old man whose natural course has been run. Peyrol's age is crucial to the tone of the novel. He cannot be compared directly to heroes like Jim, or even Verloc, who are cut off in mid career. Peyrol's active life is ended before the story begins, with his decision to retire ashore, and all that remains for him to do is to meet the obligation to the homeland to which he now returns after a lifetime at sea. There is a sense of balance at the end of *The Rover*, a sense, unequalled in any of

Conrad's other full-length novels, that the hero's achievements are well worth the price he had paid for them, a sense increased by the way in which the final pages of the novel focus upon the happiness of the survivors, Réal and Arlette, and upon their fond memories of Peyrol.

18 *Suspense*

Suspense, intended to be the great work of Conrad's late years, truncated as it remains, is somewhat longer than *The Rover*. Conrad began planning this story even before the days of *Chance* and set to work seriously upon it in 1920. Its conception therefore overlaps that of *The Arrow of Gold* and its composition was merely suspended during the writing of *The Rover*. The work, which shows promise of surpassing everything he had written since *The Shadow-Line*, was probably no more than half-way to its conclusion at the point where Conrad left it.

If we may assume that Conrad would not have altered radically what he had already written in bringing it to completion, we can relate *Suspense* structurally to the other novels of the last phase. Cosmo, the hero, is particularly like George and Peyrol in that, on his arrival in Europe in 1815, he is one who has managed to live away from the strife which has long upset the lives of the inhabitants among whom he now finds himself. Just as Peyrol, by living at sea, has avoided the turmoil of the French Revolution, so Cosmo, in the security of his remote English ancestral home, has escaped the chaos of the Napoleonic Wars. (He has indeed served under Wellington in Spain, but he has not been subject to the uprootings and conflicts of loyalties affecting the French and Italian characters of the story.) On his arrival in Genoa he meets a woman, Adèle, to whom he is attracted and whose life has been deeply involved in the affairs his own absence has avoided. Her place in the story relative to the hero seems in this respect closely akin to that of Arlette in relation to Peyrol and to that of Rita in relation to George. She appears to stand for the difficulties of life from which the wandering hero has so far preserved himself, and it is partly on her account that he is becoming embroiled in these affairs by the time the story breaks off. Cosmo cannot rest for thinking of Adèle, takes to roaming the streets at night, and is consequently caught up in Attilio's mission to deliver secret papers to Napoleon on Elba.

Napoleon, the exiled prince, hangs over the events of *Suspense* much as Don Carlos hovers in the background of *The Arrow of Gold* and as Hassim moves in the political situation of *The Rescue*. The prince represents in each case the particular cause from which the hero has so far held aloof, but to which, as the story takes off, he becomes committed. Cosmo has hitherto maintained a neutral attitude towards Napoleon, willing as an Englishman to oppose him militarily but refusing to deny his greatness or to belittle his importance. By the end of the manuscript Cosmo has already drifted into the company of Bonapartist conspirators, and his further engagement in the Emperor's cause seems most likely.

As Adèle is the heroine, so Count Helion, her husband, is the hero's rival, the unsympathetic male with a socially-sanctioned prior claim upon her. Like Ortega, he is insanely jealous; like Travers, he is rich, narrow-minded and powerful; and like Scevola he is associated with violence and revolution. Cosmo instinctively dislikes him, much as Lingard dislikes Travers and Peyrol dislikes Scevola. The story is interrupted before the two men have a chance to express their antagonism; it does not reach what, by analogy with the pattern of the three last novels, we might suppose to have been its intended second movement, in which Cosmo would have openly challenged Count Helion for possession of Adèle.

Caught between Cosmo and the Count, Adèle is typical of the heroines of the last phase. Her early life was one of sharp contrasts; just as Rita was moved from the austerity of her rustic origins to the luxury of Allègre's household, so Adèle has experienced both the comforts of aristocratic life during the *ancien régime* and the hardships of exile during the Reign of Terror. She was compromised in her marriage to the Count, which she accepted in order to win her parents' financial security, much as Edith married Travers in hopes of escaping boredom, and as Arlette tacitly accepted Scevola's protection to avoid persecution during the Revolution. As a result, like Rita, Mrs Travers and Arlette, Adèle has, by the time the story begins, abstracted herself emotionally from the world around her. Presumably she, like the other three heroines, would be re-awakened by the hero in the course of the novel, but whether Adèle would be set free, like Arlette, or, like Mrs Travers, obliged to return to her adopted course of life, is impossible to guess.

As Adèle stands between Helion and Cosmo, so Cosmo himself, like the other heroes of the last novels, would almost certainly have emerged as caught between two strong masculine figures, one representing his habitual life of non-involvement, the other his incipient commitment to the Napoleonic cause. The figure of this commitment is clearly Attilio, the Bonapartist conspirator whom Cosmo meets in the first pages of the novel, to whom he is unaccountably attracted, and in whose plots he had, by the point where Conrad left the story, become actively embroiled. The identity of the putative representative of Cosmo's disengagement is less clear. Two possible candidates appear in the story, Sir Charles Latham (Cosmo's father) and Dr Martel, but neither is sufficiently developed for his role to be definite. The strong and protective figure of Sir Charles appears only retrospectively, and the Doctor's role, as it stands, is ambivalent. Of the two, Martel, since he is on the spot and concerned in Cosmo's immediate doings, is the more likely choice. The Doctor does attempt to persuade Cosmo to leave Genoa and to forget Adèle, and it is possible that his visit to Adèle after Cosmo's disappearance would have produced some result analogous to Carter's intervention after Lingard's departure ashore in *The Rescue*.

Although Conrad's last novels are written to a basic structural pattern which seems to be shared by *Suspense*, it is not possible to infer from this the ending of the unfinished story. The last novels differ from one another in details, particularly in the moods and events of their endings. We cannot guess, for instance, whether Cosmo would triumph like Peyrol or fail like Lingard, whether he would die like the old French pirate or survive like George, or whether Adèle would be set free from her loveless marriage or constrained to live with its consequences. The patterns of Conrad's stories often remain stable while the author experiments with moral and emotional variations. It is also possible that *Suspense*, planned as it was on a grand scale, would have taken Conrad, had he lived to finish it, into yet another radical reconsideration of his fictional structure.

Part VI An Overview

We have followed a developing and changing pattern of characters and concepts through Conrad's major fictional works from his first apprentice-piece to the novel interrupted by his death. This pattern consists essentially in the arrangement of a few central character types with respect to a background of dualistic conflict. In Conrad's earliest works the conflict is a relatively simple racial antithesis of black and white, but this merges, in *The Nigger of the 'Narcissus'* and *Heart of Darkness*, into a conceptual opposition of discipline and licence, a duality which is carried into the political novels as the dilemma of a hero caught between the call of duty or humanity to involve himself in worldly affairs, and his own well justified sense that such a commitment may have fatal consequences.

The chief character, from first to last, is the hero who moves between the two poles of the conflict as between two worlds. (Up until the stories of 1910 the heroine, when present, is identified unambiguously with one side or the other, but thereafter she, much like the hero, becomes a disengaged figure subject to conflicting impulses.) The hero's problems begin when he attempts some form of compromise between the two poles of his world, either by moving under morally dubious circumstances from one to the other, or by committing himself to one side without properly discharging his obligations to the other. His pursuit of the heroine is generally tied to this compromise, either as its cause (as in *The Arrow of Gold*), or as a consequence (as in *Lord Jim*). The immediate result of the hero's relationship with the heroine is his provocation of a male rival and, sometimes, of a jealous or hostile female opponent, the anti-heroine, as well. The ultimate outcome of the compromise is the hero's confrontation by a figure of nemesis, normally a character from one of the worlds against which he has offended and an embodiment of his chief moral failings.

The pattern therefore devolves upon what is for the hero a paradoxical situation. Caught between two worlds, he finds his every attempt to move towards either one negated and frustrated by a force from the other. The negating force takes many shapes, but in most of the stories it is finally embodied in the nemesis who, in his classic form, represents both a perverted image of the hero's strivings in the world he has chosen and an effective retribution from the world the hero has deserted. This systematic and almost inflexible negation of human effort, because it is central to all his major works, we have called the Conradian paradox, the anomaly that the hero's very attempt to achieve appears, in Conrad's universe, to involve his failure.

The number of Conrad's stories which neither exhibit a recognizable version of the full conceptual pattern, nor explore some part or aspect of it, nor relate clearly to one of the major novels, is small. These, the titles mentioned only to be set aside in the foregoing discussion, can be shortly listed: *The Black Mate, The Idiots, The Brute, Prince Roman, The Partner, The Inn of the Two Witches, The Warrior's Soul* and *The Tale*. These stories total only eight, less than a fifth of the forty-four fictional titles for which Conrad is solely responsible; and, since they are all among his shorter works, the actual proportion of his output which these exceptions represent is very small. They are, besides, among his most minor pieces, stories which have no unusual merit and which have attracted critical attention only as incidental productions of an author whose greatness lies elsewhere. It therefore seems fair to conclude that this pattern of compromise and paradox was Conrad's chief and constant concern as an architect of the imagination.

Examination of Conrad's treatment of this pattern through the chronological sequence of his works reveals much about his artistic development. Most obvious is his changing conception of the hero's role, with reference to which we have divided Conrad's work into four main phases following the apprentice-period of his two first novels:

(*a*) *The early novels.* The two first heroes, Almayer and Willems, are self-involved figures activated primarily by greed and ambition, whose frustrated strivings have little effect beyond themselves.

(*b*) *The first mature phase.* The heroes from Wait to Whalley are much sharper delineations of the Conradian notion of compromise because they are themselves figures of paradox, being at once both strong and weak, idealistic and appetitive, noble and base. Each of these heroes images in himself the universal conflict in which he becomes involved. His actions are correspondingly ambivalent, being at once successful and excessive, brilliant and fatal.

(*c*) *The second phase.* The heroes of the second mature phase, which coincides with what is generally known as the period of Conrad's "political" novels, are still figures of paradox, but unlike their predecessors they attempt to avoid involvement in the conflict which rages in their environment. These heroes compromise only when, under pressure from others, they are persuaded to take action and, in so doing, to put at risk their own confortable neutrality.

(*d*) *The third phase*. The heroes of the previous phase are morally weak in so far as their initial neutrality and their efforts to maintain it are achieved at the expense of others (particularly the sacrificial figures with whom each hero is associated). The new heroes attempt a blameless neutrality by withdrawal from the world. Such are the virtual hermits Heyst, Anthony and Renouard, and such is the retiring, inactive Captain in *The Shadow-Line*. These men compromise their non-involvement, not through fear or cupidity, but from broadly humanitarian motives, generally in order to effect a "rescue".

(*e*) *The final phase*. The heroes of the last novels are also would-be rescuers, but are voluntary outcasts rather than hermits. They are caught squarely between the call of a free and morally independent form of life and the demands of a "cause" to which they become attached by circumstance, a conflict in each case imaged as between the interests of sea and land.

This progression shows that, within his pattern of conflict and compromise, Conrad was vitally concerned with the value of purposive action. The two early novels exhibit relatively simply the framework of Conrad's universe, the unspoken belief that action in pursuit of an end provokes its nemesis. The novels of the first phase explore the ambivalence of human purposes, showing in men like Kurtz and Jim that the best motives may give rise to the basest actions and that an exceptional man can be at once a danger and an inspiration. The political novels look at the special case of the exceptional man who, like Nostromo and Razumov, seeks to hide his light under a bushel. The hero who avoids decisive action and attempts to live in the shadows without committing himself on the issues which polarize his world is shown to be morally culpable. He is also seen to be unable to maintain his stance of neutrality; events recoil upon him, forcing him into a precipitous and perilous involvement, which in turn brings him, like his predecessors, to a catastrophic meeting with his nemesis.

The issue of commitment, first raised in the political novels, is further isolated for scrutiny in the novels of the third phase, where the heroes, Heyst, Anthony, Renouard and the Captain in *The Shadow-Line*, are men whose deliberate non-involvement in human affairs is neither dangerous nor parasitic. The sacrificial figures disappear from these novels, where the heroes' neutrality is achieved harmlessly. These men are persuaded to compromise their withdrawal from the world, not by threats and external pressures, as are Nostromo, Verloc and Razumov, but by a sense of compassion or duty. The introduction of the victimized heroine, whose rescue by the hero is the mainspring of the plot, underlines the selflessness of these men. Yet in two cases out of the four (Heyst and Renouard) the nemesis which the hero faces as a direct result of his action is fatal, and in another case (that of Anthony) the fatality is merely deferred.

The question of obligation versus personal freedom raised in *Chance* and *Victory* is polarized in the last novels, where each hero is caught between his wish to maintain a free and independent existence and the sense that he ought to play his part in the affairs of his fellow men. Here the compromise consists in the hero's reluctant participation in some political conflict (the rescue of the heroine, in these stories, being a separate issue), and again active involvement provokes a swift and disastrous nemesis.

There is a progressive conceptual intensification through the sequence of Conrad's major works, from the simple racial dualism of the early novels to the much more complex situations of the later heroes. The early novels present heroes (Almayer and Willems) who desert or betray the strict standards of the white world in the ultimately vain hopes of facile success in the black. Little more is involved than the illicit compromise of the easy option and its inevitable retribution. In the next phase, however, Conrad conceptualizes the question of ease versus stringency which emerges from the racial conflicts of the early Malayan stories. The background of contrasting black and white ways is retained in *The Nigger of the 'Narcissus'*, *Heart of Darkness* and *Lord Jim*, but in each of these stories the hero's movement between the two worlds is a symptom or externalization of the conflict imaged in his character between a strict ideal or code of duty and an egotistic will to achieve the personal glory of success without the risk and difficulty of following the conventionally prescribed course. The original conflict of ease and industry exemplified in Almayer thus becomes in Wait, Kurtz and Jim a conflict of licence versus discipline, the personal will versus duty and obligation.

The polarity of licence and discipline is represented in these stories by the disposition around the hero of the secondary characters. The heroines (Kurtz' native woman and Jewel) serve to draw him into the world of his compromise. The rivals in these stories (Donkin, the Manager and Cornelius) are men whom the hero encounters in the course of his compromised pursuits, men engaged in the same line of dubious conduct, but without what Marlow calls the "redeeming idea" which maintains our sympathy for the hero. On the other side, opposed to these and representing the code or ideal from which the hero has lapsed, are the anti-heroine (Kurtz' Intended) and the figures of nemesis (Allistoun, Marlow in *Heart of Darkness*, and Brown).

Of these nemesis figures the two former are straightforward symbols of rectitude, but with Brown Conrad introduces a new variety, the nemesis who confronts the hero with an exaggerated image of his own failures. Whereas Allistoun and Marlow outface their respective heroes by contrast, confronting deviation with probity and licence with discipline, Brown defeats Jim in a more complex way by showing him, not the standard from which the hero has departed, but the moral implications of his departure. Brown is Jim–Jim without the redeeming idea, but still an aspect of the hero's compromised self. Most of the subsequent nemesis figures are of Brown's type rather than Allistoun's, confronting the heroes with self-comparisons rather than contrasts. Such are Massy, Hirsch, Nikita, Jones, the deceased Captain in *The Shadow-Line*, and Jörgenson.

The effect of this alteration in the nemesis role is to make the hero's final opponent more clearly an outcome of his compromise and less of a mere retribution. Lingard in *An Outcast of the Islands* and Allistoun in *The Nigger of the 'Narcissus'* simply reassert the disciplinary authority which the hero has flouted, straightforwardly imposing restraint on those who have run to excess. Brown, Nikita, Jones and their like, while still achieving this restraining effect, do so by carrying out the implications of the hero's compromise to its nefarious logical end. In this way the reader is shown more clearly the self-destructive nature of the hero's adopted course.

The result of Conrad's development of the nemesis type intro-

duced by Brown is a deepening of the paradox of his plots. On the
one hand, as the nemesis becomes malicious and the hero's moral
inferior, our sympathy for the hero as a man of contrastingly good
intentions rises in proportion. On the other hand the development
of an obvious *alter ego* relationship between the hero and the
nemesis-villain intensifies our awareness of the darker, evil side of
the hero's nature.

As the evil in the plot is gathering around the nemesis figure, the
hero becomes less and less culpable in his motives. The novels of the
first phase are in this respect transitional, taking us from the avowed
selfishness of Willems and Wait to the self-denying purpose of
Whalley and the laudable humanitarian aims with which Gould,
the last major hero of the first-phase type, embarks upon his
compromise. The step into the next phase, taken in the character of
Nostromo and in the succeeding political novels, continues this
direction as the hero attempts to evade culpability altogether by
abstaining from commitment.

In the first phase Conrad examines the moral paradox of
purposive action; in the next, the political phase, he shows that the
paradox is generally not averted by avoidance of open activity. The
focus shifts, with Nostromo and his successors, from the moral
paradox to the logically prior question of commitment. Action may
be ambivalent, but may its attendant evils not be escaped if one
declines to take any significant action at all? Where Wait, Kurtz,
Jim and Gould make themselves conspicuous in pursuit of clear
objectives, Nostromo, Verloc and Razumov try to base their
livelihoods on refusal to act in such a way as to affect the course of
events. By avoiding the commitment entailed in purposive action
they hope also to avoid the responsibility for evil.

The hope proves vain in every case, and Conrad appears decided
that the stance of non-involvement cannot in practice be maintained. Nostromo, Verloc and Razumov are each forced by
circumstances to take compromising action. Conrad's point, however, is not so much that the action itself is dangerous as that the
attempt to avoid it is both perilous and shameful. To this end he
creates new sorts of characters, the sacrificial males (Decoud, Stevie
and Haldin), and the suffering women (Teresa Viola, Winnie's
mother and Mrs Haldin), all of whom are directly or indirectly
victims of the hero's efforts to maintain his neutrality. At the same
time, and to much the same end, Conrad revitalizes the heroine's
role. In the political novels the rather pale and stereotypical

heroines of the earlier works are replaced by deeper and fuller creations (Emilia, Winnie and Natalia) who oppose to the hero's effort at aloofness from human affairs a vital concern for the welfare of at least some of their fellow beings.

Already in the political novels the moral centre of the story is shifting from what the hero actually does to the more general issue of man's responsibility for man, a responsibility each of these heroes puts aside even before he undertakes his compromising action. The act of compromise is no longer the moral focus of the story, although it remains the turning-point of the action. Verloc's attempt on the Observatory and the subsequent sacrifice of Stevie are the outcome of an attitude and way of life he has already adopted. The same is true of Nostromo and his taking charge of the lighter, with the resultant death of Decoud, and of Razumov's betrayal of Haldin. These heroes deserve their fate not simply because of the compromises which provoke their respective figures of nemesis but more fundamentally because of the immorality entailed in their very attempts to avoid the compromise of commitment to some human group or party.

The seal is set on this phase by *The Secret Sharer*, where the hero escapes an unpleasant end and succeeds in establishing his own position precisely by taking full responsibility for another man. Instead of re-enacting Razumov's betrayal of Haldin he puts himself at risk to secure the safety of his visitor. As a result both compromise and nemesis are averted, and the paradox presented by Leggatt resolves itself with his free departure. The terms of the story, in which a strong *alter ego* relationship is established between Leggatt and the hero, show that already Conrad viewed responsibility to others as responsibility to one's self.

The interest in commitment manifested as responsibility for others leads clearly into the third phase, with its emphasis upon the rescue motif. Here the hero's neutrality becomes a studied withdrawal from society, and the sacrificial, victimized figures fade from the scene to be effectively replaced by the persecuted heroine whom the hero must try to save. In each case the heroes, Anthony, Heyst and Renouard, are initially blameless; their aloofness and withdrawal harm no one. Yet each hero, from motives of pure sympathy, engages in compromising action for the heroine's sake.

In these stories the moral focus returns to the compromise, which is now also an act of rescue. In the third phase the hero compromises a blameless and reasonably sympathetic withdrawal, which is very

different from the dubious neutralities of his immediate predecessors, by re-entering the world of action with the largely
praiseworthy intention of rescuing a victimized and suffering fellow
creature. The ironies deepen as the hero's initial withdrawal is
portrayed as more eremitical than self-seeking and as his nemesis is
the direct result of an act of rescue. Even so, the characteristically
Conradian balance of paradox is maintained. The hero's rejection
of the world, although innocent, is still presented as a course
impossible for a good man to follow consistently; Heyst, Anthony
and Renouard, just because they are sensitive and intelligent
enough to turn their backs upon the evils of society, are unable to
ignore the sufferings of others. Moreover, the rescues in which these
heroes become involved as a result of their hyper-sensitivity are, in
the cases of Anthony and Heyst, complicated by sexual attraction.
Altruistic human sympathy is not the only motive prompting these
lonely bachelors to carry off young women, and the consequent
difficulties are, at least in part, the outcome of the heroes' surrender
of their principles to their desires.

The heroes of the third phase are required to act, to compromise
their secure withdrawal by involvement in human affairs; yet the
action, however well-intentioned, is dangerous. Two heroes, Heyst
and Renouard, die as a direct result, and a third, Anthony, soon dies
accidentally and has his place taken by another. The fatal danger of
compromising action is imaged in the figure of Ransome, the weak-
hearted man who will die if he exerts himself. Action is demanded of
these heroes by circumstances, as it is of Ransome, yet because of
their weaknesses the action proves deadly.

Ransome shows that the paradox in this phase goes deeper, for
the heroes die of action, not because the action is dangerous *per se*,
but because, like Ransome, they are already susceptible. Ransome's
weakness is physical, his unstable heart, but that of Anthony, Heyst
and Renouard is temperamental. These are not ordinary men, but
men whose unusual refinements of sensibility, the same which
originally drove them to solitude, make them particularly vulnerable. They do not die simply from the consequences of their
compromising actions but also from their own excessive reactions to
them. Heyst and Renouard both commit suicide, and Anthony
choses to stay aboard his sinking ship when he might have been
rescued. Contact with the world destroys these heroes only because
their unworldly standards of goodness, the same which dictate their

initial withdrawals, deprive them of the resilience of lesser men.

The paradox of Wait and Jim, the paradox of unusual abilities combined with fatal moral weakness, thus reappears slightly altered in the heroes of the third phase. Anthony, Heyst and Renouard are men whose special perception of the evils of common life first prompts them to retreat and later makes them fatally vulnerable to pursuit. The rescue they attempt is the compromise of their principles which, by renewing their contact with the rejected world, opens the channel along which their doom pursues them.

Conrad neither endorses nor denies the view of the world taken by these heroes. Events prove too well how just are their original perceptions of worldly evil. Yet this same perception is an excess of sensibility which renders each of them unable to withstand the shock of contact when his attempted rescue brings mundane reality into his eremitical retreat. The rescue itself is at once wrong, in that it is defection from a principle which guarantees the hero's personal safety, and right in that it proves the hero's humanity and so provides the basis for the reader's sympathy. The rescue attempt, moreover, is a direct outcome of the hero's unusual perception of common evils; he is impelled to renew contact with the world by the selfsame faculty which first commands his isolation.

The compromising rescue and the paradox of the hero who is both superior to the world and vulnerable before it are the continuing preoccupations of the last novels. The superiority of these heroes is somewhat muted, however, as the piratical leanings of George, Lingard and Peyrol replace the almost saintly withdrawals of Anthony and Heyst. The heroes of the last phase are more outlaws than hermits, although, once again, the reader is encouraged to share their jaundiced view of the society they have abandoned. Less ethereal in motive than their predecessors, these heroes are hardier types; two of them survive failure and resume their outcast lives, while the third, Peyrol, dies in the course of an ultimately successful plan of action.

The chief distinguishing features of the last novels are structural. Conrad here sets out in a rearrangement of character-types the chief concepts which had evolved through the second and third phases. The hero remains, like his predecessors from Nostromo through to Renouard, a man of solitary independence. Conrad now makes him a seaman (following, in this respect, the direction of *The Shadow-Line*), and employs a series of fellow sailors (Dominic, Carter and

Symons) to stand for this life of disengaged freedom. Yet the hero, as a man of action, is unable to resist the impulse to involve himself in the shabby but serious political conflicts of landsmen (Carlism, Hassim's alliance, and the French Revolution), and in so doing he provokes a nemesis (represented successively by Blunt, Jörgenson and Réal) who identifies himself unreservedly, almost fanatically, with the cause. The hero's engagement in the cause is an act of compromise which divides him from his fellow seamen and which results in a catastrophic confrontation with the nemesis. The catastrophe comes about, as in the cases of Heyst and Renouard, because the hero is too intelligent, too sensitive and independent a spirit, to commit himself wholly to the political cause.

The heroine's part becomes more complex in these last stories. No longer simply an object of rescue, she now appears as a reflection of the hero, herself caught between the ties and obligations of her background and a will to exercise her growing freedom of spirit. The hero becomes the focus for her aspiration to independence, while her association with him, and his attempt to rescue her from the constraints of her environment, provoke the opposition of a rival.

The rivals of the last phase (Ortega, Travers and Scevola), while still obvious descendants of Omar and Cornelius, are more complex figures fulfilling a dual role. To the heroine the rival represents the ties of the world; to the hero he is the embodiment not only of sexual rivalry but also of the evils from which, before his compromise, he had cut adrift.

The hero in these stories has three alternatives, each unsatisfactory, represented respectively by the rival, the fellow seaman, and the nemesis. The rival represents the worst aspects of the world of the hero's origin, the bitter, grasping, jealous world he has rejected and abandoned. The fellow seaman stands for the life the hero choses, free and disengaged, but tainted with outlawry and, as the relationship with the heroine shows, emotionally incomplete. There remains the better side of human affairs, action accompanied by a "redeeming idea", to which the hero is drawn from his isolation. The idea, unrestrained by the sound common sense with which the hero is normally endowed, runs, like that of Kurtz, readily to excess and overtopples into a near fanaticism which the hero cannot accept. As a result the exponent of the idea becomes the hero's nemesis, confronting him with accusations of defection and disloyalty. Two of these heroes, George and Lingard, are in the end returned, empty and dissatisfied, to their lonely isolation. Peyrol, a special case, resolves his dilemma, but at the expense of his life.

A general view of Conrad's stories cannot fail to be impressed with the heavily ironic cast of his universe and the frequency with which his heroes meet tragic ends. Yet *The Rover* is not the only work to conclude on a positive note. In each of Conrad's mature phases there is at least one story in which the hero triumphs. In the first phase the failures of Wait and Jim are reversed by MacWhirr and Falk; in the second, the betrayal committed by Razumov is avoided by the Captain in *The Secret Sharer*; in the third, the Captain in *The Shadow-Line* successfully confronts the world which destroyed Anthony and Heyst; and in the final phase Peyrol, although at the cost of his life, defeats his enemies and achieves the heroine's rescue. This sequence of exceptions is of particular importance because it shows what, at each stage, Conrad felt to be the conditions for the hero's avoidance of his nemesis and for the resolution of the paradox to which most men fall victim.

The heroes of the first phase are supermen whose faults are excesses which grow directly from their virtues, from their unusual qualities of leadership and idealism. The men who succeed where these fail do so not because they are greater, but precisely because, being lesser men, they are under no real temptation to fall into the excesses which destroy their more remarkable colleagues. Falk and MacWhirr, the two heroes of this phase who survive, are simple, almost single-minded men, who are wholly untouched by the idealism, the urge to greatness, which motivates Wait, Kurtz and Jim. In MacWhirr's literalism and Falk's appetite Conrad deliberately offers a subhuman contrast to the fatal superhumanity of the other heroes of the first phase. By such dogmatic pragmatism as Falk and MacWhirr display, Conrad appears to say, the paradox of purposive action can be avoided.

The successful hero of the second mature phase is the Captain in *The Secret Sharer*. Because of the strong similarity between his case and that of Razumov in *Under Western Eyes*, it is clear that the source of his triumph lies in his response to Leggatt's appeal and his consistent loyalty to the fugitive. Leggatt, the last of a line of victimized male figures in the political novels, is saved, not sacrificed, by his hero. For this fidelity to a fellow man the Captain is excused the nemesis which overtakes his predecessors, Nostromo, Verloc, and Razumov.

In the third phase the only hero to meet unqualified success is the Captain in *The Shadow-Line*, a story whose common autobiographical root with *The Secret Sharer* is more than coincidental. Anthony's achievement is limited, both by the part played in it by Powell and by his own premature demise, and both Heyst and Renouard, as suicides, are utterly defeated in their encounters with a callous world. The Captain avoids their fate, having accepted the responsibility of command, by maintaining and reviving the energetic Burns whilst at the same time regretfully parting with the incurably debilitated Ransome. The meaning of the story, conveyed chiefly throgh these two secondary characters, is that the key to successful action lies in the kind of aggressive confrontation advocated by Burns, and in denial of the urge to withdraw, conserve and remain passive represented by Ransome. The Captain's eventual acceptance of the necessity for vigorous action and of an element of risk therewith contrasts with the defensive, indecisive measures taken against adversity by Anthony, Heyst and Renouard; and it is surely for this reason that the Captain alone of the group emerges triumphant.

Of the heroes of the final phase all survive the endings of their stories except Peyrol, yet Peyrol is the only one of them whose career results in success. Peyrol alone not only dismisses his rival but also effectually confronts his nemesis and releases the heroine to a life of happiness. Because of his age and calm state of mind, his death before the end of the novel only limits to a small degree the extent of his victory.

Peyrol's triumph is closely bound up with his fidelity to both Symons and Réal, his successful resolution of the conflicting claims of sea and land, of his past independence and his present commitments. Where George and Lingard, in attempting to balance two worlds, manage only to alienate or betray both, Peyrol is able to pay his debt to the country of his origin, represented by Réal, without breaking faith with his own former lawless way of life, represented by Symons, the ex-pirate who now belongs to the naval force of a hostile power.

The various functions of these few exceptional tales in the context of Conrad's work are brought to a focus by chronology. Putting aside the doubtful case of the unfinished *Suspense*, placing in order the titles of the remaining mature stories, and separating those with the "happy endings" just discussed, we arrive at the following list:

> *The Nigger of the 'Narcissus'*
> *Heart of Darkness*
> *Lord Jim*
>
> *The End of the Tether*

Typhoon
Falk

> *Nostromo*
> *The Secret Agent*
> *Under Western Eyes*

The Secret Sharer

> *Chance*
> *Victory*
> *The Planter of Malata*

The Shadow-Line

> *The Arrow of Gold*
> *The Rescue*

The Rover

A rough pattern emerges wherein, at or close to the end of each of the mature phases of his work, Conrad changes his mood and writes one or two stories from which the usual ironies are absent. The result is a dialogue; each group of stories poses a particular problem, to which some kind of solution is eventually proposed in an exceptional tale of a successful hero. The next group of stories then incorporates this solution, but also generates a new problem and so on.

Typhoon and *Falk* resolve the paradox of idealistic success presented in *The Nigger of the 'Narcissus'*, *Heart of Darkness* and *Lord Jim*. The offered solution is a rigorous pragmatism and studied avoidance of idealization. The political novels feature heroes whose efforts to avoid purposive action are an echo of the pedestrian common sense of MacWhirr and Falk, a determined avoidance of dangerous extremes. The new problem arises from the conspicuous selfishness of this neutrality, a selfishness which results in the sacrifices of Decoud, Stevie and Haldin, and which is ended only when the Captain in *The Secret Sharer* takes decisive responsibility for the safety of Leggatt.

The Captain's selfless intervention on Leggatt's behalf initiates the series of "rescues" which characterizes the novels of the next phase. As if hoping to emulate the Captain's triumph, succeeding heroes, beginning with Anthony and Heyst, compromise their withdrawal from the world by deliberately rescuing and taking with them at least one other person. The selfishness of the second phase is thereby avoided, but through the act of rescue something of the idealism of the first phase has crept back into the hero's character. No longer selfish in his neutrality, the new hero becomes a rescuer and, particularly in Heyst's case, a would-be saviour of beleaguered individuals from the persecutions of the world. But in setting himself up, not only apart from the world, but also in opposition to it, the third-phase hero at once provokes a reaction and, as an unsupported individual, leaves himself especially vulnerable to attack.

Anthony, Heyst and Renouard are at an opposite extreme to the first-phase heroes. Men such as Wait, Kurtz and Jim fail because their ideals involve them too much in the world, thus both provoking rivalry and falling into excess. By the time of *Chance* and *Victory* the Conradian hero has turned his back on the world; his ideal (which he now compromises in rescuing others) has become withdrawal, and his only excess, which results in his particular vulnerability, is his utter unworldliness and isolation.

At the end of the third phase the Captain in *The Shadow-Line* reverses this enfeebling trend by coming actively to grips with the malicious world (represented by the spirit of the dead commander) and by parting as a result with the well-intentioned but weak figure of Ransome. Ransome, the man who is at once the best sailor on board and yet barred by his malady from active duty, is the emblem of the third-phase heroic type, the man of exceptional intelligence and sensibility who is yet ineffective and unable to rise to the demands of worldly situations.

The departure of Ransome heralds the hero of the final phase, a man who likes his independence but who is not unwilling to take up residence among men ashore and to involve himself actively in their causes. George, Lingard, Peyrol, and, perhaps, Cosmo, are all men who have turned their backs on their native worlds to become wanderers and, in some cases, even outlaws, but none is a committed solitary of the type of Anthony and Heyst. Their problem arises, not from any unworldliness, but from the conflicting claims of their independence and of the world they have hitherto ignored.

The wheel has come full circle as the hero becomes once again, like those of the first phase, a man willing to engage actively in causes and the pursuit of ideals. Yet the case of the new hero is not identical with that of Wait or Jim because, as if through the accumulated wisdom of the intermediate protagonists, he is able to balance against the urge to involve himself in the world of human affairs a streak of detached common sense. This restraining factor, associated with the free but essentially self-disciplined life of a sailor, at once saves the hero by holding him back from the excesses of Kurtz and causes his failure by making him fall short of his worldly aims.

The last heroes are therefore placed, rather like Wagner's Wotan, between the conflicting demands of an undesirable duty and the exercise of a slightly disreputable will. Peyrol, like Wotan, discovers that his object can be attained and the conflict resolved only through a resignation of his personal interest. As Wotan fades in *Götterdämmerung* in order that the ring may be wrested from his enemies and harmony restored, so Peyrol dies in *The Rover* to remove Scevola and to preserve his friends from war and persecution. Conrad's final word is paradoxical; that through death comes victory, that worldly achievement can be won only by those prepared to put the world totally aside.

Appendix: Approximate Composition Dates of Conrad's Fiction

Almayer's Folly Sept. 1889 to April 1894
An Outcast of the Islands summer 1894 to Sept. 1895
The Sisters Feb. to March 1896
An Outpost of Progress completed July 1896
The Lagoon written late summer 1896
The Nigger of the 'Narcissus' June 1896 to Feb. 1897
Karain written spring 1897
The Return completed Sept. 1897
Youth completed June 1898
Heart of Darkness Dec. 1898 to Jan. 1899
Lord Jim May 1898 (or earlier) to July 1900
Typhoon Sept. 1900 to Jan. 1901
Falk Jan. 1901 to May 1901
Amy Foster written summer 1901
Tomorrow late 1901 to early 1902
The End of the Tether March to Oct. 1902
Nostromo spring 1902 to Aug. 1904
Gaspar Ruiz late 1904 to late 1905
An Anarchist written late 1905
The Informer written late 1905
The Secret Agent late 1905 to Nov. 1906
Il Conde Nov. to Dec. 1906
The Duel late 1906 to early 1907
Under Western Eyes Dec. 1907 to Dec. 1909
The Secret Sharer Nov. to Dec. 1909
A Smile of Fortune May to Sep. 1910
Freya of the Seven Isles late 1910 to Feb. 1911
Chance spring 1905 (or earlier) to March 1912
Victory April 1912 to May 1914

Because of the Dollars written 1913

The Planter of Malata late 1913 to Jan. 1914

The Shadow-Line written 1915

The Arrow of Gold Aug. 1917 to June 1918

The Rescue begun (as *The Rescuer*) spring 1896 and worked
   sporadically for some five years; completed autumn 1918 to May
   1919

Suspense begun in the autumn of 1912, put aside during the
   composition of *The Rover*, and left unfinished at Conrad's death in
   August 1924

The Rover Dec. 1921 to June 1922

Index

This list includes titles of Conrad's stories and names of his fictional characters. Characters are generally alphabetized under their Christian names, except (as in such cases as Verloc and Razumov) when the surname is more commonly used in the story concerned. In subheadings Conrad's stories are listed chronologically, in the order of their discussion in the text, rather than alphabetically. Page references in bold are the main ones.

THE
VISION
OF
MODERN
DANCE

THE
VISION
OF
MODERN
DANCE

Edited by
Jean Morrison Brown
University of New Hampshire

Dance Books Ltd
9 Cecil Court, London WC2

To
Janice Stille Hines
Joanna Gewertz Harris
and
Eleanor Lauer

ISBN 0 903102 54 4 (cloth)
     0 903102 55 2 (paper)

First published in the United Kingdom in 1980
by Dance Books Ltd, 9 Cecil Court, London WC2N 4EZ
by arrangement with Princetown Book Company

PREFACE

The history of modern dance is one of strong-minded, independent individuals. The leaders of each succeeding generation, in breaking away from their mentors, created according to their own personalities and times. When these new leaders became established, they in turn became the focus of rebellion by younger dancers, often their company members, who began to choreograph, develop their own techniques and means of artistic expression in movement, and establish their own schools and companies. As a result, the newest modern dance remains true to the spirit of innovation that motivated its originators, although its external form has changed drastically.

In the early days, the search was to gain, in the words of Louis Horst, "inner sensitivity to every one of the body's parts, to the power of its whole and to the space in which it carves designs. The great quest was to find ways to attain this sensitivity and manners in which to discipline it for communication." This was the heritage of the originators, carried on and furthered by their successors.

The evolution of American modern dance over the last seventy-five years reflects conceptual changes that can be found in all the arts. In some cases there has been direct and significant mutual exchange between dancers and other artists. Like the contemporary trends in the other arts, modern dance affords creative individuality through wide-ranging subject matter. The continuing rebellion against the traditional past, as a renewing self-assertion, has brought forth the highly individual statements that characterize the works of present-day artists.

The aesthetics of modern dance lies in the integration of movement and meaning through three-dimensional kinetic design, which is restricted only by the anatomical limits of the human body and the artist's conceptualization. Even at its most expressive, dance is nonliteral, employing abstractions and exaggerations of movement to create an illusion in time-space through the use of force. Spatial design is realized in part by plastic positioning and in part by trace designs created through movement of parts or of the whole body. Rhythmic design is achieved by time-force interactions in space, creating dynamics.

Because dance is a time-space, nonverbal art, many dancers do not express themselves readily in words. Others, however, are most articulate. The early modern dancers seem to have felt an especially strong need to give verbal expression to their beliefs.

The selections presented here are dancers' statements of their philosophies. They span the historical scope of modern dance, from those who paved the way for its development to the present, and reveal the overall changes in modern dance during the twentieth century, which have nevertheless occurred within the framework of a common theoretical outlook. In many cases, a statement, although written at an early period in the artist's development, reflects a philosophy that, in essence, remained unchanged during the course of his or her career. Others simply express a position at one point in the artist's development. Many important dancers are not included, primarily because they have been too busy with dance and dancing to write about it.

The idea for this book came from *Dance as a Theatre Art,* edited by Selma Jeanne Cohen. I was spurred on by the continuing search for a suitable text for my course, Modern Dance I, which is part dance technique and part lecture, at the University of New Hampshire.

No book is a solitary effort. For this one, I wish to thank most sincerely:

Professor David Magidson for the initial push;

Professor Allegra Fuller Snyder for the opportunity to work at UCLA as a Visiting Scholar in the Dance Department, and Professor Emma Lewis Thomas for early suggestions on the manuscript;

Genevieve Oswald and the staff of the Dance Collection at the New York Public Library at Lincoln Center for valuable assistance;

The staff of the Harvard Theatre Collection at Harvard University for the opportunity to use that resource;

Professor Louis Hudon for translation from the French of a manuscript by Isadora Duncan;

Susan Edwards, Joanna Gewertz Harris, Eleanor Lauer, Ernestine Stodelle, Marian Van Tuyl, and Theodora Wiesner for perceptive and thoughtful criticisms and suggestions on the manuscript;

Deborah Jackson for typing and retyping;

Charles Woodford for much patience and assistance;

And last, but never least, my husband, for constant support.

Acknowledgments

Isadora Duncan. *The Art of the Dance.* New York: Theatre Arts Books, 1928. *My Life,* New York: Liveright Publishing Corporation, 1927. Unpublished manuscript, Harvard University Theatre Collection. WNET Great Performances: Dance in America, *Trailblazers of Modern Dance,* 1977.

Loie Fuller. "Light and the Dance." In Fuller, *Fifteen Years of A Dancer's Life.* Boston: Small, Maynard & Co., Inc., 1913. (Brooklyn: Dance Horizons, 1976.) .

Ted Shawn. "Constants—What Constitutes a Work of Art in the Dance." In Shawn, *Dance We Must.* Pittsfield, Mass.: The Eagle Printing & Binding Co., 1940, 1950, 1963. (New York: Haskell House, 1974.)

Mary Wigman. "Stage Dance—Stage Dancer (1927)." In Wigman, *The Mary Wigman Book.* Edited and translated by Walter Sorell. Middletown, Conn.: Wesleyan University Press, 1975. Copyright © by Walter Sorell, by permission of Wesleyan University Press.

Martha Graham. "Graham 1937." In Merle Armitage, ed., *Martha Graham.* Los Angeles: privately printed, 1937. (Brooklyn: Dance Horizons, 1966.)

Doris Humphrey. "What a Dancer Thinks About." Unpublished manuscript. Dance Collection, New York Public Library at Lincoln Center.

Charles Weidman. "Random Remarks." In Walter Sorell, ed., *The Dance Has Many Faces.* 2d ed. rev. New York: Columbia University Press, 1966.

Hanya Holm. "Hanya Speaks." In Walter Sorell, *Hanya Holm: Biography of an Artist.* Middletown, Conn.: Wesleyan University Press, 1969. Copyright © 1969 by Wesleyan University, by permission of Wesleyan University Press.

Merce Cunningham. "You have to love dancing to stick to it." In Cunningham, *Changes: Notes on Choreography.* New York: Something Else Press, 1968. Copyright © 1968 by Merce Cunningham.

Erick Hawkins. "a little house to understand and protect it." *Dance Observer* 27, no.2 (1960).

José Limón. "On Dance." In Fernando Puma, ed., *Seven Arts #1.* Garden City, N.Y.: Doubleday & Co., Inc., 1953.

Anna Sokolow. "The Rebel and the Bourgeois." In Selma Jeanne Cohen, ed., *The Modern Dance: Seven Statements of Belief.* Middletown, Conn.: Wesleyan University Press, 1965. Copyright © 1965 by Wesleyan University, reprinted by permission of Wesleyan University Press.

Alwin Nikolais. Excerpts from "Nik: A Documenary." Edited by Marcia B. Siegel. *Dance Perspectives* 48 (1971). Copyright © 1971 by Dance Perspectives Foundation. Reprinted with permission.

Anna Halprin. "The Process is the Purpose." An interview with Vera Maletic. *Dance Scope* 4, no. 1 (1967-1968) Copyright © 1968 American Dance Guild.

Judith Dunn. "We Don't Talk about It. We Engage in It." *Eddy* 1, no. 2 (1974).

Yvonne Rainer. "The Mind Is a Muscle." *Work 1961-73.* Halifax: The Press of The Nova Scotia College of Art and Design; New York: New York University Press, 1974.

Pilobolus. "Talking with Pilobolus." An interview with Elvi Moore. *Dance Scope* 10, no. 2 (1976). Copyright © 1976 by American Dance Guild.

Trisha Brown and Douglas Dunn. "Dialogue: On Dance." *Performing Arts Journal* 1, no. 2 (1976).

Rod Rodgers. "Don't Tell Me Who I Am." *Negro Digest.* 18, 1968.

Photographs

From the archives of the Dance Collection of the New York Public Library at Lincoln Center:

Isadora Duncan, photographer unknown

Loie Fuller in *Serpentine Dance,* drawing by Toulouse-Lautrec

Ruth St. Denis in *Incense,* photographer unknown

Ted Shawn, photographer unknown

Mary Wigman in "Schwingende Landschaft" from *Sommerlicher Tanz*, photograph by Charlotte Rudolph

Martha Graham in *Cave of the Heart*, photographer unknown

Charles Weidman, photographer unknown

Hanya Holm in *Icon,* photograph by Charlotte Rudolph

Erick Hawkins in *John Brown*, photograph by Alfredo Valente

José Limón, photograph by Zachary Freyman, by permission of the photographer

Anna Sokolow, photographer unknown

Alwin Nikolais, photograph by Basil Langton

Pilobolus in *Monkshood Farewell*, photographer unknown

Trisha Brown, photograph by Peter Moore.

By permission of Charles Humphrey Woodford:

Doris Humphrey in *Theater Piece*, photographer unknown

By permission of the Cunningham Dance Foundation:

Merce Cunningham, photograph by Penny Brogden.

By permission of Anna Halprin:

Anna Halprin, photographer unknown.

By permission of Peter Moore:

Judith Dunn in *Witness II.* photograph by Peter Moore, © 1963.

Yvonne Rainer, photograph by Peter Moore, © 1963.

By permission of Douglas Dunn:

Douglas Dunn, photographer unknown

By permission of Rod Rodgers:

Rod Rodgers, photographer unknown.

TABLE OF CONTENTS

Part One

THE
FORERUNNERS

INTRODUCTION

Modern dance is usually regarded as a uniquely American, twentieth-century art form. However, as all rebellions evolve from precedents, so the antecedents of modern dance can be found in nineteenth-century Europe.

The French singer François Delsarte (1811-1871) delineated basic principles of movement and expression in movement. His theory, formulated in the *Science of Applied Aesthetics*, divided the body into three zones, with each zone further divided into three sections for the purpose of expressive gesture. Movements were assigned to one of three basic categories: successions, parallelisms, and oppositions. These theories were originally developed for actors and musicians, but they later reached dancers through the efforts of his disciples and ultimately revolutionized dance.

Emile Jaques-Dalcroze (1865-1950) was born in Vienna but performed his major work in Geneva. He developed a system of rhythmic exercises called *Eurythmics*, which were designed to foster music students' expressivity by creating a greater feeling for the movement inherent in the music. His connection with Delsarte is uncertain, but exposure to Delsartean theories seems probable. Early modern dancers studied Eurythmics in order to foster rhythmic sensitivity.

Rudolf von Laban (1879-1958), the son of a Hungarian diplomat, studied with a disciple of Delsarte and is reported to have studied ballet as well. He established a school in Switzerland and then one in Germany, where he trained movement choirs until 1938, when he moved to England. He invented a notation system called *Labanotation*, now widely used in recording and reconstructing choreography. His *Effort-Shape* theories have been incorporated into dance education and dance therapy, while his space concepts may still be seen in the work of dancers who carry on the tradition of German modern dance.

In America, disciples of Delsarte, including Genevieve Stebbins, Steele Mackaye, and Mrs. Richard Hovey, taught

his work in the late nineteenth century. Stebbins studied in
Europe with a disciple of Delsarte, then toured the U. S., giv-
ing lecture-demonstrations while dressed in a Greek tunic.
Mackaye studied with Delsarte himself and then developed
the principles into a system of exercises called *Harmonic
Gymnastics.* A Delsarte craze ensued throughout America.
Mrs. Richard Hovey studied in France with Delsarte's son,
Gustave, who had evolved a movement system similar to
Mackaye's. These disciples and others influenced the Ameri-
can dancers who created the climate out of which American
modern dance eventually arose.

Isadora Duncan and Ruth St. Denis were born at about the
same time (1877-1878) on opposite sides of the American
continent. Both had dominant, liberated mothers who im-
parted to them the principles of François Delsarte; both had
brief stints in show business before traveling to Europe; and
both were influenced by Loie Fuller, another American dancer, who was the rage of the Folies Bergère.

The rebelliousness that has characterized the leaders of
modern dance has its origins in the work of St. Denis, Duncan, and Fuller. At a time when women were corseted, dis-
enfranchised, and denied access to education and jobs, these
three women lived a liberated existence and expressed a freedom in their art that relatively few other women possessed.
They freed their bodies by discarding the conventions of Vic-
torian costume; they sought to synthesize movement and expression. In short, they sought individuality.

Both Duncan and St. Denis opened their minds by reading
and doing research in museums as well as by traveling extensively. Images from the past inspired both with visions of the
future of dance, and both expressed their philosophies in writing. The followers of Isadora Duncan inherited a style and a
point of view that has had a far-reaching influence on American modern dance, as has the legacy of Ruth St. Denis, which
became meshed with that of Ted Shawn.

At the time that Duncan, St. Denis, and Fuller were liberating themselves through dance and winning public esteem,
dance was still a taboo profession for American men. It took
courage for Ted Shawn, a former divinity student, to become

a dancer. He first toured the vaudeville circuit. Although he had seen Ruth St. Denis dance in 1911, it was not until 1914 that he auditioned for her and became her partner, and then her husband. In 1915 the couple founded Denishawn, a school that dominated American theatrical dancing for the next fifteen years.

Oriental dance and ballet were taught at the school, as well as yoga, Delsartean theories (taught to Ted Shawn during this period by Mrs. Hovey), and a wide variety of ethnic dance styles. The dances choreographed by St. Denis and Shawn reflected the philosophy of the school: expressive, eclectic works on ethnic and/or religious themes that treated existing dance forms in new ways.

At the height of its success, the Los Angeles-based Denishawn franchised schools from coast to coast, which were run by former students. There were also two touring companies, one directed by "Miss Ruth" and the other by Shawn. Men were included in both the schools and the companies, for one of Shawn's ambitions was to restore to male dancing the respect it had commanded in ancient Greece.

Although Denishawn encompassed all forms of dancing, the vision of its founders fell short of accepting diverging theories. Their blindness to innovation on the part of company members, together with personal difficulties and unrealistic expectations for a "Greater Denishawn"* in the year of the stock market crash, eventually led to Denishawn's demise.

During this same period Mary Wigman established her school of German modern dance in Dresden, Germany, in 1920. She had studied with both Dalcroze and Laban, and she strongly influenced the course of German modern dance for the next fifty years. Branches of the school were set up throughout Germany, with a New York branch established in 1931 (directed by Hanya Holm), following her first American tour. She undertook her third and final American tour with her company in 1933.

---

*"Greater Denishawn" encompassed a vision of expansion which took the form of plans for centers on both the East and West coasts.

Isadora Duncan had a tremendous and long-range impact on dancers, artists, and society as a whole. A feminist in the most contemporary sense of the word and a radical whose rebellion, particularly against ballet, was complete and far-reaching, she was also a Romantic. The writings of Nietzsche, Rousseau, and Walt Whitman influenced her greatly, and she performed to the music of Gluck, Wagner, Schubert, and Chopin, among others.

Isadora believed that dance should come from and be an expression of the spirit, inspired by nature; anything else was stilted and artificial. She felt that her philosophy was best exemplified in ancient Greek civilization, and her basic costume was a Greek tunic.

She found little acceptance in her native country. From 1899, she lived and performed in Europe, where she enjoyed sensational success, especially in Russia. She inspired artists, poets, and musicians. In 1908 and again in 1914 she returned to the United States to perform, but Americans disapproved of the liberated life style that pervaded her art.

EXCERPTS FROM HER WRITINGS

In spite of her several attempts to establish schools in Germany, France, and Russia to continue her vision, Isadora's lifelong dream was repeatedly frustrated. Part of the difficulty was financial; part was her unwillingness to systematize her art and her inability to transmit her spirit; part was her frequent absence from the school. However, the essence of her vision and her rebellion remains with us, and continues to influence dancers today.

Isadora Duncan (1877-1927)

In a moment of prophetic love for America, Walt Whitman said: "I hear America singing," and I can imagine the mighty song that Walt heard from the surge of the Pacific over the plains, the voices rising of the vast Choral of children, youths, men and women, singing Democracy.

When I read this poem of Whitman's I, too, had a vision—the vision of America dancing a dance that would be the worthy expression of the song Walt heard when he heard America singing. It would have nothing to do with the sensual lilt of the jazz rhythm: it would be like the vibration of the American soul striving upward, through labour to harmonious life. Nor had this dance that I visioned any vestige of the Foxtrot or the Charleston—rather was it the living leap of the child springing toward the heights, towards its future accomplishment, towards a new great vision of life that would express America.

I see America dancing, standing with one foot poised on the highest point of the Rockies, her two hands stretched from the Atlantic to the Pacific, her fine head tossed to the sky, her forehead shining with a Crown of a million stars.

***

I was born by the sea . . . my first idea of movement of the dance, certainly came from the rhythm of the waves. . . .

***

The great and only principle on which I feel myself justified in leaning, is a constant, absolute, and universal unity which runs through all the manifestations of Nature. The waters, the winds, the plants, living creatures, the particles of matter itself obey this controlling rhythm of which the characteristic line is the wave. In nothing does Nature suggest jumps and breaks, there is between all the conditions of life a continuity or flow which the dancer must respect in his art, or else become a mannequin—outside Nature and without true beauty.

***

It is the alternate attraction and resistance of the law of gravity that causes this wave movement.

***

Every movement that can be danced on the seashore, without being in harmony with the rhythm of the waves, every movement that can be danced in the forest without being in harmony with the swaying of the branches, every movement that one can dance nude, in the sunshine, in the open country, without being in harmony with the life and the solitude of the landscape—every such movement is false, in that it is out of tune in the midst of Nature's harmonious lines. That is why the dancer should above all else choose movements that express the strength, health, nobility, ease and serenity of living things.

***

When I have danced I have tried always to be the Chorus; I have been the Chorus of young girls hailing the return of the fleet; I have been the Chorus dancing the Pyrrhic Dance, or the Bacchic; I have never once danced a solo.

***

Now, I am going to reveal to you something which is very pure, a totally white thought. It is always in my heart; it blooms at each of my steps. . . . The dance is love, it is only love, it alone, and that is enough. . . . I then, it is amorously that I dance; to poems, to music, but now I would like to no longer dance to anything but the rhythm of my soul.

***

Is it not true that all the graces of God are upon woman. . . that all the marvelous litheness of the animal, that the gestures of the flower are in her? So, if she has all the gifts, she is the reflection of the world. She is also like a garland suspended between reality and the ideal. . . . She can, with all her gestures, represent all ideas. If the gesture is right, the idea is beautiful.

She is the proud huntress, the virgin Walkyrie, Botticelli's Spring, the lascivious nymph, the intoxicated Bacchante, Antigone in tears, the mother at the cradle, the supplicant at the altar, the priestess in the sacred grove, the lewd and the chaste. . . . Finally, she is a fresco of changing grace, her body floats and undulates like silk in the wind, princess of rhythms performing the dance in the garden of life.

***

Oh, what a field is here awaiting her! Do you not feel that she is near, that she is coming, this dancer of the future! She will help womankind to a new knowledge of the possible strength and beauty of their bodies, and the relation of their bodies to the earth nature and to the children of the future. She will dance the body emerging again from centuries of civilized forgetfulness, emerging not in the nudity of primitive man, but in a new nakedness, no longer at war with spirituality and intelligence, but joining with them in a glorious harmony.

This is the mission of the dancer of the future. Oh, do you not feel that she is near, do you not long for her coming as I do? Let us prepare the place for her. I would build for her a temple to await her. Perhaps she is yet unborn, perhaps she is now a little child. Perhaps, oh blissful! it may be my holy mission to guide her first steps, to watch the progress of her movements day by day until, far outgrowing my poor teaching, her movements will become godlike, mirroring in themselves the waves, the winds, the movements of growing things, the flight of birds, the passing of clouds, and finally the thought of man in his relation to the universe.

Oh, she is coming, the dancer of the future: the free spirit, who will inhabit the body of new woman; more glorious than any woman that has yet been; more beautiful than the Egyptian, than the Greek, the early Italian, than all women of past centuries—the highest intelligence in the freest body!

Loie Fuller, born in Fullersberg, Illinois, was another
American who found a more receptive atmosphere
in Europe than in her native country. After a start in
the American theater, she went abroad. Arriving in
Paris in 1892, she was a great success from the
night of her debut at the Folies-Bergère.

The spectacular effect of Fuller's dance resulted from
her use of colored theatrical lighting playing on and
through the voluminous folds of silk that were her
costume. At the time, light refraction had only
begun to be studied by scientists, and electric stage
lighting had just come into use in the theater. In the
other arts, Impressionist painters such as Claude
Monet and Camille Pissarro, and music composers,
notably Claude Debussy, were attempting to capture
light refraction in their works. The artists of Art
Nouveau accepted the American dancer as a revolutionary artist.

LIGHT AND THE DANCE

Miss Fuller invented many new pieces of theatrical
lighting equipment, traveled with a large number of
technicians, kept her techniques a closely
guarded secret, and complained of imitators
who, she felt, detracted from
her success. She toured widely
abroad and in the United
States during her career. Although she turned
from solo to group choreography around
the turn of the century and founded a school in 1908,
neither her works nor her school lasted. The value
of her innovations is only now receiving recognition.

Loie Fuller's discovery of the effect of light on cloth
is described in this chapter from her autobiography.

Loie
Fuller
(1862-1928)
Since it is generally agreed that I have created
something new, something composed of light,
colour, music, and the dance, more especially
of light and the dance, it seems to me that it
would perhaps be appropriate, after having
considered my creation from the anecdotal
and picturesque standpoint, to explain in more
serious terms, just what my ideas are relative

to my art, and how I conceive it both independently and in its relationship to other arts. If I appear to be too serious I apologise in advance.

I hope that this theoretical "essay" will be better received than a certain practical essay that I undertook, soon after my arrival in Paris, in the cathedral of Notre Dame.

Notre Dame! The great cathedral of which France is justly proud was naturally the objective of one of my earliest artistic pilgrimages, I may say of the very earliest. The tall columns, whose shafts, composed of little assembled columns, rise clear to the vaults; the admirable proportions of the nave; the choir, the seats of old carved oak, and the railings of wrought iron—this harmonious and magnificent pile impressed me deeply. But what enchanted me more than anything else was the marvellous glass of the lateral rose windows, and even more, perhaps, the rays of sunlight that vibrated in the church, in various directions, intensely coloured, as a result of having passed through these sumptuous windows.

I quite forgot where I was. I took my handkerchief from my pocket, a white handkerchief, and I waved it in the beams of coloured light, just as in the evening I waved my silken materials in the rays of my reflectors.

Suddenly a tall imposing man, adorned with a heavy silver chain, which swung from an impressive neck, advanced ceremoniously toward me, seized me by the arm and led me toward the entrance, directing a conversation at me which I appreciated as lacking in friendliness although I did not understand a word. To be brief he dropped me on to the pavement. There he looked at me with so severe an expression that I understood his intention was never to let me enter the church again under any pretext.

My mother was as frightened as I was.

Just then a gentleman came along, who seeing us completely taken aback, asked us what had happened. I pointed to the man with the chain, who was still wrathfully surveying us.

"Ask him about it," I said.

The gentleman translated the beadle's language to me.

"Tell that woman to go away; she is crazy."

Such was my first visit to Notre Dame and the vexatious experience that my love of colour and light caused.

When I came to Europe I had never been inside an art museum. The life that I led in the United States had given me neither motive nor leisure to become interested in master-pieces, and my knowledge of art was hardly worth mention-ing. The first museum whose threshold I crossed was the British Museum. Then I visited the National Gallery. Later I became acquainted with the Louvre and, in due course, with most of the great museums of Europe. The circumstance that has struck me most forcibly in regard to these museums is that the architects have not given adequate attention to considerations of light.

Thanks to this defect I get in most museums an impression of a disagreeable medley. When I look at the objects for some moments the sensation of weariness overcomes me, it becomes impossible to separate the things one from another. I have always wondered if a day will not come when this problem of lighting will be better solved. The question of il-lumination, of reflection, of rays of light falling upon objects, is so essential that I cannot understand why so little impor-tance has been attached to it. Nowhere have I seen a mu-seum where the lighting was perfect. The panes of glass that let the light through ought to be hidden or veiled just as are the lamps that light theatres, then the objects can be ob-served without the annoyance of the sparkle of the window.

The efforts of the architect ought to be directed altogether in that direction—to the redistribution of light. There are a thousand ways of distributing it. In order that it may fulfill the desired conditions light ought to be brought directly to pictures and statues instead of getting there by chance.

Colour is disintegrated light. The rays of light, disin-tegrated by vibrations, touch one object and another, and this disintegration, photographed in the retina, is always chemically the result of changes in matter and in beams of light. Each one of these effects is designated under the name of colour.

Our acquaintance with the production and variations of these effects is precisely at the point where music was when there was no music.

In its earliest stage music was only natural harmony; the noise of the waterfall, the rumbling of the storm, the gentle whisper of the west wind, the murmur of the watercourses, the rattling of rain on dry leaves, all the sounds of still water and of the raging sea, the sleeping of lakes, the tumult of the hurricane, the soughing of the wind, the dreadful roar of the cyclone, the crashing of the thunder, the crackling of branches.

Afterwards the singing birds and then all the animals emitted their various sounds. Harmony was there; man, classifying and arranging the sounds, created music.

We all know what man has been able to get from it since then.

Man, past master of the musical realm, is to-day still in the infancy of art, from the standpoint of control of light.

If I have been the first to employ coloured light, I deserve no special praise for that. I cannot explain the circumstance; I do not know how I do it. I can only reply, like Hippocrates when he was asked what time was: "Ask it of me," he said, "and I cannot tell you; ask it not and I know it well."

It is a matter of intuition, of instinct, and nothing else.

Sight is perhaps the first, the most acute, of our senses. But as we are born with this sense sufficiently well developed to enable us to make good use of it, it is afterward the last that we try to perfect. For we concern ourselves with everything sooner than with beauty. So there is no reason for surprise that the colour sense is the last to be developed.

Yet, notwithstanding, colour so pervades everything that the whole universe is busy producing it, everywhere and in everything. It is a continued recurrence, caused by processes of chemical composition and decomposition. The day will come when man will know how to employ them so delightfully that it will be hard to conceive how he could have lived so long in the darkness in which he dwells to-day.

Our knowledge of motion is nearly as primitive as our knowledge of colour. We say "prostrated by grief," but, in reality, we pay attention only to the grief; "transported with joy," but we observe only the joy; "weighed down by chagrin," but we consider only the chagrin. Throughout we place no value on the movement that expresses the thought. We are not taught to do so, and we never think of it.

Who of us has not been pained by a movement of impatience, a lifting of the eyebrows, a shaking of the head, the sudden withdrawal of a hand?

We are far from knowing that there is as much harmony in motion as in music and colour. We do not grasp the facts of motion.

How often we have heard it said: "I cannot bear this colour." But have we ever reflected that a given motion is produced by such and such music? A polka or a waltz to which we listen informs us as to the motions of the dance and blends its variations. A clear sparkling day produces upon us quite a different effect from a dull sad day, and by pushing these observations further we should begin to comprehend some more delicate effects which influence our organism.

In the quiet atmosphere of a conservatory with green glass, our actions are different from those in a compartment with red or blue glass. But usually we pay no attention to this relationship of actions and their causes. These are, however, things that must be observed when one dances to an accompaniment of light and music properly harmonised.

Light, colour, motion, and music.

Observation, intuition, and finally comprehension.

Let us try to forget educational processes in so far as dancing is concerned. Let us free ourselves from the sense that is ordinarily assigned to the word. Let us endeavour to forget what is understood by it to-day. To rediscover the primitive form of the dance, transformed into a thousand shapes that have only a very distant relationship to it, we shall have to go back to the early history of the race. We then get a notion [of] what the origin of the dance must have been and what has made it what it is to-day.

At present dancing signifies motions of the arms and legs. It means a conventional motion, at first with one arm and one leg, then a repetition of the same figure with the other arm and the other leg. It is accompanied by music, each note calls for a corresponding motion, and the motion, it is unnecessary to say, is regulated rather by the time than by the spirit of the music. So much the worse for the poor mortal who cannot do with his left leg what he does with his right leg. So much [the] worse for the dancer who cannot keep in time, or, to express it better, who cannot make as many motions as there are notes. It is terrifying to consider the strength and ability that are needed for proficiency.

Slow music calls for a slow dance, just as fast music requires a fast dance.

In general, music ought to follow the dance. The best musician is he who can permit the dancer to direct the music instead of the music inspiring the dance. All this is proved to us by the natural outcome of the motives which first impelled men to dance. Nowadays these motives are forgotten, and it is no longer considered that there should be a reason for dancing.

In point of fact the dancer on learning a piece of new music, says: "Oh, I cannot dance to that air." To dance to new music, the dancer has to learn the conventional steps adapted to that music.

Music, however, ought to indicate a form of harmony or an idea with instinctive passion, and this instinct ought to incite the dancer to follow the harmony without special preparation. This is the true dance.

To lead us to grasp the real and most extensive connotation of the word dance, let us try to forget what is implied by the choreographic art of our day.

What is the dance? It is motion.

What is motion? The expression of a sensation.

What is a sensation? The reaction in the human body produced by an impression or an idea perceived by the mind.

A sensation is the reverberation that the body receives when an impression strikes the mind. When the tree bends and resumes its balance it has received an impression from the wind or the storm. When an animal is frightened its body receives an impression of fear, and it flees and trembles or else stands at bay. If it be wounded, it falls. So it is when matter responds to immaterial causes. Man, civilised and sophisticated, is alone best able to inhibit his own impulses.

In the dance, and there ought to be a word better adapted to the thing, the human body should, despite conventional limitations, express all the sensations or emotions that it experiences. The human body is ready to express, and it would express if it were at liberty to do so, all sensations just as the body of an animal.

Ignoring conventions, following only my own instinct, I

am able to translate the sensations we have all felt without
suspecting that they could be expressed. We all know that in
the powerful emotions of joy, sorrow, horror, or despair, the
body expresses the emotion it has received from the mind.
The mind serves as a medium and causes these sensations to
be caught up by the body. In fact, the body responds to
these sensations to such an extent sometimes that, especially
when the shock is violent, life is suspended or even leaves the
body altogether.

But natural and violent movements are possible only in the
midst of grand or terrible circumstances. They are only occasional motions.

To impress an idea I endeavour, by my motions, to cause
its birth in the spectator's mind, to awaken his imagination,
that it may be prepared to receive the image.

Thus we are able, I do not say to understand, but to feel
within ourselves as an impulse an indefinable and wavering
force, which urges and dominates us. Well, I can express this
force which is indefinable but certain in its impact. I have
motion. That means that all the elements of nature may be
expressed.

Let us take a *"tranche de vie."* That expresses surprise,
deception, contentment, uncertainty, resignation, hope, dis-
tress, joy, fatigue, feebleness, and, finally, death. Are not all
these sensations, each one in turn, humanity's lot? And why
can not these things be expressed by the dance, guided intelligently, as well as by life itself? Because each life expresses one by one all these emotions. One can express even the
religious sensations. Can we not again express the sensations
that music arouses in us, either a nocturne of Chopin's or a
sonata of Beethoven's, a slow movement by Mendelssohn,
one of Schumann's lieder, or even the cadence of lines of
poetry?

As a matter of fact, motion has been the starting point of
all effort at self-expression, and it is faithful to nature. In
experiencing one sensation we cannot express another by
motions, even when we can do so in words.

Since motion and not language is truthful, we have accordingly perverted our powers of comprehension.

That is what I have wanted to say and I apologise for
having said it at such length, but I felt that it was necessary.

Ruth St. Denis found her primary inspiration in the exoticism of the Orient. Dance was very much a spiritual experience for her, at once sensuous and mystical. Born in Somerville, New Jersey, she performed in New York and Europe for a number of years before her marriage to Ted Shawn. Together they established Denishawn, where "Miss Ruth" taught Oriental dance and also choreographed for and performed with the Denishawn company, which toured widely throughout the United States for the next ten years. During this period, with the help of Doris Humphrey, she developed "music visualizations."*

Following her separation from Ted Shawn and the dissolution of Denishawn in the early 1930s, St. Denis remained in New York City. There she founded

THE DANCE AS LIFE EXPERIENCE

the Society of Spiritual Arts and a Church of Divine Dance, and her rhythmic choir performed in several large churches as well as at the 1939 World's Fair. During World War II, St. Denis returned to Los Angeles, where she worked in an airplane factory for a few months before opening a studio. On her seventieth birthday the Church of Divine Dance was refounded in Los Angeles. St. Denis remained active in religious dance until shortly before her death.

The following article is taken from Denishawn Magazine, which was published by the school for only two years (1924-1925). A typical issue included essays written by St. Denis and Shawn, as well as poetry by St. Denis.

Ruth St. Denis (1877-1968)

I see men and women dancing rhythmically in joy, on a hilltop bathed in the saffron rays of a setting sun.

*Music visualization is the translation of musical structure into movement.

I see them moving slowly, with flowing, serene gestures, in the glow of the risen moon. I see them giving praise; praise for the earth and the sky and the sea and the hills, in free, happy movements that are projections of their moods of peace and adoration.

I see the Dance being used as a means of communication between soul and soul—to express what is too deep, too fine for words.

I see children growing straight and proportioned, swift and sure of movement, having dignity and grace and wearing their bodies lightly and with power.

I see our race made finer and quicker to correct itself—because the Dance reveals the soul.

The Dance is motion, which is life, beauty, which is love, proportion, which is power. To dance is to live life in its finer and higher vibrations, to live life harmonized, purified, controlled. To dance is to feel one's self actually a part of the cosmic world, rooted in the inner reality of spiritual being.

The revelation of spiritual beauty in terms of movement is the natural and inevitable progression of life and art; and the word Dancer should rightly mean one who expresses in bodily gesture the joy and power of his being.

Dancing of late years has been degraded to the narrow limits and low level of professionalism—of mere mechanical proficiency, associated always with the most frivolous and ephemeral phases of the stage. But this day is fading. We are slowly advancing beyond this stage of obscuration and perversion. We are turning our gaze inward, learning to seek there the divine sources of the dance, to the end that it may flower into new and more glorious forms of beauty and worth.

We dancers today are struggling and sacrificing and working so that at some precious hour in the future we may live! In truth, we are living now. Behind the veil of our actual, common days is the Eternal Now which is seeking ever to reveal itself—to shed light on the confusion of our heavy hours. But the power of the dance to release the soul is still buried under the weight of the binding and artificial world we have created for ourselves—in which there is no time to know, and no space to move.

The Eternal Now of the Dance includes both past and future. It includes the knowledge and assurance that in the past bodily gesture was the first communication of the simple needs of primitive man, and it includes the vision of the future in which the Cosmic Consciousness, to which man gradually attains, will find expression in finer bodies and more beautiful and articulate gesture.

We can not, of course, communicate, in any language, what we do not feel or know. But in modern times we have used almost exclusively the language of the intellect—speech— to express all states and stages of our consciousness, and by so doing we have inhibited and dwarfed the physical and emotional beauty of the self, while the spiritual consciousness has sought entirely other means for its expression, not knowing that dancing in its nobler uses is the very temple and word of the living spirit.

It is largely from this error that the sense of separation between body and spirit has grown. In reality, each individual self creates and governs its own organ of expression, and with this organ its communication with the world.

Let us, therefore, regard the dance fundamentally as a Life Experience, as the primitive and ultimate means of expression and communication. Let us see in the free, spontaneous dance of every child the beginning of the universal language, and the universal art, which, largely unconscious to himself, grows bodily into words, telling of illusive and exquisite moments of the hidden self; and later flowers into forms of art that will heal the world of some of its artistic sins.

To know this experience, even in a slight degree, to have space and light and music, a real sacrifice is necessary. The physical elements of our present life are designed for other uses, and our days are crowded with profitless confusions. Let there be more beauty and harmonious activity experienced *by* the individual, less merely *for* him. That is the purpose of the Dance. He has too much now of concert, stage, vaudeville and movies. We are continually urged to go and see this opera or that concert—always to be the silent, negative part, providing an audience and support for another's hours of joyous experience. (Let us not forget that the artist's joy is in his work. It is only in the discord of the artist's environment that his suffering lies.)

How much of our precious time is wasted by impositions from without—by having our minds defaced and poisoned by pictures that confuse and weigh down the spirit, in the name of art, because we do not know how to release the divine urge to strength and beauty within ourselves!

Pure dance has no bounds. The infant begins to dance at its mother's knee. Old age should have its gestures to express love and serenity no less. Each period of life has its own activity, its own beauty, and it is stupid and futile to attempt, as we do on the stage in the name of art and entertainment, to force or retard the natural unfolding of the spirit from youth to maturity.

Artificial and limited ideas of the dance have done cruel and grotesque things to its servants, as, indeed, they have to most artists of the stage. The spectacle of a singer or dancer or actor continuing on the stage in parts too young for him is tragic enough—but still more tragic is the situation of the artist who, in his maturity, having grown to the most interesting and beautiful stage of his consciousness, is forced to withdraw from his active career because of the childish demand of the public for mere youth. Some day our conceptions will expand to take in, with the loveliness and freshness of childhood, the gracious dignity of age, in art as well as in life. Here the dance will unfold many truths of being, many unknown or unseen joys possible to us in the very midst of our common days.

Make way for the dance! See if it does not repay a thousand fold. It will enlarge the horizon, give meaning to many things now hidden, new power to the self, a new value to existence.

Dancing as a life experience is not something to be taken on from the outside—something to be painfully learned—or something to be imitated.

Dancing is the natural rhythmic movements of the body that have long been suppressed or distorted, and the desire to dance would be as natural as to eat, or to run, or swim, if our civilization had not in countless ways and for divers reasons put its ban upon this instinctive and joyous action of the harmonious being. Our formal religions, our crowded cities, our clothes, and our transportation are largely responsible for the inert mass of humanity that until very lately was encased in collars and corsets. But we are beginning to emerge, to throw off, to demand space to think in and to dance in.

Oh, dancers and lovers of beauty everywhere, come, let us reason together and see if we can not make a better world, "one nearer to our hearts' desire!"

For I see a place of magical Beauty, that is and is not of this world that we know, a world created of familiar things, but arranged in a new and harmonious order.

I see a life lived that bridges the two worlds, the inner and the outer, concept and expression, Nature and Art.

I see groves of meditation, where Truth is learned and loved, and halls of Beauty, where the divine self is expressed.

Ted Shawn, the one-time divinity student from Kansas City, Missouri, shared with his wife, Ruth St. Denis, a belief in the validity of dance as religious expression. Many of the dances he choreographed had a religious or ethnic base, and often the two themes were combined. He choreographed, performed, and shared the direction of the Denishawn company and was also responsible for the development of the Denishawn school. His study of Delsarte's theories had a profound effect on him, which carried over into his teaching.

CONSTANTS— WHAT CONSTITUTES A WORK OF ART IN THE DANCE

His eclectic approach to dance education was later reflected in the "University of the Dance," which he established at Jacob's Pillow, his summer school of dance in the Berkshire Mountains of western Massachusetts. "The Pillow" continues today, much as he founded it. In the 1930s, after the collapse of Denishawn, he formed the Company of Male Dancers, a dance company that toured widely across the country. Although separated, Shawn and St. Denis remained close friends. In 1964 they danced together for the first time in over thirty years, in celebration of their fiftieth wedding anniversary.

Ted Shawn was articulate on the dance and published a number of books. The following essay is taken from a collection of lectures that he delivered at George Peabody College.

Ted Shawn (1891-1972) Philosophers have tried to tell us that all life is a continuous flux—that nothing is permanent but change. But, somehow, the human soul continually reaches out for something permanent, something enduring. We crave solidity and the eternal in the midst of all evidence that everything is elusive and impermanent. Perhaps it is only wishful thinking on my part, but I believe that this eternal desire of the soul is the greatest argument for the value of "constants" in art. For in art we create our ideal worlds, and in the ideal world of the universal man, there are constant, enduring and never-changing qualities.

In relation to the dance, these constants have two aspects: the physical and the—shall I say?—spiritual (at least spiritual in the sense of art-values).

In the physical realm, the constants are what we, as dancers, must all have and what, critically, we have the right to expect of other dancers. These are bodily skills, mind-body coordinations, disciplines.

No matter what type of dancing is done there are certain things that must be mastered: the dancer must be light, i.e., able to leave the floor by leaping or jumping, and land with elasticity, so as not to jar his body or make a noise. He must have mastered all those fundamental movement patterns which I have elucidated at greater length in my monograph: "The Fundamentals of a Dance Education"—swinging, walking, running, leaping, jumping, falling, torsion, bending, shaking, oppositions, parallelisms, successions, the "alphabet" of those movements out of which dance steps are made; he must be the master of the twin principles of tension and relaxation, and must be able to maintain balance perfectly whether at rest or in motion. He must have his body so trained and so co-ordinated that the idea, be it kinetic, musical or dramatic, is expressed by his whole body as a unity. He must know thoroughly the patterns of construction of dance in relation to all three dimensions of space, and in relation to that fourth dimension of the dance: time. He must be trained in the relation of the dance to music so that, when dancing to music, his movement and the music seem the twin emanation of one impulse, and he must master the relationship of himself to a group of other dancers in an almost infinite variety of patterns. In addition to this he must apprehend all the different *qualities* of movement, and be able to produce these qualities as surely as the organist pulls out the stops on his organ. He must acquire a rich vocabulary of movements, so that he can improvise as easily as he indulges in a pleasant and exciting conversation, never stopping to think what word to use, nor how to form his sentence grammatically. And he must have acquired and mastered a technique (many techniques, really) or else build a technique for himself, by doing which he has administered to himself a more severe discipline than if he had been trained in the technique of others.

These, then, are constants—we must deal with all of these if we expect to dance ourselves, and we have a right to expect these in dancers we see, and fairly judge the value and quality of the performance by the degree the dancer shows us how he has absorbed, mastered and practically forgotten these constants.

But beyond these physical constants there are the greater constants. For no matter how cleverly a dancer dances, no matter how disciplined and technically proficient he be—if the dance he performs is inexpertly constructed, and the content worthless or thin, we are disappointed and "let down."

These greater constants are those which we look for in the dance itself—the dance as a work of art—where we are judging the work of the composer, the author, that is, the choreographer.

In actual physical performance, the dance has many unique problems which are not shared by any other art form, but the standards by which we judge a dance as a work of art (the dance in itself, as distinct from the performance of it) are almost the identical standards by which we judge a work of art in any other medium.

First, there should be complete clarity in the mind of the creator as to what he intends to do (that is, to say, in his own particular medium of the dance). He may wish to create a mood, or he may wish to tell a story, or he may wish only to take a "seed" of basic movement, and let it be organically developed into a final complicated-yet-simple product. Whatever his aim, the choreographer must not be confused as to his intention, his method, his stylization, the special technique used, or the result will be hybrid, confusing, neither one thing nor the other.

Second, there must be unity of style in the composition, one quality of movement must remain throughout. This does not mean that there can be no variety, but that the variety must be within the unity. The work as a whole must be of one stuff, as an emerald is all emerald—crush it to powder, and each tiny pinch of that powder will still be emerald. A fragment of a Greek vase is instantly recognizable, and each fragment of any dance which is a work of art should be sufficiently stylized to identify the whole from which it was taken. And, within this unity, the work must cohere—it must be solid in its construction, so that there are no joining places left visible in the finished product—but it seems to have been quarried out of one piece.

This means that the dance must have sequence, each movement done must lead inevitably into the next movement, so that one could not imagine any other movement being possible as successor to the movement just done.

And this implies, absolutely, architecture. The whole dance, as a work of art, must be constructed as well and carefully as a beautiful building, which is beautiful not only because of its materials and ornamentation, but also on account of its design, its proportions; because it has a solid foundation, and because its walls are solid and capable of supporting the roof. A dance work of art must have beginning, development and climax—just as a building has foundations, walls and roof.

Since the dance is almost universally accompanied by music, there are certain constants in that relationship, too. The dance must have in it all the qualities that the music has and provide, in replica, all the elements of the music. Of course, the foundation is rhythm—the without-which-nothing—the thing on which all rests. But, as music has harmony so must the movement be harmonious within itself and with the music. Even if one is dancing to the apparent dissonances of modern music, there must be a harmony between the distortion—consciously and intelligently used—of the body and the distortions of tone from the accepted norm. All the values of time, duration, stress, dynamics and form inherent in the music, must be equally inherent in the dance work of art.

Much has been and still is said about kinesthesia, about dance being kinetically created, but this is one only of the legitimate starting points for the creation of a dance, and it never excuses formlessness in the finished product. Many things that are permissible in the studio as training, as experimentation, as discipline, are not permissible to offer to an audience as a dance work of art. Many people who are interested in the dance may enjoy visiting a class and watching the training process, but studio exercises should be confined to the studio, and never be brought to an exhibition program of the supposedly finished product.

We hear the word "stylized" a great deal in regard to the dance. This refers to what I said about unity. A dancer may choose to do a dance in the style of the hieratic wall paintings of ancient Crete, or in the style of a Javanese dance, or a Spanish dance. In this case, this style must predominate, govern and discipline every movement, and even the dance as a whole. The dancer may develop such a strong individual style that his movement may be "stylized" and yet not be classifiable as belonging to any actual style such as those mentioned above; yet within his own style he maintains a unity of quality and is disciplined by his own imposed limitations.

"Distortion" is another word much discussed in the dance today. From a certain angle, all art is distortion, in that it is not a photographic, mechanical reproduction of nature. The artist chooses from out of the vast superfluity of nature that which he wishes to use, shapes that to his own purpose, and so "distorts" it from its original form and shape. But "distortion" is a dangerous word, for many people seem to think that wrenching things blindly into grotesque shapes has value in itself. Those who have revolted unintelligently from the ballet tradition and technique seem to believe that the exact opposite of the rules of the ballet will give some strangely desirable result. This produces movement without real significance—or perhaps it has some significance: that of the naughty child who makes faces to show that it doesn't like a person.

Do not be afraid that, because you are teachers, and especially teachers in Physical Education, that all this talk about "art" is beside the point. It is very definitely to the point, because the dance is art, or it is nothing. It is not merely a means of exercising, or promoting health, or building a strong symmetrical body. It does all these things, and better than any other means of physical education, but these are all by-products. An art activity is the deepest, richest, most worth-while activity of mankind. It is work and it is play—the most delightful play ever known, and "that work most worthy of man's perfected powers." We must be conscious of the dance as art even when we are teaching the simplest beginning fundamentals, and try to awaken that attitude towards the dance in all our pupils. The value of the dance, its greatest value, is in the "intangibles." Success in the dance cannot be measured by a tape, weighed on scales, nor timed with a stop-watch. It demands an awareness and sensitivity in the dancer's soul and in the soul of the beholder who partakes vicariously, empathetically, in the dance—and it is the development, strengthening and cultivation of this awareness which is the teacher's most important job.

You must clear your mind of all misconceptions of what art means—get out of your head, if possible and if you have any of that feeling there, that art is something in museums, something remote and precious. Art is experience, vital experience, and nowhere does one experience the reality of art so greatly as in the dance. Here the constants of beauty, ease, proportion, vitality, technical mastery, of the communication of ecstasy to the beholder, are within one's body-soul—they are as much you as your blood and your breath. And the greatest constant of all is that here in the dance we experience a rhythmic beauty, the activity of God Himself.

Mary Wigman, a native of Germany and a student of Dalcroze and Laban, developed a new dance form that has often been called "absolute dance." It was a unique combination of her training, her personality, her Germanic heritage, and the atmosphere of pre-Nazi Europe. Often expressionistic, it was similar to the work of German Expressionist painters, notably Emil Nolde, who had a direct influence on Wigman. Her works ranged from gentle dances of nature to the macabre. She believed that "art grows out of the basic cause of existence."

STAGE DANCE-
STAGE
DANCER

Wigman was the leading force in German modern dance for some fifty years. Her school, founded in Dresden in 1920, developed branches all over Germany, and also one in New York. During World War II she lived in Leipzig, where she taught only a small number of students, but in 1949 she reestablished her school in West Berlin and continued to teach until blindness and old age forced her to retire in the late 1960s.

The essay reprinted here was originally written in 1927, yet Wigman's ideas have the ring of timeless truths.

Mary Wigman (1886-1973)

We find ourselves in a process of change as far as the dance is concerned: abandonment of the classical ballet in favor of an expression representing our time. On the one hand, it would indicate a deterioration of the classical ballet and the traditional corps de ballet at the opera houses. On the other hand, the advance of a few personalities in the dance field to whom the ballet denied the expression of their creative ideas because of its set vocabulary and style.

What are we looking for? To attune our inmost feelings to the mood of our time. Everywhere appear solo dancers and dance

groups. A wild mixture of good and bad accomplishments, bold attempts, and daring experiments results in apparent confusion—a condition which, on second thought, is quite natural. Can we expect from this hardly twenty-year-old child of our time that it should have its own tradition by now? Even if one invokes the usual slogan about the speed of our time, one cannot demand the impossible.

Our dance would be of little meaning and would have no life nor enduring quality at all had we already conquered it to such an extent that its possibilities were clearly defined, its style set, and its development decided upon. We had better be patient and wait until the unorganic parts get lost and the pure fulfilled form becomes crystallized. It cannot be denied that our body awareness was unknown to any former generation the way it is now. Interest in physical movement, from all kinds of sports to artistic dancing, is now alive and will remain so. The strengthening and ennobling of the body as well as body expression have become slogans which may make sense but can only turn into fulfillment generations later. Genuine accomplishments need time to mature even in our fast-paced life.

The confusion in the field of movement is great and yet not so great as it may appear to the uninitiated. There may be many systems and methods of gymnastics, but they all point to one purpose: to control the body for the body's sake. The ultimate and noblest meaning of the dance can have one aim only: the living work of art presented through the human body as its instrument of expression. The manifoldness of dance expression was overwhelming and confusing after its divorce from the set world of the classical ballet. Gradually, the dance scene can more easily be surveyed. Even the skeptic will have to admit that the so-called "modern" dance has gained a great deal of ground in the short time of its existence, and not only in its own artistic right, but also in its effect on all other art forms.

Two essential types of creative dancing are the *absolute* dance and the *stage* dance. A parallel can be found in music. The absolute dance is independent of any literary-interpretative content; it does not represent, it is; and its effect on the spectator who is invited to experience the dancer's experience is on a mental-motoric level, exciting and moving. If it still happens that we see in absolute dancing any definable action in a theatrical sense, then the fault lies only partly with the dance creation. The difficulty usually lies with the spectator, who has not yet learned to absorb dance as pure dance without seeing in it some perceived or imagined imagery. The stage dance works with the same means as the absolute dance, but it is predetermined by the "scenic" event. The decorative element is evoked by set, lighting, and costume. The main accent is no longer on the dance itself but on the total stage event.

Pantomime is one of the purest forms of the stage dance when it interprets meaningful action by means of mere dancing. The actor's pantomimic gesture has been completely absorbed by the [silent] film. What music is to the opera, pantomime is to dance. Pantomime need not be limited to the old-fashioned shepherd's plays or idylls and harlequinades; all doors are open to pantomime in whatever can be represented by means of the dance, from symbolic events to the most realistic happenings.

It has been said that the stage dance has not stood the test and the dancers proved a failure. This may be true in certain cases, but cannot be applied to all contemporary dance accomplishments. I would like to shed light on this situation in showing how it looks to me. Not only is the modern dance too young to be up to all the requirements imposed upon it, nor is the dancer sufficiently mature to fulfill all the demands asked of him. There are very few stages in Germany that have a homogeneous dance group trained in the modern dance idiom. In most cases the young dancers become a part of an established classical ballet ensemble. And these ballet groups are not only differently trained, they are no longer able to do justice to the spirit of our time. The artistic results of such a dance group, diversely oriented, cannot be satisfactory, at least not overnight. More often than not, well-meant attempts are doomed to failure. In most cases a compromise is found between the two techniques, and "modern" is being danced today, then again "classic" tomorrow, without adhering to the one or the other.

Hardly anyone of the gifted young people turning to the dance wants to become a ballet dancer—at least, at the moment here in Germany. They all want to dance the way they feel, and the dancer's sensibility is rather uniform and directed toward expressing the spirit of today's generation, however inadequate his artistic expression may be. Today's dancers—who, in contrast to former times, do not exclusively belong to a certain stratum of society but come from all walks of life—expect more from the dance as a profession than to make a living. They see in the dance a possibility to express their very being, they envision the stage as a place of artistic creation where they can develop their abilities and fight for new ideas. It is no longer enough for our youth—regardless of how far advanced he is as [a] dancer—to take part in the ballet episode of an opera, to hop around in a peasant *Reigen,* or to cross the stage in the role of a page carrying an orb made of papier-mâché. He asks for more and has a right to do so. He asks for tasks for which it pays to work and struggle, and it often enough happens that, after a short while, he loses interest and tires of the little ability he has acquired.

We certainly do not find the same condition everywhere, and there are theatres in Germany where the dance gets full attention and the dancer is able to prove himself. But it also happens that after acceptance of the first bold attempts, the interest of the public and press in the new dance group wanes, and sometimes also a sudden disinterest in the theatre administration makes things difficult for the dancers. One loses patience when the young and motley ensemble does not achieve a uniform capacity within one season, or when the choreographer does not display a stunning dance idea each month. From where should they all come, the perfectly trained dancers with masterly accomplishments, the unusually gifted balletmasters and choreographers and dance composers? They do not have the time to develop and to prepare themselves, inwardly and outwardly, for the responsibility of their profession.

We must not overlook that our time is characterized not only by many positive as well as negative accomplishments, but also by a serious economic crisis. Who, nowadays, can still afford to finish any of his studies? The young dancers are—like any other working people—the bearers and victims of our time. Almost without exception, after one or two years of study they must make a living. How can they accomplish anything close to perfection under such conditions? They need the theatre not only as a place to work in, but also for their extended study. Above all, they need a guiding spirit in the theatre whom they can trust and who would undertake to further their study. But this ballet-master, who ought to be a choreographer and, if possible, a composer at the same time (for there are no ready-made modern dance works which can be rehearsed and performed) usually comes to his position under similar circumstances. He too has not enough experience and an insufficient store-house of imagination to enable him to stage one work after the other.

It may be well to compare the developing career of a conductor with that of a modern choreographer. In his studies during many years at a conservatory and at colleges the conductor must first prove that he really is a "musician." He must master the piano and know the other instruments, he must be able to read a score, must be familiar with all styles of music from the classic to the avant-garde composers. If, after the completion of his studies, he succeeds in obtaining a post at a theatre, he does not start in a leading position and is not immediately charged with difficult tasks. He first acts as a coach and assistant to the chief conductor of the house. He thus starts the second half of his studies and knows that it may take a couple of years before he will lead the orchestra. In case he proves to be a strong talent, a musician and conductor of some merit, he will undoubtedly be noticed and his ability will become known despite all the difficulties which any ambitious young talent must face in a theatre following traditional concepts. Such an intermediate period is nonexistent for the choreographer. After much too little study and without any practical experience in the theatre, he takes over a position which is just as responsible as the one of a conductor.

My personal experiences have made it clear to me how difficult it is to train and develop a dance talent and to integrate it into a dance ensemble. It cannot be pasted on from the outside, it only comes about within a spirited, ideal workshop. Every young person has a strong feeling for a common cause, and, when handled with understanding, the individual will and desire for self-expression will never come in conflict with the teamwork. The necessary raising of the individual and total accomplishments is possible only if one can muster the patience to protect and further each individual talent within the team, to utilize the given abilities creatively within the framework of the projected dance itself.

The concert stage where the modern dancer first maintained himself, with the theatres not yet open to him, could be taken as a criterion for his accomplishments, as the touchstone for his potentialities. However, it presupposes a certain maturity not only of the dancer, but also of the public invited to share the dancer's experience and to criticise him. And it must be said once and for all that the public has to take its share of blame for innumerable incompetent dance performances. As long as it will remain in the habit of applauding a few nice legs of girls who, with their best intentions, stamp their rhythms, as long as mere ambition and misunderstood individual pride can present themselves under the guise of dance, neither will the chaos in the field be set right nor will the level be lifted. We must reach the point where, above and beyond everything else, the dance is evaluated as a work of art and the dancer as the interpreter of an art form, as is done in all other arts. But we must also learn to discriminate between the gratification of personal vanity and a young talent testing its mettle for the first time. The right to appear in public may be a question of talent and creative ability, but even more so of personality, of the stage magnetism which one cannot teach nor learn.

By no means do I want to create the impression that I wish to apologize for dance and dancer with these words, or protect mediocre and bad artistry. I think I have sufficiently proved through my own work as a dancer and choreographer that the demands imposed on myself and my students are not small and have contributed to a higher level of dance creation in many ways. But for the sake of a better future development of the dance I deemed it necessary to approach the dancers with my thoughts about them and their craft and also to do justice to the situation in which they find themselves today. Our dance is born of our age and its spirit, it has the stamp of our time as no other art form has. I wish that our contemporaries would become fully aware of their responsibilities toward their own and most alive creation, the modern dance. It does not suffice to support occasional feats of accomplishment. They ought to prepare with the dancer the ground for the unfolding of the art's future.

Part Two

THE
FOUR
PIONEERS

INTRODUCTION

Called at various times "Papa Shawn" and the "Father of American Dance," Ted Shawn was the kind of parent who required submission and inspired rebellion in his offspring. The first of the famous Denishawn "children" to leave the fold was Martha Graham in 1923. Although Shawn had been her primary teacher and had featured her in his dances, she felt that she must strike out on her own.

The next defectors from Denishawn left in a group in 1928, joining forces for the next sixteen years. Doris Humphrey, star performer and main teacher in the Denishawn school; Charles Weidman, also a performer and teacher there; and Pauline Lawrence, school accompanist, together established the Humphrey-Weidman Dance Company in New York City. These "unholy three" were voted out of Denishawn for disloyalty when Humphrey and Weidman refused to give up their experiments with movement to tour with the Ziegfield Follies. The tour was to raise money for "Greater Denishawn," at that point, a huge, unpaid-for house in the suburbs of New York City.

Shortly before that confrontation, Humphrey had been chided by Shawn for not teaching straight Denishawn technique in classes. Instead, she had been testing the discoveries she was beginning to make about dance movement.

Paramount among these, and the basis for the technique she was to develop, was her concept that dance takes place in an arc of unbalance, that is the motion which occurs between the vertical (standing) and the horizontal (lying down) positions. This is the basis of the Humphrey Fall and Recovery Theory.

Martha Graham had also begun to develop a new dance technique which continued to evolve out of her choreography during her entire career. The style which she developed was sharp, angular, and percussive; the most distinctive movement, in her technique, the contraction and release involving the torso, resulted from her observations of breathing.

This was the beginning of American modern dance. For the first time American dancers were creating new movements for new subject matter, and reflecting their own era rather than a previous one. Their movements evolved from the meaning of the dance, rather than from previously learned steps developed by peoples of a different culture. In the process of finding new techniques to express their art, these modern dance pioneers broke the existing rules; indeed, that was their intent, for they were anti-Denishawn, anti-ballet, anti- the past.

The percussive, angular, and often distorted movements of early modern dance expressed the tensions of contemporary life. Similar developments in other arts resulted in the Cubist paintings of Picasso and Braque and the dissonant music of Hindemith and Schoenberg. At the same time, dance ceased to be regarded primarily as entertainment, and through the new aesthetics, it achieved the status of a serious, creative, independent art form.

All levels of the dancers' space were used, resulting in a relationship to gravity that was in direct contrast to the *danse verticale* of the Romantic ballet. The torso became fully active as it was freed of its balletic rigidity, and the dancers angled their limbs, in contrast to the extended line of ballet. Interestingly, many of these movements can be traced to the Denishawn origins of the pioneers, particularly to the Oriental and Delsartean influences. The difference between the old and the new was that these modern dance originators used the principles they had learned from Denishawn to create new movements. Their first dances accordingly showed a lingering Denishawn influence, but in time they worked away from it, although their warm-up exercises continued to include a combination of yoga and ballet.

The dancers' costumes and stage settings were extremely simplified, often to the point of starkness. The dance itself was performed either to music written for it by a contemporary composer or to no music at all; occasionally, music of the pre-classic or classic period was used. The dancers performed wherever they could: in lofts, studios, and small theaters in New York City, and in colleges and university auditoriums and gymnasiums throughout the country.

Critics played an important role in bringing this avant-garde movement before the public eye and in expanding its small but devoted following. John Martin, a staff critic for *The New York Times* from 1927 to 1962, had a background in theater but soon began covering modern dance performances extensively, becoming the foremost champion of the fledgling art and the first "dean" of dance critics.

By the time that Louis Horst founded *Dance Observer* in 1934, he was already an old friend of the modern dancers. As a musician he had accompanied classes and performances at Denishawn. He left when Martha Graham did, becoming her advisor, critic, and music composer. In addition, he developed a formal approach to the teaching of dance composition, which has been experienced by countless students over the years. This approach uses art forms and styles from all periods of human history except that in which ballet developed. *Dance Observer* presented reviews, articles, and advertisements devoted principally to modern dance, and Horst continued monthly publication until his death in 1964.

Walter Terry, who studied with Shawn, Graham, Humphrey, Limón, and others, began his career as a critic in 1936. Long associated with the *New York Herald-Tribune,* he is now the dance critic for the *Saturday Review.* Martin, Horst, and Terry have all written definitive books on dance.

In 1931 Hanya Holm came from Germany to open the New York branch of the Mary Wigman School. She had studied with Dalcroze, Laban, and Wigman before becoming a Wigman company member and teacher. By 1936 she had established the Hanya Holm School and Company, and the New York Wigman School was dissolved. German modern dance, which up to this time had developed parallel to American modern dance, was thus injected into the mainstream of American modern dance. This dance form, characterized by its use of space and of improvisation as a teaching tool, has retained its uniqueness through the followers of the Laban-Wigman-Holm tradition in this country.

Modern dance coalesced as a movement through the efforts of two far-sighted young women, Martha Hill and Mary Jo Shelly, who established the Bennington College School of the Dance in 1934. There they invited the leading modern dancers to teach and create. Martha Graham, Doris Humphrey, Charles Weidman, and Hanya Holm were the permanent faculty from 1934 until its closing in 1941.

The economic stability, the artistic freedom, the space, and the chance to perform gave these four pioneers the opportunity to focus their energies on the creation of larger works during the summer months. Some of these works composed and presented there remain as milestones of modern dance, such as *Deaths and Entrances* and *Letter to the World* by Martha Graham, *With My Red Fires* and *Passacaglia and Fugue in C Minor* by Doris Humphrey, and *Trend* by Hanya Holm.

World War II began a period of disruption in the careers of the pioneers. The Bennington School of the Dance closed; male dancers were drafted into the armed forces; tours of the "gymnasium circuit" of colleges and universities, long a financial mainstay of modern dance companies, declined. Financial difficulties forced the disbandment of the Hanya Holm Company in 1944. Miss Holm turned to choreography for Broadway musicals while continuing to teach at her New York studio and at the Colorado College summer sessions.

Nineteen forty-four also saw the end of Doris Humphrey's performing career, owing to an arthritic hip. For a brief time she considered total retirement. But then she found a vehicle for her creativity in José Limón, a former member of her company who had just been released from the U.S. Army. She became artistic director for his company and composed some of her best-known works for it. She also continued to teach choreography.

Following the breakup of his partnership with Doris Humphrey in 1940, Charles Weidman continued to teach, choreograph, and maintain a company and studio theater. Because he had depended heavily on her, he found it difficult going alone as his financial problems grew. However, in spite of the drawbacks, he was able to choreograph a number of important works in the years that followed.

Of the original four pioneers, only Martha Graham was still in full command of her performing powers at the end of World War II. And the peak of her creative career was still ahead of her.

Two other important dancers of this generation were Helen Tamiris and Lester Horton.

Helen Tamiris combined ballet and Delsartean theory learned from Irene Lewisohn to create her own style of modern dance. In 1930 she attempted to unify modern dancers through the cooperative performances of the Dance Repertory Theater, but unification was not to be realized for another thirty years. Together with her husband, Daniel Nagrin, she founded the Tamiris-Nagrin Company in 1960, which was dissolved with her death in 1966.

Influenced by Denishawn, Mary Wigman, the Japanese dancer Michio Ito, American Indians, and ballet, Lester Horton organized a dance company in Los Angeles in 1932, which was notable as the first company to include blacks. Although he was aware of the activities of the modern dancers in New York, he preferred to work in isolation from them. Following his untimely death in 1953, some of the dancers from his company continued their own careers, including Alvin Ailey, Carmen de Lavallade, Bella Lewitzky, Joyce Trisler, and James Truitte. Through these dancers Horton's eclectic, individualistic technique and choreography have been kept alive.

*Born near Pittsburgh and raised in Santa Bar-
bara, Martha Graham, like Isadora Duncan,
Ruth St. Denis, and Doris Humphrey, had a
remarkably strong mother who encouraged
her. She began her early days of dance as a
student and performer at Denishawn, where
she worked principally with Ted Shawn. She
made her debut there in 1919 and remained
until 1923.*

*Her first independent concert, given in New
York City in 1926, had eighteen dances on the
program, performed by her and three other
women. Throughout her evolving periods
and styles, strong, dynamic women of history
and literature have provided the inspiration for
many of the roles she created for herself in her
works.*

*The Martha Graham School of Contemporary
Dance was founded in New York in 1927.
The dance technique that is still taught there
developed out of movements she created for
her choreography. As her technique was taught
and retaught by many other dancers, it became
codified and systematized.*

GRAHAM
1937

*Martha
Graham
(1894-)*

*The long span of
of Graham's career
has contributed to and set
the pace for the establish-
ment of modern dance as a valid, independent
art form, and her company has provided the
starting point for many of the major choreographers who have followed her. Since her retirement as a performer in 1969, she has continued
to choreograph for and to direct her company.
In 1976 she celebrated the fiftieth anniversary
of the founding of her company with a gala performance and the premiere of* Lucifer, *performed
by Margot Fonteyn and Rudolf Nureyev. Thus
her rebellion has come full circle.*

*Graham's philosophical outlook, as expressed in
this essay, has remained unchanged throughout
her career.*

Throughout time dance has not changed in one essential function. The function of the dance is communication. The responsibility that dance fulfill its function belongs to us who are dancing today.

To understand dance for what it is, it is necessary we know from whence it comes and where it goes. It comes from the depths of man's inner nature, the unconscious, where memory dwells. As such it inhabits the dancer. It goes into the experience of man, the spectator, awakening similar memories.

Art is the evocation of man's inner nature. Through art, which finds its roots in man's unconscious—race memory—is the history and psyche of race brought into focus.

We are making a transition from 18th to 20th century thinking. A new vitality is possessing us. Certain depths of the intellect are being explored. Great art never ignores human values. Therein lies its roots. This is why forms change.

No art can live and pass untouched through such a vital period as we are now experiencing. Man is discovering himself as a world.

All action springs from necessity. This necessity is called by various names: inspiration, motivation, vision, genius. There is a difference of inspiration in the dance today.

Once we strove to imitate gods—we did god dances. Then we strove to become part of nature by representing natural forces in dance forms—winds—flowers—trees.

Dance was no longer performing its function of communication. By communication is not meant to tell a story or to project an idea, but to communicate experience by means of action and perceived by action. We were not speaking to that insight in man which would elevate him to a new strength through a heightened sense of awareness. Change had already taken place in man, was already in his life manifestations. While the arts do not create change, they register change.

This is the reason for the appearance of the modern dance. The departure of the dance from classical and romantic delineations was not an end in itself, but the means to an end. It was not done perversely to dramatize ugliness, or to strike at sacred tradition—to destroy from sheer inability to become proficient in the technical demands of a classical art. The old forms could not give voice to the more fully awakened man. They had to undergo metamorphosis—in some cases destruction—to serve as a medium for a time differently organized.

The modern dance, as we know it today, came after the World War. This period following the war demanded forms vital enough for the reborn man to inhabit. Because of the revitalized consciousness came an alteration in movement—the medium of dance, as tone is medium. Out of this came a different use of the body as an instrument, as the violin is an instrument. Body is the basic instrument, intuitive, instinctive. As a result an entirely contemporary set of technics was evolved. While it had points of similarity with the old, that was because it was based on the innate co-ordination of the body which is timeless. With this enhanced language, and the more vitally organized instrument, the body, we are prepared for a deep, stirring creative communication.

All of this has nothing to do with propaganda as known and practiced. It only demands the dance be a moment of passionate, completely disciplined action, that it communicate participation to the nerves, the skin, the structure of the spectator.

For this to be accomplished, however, it means that the communication be valid to the twentieth century man. There has been swift transition in this present recurrence of the modern dance. There was a revolt against the ornamented forms of impressionistic dancing. There came a period of great austerity. Movement was used carefully and significantly. Subject matter began to diverge—the dancer emerged from the realm of introspection. The dance began to record evolution in man's thinking. An impassioned dynamic technic was needed and gradually appeared. Dance accompaniment and costume were stripped to essentials. Music came to be written on the dance structure. It ceased to be the source of the emotional stimulus and was used as background. Music was used almost in the same sense that decor had been used in the older dance to bring the emotional content of the movement into focus for the spectator. As dance evolved into larger forms, music began to evolve also. The composer gained a greater strength and a more significant line from composing to meet the passionate requirements of the dance.

Then arose a danger. With music no longer acting in that capacity, what means to employ for focus—a focus suited to the eyes of today? Dance can remain for a time an authentic, creative experience for the comparative few. There are those for whom focus is possible—because of their awareness and their response to the artist and his medium. But for the many the focus is not sharp enough to permit clear vision. At this point the responsibility rests with the dancer-choreographer. Now it seems necessary that the focus be made through sight.

While music for the dance is still transparent and exciting as an element, we still use the perennial black velvet curtain of another period as background. They were first used for the dance I believe by Isadora Duncan. She used them, from the same need we have today, to bring focus upon the dance, and she succeeded. But the dance today is another dance, brought into emergence by another orientation. Perhaps what Arch Lauterer calls "space man" will be as necessary to the dance of the future as the composer. All of life today is concerned with space problems, even political life. Space language is a language we understand. We receive so much of sensation through the eye.

It is understood without question that presentation can never take the place of the dance. It can only cover bad and unauthentic dancing as music was long able to do. But this evolved presentation will have nothing to do with dance decor in the older sense, which was basically a painting enlarged for the stage. At best it can only be an *accent* for the dance, evolved after the dance is finished. Dance decor can, I believe, serve as a means of enhancing movement and gesture to the point of revelation of content.

I refuse to admit that the dance has limitations that prevent its acceptance and understanding—or that the intrinsic purity of the art itself need be touched. The reality of the dance is its truth to our inner life. Therein lies its power to move and communicate experience. The reality of dance can be brought into focus—that is into the realm of human values—by simple, direct, objective means. We are a visually stimulated world today. The eye is not to be denied. Dance need not change—it has only to stand revealed.

When Doris Humphrey reached Denishawn in 1915, she had already had many years of dance study in her hometown of Oak Park, Illinois, as well as some teaching experience. She soon became a teacher at the school and a leading performer with the Denishawn Company. In addition to assisting Ruth St. Denis with choreography, she created dances of her own, which became part of the Denishawn repertoire.

By the time Doris Humphrey left Denishawn in 1928, she had begun choreographing in a totally new style, and she had developed a fundamental theory of movement that became the basis of her technique. Together with Charles Weidman, who left Denishawn at the same time, Humphrey founded the Humphrey-Weidman Dance Company, based in New York. Both partners taught, choreographed, and performed together in each other's works for the next sixteen years. When the

WHAT
Humphrey-Weidman Company was disbanded in 1945, she be-

A DANCER
came the artistic director for the company of José

THINKS
Limón and continued to display her ability

ABOUT
as a master choreographer with a mature sense of artistry. Always articulate, she set forth her choreographic principle in The Art Of Making Dances, *which was published shortly after her death.*

The following essay, written about 1937 as the first chapter of a book that was never completed, describes an insider's view of dance.

THE DANCER ANSWERS SOME QUESTIONS

Doris Humphrey (1895-1958)

On reflecting about a long career in the theatre as a dancer, I recall numerous people who have offered me questions and remarks, usually in a pressing crowd backstage after a performance. Since I had no time to answer them properly then, my conscience, or is it my egotism, prompts me to send the answers out into space, hoping that the woman in

Oklahoma who liked it but didn't know why, and the student in California who thought it must be good exercise, but "what is it all about?" will chance to read this book and be wiser. These people, who are fairly numerous, must be the visible seventh of an iceberg that reaches into the cold, dark depths of America, and it is my hope that some of these may be thawed out too. In case I should seem, in the following pages, to be pouncing too much on the least intelligent members of our audience, may I say that there are hundreds of people who have been most appreciative, and who have said just the right things to warm the heart of any creative artist. My intention, however, is to crusade and not to eulogize; hence the attack on the misunderstanding that exists about the Modern Dance in the mind of that most important person in the theatre—the ultimate consumer.

One of the things often said to me in a backstage crush is: "You must be glad you took up dancing. It's such nice work. But don't you get awfully tired? You do three or four hours [of] rehearsal, besides the performance. My! I'd be dead, but I suppose you like it and it *is* nice work." One of these speeches has the effect of paralyzing me, and a feeble "yes" is about all I can manage at the time. The implications are so staggering that it certainly will take many words to try to strip off the layers and layers of asbestos wrappings overlaying the true responsiveness to the dance which I firmly believe everyone possesses. "Taking up dancing" perhaps enrages me most as a phrase. Dancing, by implication, is a hobby which one "takes up," like gardening or rug weaving, and what makes it "nice work" is that people will pay to see it or learn it. It obviously makes you tired sometimes, and this confuses our poor stupid one. Why work to the point of exhaustion? That can't be much fun. This is, no doubt, put down to the inexplicable vagaries of artists, who are notoriously lacking in common sense. They just let their enthusiasms run away with them. Once a man told me that, during a long passage when I was lying on the floor in one of my dances, all he could think of was rushing up on the stage with a blanket. The dramatic scene that was going on at the same time passed him by because he could not forget that females do not lie partially nude on cold floors. It isn't sensible to pursue even nice work that far.

The next remark of my original questioner, that "I'd be
dead doing that," reveals another terrific gap in her perceptions (usually it's a women; no man of the same calibre
would imagine doing it at all¹).   The highly trained body
of the dancer is as different from that of the non-dancer
as an antelope from an ox. They both breathe and move
their legs and have similar nervous systems so they both
belong to the animal kingdom, but the ox is a handsome,
dignified, and integrated creature the way he is and wouldn't
dream of overstepping the limitations of his species or care
to embarrass the antelope with suggestions as to how *he*
would look bounding from crag to crag like that. Parenthetically, however, the similarities in physical construction
and function between our two kinds of human animals are
quite sufficient to make the layman understand the dancer,
given a direct and simple approach, with no nonsense about
the dancer's function being a kind of glorified fancy-work.
Of this, much more later.

   I should like our audiences to know: first—that one does
not "take up dancing" in my kind of theatre, any more than
Aimee McPherson took up evangelism, or Geraldine Farrar
singing.   The dancer is born with, or cultivates an overwhelming desire to dance, and to communicate his findings
about life in this medium. No, he doesn't think of dancing
as "nice work," or as a way to make a living, but as an imperative urge, a call. He wants to make his art mean something to people, not superficially as entertainment, but to
their real selves, the selves they bring to living and that they
sometimes bring to be fed at the springs of the other arts,
notably music and literature. In other words, he wants to
make it significant.

SIGNIFICANCE IN THE DANCE VERSUS LITERATURE

Significance can hardly be justified in the eyes of non-dancers
without some explanation. They may ask, and often do:
"Why make the Dance significant, when there is already
at hand such a completely expressive medium as literature?
I think dancing should be graceful." The thought of
significant dancing perplexes the modern mind, which is

trained to slide easily from idea to expression only in well-greased literary channels. In fact, the idea of art, with the exception of literature, conveying anything other than simple conceptions of the beautiful, is quite unfamiliar. People on the whole are slaves of "The Word" and the tendency is to believe that if it cannot be written it cannot be said at all, or even that it does not exist. As an extreme instance of this: I once knew a man who did not learn to write until he was twenty-five years old. When he did, however, the revelation of "The Word" took tremendous hold on him. In his idle moments he would write his name on a scrap of paper, and gaze at the miracle of it for fifteen minutes. "The Word" made him an entity. It confirmed an existence of which he had entertained some doubt until he learned to write it down. He typifies the prejudice of our times towards the exclusive expression of the Self through the medium of words, which certainly are indispensable for the ordering of groceries, or the writing of a treatise on political economy, but in my opinion are by no means able to express the whole man. "The Word" is easier for man. It comprehends his daily living, but at the same time its limitations restrict his cultural life. The simplest mind unconsciously admits that it is not enough to be able to speak. How often do we hear such a phrase as: "Words cannot describe it." This comes even from people who have a large vocabulary. Heretofore man expressed his noblest self in dance and gesture, until the word-mongers put him to sleep with their dreary drugs and grabbed the ordering and governance of ritual for themselves. Then "The Word" was made more important than the act, so that now religion is a doleful mumbling in church pews and the philosophy of life is a tangle of incomprehensible phrases in a book.

The dancer and artist deplores this tendency to restrict the expression of the grandest impulses of humanity to agitations in the larynx and to words and more words in a book. The dancer believes that his art has something to say which cannot be expressed in words or in any other way than by dancing. He recognizes that he is the lineal descendant of those ancients who expressed their innermost feelings in dance and gesture long before language became common.

He is, in a sense, a throwback. He is aware of that but believes that his art is rooted so deeply in Man's fundamental instincts that he can read back into His unconscious remembrance, before the atrophy of civilization set in, and move Him profoundly without a word being spoken. This is so little recognized among laymen that such a conversation as this, between a college girl and myself, took place recently: She asked—"How much do professional dancers have to study?" On my replying that students often dance five or six hours a day for several years, she said: "I don't mean the steps, but really study, you know, from a book." To me this is both horrifying and pathetic. There are times when the simple dignity of movement can fulfill the function of a volume of words. There are movements which impinge upon the nerves with a strength that is incomparable, for movement has power to stir the senses and emotions, unique in itself. This is the dancer's justification for being, and his reason for searching further for deeper aspects of his art.

But the reaction of his potential audience, except for a few, puts the artist in the position of having to defend and explain. Actually very few people understand the basic element of the dancer's art, or appreciate the impulse which provokes the modern dancer to enlarge it. Yet the explanation is quite simple if the reader will try to forget his prejudices, and examine his reactions to movement of any kind, and then translate it into terms of dancing.

MOVEMENT SPEAKS VOLUMES: KINESTHESIA IS THE WORD FOR IT

Who, for instance, has not felt a thrill of violence as a train rushes past, or not experienced the quieting effect of still water? These sensations are examples of the two extremes of our response to movement; on the one hand, the terror inspired by movement out of our control; on the other hand, the negative response we have to absolute rest. Neither sensation in its ultimate sense is emotionally bearable, the one being confusing, the other boring. Between the two, however, lies a whole range of movement with definite degrees of stimulation and response. Allied to this response to the static and the dynamic is the response to balance and unbalance. John Martin, in his "American Dances," has explained this phase of my work in the following words:

In its structural sense, movement is "The arc between two deaths." On the one hand is the death of negation, motionless; on the other hand is the death of destruction, the yielding to unbalance. All movement can be considered to be a series of falls and recoveries; that is, a deliberate unbalance in order to progress, and a restoration of equilibrium for self-protection. Thus is typified the basic life struggle for maintenance and increase. A more dramatic medium, or more inseparable from human experience could hardly be imagined; it is inherently both exciting and relevant. The nearer the state of unbalance approaches the dangerous the more exciting it becomes to watch, and the more pleasurable the recovery. This danger zone, which life tends to avoid as much as possible, is the zone in which the dance largely has its existence.

The only author on esthetics I have ever read who perceived this same fundamental relationship of balance and unbalance to all art, is Ozenfant, the French painter and teacher who, in a chapter on "Constants," in his book *Foundation of Modern Art,* shows a diagram of a man falling and states that all form is the echo in us of the awareness of gravity, and that the unconscious participation in the constant falling and recovering of all moving objects is the basic of a universal language of feeling. Not a word about dancing as the supreme manifestation of this language occurs in the book. In fact, no mention is made of the dance whatever. In this respect, M. Ozenfant is in complete accord with at least ninety-nine percent of the world's authors of books on art. This obtuseness on the part of authors is a tempting subject, but being far too busy to pursue, single-handed, a fight with esthetes who ignore the dance as the mother of the Arts, I had best proceed with an explanation of the stuff the Dance is made of.

The sense which perceives and responds to the stimuli of balance and unbalance, stasis and movement, is rooted in the muscles and is known to dancers and students of physiology as Kinesthesia. It is the Modern Dancer who claims, by instinct and training, to have a special conscious-ness of kinesthesia. For him it is an instrument for promoting an esthetic experience appealing to senses to which no other

art appeals. Not only this, but the special claim of the Modern
Dancer is that he, and only he, by painstaking search, has
rediscovered and re-applied the laws of kinesthesia so that
the dancer appears as a human being on the stage and not a
machine for making geometrical lines in space. Or, rather,
this is what I claim that I do. Unfortunately, it is not possible
to assert that all modern dancing looks human and not
geometric. In general, however, it would be easier for a
theological student to deny God than for the dancer to deny
the existence of kinesthesia. His special perception of it
makes it imperative for him to use it. That is why he dances
instead of writing a book.

Kinesthesia is a rudimentary response in most people,
and there is a great need for a fuller consciousness of this
special sense for it to be ordered and made comprehensive.
Only thus can audiences really enjoy modern dancing. This
sense needs to be enlarged by education and training; nothing
else about us has been so much allowed to atrophy. When
man ceased to run and leap for his food the decay of the
kinesthetic sense began. With this defection the universal
interest in dance and ritual also declined, and as man
labored slowly outwards and upwards to the heaven of
industrial civilization where his food comes with the nuts
and bolts of the assembly line, so did he lose any sympathetic
perception of dance movement which extends beyond the
piston one-two of the Rockettes' leg drill.

But this situation is not entirely hopeless. The further
increase in leisure time arising out of our industrial growth
has helped to increase play and athletics and most particularly
the ballroom dance and the folk dance. These will partially
restore to the layman some of the perceptiveness of his
kinesthetic sense.

DANCING IS LIKE MUSIC

One of the things that makes the language of kinesthesia
difficult from the dark side of the footlights is that it is
abstract. Its scope is roughly parallel with that of music.
Like music, it has psychic overtones to which one responds
and which give one definite emotions not clearly described.
This in the dance is called Metakinesis, or emotional meaning

overlaying kinesthesia, and can be the whole reason for a dance; for a dance composed without any story does have, for whoever looks for it, a great deal of meaning. This meaning is for him alone; that is, it belongs with those profound, almost incomprehensible, responses within us, of which we can scarcely tell because they defy the telling.

Everyone is familiar with these strong but difficult-to-define responses when it comes to music. The symphony, for example, is abstract; it does not tell a story, yet great masses of people are profoundly stirred by the marvellous interplay of tone, rhythm, melody and harmony. These elements in the hands of a great composer recall experience, purge and elevate the spirit, and, by organizing harmony against disharmony, help to make the tragedy of living bearable. The very fact that music such as this is abstract makes it powerful. Each one who listens may interpret the sounds in his own way; it speaks to him directly, unhampered by a certain kind of circumstance. The traditional contrast to this is Opera, where the intricacies of the plot may interest you; on the other hand, they may distract you from the music and your personal drama. Then again, the appearance of a real pair of lovers—in Tristan and Isolde—may meet your demands of romantic love but often it is more thrilling to listen to the music either canned or on the concert stage.

Abstract dancing is analogous to abstract music. The same elements are there—the tone, rhythm, melody and harmony, with the addition of the kinesthetic appeal only possible in the dance. This means that, to a sensitive onlooker, there is a constant stream of primitive excitement going on inside him; movement and gestures by the dancers, that have been submerged in his subconscious mind, seem to come alive in him; he is young, supple, strong. He sees re-enacted urges and releases that he has had only words for, efforts and successes, and failures, all more dynamic for being expressed in movement. He sees models of dynamic equi-librium; units running, falling, leaping, whirling, not dis-integrating but always balancing out into a logical con-tinuity of creative line. Or perhaps the choreographer will give him, as a contrast, the horrid bogeyman—Disharmony—staggering drunkenly through a group where freedom means anarchy, and the conflicting elements do not yield to logic and reason. Again, the mass pattern of the dance may hold the mirror up to humanity. It can indicate its vulgar grimacing images, scrambling and competing in wild riotous disorder. It catches the audience in the theatre in a sober and reflective mood and shows it the image of the drunken, orgiastic confusion which is optimistically called Civilization, and to which it returns once it steps outside. It is like playing to an alcoholic a victrola record of his previous night's indiscretions. Before the audience leaves, however, the dancer gives it an object lesson in the smoothness of line, beauty of form, and clarity of purpose a group can achieve by the co-ordination of its parts and the mutual co-operation of the individuals composing the group. Again, for instance, the aspect of the eternal triangle is presented in its abstract form. The bickering of the opposed A, B and C becomes a jarring rhythm creating a feeling of discomfort in the audience and the resolution of the triangle in terms of harmony, because it is pleasurable, creates an intellectual bias towards such a solution.

WHAT DOES IT MEAN TO YOU?

Sometimes the interpretation by an audience is quite different from that the choreographer intended, but this does not disturb him in the least, or, shall I say, it does not disturb me. An A, B, and C theme may mean international complications to some. This is quite alright as long as it means something to them. I don't even mind the quite far-fetched explanation such as the one that came to my ears about my "Bach Passacaglia in C Minor." At a certain point in this abstract composition one dancer walks on the backs of certain others with an heroic and rather haughty stride. The left wing said this was Capitalism walking on the backs of Labor, and when Labor finally arose and dominated the scene, their joy was complete. The idea I had used was Courage and Faith in the face of adversity. Far from being contrite over the charge, which I frequently have from critics, that such and such an abstract dance is vague, and that it might mean different things to different people, I say let them fit the dance into their own experience; this is the power and the glory of abstraction. Must Cesar Franck's symphony be about Adolphe, who was sitting one day in a garden overlooking the Rhine, when Anna, a beautiful young girl, walks by, reminding him of his lost love in the Bavarian Alps? Only if you are ten years old I should think.

I wonder if any of this will answer the lady from Oklahoma?

In 1921 Charles Weidman found his way to Denishawn from Lincoln, Nebraska, and became a member
of the company, performing frequently as Martha
Graham's partner. It was at Denishawn also that he
met Doris Humphrey, which led to an association
that lasted more than twenty years.

As a choreographer he is best known for his satirical
and whimsical comedies. However, he also created
important dances on serious subjects and choreographed several Broadway shows. Like Miss Humphrey,
he had an infallible sense of good theater. He also
had a natural spontaneity of expression and the
ability to single out human traits.

Following the breakup of the Humphrey-Weidman
Company, his artistic and personal life began to decline, although he continued to maintain a school and
choreograph for his own company and for the New
York City Center Opera. After reaching a devasta-
tingly low point in the mid-1950s, he sought to re-
build his career. He opened a new studio, the Expression of Two Arts, which was a miniature replica

RANDOM
of the old Humphrey-Weidman
Studio Theatre. There, in an in-

REMARKS
adequate space,
surrounded by a
few loyal followers, he kept alive his old works and
choreographed new ones. The last years before his
death brought a new wave of support from the
dance world.

Charles Weidman, more a doer than a writer, made
the following statement for the second edition of
The Dance Has Many Faces (1966).

Charles I have always believed that the audience and
Weidman the performer are indivisible. Both artist and
(1901-1975) audience enter the house—although through
different doors—from the same street. They
have both seen the same headlines, left the
same world of reality behind them. And
while the artist puts on his make-up, the audience leaves its everyday disillusionment in
the checkroom.

Real art can never be escape from life. In histrionic terms, illusions are not false impressions or misconceptions of reality. The world of illusion which the audience expects from the artist is, in fact, the world of their real selves, the image of their own world, the translation of their hopes and fears, their joys and sufferings into the magic of the stage.

The artist must not run away from himself, from his "center of being." He is the bearer of a message, and it is his responsibility to tell it—in whatever medium it may be—intelligibly, forcefully and with his utmost artistic ability. He may sometimes fail in the delivery of his message, but he must never fail in his purpose.

It is often said of the modern dance that it is not easily understood, that its silent language of movement is so intricate as to veil its meaning. But since any dance presentation lives only while it is being performed and since it can hardly be preserved for later in files and books, it would utterly fail to accomplish its task or even to justify its existence could it not clearly convey its message. Only poets, musicians, painters or sculptors can dare challenge their contemporaries with their media of art and yield to the judgment of posterity. The dancer can do this as little as can the actor or singer. L'art pour l'art is for him the death sentence expressed by his own feeble attempt to convince his audience.

I have always been impatient with the "art pour l'artist." Clarity and understandability has remained the basis of my dance creations. Their intent, concerned with human values and the experience of our times, must be carried by the fullest emotional impact the artist can muster. Then, with the conception of the idea, the intelligibility of its message and the emotional intensity of presentation, the artist's primordial task is fulfilled and—however his artistic deliverance may be judged—his sincerity cannot be doubted.

Some may say that I am going too far when I desire to make my dance creations as easily understandable as a movie. But this may explain why more and more I have come to believe in the pantomimic dance drama. The word "pantomime" does not mean to me the presentation of a dumb show, as most dictionaries define it, or the mere telling of a story or action without the use of explanatory words. To me it is the transport of an idea into movement, the animation of the feeling behind the idea, an animation in which suddenly all commas and periods, all silent moments of an unwritten play become a reality in movement. Moreover, it may be likened to that emotional sequence of a growing world of images which we may experience when listening to a symphony, full of logical continuity and expressiveness where words might seem feeble and music inadequate.

I may be prejudiced in favor of the pantomimic dance, because I have found that my gift as a dancer is essentially tied up with my dramatic talent as an actor, or—let us better say—as a mime. The modern mime must be a modern dancer, and as such his entire body must be alive. This cannot be acquired by emotional experience, only by hard physical training. It may be best called bodily awareness. In order to test this bodily awareness in one of my dance compositions, I went so far as to exclude the face, i.e., the facial expression, completely from the pantomimic presentation.

Any idea being projected produces its specific movement and gesture pattern which is, in itself, purely abstract. Though, basically, pantomime is not mere storytelling, a story may be, and usually is, achieved by what is done. But to attain such ends, the means must be determined by strict form, since form alone leads to artistry.

In seeking to reach my audience and to convey my message in the easiest understandable manner, I often chose the channels of humor. There are various kinds of humor, but first and foremost it must be said that, whenever a humorous element is required, it can come only from the performer himself and must be projected by him.

In the beginning I employed the most obvious humor, the sadistic type of humor, the effect of which is almost guaranteed with every audience. However, with time, I was continually looking for a broader expression of what I wanted to achieve, and I attempted to abstract the essence of any emotion projected through movement. Here is an example. Instead of being frantic as, let us say, a minstrel would be when a bucket of water is thrown over him, I tried to convey the same idea without impersonating a minstrel and with no bucket of water causing the emotion. This attempt finally crystallized into a dance called *Kinetic Pantomime*. In this composition I so juggled, reversed and distorted cause and effect, impulse and reaction that a kaleidoscopic effect was created without once resorting to any literary representation.

It has been a long and arduous way from this comedy pantomime to Thurber's *Fables*. But my basic approach to subject matter, though it has widened and developed, has never changed. Content and form are equally important to my choreographic pantomimes. I have never believed that artistry can be achieved without adhering to the strictest form, nor that the heart of the public can be reached, if the artist is blind to the life that surrounds him or tries to shut himself off from it by escaping into mere fantasy and romance. Art demands that we be part of life and merge with it. Art and life are as indivisible an entity as the artist and his audience.

The German dancer, Hanya Holm, along with Martha Graham, Doris Humphrey, and Charles Weidman participated in the Bennington College School of the Dance in the 1930s. She was actually a second-generation modern dancer, having been a member of the Wigman company in Germany. The success of Miss Wigman's tours in the United States in 1930 and 1931 encouraged her to ask Hanya to come in America in 1931 to establish a New York branch of the Wigman school. By 1936 Hanya had realized that German modern dance was not entirely appropriate for Americans, and she decided to develop her own school, company, and style.

HANYA SPEAKS

Although forced to disband her company in 1944, Hanya continued to maintain a studio in New York. Since 1940 she has taught summer sessions in modern dance at Colorado College. Choreographically, however, she turned to musical comedy on Broadway, her best-known contribution being "My Fair Lady." Her former students, who include Alwin Nikolais, Don Redlich, Nancy Hauser, and Valerie Bettis, have retained in their own work much of that which is unique in German modern dance, particularly the space concepts.

"Hanya Speaks" deals largely with Hanya Holm's philosophy as a teacher of dance.

Hanya Holm (1898-) You are your own master and student. There is no value in copying what someone else has done. You must search within your own body. What you discover there will be for your own benefit. Others can give you the means, the tools, but they cannot do it for you. The art of dancing is in no book, nor can you take it with a spoon or in [the] form of pills. Dance can only result from your own concentration and understanding. When you do stretches, sit-up excercises, or whatever you may be doing, you are doing it for one purpose only: you want to make an instrument out of what is otherwise a mere body.

* * *

There is a difference between acting a movement and actually doing it. In the final analysis it is meaningless to count the amount of jumps you can do, because one small gesture which is right and proves the oneness of purpose in what is being done will far outweigh everything else.

* * *

Finding something is the greatest thing that can happen to you. If you are searching you will make new discoveries, but searching is not easy. You cannot help facing movement blocks that will stand in your way. No one can remove these blocks except you yourself, and only when you are able to remove them will you eventually discover yourself. This is the only way you can improve and grow into something big.

* * *

You need an enormous amount of inspiration within yourself. Don't wait for someone to light a candle within you or place a bomb under you. A bomb causes external excitement which is quite the opposite from the excitement you should have. The excitement must come from your inner focus. There can be no inner focus if you are not aware of what the head is doing, what the arm, the trunk, the back is doing. The entire body must be knowledgeable before there can be an inner focus. The same moment you discover that focus you will burst forth in your outward appearance. Your audience will recognize it immediately. The people won't have to look inside of you for emotional overtones. Your chest will be right, your hip will be right, you will have a carriage that is supported and that is right for that which is intended.

* * *

Let's face it, the art of dance is much bigger than any one of us. We are ants in relation to what dance is, but it is an honor to be that ant. Don't say, "Oh well, we did that, and I kicked my leg five inches higher than she did." Who cares? Did you understand the movement? That is what matters.

* * *

Don't swallow everything hook, line, and sinker. Absorb! React! There isn't such a thing as *"the"* gospel. Don't expect a compliment unless you deserve it. When you do receive a compliment take it at its face value. Good dance instructors do not throw around compliments. They don't throw them away. If you are dissatisfied because of lack of praise, see why you are dissatisfied. Is it the teacher's fault or yours?

* * *

Your enemies are not those about you in the studio, but your own imperfections. You can't fight yourself if you run away and refuse to see yourself.

* * *

On stage there is no use pretending you are an ostrich with your head in the sand. The audience recognizes everything you are trying to hide. Every gesture you make reveals something of you. Don't think you can hide behind a gimmick, or a little bit of extravaganza you have learned to master with great flourish. Even the simplest movement will be marvelous if it is fulfilled by you, by your real self. When you dance you are naked.

* * *

There is no easy short cut to learning how to dance. Don't walk around lamenting that you "didn't feel right, or you didn't feel this or that, or the movement wasn't right for you, or you were out late last night." You have no excuse. You must function right there where the demand is made. Your whole life with its ups and downs must be focused. This doesn't mean that you have to live like a bird in a cage. On the contrary, open up and fly out. That little magnet in the center holds you together. Master whatever comes your way and enjoy the mastering. Unless you are challenged there is no work, there is no accomplishment, there is nothing of value, there is no test of your strength. Strength has to be challenged, otherwise it is lost. Challenges are just as important to life as eating, perhaps even more so.

* * *

Watch little children when they hear some music. They throw themselves around and onto the floor and jump up again. They don't get hurt. They don't care. They enjoy it. They fall down a second time and roll over and laugh it off. You should be able to do the same thing but you kill it with fear. They have no fear. Art is living. It is not just craftsmanship, It is the flow of love. There is that meeting place of the body and the soul and the spirit that gives you control.

* * *

A walk is of no value unless it is of the nature that you can change it. You should be able to do an angry walk, a floating walk, a sombre walk, a determined walk cutting into space. You must be able to change it to fulfill the inner demand of what you want the walk to be. If you can follow only one pattern which is very thoroughly ingrained in you, then you have closed the doors to all of that which is expressional.

* * *

What you are capable of is so marvelous that it is almost impossible to imagine what you could do if you achieved it. Don't say you can never get there. Get as far as you can with a full heart and with full conviction, then try to drive on a little further. To achieve something takes strength. You are not born with that strength, you have to gain it. Don't look at your exercises as something to make your muscles hurt, but as something that will help you to improve yourself. Know that you are a human being, that you are able to take

life as it is. Life is not an escape. It is not an excuse. It is not
idle cowardliness. You must think, "I can do more this year
than I did last year because I have grown meanwhile."
Don't dull yourself with copying something or someone,
remember that sometimes you absorb much more through
your pores than through your head.

* * *

You must be humble in relation to your steady progress.
Be thankful for what you have but recognize that you haven't
gotten it all. We are all but a small part of what remains to
be discovered, to be found out. Those who have attained
even a great deal know that there still lie out there somewhere
a thousand things yet to be discovered. You will find out
that one life is not enough. You will want to have several
lives in which to discover what there is to be discovered.

* * *

The right way of developing is to go at a steady pace and
to get the most out of every situation. When you have
reached a platform, look for the stairs leading up to the next
platform. But be patient, don't want success too fast. Learn
to wait. The platform on which you stand must not be an
illusion. Above all, it must be deserved. It is impossible to
remain for very long on a high platform if you don't have
an absolute knowledge of what you are doing. Operate
within your own ability. Do not try to conquer things
which are too far above you. They may kill you. Sooner or
later it will show that you have no base, that you are just
a hollow front. Audiences are very cruel with hollow fronts.
They will say, "Show me!" and if you don't show them they
will let you fall flat two miles down to your death. Go the
straight, direct way, don't skip anything. Never think that
you are better than anyone else. It is the nature of our
existence on this earth that no one is better than anyone
else.

* * *

At the end of the forties when George Balanchine moved with his company into the City Center, we had long meetings together, and I favored the idea of making a corps of ballet dancers and a corps of modern dancers. There were many talented people in and around New York City, and I wanted to bring them together to form a company for which various choreographers of the modern dance would come in and choreograph .with the pool of chosen dancers. The ballet accomplished this but the modern dance did not. The various choreographers would not let go of the members of their companies. This kind of isolationism among modern dance choreographers has caused the audiences to take sides, and thereby modern dance has failed to achieve recognition as a unit. It was planned to include all styles of choreography in the company—so this was not their reason for holding back. The problem was that their ego [s] would not allow them to let go of the group of dancers they had clustered around themselves. About fifteen years later the same attempt was made, the same people came together and wanted to pool a group of dancers, but they could not get the necessary financial backing. No one was willing to take the risk. Modern dance had done too thorough a job of scattering itself in a thousand different directions.

* * *

You can do a lot with very little if you only know how. If you have something of value, if you have a plan, if you know what you are undertaking, if you have the intelligence to do it, you can accomplish it with very little help. If you can prove that you *have* something, the help will come.

* * *

If you haven't the knowledge to implement a modern dance program, teach folk dance. Folk dance has form, organization, step patterns, relationships, and continuity. It is wrong to try to abstract when you don't even know what the word means. I constantly see abstractions of themes that are nothing more than miserably performed, dull conceptions of what the theme means. Do the forms that

can be done at your level. An Irish jig takes great skill. A
Yugoslavian folk dance is very difficult to accomplish. These
are good forms which you can do if you lack the knowledge
of making up your own. One should not look down on the
forms established in folk dancing. Folk dancing is a highly
developed skill. Skilled folk dancers have the feeling for
rhythm and understand the responsibility one has to a
beat and a pulse. You should see them do sword dances,
you should watch the position of their feet. They are
beautiful. If you can accomplish all of this, you are well on
your way to becoming a good modern dancer.

* * *

I will never forget the great experience I had in the
Cathedral in Strasbourg. It was dark inside the Cathedral
so that you could not see clear to the top. It had the effect
of funneling your whole attention upward. Light was coming
through a beautifully painted window and caused a stream
of reflection which hit an altar with a crucifixion scene. It
had the most unbelievable effect of arresting your step,
of making you stand still, of giving you a heightened sense
of being. How many times does this happen? I have been
in St. Peter's in Rome and in all of the major cathedrals in
Europe but none struck me with that kind of meaningful
space. There was a tension inside that church which created
the constant feeling of being uplifted.

* * *

Your dances must be built from something within your
self. It does not have to be concrete. It may be a very
intangible thing. It may have a very wonderful, ethereal
reason. You cannot do a dance and then decide what it is.
Form has to come out of that to which it is related. That
which causes the behavior determines the form.

* * *

If a decoration is placed on a basic structure without
feeling for the structure, it will be destructive. Decoration

should be used only if it serves to enhance the form and brings out more than the basic naked form can do by itself. Some forms need a diversified statement. Others do not because they are self-sufficient. You must train your senses, taste, and judgment. Training means experience. Judgment is not learning what is black and white.

* * *

Life cannot be superimposed upon a piece of art. If it doesn't have it, it will never have it. The message of life must be given a work at birth. It is the same with us. If we do not have it, we will never have it. We cannot learn it out of a book, it must be learned by experience. It comes with the fine things like the fragrance of a rose.

* * *

Art is projected through the clarity of its form. It is the sum total of something. Something spiritual comes across which is not broadcast through the deed itself, but is manifested in the manner in which you did it. The "how" in which you do it is extremely important. It requires discipline.

* * *

Form is the shape of a content. Form without content becomes form for the sake of form. Inspiration has to be there to make a form live. The form should contain the original impetus out of which it was created. If the form emerged from an emotional ingredient, then that emotional ingredient must be there.

* * *

You should not dance academically. It has no departure, no breath, no life. The academician moves within a group of rules. Two plus two are four. The artist learns rules so that he can break them. Two plus two are five. Both are right from a different point of view.

* * *

An example: a rule is that your knee has to be over your toe when you perform a plié. Sometimes you have to turn the knee in and break the rule. If you know the rule and technique, then you can bring that knee in without getting hurt. For some things the knee must be in in order for the shape and form to be right according to that which you are communicating. Another rule is that when walking you transfer the weight from straight knee to straight knee with an adjustment of the general velocity. You may want to walk in an awkward way with hanging knees for the reason of getting an idea across. You have broken the rule of walking right, but you have entered a form through which you could communicate. Yet if you don't know the rules you won't know how to break them. You might make the baggy knees the norm and the shuffling forward the rule. If you don't know the rules you won't know what to go away from, and there are millions of departures. Your form will often demand that you break rules.

* * *

There are a thousand points of view. Hindemith and I were at the same conservatory in Frankfurt. We both received the same kind of basic training. Then he departed in the way of finding out how music could be made. He used combinations of many different kinds, the twelve-tone scale, the cacophony, the dissonances, broad chords requiring more than ten fingers. He became absorbed in tone qualities and the tone relationships of intervals, but before he died he came back to the classic style. You can work, for example, with just the hands and arms and develop them to the nth degree until they are marvelous—but you will come to a dead end where it will be necessary to return to the body in order to incorporate your findings into the body as such in order to go on moving.

* * *

There are books written about circles and squares. The ancient people understood them. You will find them amongst the old Egyptian ruins. Some of the old Mayan ruins were temples with a circle or a square of stone tops which were of great significance. No one originated these forms. They have always existed. One day while walking about Rome I came upon a church called St. Clement. There was an entrance at one of its sides leading downstairs. Two flights below the church was an ancient heathen worship ground. After passing several hallways which were very low, I came to a chamber with seats around the outside. In the center was a square altar. The old mystical signs were still visible everywhere in the room. They had been hammered into the stone. The worshipers had worn away the earth where they had been sitting. On top of this chamber was a very common assembly hall and on top of that was the church. The more intelligent the ancient peoples were, the more mystical was the form in its use and significance. There is more to a round than just making a circle. You will have to run in circles for many days before you will know what a circle is. Then all of a sudden you will realize that you are not yourself anymore, that your space is dynamic and powerful and that you have to master that force. Turning is almost a dervish exercise with the world suddenly going around and you feeling very calm and quiet. If you work for half a year on circles, your turns will become different.

* * *

Style requires a certain form, and you have to stick to that form. You have to discipline yourself to it, or you will not get a good theater piece. The characteristic has to be maintained in every aspect of the work. Even a walk has to be practiced. There are a thousand walks. If you don't know which walk to do, you will just wobble and walk as best you can, but nothing will be created by it. A walk without a characteristic is as good as nonexistent, it is pitiful. It would be better to lower the curtain and go home.

* * *

The line between emoting and emotion is different with each person. You have to discover within yourself when your technique arrives at a point where your movement becomes an experience as such. You must master the physical experience so that it becomes a kinesthetic experience. You will discover through this kinesthetic experience that a relationship is established within the body which coordinates the flow of movement and the flow of animation. You will find out that movement can contain only a certain amount of emotion before the emotion outdoes the physical experience. When this overtaxation happens, you have overdrawn. Emotion is a stimulus, not an end result. It is arrived at but not emphasized. Emotion is the stimulus which gives the movement its coloring, its reason for being. Since the emotion is the stimulus for the movement, it is, therefore, both the stimulus and a part of the end result.

* * *

The face is of course the mirror of all that goes on, but it should not be more prominent than is intended and it should not substitute for all that which isn't going on in the body. Facial muscles are very small and very sensitive. If the face does too much it turns into mugging. The face becomes a thing in itself. It overdoes things because the body doesn't understand what to do and therefore the face substitutes. The face should have a relationship to the whole attitude. It should enliven the attitude and complement it. A dancer's face is not a mask. I sometimes look at the eyes instead of looking at the movement and I very often see absolutely dead eyes inside a multiple-moving body.

* * *

Your body is your language. Cultivate your language. Be able to say what you want. If you are supposed to be in second position with your bottom sticking out, then it is right according to the form. If your bottom is not supposed to be sticking out and it is, it is an insult to the form. The form is changed from a form into nothing. A form is a silent thing which has achieved a shape. The shape will be as exciting as that which you put into it. It will be clear only as you give it clarity. It can have only the shape which you give it. It can achieve life only because you have given it such. The responsibility is yours.

* * *

Check yourself and see if you are willing to sacrifice yourself for something that is bigger than you are. You must know to what you have put your mind. If you are in dance just to satisfy your ego, then be a nice admirer but get out of the field. If you are dabbling in dance just for your own satisfaction, go right ahead, but don't pass on your half-knowledges to people who are searching. Dance is the noblest art there is. Sacrifice is necessary, even if that sacrifice is your ego. This does not mean that you should become a limp rag and let everyone wipe his dirty feet on you. Your inner self must give you hope, strength, belief, a power of dedication without resorting to the ugly thing of cheating. Make-believes are not worth anything; they have their own doom written within themselves; they only wait for you to find out, and by the time you do find out you will have wasted years and years and years. Waste you must, but waste in the right direction.

* * *

The inner man is a fine little point where your being comes together. If you could externalize it, it would not be bigger than the head of a pin. In size of volume it is not a fraction of a fraction of an atom. This inner man is like the center of a hurricane. The secret of a hurricane is its eye. The eye is calm. If you destroy that eye you destroy the hurricane. If you can't be as calm as the eye of the hurricane which holds all the answers to the devastating storm of the outside, you can't hold yourself up in the world of dilemma and battle. There is no force that does not come from an utter calm. Sensitivity, the power to absorb and to register, is the calm of the eye which starts that outer passion and tremor.

* * *

When you have discovered that inner self, you can call yourself a dancer, but don't get snooty about it. Dancers don't live in ivory towers. If you put that inner man on a scale, it wouldn't weigh more than a hundredth of an ounce. The more you know, the humbler you become, if you really know it. This is growing, studying, living. Dance is life. Know that you are alive.

Part Three

THE
SECOND
GENERATION

INTRODUCTION

The first of the second-generation performing groups was a unit of the Workers Dance League, which had been started in the early thirties by students of the New York Wigman School. Concerned for the social ills of the world, they gave performances in trade union halls for labor groups and gained the support of the Communist party. Over the next ten years many young dancers joined the group, during which time it lost its radical leanings. It had become the New Dance Group, from which evolved in 1942 the performing trio of Jane Dudley and Sophie Maslow of the Martha Graham Company, and William Bales of the Humphrey-Weidman Company. Their New Dance Group Studio offered modern dance classes.

Many of the early members of the second generation began choreographing independently while they were still members of the parent dance company. Among them were José Limón and Sybil Shearer of the Humphrey-Weidman Company, Valerie Bettis of the Hanya Holm Company, and Anna Sokolow, Merce Cunningham, and Erick Hawkins of the Martha Graham Company. Interestingly, in spite of a continuing philosophical rejection of ballet, some of these dancers studied it and used certain aspects of it in their own techniques.

Opportunities for younger dancers began to grow. In 1936 the first series of Sunday afternoon concerts at the 92nd Street Young Men's Hebrew Association in New York City was instituted, offering young dancers a setting in which to make their debuts. Classes were also held at the YMHA, enhancing its position as a center for modern dance. In 1940 the Humphrey-Weidman Company opened a studio theater in which to give their performances, and also made it available to younger dancers.

In 1948 the Bennington School of the Dance was reinstituted at Connecticut College, with Martha Hill and Ruth Bloomer as codirectors. With better performing and studio facilities than those that had been available at Bennington, modern dance had a new summer home.

During the fifties, efforts were directed toward bringing modern dance to larger audiences. The Martha Graham Company had already performed in Broadway theaters, and other companies began to follow suit. Indeed, they were virtually forced to do so in order to be reviewed in the two influential newspapers, *The New York Times* and the *New York Herald-Tribune.* Touring to colleges and universities surpassed prewar levels as the strength and budgets of college dance programs grew.

Most dance companies continued to operate on a shoestring although, for some, increased recognition brought welcome financial assistance. For the first time, foundations began giving grants to a few modern dancers, although most of the money still went to ballet companies. Beginning in 1954, some modern dance companies found themselves used as instruments of U.S. foreign policy, giving State Department-sponsored tours. In fact, for the next fifteen years the Martha Graham Company was not seen in the United States outside of New York City. On the whole, it seemed that the financial problems of modern dance companies were lessening and that the art form had indeed arrived.

During the decade of the 1950s, men began to take over the major leadership of modern dance, despite the continuing social stigma against male participation. José Limón began the José Limón Dance Company in 1947. With Doris Humphrey continuing as his artistic advisor and choreographer until her death, he became one of the most prominent figures in modern dance. He developed a strong, visually striking style for his dances, which were often based on religious or historical themes. As the size of his company grew, he became a master of large group choreography.

In the same period, the avant-garde leaders of modern dance, Merce Cunningham, Erick Hawkins, and Alwin Nikolais, advanced style that differed widely from one another and from all other dancers. Each had broken away from the style of his mentor (Cunningham and Hawkins had worked with Martha Graham and Nikolais had worked with Hanya Holm). Influenced by other artists, each developed a unique approach to the use of music, sets, costumes, and above all to choreography and movement. Costuming was revolutionized by the invention of Helanca; leotards and tights became the sole costumes, creating the unisex look. In the sixties the Moog synthesizer, the computer, and other electronic devices were used to create new music by and for them. Projections of slides onto the stage added a new visual dimension. Sets utilized contemporary materials, such as the helium-filled pillows created by Jasper Johns for Cunningham's *Rainforest.*

Even though these artists became established in the dance world, continued exploration and discovery kept them in the avante-garde of modern dance into the 1970s. Other, younger men also have made significant contributions. Murray Louis, principal dancer with Alwin Nikolais, continued to perform with the Nikolais company after establishing his own company. A dancer's dancer, often humorous, he has a gift for kinetic timing.

Paul Taylor, a former member of the Martha Graham Company, began by experimenting with nondance, in the spirit of the avant-garde. As time passed, however, he explored many diverse styles, some balletic, some highly energetic, others in a narrative vein. His company has become one of the most popular in America.

Alvin Ailey took over direction of the Lester Horton Company for a while after Horton's death in 1953, and then struck out on his own. In blending his black heritage with his dance background, he has created enormously popular and exciting works, and his choreographic career has soared.

Of the women of the second generation, Anna Sokolow spent a number of years in Mexico, Sybil Shearer moved to Illinois, Valerie Bettis worked both on and off Broadway, Jean Erdman, Pearl Lang, Mary Anthony, and others had small companies that did not have the impact of the larger ones. Bella Lewitsky of the Horton Company remained in California and was not seen in the East for more than a decade.

During this period, modern dance began to evolve from an expression of the human condition to the presentation of movement for its own sake. Many of those who continued in the earlier tradition used dance as an expression of the concerns of mid-twentieth-century America.

Merce Cunningham has been a maverick for twenty-five years. Simply by going in his own direction he has had a far-reaching impact on modern dance. The dances that he has choreographed exist for themselves rather than for expressive content. He has eliminated dependence on music by allowing the dance to coexist with the sound; he has developed "chance" choreography which avoids usual or expected movement sequences. He has decentralized the dancers by dispersing them on the stage, allowing the individual abilities of each to thrive.

His dance beginnings seem conventional: tap dance lessons in his hometown of Centralia, Washington. The relatively early influence of avant-garde composer John Cage, who was teaching at the Cornish School of Music in Seattle while Merce was a student there, has had a lifelong impact on him. His later associations with artists Robert Rauschenberg and Jasper Johns have also been influential.

YOU HAVE TO LOVE DANCING TO STICK TO IT

In 1939 Cunningham attended the Bennington School of the Dance at Mills College. He then went to New York to study with Martha Graham and at the School of American Ballet, making his debut with the Graham Company as a soloist in 1940 and performing with her for the next five years. He began choreographing during that time, and in 1953 he established the Merce Cunningham Dance Company.

Cunningham has coupled a completely down-to-earth attitude with a sense of humor and an open point of view. He has been a major influence on the young avant-garde while continuing to work at the forefront of modern dance and remaining open to new possibilities. In 1965 he began to choreograph dances for spaces outside the theater, notably for museums and gymnasiums. In 1977, almost twenty-five years after he began his company, he finally gave a performance in a Broadway theater.

Merce Cunningham (1919-)

The choreographic philosophy that is expressed in the following statement continues to pervade his work.

you have to love dancing to stick to it.   it gives you
nothing back, no manuscripts to store away, no paintings
to show on walls and maybe hang in museums, no poems to
be printed and sold, nothing but that single fleeting
moment when you feel alive.   it is not for unsteady souls.

                              and though it appeals through the eye
                              to the mind, the mind instantly rejects
                              its meaning unless the meaning is
                              betrayed immediately by the action.
                              the mind is not convinced by kinetics
                              alone, the meaning must be clear, or
                              the language familiar and readily
                              accessible.

the kinesthetic sense is a separate and fortunate
behavior.   it allows the experience of dancing to
be part of all of us.

                    but clarity is the lowest form of
                    poetry, and language, like all else
                    in our lives, is always changing.
                    our emotions are constantly being propelled by some new
                    face in the sky, some new rocket to the moon, some new
                    sound in the ear, but they are the same emotions.

you do not
separate
the human being
from the
actions he   it is hard for many people to
does, or   accept that dancing has nothing
the actions   in common with music other than
which sur-   the element of time and division
round him,   of time.   the mind can say how
but you can   beautiful as the music hints at,
see what it   or strikes out with color.
is like to
break these   but the other extreme can be seen
actions up   & heard in the music accompany-
in differ-   ing the movements of the
ent ways, to   wild animals in the Disney films.
allow the   it robs them of their instinctual
passion, and   rhythms, and leaves them as car-
it is pas-   icatures.   true, it is a man-made,
sion, to ap-   arrangement, but what isn't?
pear for each
person in his
own way.

the sense of human emotion that a
dance can give is governed by familiarity with the language, and the
elements that act with the language;
here those would be music, costume,
together with the space in which the dance happens.

      joy, love, fear, anger, humor, all can be "made clear" by
      images familiar to our eyes.   and all are grand or meager
      depending on the eye of the beholder.

              what to some is splendid entertainment,
              to others merely tedium and fidgets;
              what to some seems barren, to others
              is the very essence of the heroic.

and the art is not the better nor the worse.

Erick Hawkins, a native of Trinidad, Colorado, majored in Greek studies at Harvard University and studied ballet before he became a modern dancer. Between 1935 and 1939 he danced with the American Ballet and Ballet Caravan. But in 1938 he joined the Martha Graham Company and left his ballet career behind, becoming Miss Graham's principal partner, and later her husband. In 1947 he began to choreograph, and in 1951 he left Martha Graham to establish an independent life and career.

A LITTLE HOUSE TO UNDERSTAND AND PROTECT IT

Hawkins developed a theory of dance that is radically different from Graham's, one that emphasizes ease and the free flow of movement, together with an Oriental gentleness. He believes that dance should be a visually sensuous experience. This philosophy has pervaded his dances for the last twenty-five years.

Contributing to the quality of Hawkins' work for most of that time has been his composer, Lucia Dlugoszewski. Her onstage performances, given while kneeling in front of musical instruments that she has invented, offer a new dimension to the visual experience of the dance.

Hawkins, who maintains a studio and company in New York, is one of the most articulate modern dancers, and the essay here epitomizes the quality of a Hawkins dance.

Erick Hawkins (1917-)

Dance today in the western world is an art that has just been born.

Therefore we have now two pleas: not only for the new image in an established art, but for the new image in a new art.

(Of course, in somewhere and somehow, dance has always existed even in the west, but on the whole stream of ideas of western culture, it has only been a parenthesis.)

Once born, this dance must grow. It cannot be codified and repeated without the delight in its own day to dayness. Its only tradition is to discover truth for that day.

Every day the mystery must be performed.

Yet the mystery is only the same mystery of every day.

The noise outside is deafening. Someone must say, "sshh," "listen!"

No critic can write this vision, that will create young new dancers. No critic can call the modern dance dead. Only the dancer who loves will have the love to see it live, and call out, "Lazarus, come forth!"

Few people are innocent enough to come to a bright light and see the light or anything for we live with eyes shut tight by no's and it often takes the right word to say "open! this is yes!" And what work could anyone propose? Buddha's ultimate word was lifting the flower in his hand. We have had too much honking of horns to understand such silence. Actually only the shouted word is the reigning favorite of our time. Among the Balinese every man dances. Among the Hopis I have seen men from four (when they began) to a clan chief (of ninety-two) dance. Among us what does everyman do? Read the newspaper?

Ever since I was a little boy living in my culture I couldn't help but sense that something was not quite right; that all the answers had not yet been given; that something had not yet been born that desperately needed to be born. It was too much a culture of deadness and deathliness and ugly bodies. I have always wondered whether every child as he or she grows up arrives at a strange and sorrowful disillusionment when he sees the miracle of the body spoiled and degraded in the adult world. Our only image really for the body is equated with pornography. Our image of dance has always been of something we could never be—that of the fat old sultan owning his pretty little dancing girls.

The truth of art has never been the peacock feather to titillate the fat old caesar. It could never be something he could buy, something outside his own body, to really be. And if it were within him, it could never let him be the fat old caesar. Art has *never* been a luxury; always the deepest force to keep us alive . . . (more than any food or drug).

The dance is the truth, within each person's own special body-that-will-never-happen-again (somehow the ourselfness inside the world). This has been the real revolution of modern dance.

Real-ly speaking, the whole nature of the spirit is the creating of beautiful flesh, and to deny the flesh is to *muzzle* the spirit and therefore to deny the spirit.

The "now" of word-poetry and of music has been slightly unhinged by the bookbinder and the recording machine. But dance, more than any other art, still exists only in the "now" and no place else. This might make it less attractive and less profound to our world so bent on hanging on to each hard complacent thing (even though our dying would never understand).

For me, the momentness of dance is one of its most precious gifts. Actually only the nowness of ourselves really exists; that true seeing of time; in the quiver; in the inside of our seeing and not on the outside horribly on the face of a clock. I want to perform that act which we call moving which really is the insides of our seeing. This is what I want to do more than anything else in the world.

But the dance does not occur until the one who watches sees it as well as the one who dances dances it; until the dancer is sitting in the audience as well as standing on the stage.

I am tired of constantly presenting and seeing presented modern dances as some tiny mysterious naked baby without any little house to understand and protect it. I would like to try to build a little house out of the only materials that can really be found lying around in the streets of our culture—the written words. Architects, painters, and composers of the last fifty years have certainly discovered the power of this material to proclaim the birth of their own. Witness: Frank Lloyd Wright and Le Corbusier, Stravinsky and Schoenberg, Kandinsky and Klee. Now is the time for the dancer, the time of now.

Never any more than today has the world needed artists. From the time of Christ, and even before, the oracle has ever told us to be as the little child and enter the kingdom of heaven and yet every day we see some six-year-old dragging his imaginationless sixty-year-old body around before us to destroy us. The little child is disappearing off the face of the earth and only the artist with his deep love can ever hope to resurrect such an image. For even one person to move beautifully would be to give the possibility of beautiful movement to everyone in the world.

For to move beautifully is to be the little child; the human reality at its most total awareness of the material of living more unfixable than the very aliveness of any man's life.

José Limon was born in Culiacan, Mexico, and grew up in Los Angeles. In 1928 he went to New York to study painting, but a performance by the German dancer Harald Kreutzberg so inspired him that he enrolled in classes at the Humphrey-Weidman studio shortly afterward. Limón studied and danced with the Humphrey-Weidman Company from 1930 to 1940. He also began choreographing independently and organized the Little Group, which performed at the Humphrey-Weidman studio. In 1937 he was a recipient of a Bennington School of the Dance Fellowship. From 1940 to 1942 he toured the West Coast with May O'Donnell, a former member of the Graham Company. After serving in the U.S. Army during World War II, he formed a trio and placed it under the artistic direction of Doris Humphrey, a position she held until her death. During that time the company grew in size and became one of the major dance companies in the United States.

ON DANCE

Many of Limón's dances reflect his Mexican-American heritage, and some clearly exhibit the love of music that he inherited from his father, who was an orchestra conductor. One of his main concerns was to present "the grandeur of the human spirit and the basic tragedy of man." His dance style was magnificently strong, masculine, and elegant, traits that are apparent also in the following essay.

José Limón (1908-1972). The Dance is all things to all men. Parents are delighted and amazed at the instinctive response of their infant to music. "Look, he's dancing." Children do not walk to school. They run, skip, hop, leap: they dance to school, or into the dining room, or up the stairs to bed. The adolescent is notorious for his nervous, jittery dances. And love's young dream: imagine our early romances without a waltz by moonlight! We discover the rapture and intoxication of love during the dance. And even maturity finds a new dimen-

sion to the weary business of existence during the sedate
ritual of the ballroom: a suspension, a surcease, an inexplicable lifting of the spirit, when even the corns cease to hurt.
The dance is an atavism. It has been with us since we became
humans, and no doubt even before that. It will be with us
to the end. It is a human necessity, profound and not to
be denied. Puritans have banned and proscribed it at various
times as the work of the Devil, happily without success. I
believe that we are never more truly and profoundly human
than when we dance.

It is religion. In primitive societies it solemnizes birth,
puberty, marriage, and death, the seasons, the sowing and the
harvest, war and peace, and to this day in our western world,
young boys dance to the Virgin before the high altar in the
Cathedral in Seville, and the Indians in Mexico and the South-
west dance their religion.

It is joy. I have seen sober, middle-aged people lose themselves utterly in congas and square dances. Young people
would not be young without their dances, those rituals which
celebrate the ineffable joy of being alive.

It is pleasure. Think only what musicals would be if you
were to leave out the dances, and can you imagine a circus
without the dances of the clowns and the acrobats? For
certainly the buffoons are dancing. And what the performers
on the trapezes and tight ropes do is a very exciting sort of
dance.

It is art. Some of the most sublime and creative works
of man in the twentieth century have been accomplished by
dancers. It is an inspiring panorama, both in Europe, with
the traditional dance, and here in this country with the so-
called Modern Dance. This latter aspect of the art of the
dance, which is the one that I serve, has been referred to by
various names, such as the "Serious Dance," the "Concert
Dance," the "Creative Dance," etc. It has made some very
great contributions to the art. It has influenced greatly
the traditional dance. But I think that its greatest contribution lies in giving the dance to the individual. It has broken
with the great orthodoxy of the traditional Ballet, and given
validity to personal expression. Since one human being
differs from another, this has often led to painful results.
But in the case of the disciplined artist, this liberation has
given us, in this country, certainly, the most exalted art.

The dancer is fortunate indeed, for he has for his instrument the most eloquent and miraculous of all instruments, the human body. My teacher, Doris Humphrey, when I first came to her studio as an unpromising but dedicated beginner, told us something I have never forgotten. She said, "The human body is the most powerfully expressive medium there is. It is quite possible to hide behind words, or to mask facial expression. It is conceivable that one can dissimulate and deceive with paints, clay, stone, print, sounds. But the body reveals. Movement and gesture are the oldest languages known to man. They are still the most revealing. When you move you stand revealed for what you are."

This great power of expression is ours from the day we are born to the hour of our death. With most human beings it remains largely unconscious. We dancers use this faculty consciously. But it is subjected to long and arduous discipline. The body must be made strong and supple. It is subjected to the exercises of the traditional Ballet and the modern dance techniques to train it in balance, control, elevation, speed, coordination, and exactitude of execution. But to me the most fascinating part of our craft lies in a great search. We explore the possibilities and potentialities for movement inherent in every part of the body. I like to compare it to the symphony orchestra, with its tremendous range and variety of sound, from the robust and percussive to the delicate and subtle. I like to devise exercises and studies which focus on a certain part of the anatomy. This section is isolated, so to speak, and made to move in as many conceivable ways as possible, so that one may become aware of its complete range and capacity, in the same manner that a musical composer must know what each instrument in the orchestra can do. There are exercises, first and foremost, for that great source of movement, the breath center. Then there are others for the shoulders, the ribs, pelvis, knees, feet, elbows, hands, and the head. Each of these regions of the body possesses its own special qualities of movement, and has great possibilities.

Take the head. Leave aside such important means of expression as the eyes and the mouth. The head, from the perpendicular, can be made to hang forward on the chest, or fall backwards as far as the cords of the neck will permit. It can rest sidewise on either shoulder. It can describe a complete circumference, touching the four points just mentioned. Beginning with these simple and rudimentary directions one can devise such complex and endless variations to the movement of the head that, given creativeness and imagination, entire dances can be based on these. The head can be an erect proud symbol, or droop abjectly, or roll in drunken ecstasy and abandonment. It is capable of great pendular convolutions, or infinitely contained, minute gestures. Within its orbit it can move in tilted diagonals, tangents, and obliques, which give it a great expressive range.

The chest can be made empty, to fall inwards and downwards to an utter inversion, a defeat. It can rise with the breath, like a plant growing up and out from the pelvis, and there be suspended, noble and affirmative and aspiring. It can extend beyond this to attitudes of pride and arrogance, and overextend further to the comic, the pompous, the absurd. This region of the chest, the breath, is the fecund source of movement, and its range is limited only by one's inventiveness and imagination.

The shoulder closes forward, and opens backward, and can be lifted or lowered, and made to rotate to describe a full circle. This part of the "orchestra" is capable of small and delicate movement. It can describe with subtlety and nuance.

The area of the ribs can expand and contract, giving the torso great flexibility and fluidity. The ability to bend, to fall away from the balance and poise of the perpendicular into the excitement of the unbalance, the oblique, the wild Dionysian regions, is centered in this part of the body.

The pelvis has a great potency. When it is held in centered discipline it polarizes the body into a powerful and beautiful column, in perfect harmony with the earth's gravity, serene and Apollonian. From this axis, the pelvis can thrust forward, pull backwards, move from side to side, and describe a complete circumference, and in so doing generate a labyrinth of movement and gesture which can make the body into a graceful object of poetry and lyricism, or break it into crude and violent shapes, discordant and brutal.

In the dramatic language of the dance the use of the knees offers a great paradox. They can project the body into the air, and propel it through space. When locked into a stretched tautness, they raise and suspend the body where it seems to float and deny the pull of gravity. On the other hand, by bending they lower the body to the earth, to a surrender and a death. The inward rotations of the knees create primitive or grotesque attitudes. The outward manipulations lend elegance and expansiveness. The use of the knee-level in the Modern Dance has opened a remarkable new territory. I have seen some stunning passages executed on the knees in the works of Martha Graham and Charles Weidman.

Our contact with the earth with and through the foot gives this part of the dancer a special significance. It is the "radix," and like the roots of plants, it gives the dancer the substance and sustenance of the earth. The use of the foot reveals the entire philosophy· of the dance. Surely there is no greater contrast than that between the dance on the points, which seems to etherealize completely the human form, and the use of the bare foot in the contemporary dance. The first came into being through the poetic imagination of the Romantic period, when the dancer was not human, but a supernatural creature borne by the zephyrs. The bare foot came to us through the great rebel, Isadora Duncan. It is a very expressive part of our instrument, supple and beautiful in itself, capable of many more things than being brought to an elegant point. It can be, in the right hands, so to speak, almost as eloquent and expressive as those hands themselves. When emphasis is placed on the heel of the foot a strength and robustness is attained. It can articulate, twist, roll, rotate. It can speak with tenderness or violence. It has grown to be symbolic of the revolt against the academic dance. Duncan, in her search for a new language for the dance of our time, discarded not only the corsets but the slippers. Her successors in post-World War I Germany and the United States followed in her bare footsteps. In a stricken and turbulent century they created a new language of the dance which could say something about the present world and its tragic realities. The use of the foot in its naked and unfettered beauty was as necessary to the new dance as was the toe-slipper to that of a less disillusioned, less harassed age.

The elbow can articulate in the same fashion as the knee, with the exception that it cannot project the body into the air. It can, however, play an important part in supporting it when the dancer uses the floor level, in falls. This flexible joint gives the arms a rich, flowing quality. The stretching of the joint gives the arm an extended power. The acute bend, with the resultant angularity, opens an entire region of expression, very much related to the cubistic in painting and the dissonant in music. The inward rotations of the flexed or rounded elbow create an inverted, minor tonality in movement, while the opposite, or outward manipulations suggest an open, major one.

One of the most eloquent of the voices of the body is the hand. It is its function to give completion to movement and gesture. The hand is the seal upon the deed. A powerful gesture with the body cannot fully convince unless the hand is in accord with it, nor can a subtle, restrained one be completely so without having the hand in full consonance. The hand can be said to breathe like the lungs. It expands and contracts. It can project movements seemingly to infinity, or gather them back to their source within the body. It is a mouthpiece, a moderator. It has a brilliant range, capable of complexities and subtleties unequalled by other regions of the dancer's "orchestra." It is the abettor of all that the dancer intends. It is unthinkable, a dance without hands.

These are the rich resources of the body. These are the voices. They must be disciplined and developed so that they can speak with truth and power. This necessitates the study of the quality of movement. A single gesture can be phrased in different ways: smoothly, sharply, slowly, rapidly. It can be performed in its entirety, or broken into its component parts. The basic and all-important principle is never forgotten, that movement, in order to have power and eloquence and beauty must spring from the organic center of the body. It must have its source and impulse from the breathing of the lungs and the beating of the heart. It must be intensely and completely human, or it will be gymnastics, and be mechanical and empty. It is this quality, this inflection in the movement that creates that magic in the theater which dance alone can create. Complete mastery of the nuance and color in gesture and movement is the goal toward which the dancer works continually, for this command is what gives his utterance import and validity.

This highly trained, responsible instrument we dedicate to a single idea: that the dance is a serious, adult art, every bit as serious and adult as serious music, painting, literature, and poetry. The oldest of the arts need not exist only as entertainment. It has a great tradition to uphold and by which to be guided and inspired. The American Dance has an imposing gallery of the illustrious. The entire artistic life of the West has felt the impact of Isadora Duncan, the Inceptor. Ruth St. Denis and Ted Shawn pioneered the Wilderness, and took the magic of the dance to the remotest corners of the earth. Their organization was the womb which brought forth Martha Graham, Doris Humphrey, and Charles Weidman. The accomplishments of these children of Denishawn rank with the highest in the cultural story of America. Each has made Art and Civilization in his own very special way. Graham the dark flame, the personifier, the dithyrambic. Humphrey the symphonist, the molder, author of mighty works. Weidman the inspired clown, the Harlequin from the prairie.

These artists have given us something priceless. They have restored the dance to its ancient function, and proven to the modern world that it can reveal, instruct, and ennoble. It can exalt. It can ritualize the great tragedies and ecstasies of man. It is in its power and province to reaffirm the dignity of man in an age that desperately needs this affirmation. Never have the arts been so much needed, nor so challenged, as in these times of mechanized bestiality, when the human species seems possessed by a suicidal frenzy. Surely the Dance can remind us of the greatness of man's spirit, and of his creativeness, not his destructiveness. The Dance is many things. It is a Power. It can help stem the putrefaction and decay gnawing at the heart of human courage, and withstand the philosophies of doom and surrender. The dancer can use his voice to call for reason out of unreason, and order out of disorder. That has always been the high task of the artist. The great Goethe, as death engulfed him, cried "Light, more light." The contemporary artist can do no less than to dedicate the power of his spirit and the flame of his art to bring light to the dark places.

The daughter of Polish immigrants, Anna Sokolow grew up on the Lower East Side of New York City. Against her mother's wishes, she first studied dance with Bird Larson, then with Blanche Talmud, Martha Graham, and Louis Horst at the Neighborhood Playhouse, at that time located on Grand Street. At the age of fifteen she left home and school to join the Martha Graham Company, with which she performed until 1938.

While a member of the Graham Company she choreographed and performed independently, beginning in 1933 to present her dances through the Workers Dance League. From the early forties she spent six months of each year in Mexico,

THE
teaching and performing with her company there, the Blue Dove (La Paloma
REBEL
Azul). In the early fifties she returned to
AND THE
New York and became associated with the New Dance Group, but she
BOURGEOIS
soon left for Israel to work
with the Inbal Yemenite Group. At this time (1953) she discontinued her own performing career. In 1962 she formed the Lyric Theater Company in New York. In recent years she has been choreographing on a freelance basis and is currently the resident choreographer for the Daniel Lewis Dance Repertory Company.

Throughout her choreographic career, her dances have been based on intense, passionate social comment. Always a realist, her works might be compared with the "ashcan school" of American painting of the early twentieth century.

This essay which was first published in Dance Magazine (July 1966) is a classic statement in modern dance.

Anna I hate academies. I hate fixed ideas of what a
Sokolow thing should be, of how it should be done. I
(1915-) don't like imposing rules, because the person, the artist, must do what he feels is right, what

he—as an individual—feels he must do. If we establish an academy, there can be no future for the modern dance. An art should be constantly changing; it cannot have fixed rules.

The trouble with the modern dance now is that it is trying to be respectable. The founders of the modern dance were rebels; their followers are bourgeois. The younger generation is too anxious to please, too eager to be accepted. For art, this is death. To young dancers, I want to say: "Do what you feel you are, not what you think you ought to be. Go ahead and be a bastard. Then you can be an artist."

The modern dance should be non-conformist. We should not try to create a tradition. The ballet has done that, and that's fine—for the ballet. But not for us. Our strength lies in our lack of tradition. Some say that the big change came in the late 1920s, and now is the time for the modern dance to assimilate and solidify. That's all wrong, because it is like building on still another tradition. Without change there can be no growth, and not enough change is going on today.

My quarrel with this generation is that they copy their teachers, and it's their own fault. They don't want freedom; they want to be told what to do. Why don't they realize they don't have to believe everything teacher says? They ought to disagree; they ought to argue.

Of course it's not all the fault of the student. Too often, teachers are merely polite when they should be provocative. They ought to shock. Look at Louis Horst. At eighty, he was still fresh and bold. The good teacher does not teach rules; he stimulates. He shows the students what he knows and inspires them—to go and do something else.

Learning rules cannot produce an artist. What is an artist? What is the nature of the creative process? These are things we can't know; they can't be explained. The creative teacher opens doors for his students to see what life is, what they are. They have to take it from there.

It is easier and quicker to teach by rule, but in the end it's no good. To learn to choreograph, you just have to mess through it for a while. Most people feel they have to "fix" a dance, they have to make it "neat." No—it's better to have disordered life, but to have life. The modern dance is an individual quest for an individual expression of life.

The new generation have not really faced themselves; they don't know what it is they want to say. Most of their choreography is vague. It doesn't come organically from the person. It can't, because the choreographer doesn't know who he is or how he feels. So he tries to cover up his confusion by giving his dances fancy titles, by being intellectual. Dance is not intellectual. It deals with deep emotion.

Choreography always reflects the character of the creator. We see in the person's work what he asks from life and from art. Some want only to be entertained, so they offer us only entertainment. Others see life as a tremendous, mysterious force, and this is reflected in their work. Of course there are times when we want to be entertained. Life is not all deep emotion. Art should recognize all our needs.

I don't believe in ivory towers. The artist should belong to his society, yet without feeling that he has to conform to it. He must feel that there is a place for him in society, a place for what he is. He must see life fully, and then say what he feels about it. Then, although he belongs to his society, he can change it, presenting it with fresh feelings, fresh ideas.

The important thing is that the art being created now be related to now, to our time. The artist must be influenced by his time, conditioned by the life around him. If he is not, his viewpoint is limited by the past, and turns back instead of going forward. If he draws on the ever-changing life around him, his work will always be fresh and new. Art should be a reflection and a comment on contemporary life.

Yet some people are afraid to use life, feeling that art should be something apart, something isolated from reality. I once had a student in Israel who had been in a German concentration camp. You would never have known it from the windblown *schöne tänze* that she composed for me. They amounted to—nothing. I asked her: "Why don't you use your experience?" Then she created a marvelously powerful study based on the reality she had known.

Anyone, however, can have a good idea for a dance. In itself, that's not enough. There must be form as well as concept; both matter—what you feel—and how you express it. First, the choreographer sees his idea in terms of movement, as the painter sees his in terms of color, line, and mass. This happens spontaneously. Movements are not intellectually contrived but are evoked by emotional images. The only intellectual process is the one that puts these spontaneously conceived movements together into a form that works as as whole.

A sense of form, a feeling for construction, can be learned. But there are no rules. How, then? Well, you look at forms, at structures around you. Look at the shape of a box or a bottle; look at the lines of a table. It is easier to see form in life today than it was in the era of the Baroque, when forms were all covered with ornamentation. I don't like elaborated design. I like naked structure. In the theatre, I am anti-décor and anti-costume.

Progress in art comes through the quest for new forms. The artists I most admire are the ones who have dared to break with traditional forms—artists such as Joyce and Picasso and Balanchine. Pure form is not cold, because it is an abstraction from reality; its source is life itself. Form for form's sake is dull, contrived, intellectual. True form comes from reducing reality to its essential shape, as Cézanne did with the apple. In the hands of an artist, form is emotional, exciting. You feel that there is a reason for everything being there, just as it is. There is nothing superfluous, because the artist has stripped his work down to the bare essentials. And an audience responds emotionally to this purity, this inevitability of form, which is beauty.

It takes courage to be so simple. I dig Balanchine because he is daring in his simplicity. Look at the last movement of *Ivesiana*—the dancers just walk on their knees. This is bold; it's modern. It's ballet, but it's modern.

I think there will always be a basic, technical distinction between modern dance and ballet, because the modern conception of training is different. But in dance works there should be no idioms. It's not technique that makes a dance modern; you can have a modern dance on pointes. It's not subject matter, either. Tudor's *Pillar of Fire* has a romantic story like *Giselle,* but it doesn't reflect the conventional concept of romance. It's a difference in point of view. The modern attitude does not eliminate fantasy or romantic and poetic ideas. But we don't handle them the way the nineteenth century did. We are not representational; we are imaginative.

I have never told stories in dance, though I have always been strongly dramatic. I never plan a dance. I do it, look at it, and then say: "Yes, I see what I am trying to do."

For me, *Lyric Suite* was a turning point. It was then that I began to find a language of movement for myself. I see no reason to fight a personal language; it's an organic statement of the person. But one must not rest on it. The important thing is to stretch the personal vocabulary so that it does not remain static. This does not mean changing its essential nature. One can remain one's self without repeating a statement

When I first heard the *Lyric Suite*, I was fascinated with Berg's music, because I could see nothing lyric about it. Then it began to evoke dance images for me. After it was done, I saw the first movement as an expression of man; the second, as the quality of woman.

Rooms was choreographed without music. I wanted to do something about people in a big city. The theme of loneliness and noncommunication evolved as I worked. I like to look into windows, to catch glimpses of unfinished lives. Then I ask: "What is there, and why?" Then I thought of using chairs as if they were rooms, each dancer on his own chair, in his own room, isolated from all the others though physically so close to them.

Jazz was the right music for *Rooms*. I have always been interested in jazz; I find it one of the greatest and most profound expressions of our times. It makes me think. In *Rooms*, jazz was used for the dramatic and psychological depiction of individuals. In *Opus 58* I used jazz for an overall aura of the sounds and rhythms of today. I wanted the feeling of a new era, one where life is violent and precarious, and the individual seems unimportant.

Then came *Dreams*, which was my indictment of Nazi Germany. When I started, I had only the idea of dreams, but they became nightmares, and then I saw they were related to the concentration camps. Once this had happened, I intensified the theme by focusing on it.

In *Opus 63* I just started out to do something in unison movement. But the work talked back to me. After a wild Bossa Nova, with everyone going at each other, I ended it with the dancers just walking. It had a quality of strength, like religion; a belief that the spiritual thing will survive. But my works never have real endings; they just stop and fade out, because I don't believe there is any final solution to the problems of today. All I can do is provoke the audience into an awareness of them.

"Nik" was a musician and then a puppeteer before beginning his career in dance, and these roots are reflected in his dances. In them the accoutrements of the theater—lights, props, costumes, sets—are so thoroughly integrated with the movement that the visual result is indeed kinetic art. His dances used mixed media before the term was invented. When modern technology caught up with Nikolais, he was ready, using it to extend his works further. Some have called his dances otherworldly or inhuman, some have seen similarities to the Bauhaus Theatre of the 1920s in Germany.

EXCERPTS FROM "NIK: A DOCUMENTARY"

"Nik" was born in Southington, Connecticut, of Russian and German ancestry. The German modern dance had a definite influence on the young Nikolais. In 1933 he attended a performance by Mary Wigman and was so impressed with her use of percussion that he went to study with Truda Kaschmann, a former student of Wigman's. At the Bennington College summer sessions he came in contact with Hanya Holm, and after serving in the Army during World War II, he went to New York to study with her.

In 1948 he began the association with the Henry Street Playhouse on the Lower East Side of New York that provided him with a home base for almost twenty-five years. In the early fifties he retired from performing to devote himself to choreography and teaching. In 1970 he left the Henry Street Playhouse and founded the Chimera Foundation for Dance and the Louis-Nikolais Dance Theatre Lab with Murray Louis, his associate and principal dancer since 1949.

These excerpts from "Nik: A Documentary" contain the artistic philosophy of Alwin Nikolais.

Alwin Nikolais (1912-)

It is abrasive to one's ego to be an esthetic revolutionary. A long time passes before language catches up with the germinal machineries of such a change. Consequently only

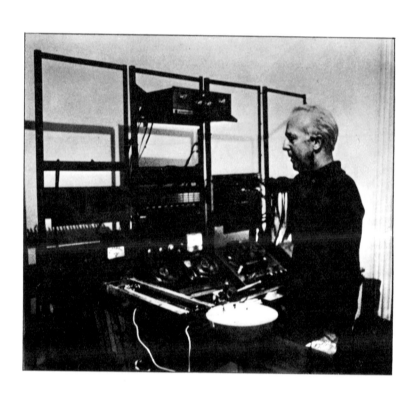

peripheral descriptions are given into the archives of one's time, and any verbalization in depth is not all guaranteed even at a later time. This is so in the temporal art of (dance) theater particularly.

In my own case, I look back with a sort of wonderment at the things I did—intuitively—in innocence—mixed, of course, with some indulgences and an occasional escapism. There were so many things that happened—profound and foolish, playful and diabolically real.

First came the annoyance with the self-expression rampant in the late 40s. The self as the sole germinal point of all value. It was as if an immaculate conception took place—as if one's presence was a self-induced miracle, and each gesture was a radiant gift bestowed upon the environment and whatever existed within it. There was little acknowledgment of external source or heritage. In most cases the stimuli derived from neurotic frictions. These were treasured as events of great import and merely reliving the situation was thought an act of choreographic merit. Behavior more worthy of clinical study than art was placed on stage in enthusiastic and somewhat orgiastic profusion.

I found myself realizing a new philosophy and consequently creating new techniques. Perhaps it was that I had the philosophy but had to clarify it to myself. I recognized the pattern of religious dynamics—particularly in the Christian belief where man, built in the image of a god, created a direct line of energy from that concept—there was an imagined spiritual umbilical cord nourishing him. In this fantasy he built moralities and laws. He built life on this basis and created art despite it.

It was Darwin who cut this cord. Man, dangling like putti from a cord from heaven up above, flopped in the morass of primordial ooze. He did not realize that instead of being the embodiment of an ageless bewhiskered god, he was for the first time given not only a foot upon the earth, but a place within the sun—and more importantly, an entity—albeit a microscopic one—in the universe. Man's definition changed—his energy and life source were re-routed. His whole physical environment structured upon the basis of godliness—this pipeline to his god was severed and he had only himself.

If Darwin ruined man's concept of his divinity, Freud gave the final blow by exposing his uglies. With ties to god cut, now his self-expression had no parentage other than his personal itch. He turned his reverence to himself—uglies and all. Again art happened despite this. Man was now stuck with a sex-dominated libido. He was now man-god—self-important— inviolable—the thing from which all blessings flow.

With Einstein, again life dynamics changed. The circuitry again repatterned—but whereas before there were semi-permanent patterns, now the patterns changed to suit the venture. Man was permitted variable vistas.

Yet with a whole civilization system built upon the idea of proprietary rights not only of the flesh but land as well, a fixed point was an essential to life, like the tonality of the old Western musical system. There was always the "Do," and the sonata of living was always in accord and in reference to it. Perhaps the jump in divorce rates and Schoenberg's 12-tone system of music were not strange bedfellows. The itch to be flexible—to shift the "Do."

* * *

My total theater concept consciously started about 1950, although the seeds of it began much earlier I'm sure. First was expansion. I used masks and props—the masks, to have the dancer become something else; and props, to extend his physical size in space. (These latter were not instruments to be used as shovels or swords—but rather as extra bones and flesh.) I began to see the potentials of this new creature and in 1952 produced a program called Masks Props & Mobiles. I began to establish my philosophy of man being a fellow traveller within the total universal mechanism rather than the god from which all things flowed. The idea was both humiliating and grandizing. He lost his domination but instead became kinsman to the universe.

* * *

With the breakdown of story-line, choreographic structure necessarily changed. With the further breakdown of physical centralization—the lid was off. Logic of metronomic and sun time was no longer necessary. Time no longer had to support logical realistic events. It too could be decentralized but more importantly, breaking the barrier of literal time throws the creator into visions and possible motional itineraries way beyond the literal visions (particularly if physical emphasis is subdued). The time-space canvas was now free. The ecology of the space canvas now could be balanced—no dominant Aunt Minnie—no nonreturnable bottles grinning out of the landscape. Now we are permitted visions into the world in which we live and perhaps even into the universe. We might even, then, return to the vision of self but placed more humbly into the living landscape, adding grandeur to vision of self—not in proud pigeon arabesques but as consonant members of the environment—enriched by the resonance of that which surrounds us, a shared energy interplaying with vital discussions rather than domineering argument.

* * *

I was all for understanding the landscape of self by sensing the presence of the sun and the ant within it. I hoped as well to find the universe and the microbe—then I dared to smash these boundaries to explore into the mystical blackness of primalities—motion as an art—void of physical vision despite the fact that physical vision was the means by which we perceived the wondrous blackness. I don't mean to imply that all humanistic identifiable art was without dimension. Surely Martha had wondrous blackness but it was always subservient to the figure.

What preposterous expectation—to ask a dancer to give up self-presence to expose motion—through him rather than on him.

* * *

Dancers often get into the pitfall of emotion rather than motion. To me motion is primary—it is the condition of motion which culminates into emotion. In other words it is our success or failure in action in time and space which culmi-

nates in emotion. This drama of action is universally understood by Chinese, Africans, South Americans and the Zulus.
We do not have to be educated to understand the abstract
language of motion, for motion is the stuff with which our
every moment of life is preciously concerned. So in the final
analysis the dancer is a specialist in the sensitivity to, the perception and the skilled execution of motion. Not movement
but rather the qualified itinerary en route. The difference
may be made even clearer by giving the example of two men
walking from Hunter College to 42nd and Broadway. One
man may accomplish it totally unaware of and imperceptive to
the trip, having his mind solely on the arrival. He has simply
moved from one location to another. The other may, bright-
eyed and bright-brained, observe and sense all thru which he
passes. He has more than moved—he is in motion.

* * *

I have often tried to trace my path of development. It has
by no means been a clear-cut progress. The first chore was to
drive—coerce—bludgeon—love and bribe the dancer to extri-
cate himself from the patterns of self-clinical and cathartic
indulgence and place him in skilled conversation with the
environment and the things and happenings within it. Here I
meant not just a presence in space—a place free of obstacles
in which one could cavort, turn, kick legs, wrestle with fellow
dancers. I meant much more than orientation.

I looked to space as a potential 3-dimensional canvas
which even in the most simple terms allows and invites a
sense of relationship. One's realized presence within space
creates an accoustical sounding board even before the dynamics of action takes place. But—how difficult to teach the performer that presence alone in this instance is insufficient.
How to teach the dancer to make himself right in any part of
a space structure by acknowledging with his body the proportions and dynamic vitality of that relationship—just as a
painter can qualify a line anywhere on the canvas by virtue
of its position and structure—and make it beautiful.

Now when the dancer by his action creates other linear
boundaries or volumes of space these also are made visible
and alive by the textural behaviorism of his body—all of this

taking intense realization and concentration of the dancer upon the spatial involvements. If he cannot do this—the involvements will be dead—without audibility—they remain unspoken—in reality—unperformed. The relationships exist only as symbols—unexplained.

Let's take the space environment as I outlined above and qualify it further by the presence of another dancer or several dancers—all alive and responsive to the spatial behaviorism as it is activated by their orchestral involvement with it and each other. Suppose we think of time and shape in the same terms—not involved in the drama of boy meets girl—nor even in humanistic presence—but rather as dynamic musicalities of action of fabulously sensitive instruments, reminding one of things beyond the physicalities of the instruments—yet seen through them. Abstract expressionism? Perhaps—but basic dance—relieved of the romantic fallacy of the inviolability of a dull fat arse (or a puny skinny one—for that matter). Here our identification is with the rumblings and utterings and songs of generative primal stuffs—the stuffs which disclose and qualify not only the dimension of nature—to which man belongs—but of man as well. Dehumanization?

From the point of view of mathematics, dynamics, dispersion of visual and auditory events and energies I caused the whole upset to dance dynamics. Whatever anyone else might have done or still is doing within that or this period of so-called avant-garde dance theater, this particular creative vision seems to be peculiarly my own—and is still often misinterpreted and mostly unexamined in terms of its basic social and esthetic germination. Most interpretations still evolve around the Nureyev principle and the brother-in-spirit identifications with humanistic events on stage no matter how abstractly whacky the dance gesture might be. It's still Nureyev or Fonteyn doing it. Bare-assed or dressed—frontal or back-al—jeans or tutus—whiskers or wigs. Of course the specialists are bewildered. Reminds me of a shoe store man in Hartford. He often stood outside his shop. When I passed he never said "Hello" to me—it was always to my shoes.

* * *

I consider myself to be somewhat of a greybeard not far from half a century in the "business." There are simple mathematical facts in such a lengthy and deeply saturated involvement. It is impossible to survive that length of time in an art without accomplishment, a sense of humor, and I'm inclined to add, a certain attraction, innocently or otherwise, towards vulgarity. This is aside, of course, from the hysterical search for beauty. During the course of this adventure, one measures himself against a million things, incidents, experiences, involvements. One takes one's esthetic temperature 10 billion times—always curious, always questioning and most always doubtful, at least on the surface.

Behind it all there develops an inward assurance—fortified over the years as one tests oneself—first upon relatives and friends—next upon cities of people, then upon nations and then the world. Historical presence, social dynamics and fortuitous timing can cause storms, sometimes swamping your craft and other times lifting it on wind-wings.

Your welfare is greatly a matter of whether your esthetic vision coincides with the whims of history in progress. Even the weather matters. At this time I am back in the U.S. one month following a 4-month tour of Europe, the Near East and a bit of Africa. It was a glorious magic carpet tour. Paris, Lisbon, Vienna and Teheran were ecstatic. Seven thousand each night in the 3rd-century Roman theater in Carthage thrilled us no end. Playing on top of the old walls in Dubrovnik and the ancient Diocletian palace in Split added more glamour. But London! Carolyn [Carlson] was ill and had left the tour. The company was a wreck—tour tired. Our tech people got involved in some misunderstandings, causing an hysterical delay in set-up—even holding the audience until we were technically ready. A heat wave hit London and no air conditioning, not even good ventilation in the theater—and to top it off we were booked at the tail end of an oversaturated dance season to which the Londoners responded half-heartedly. That we survived the 3-week season at all was a miracle. Obviously critical response in London—although good—was not anywhere nearly as fine as Vienna or Paris. The works, of course, were the same. Now had we not had brilliant receptions in so many other places one would begin to question validities. Then one begins to think of the British as people. Is their esthetic Rorschach as good as the French or Viennese? Then I remembered the hysterically ecstatic reception 2 years earlier in London. This time the Londoners complained about missing Murray and Phyllis Lamhut too—and I thought Oh Gawd—it's the Nureyev syndrome again and I was angry.

Then there was the difference in reception to different pieces. The French loved *Echo*—the British were somewhat indifferent. Some pieces are apt to vary in different countries. (I avoid my humorous pieces in Italy because the Italians do not respond to them at all.)

Anyway—in just this one instance you can see that it is essential for the artist to fortify himself against such experiences and to have great knowledge and sense of value for his own work. It is not ego or immodesty, it is simply an inner and necessary assurance gained in a vast number of experiences and over a very long time. At this point in a career it is almost impossible to make the wrong stroke upon the canvas. It is mathematically unreasonable. And if the artist does make the mistake he certainly will see it and will not exhibit the canvas.

Part Four

THE
NEW
AVANT-GARDE

INTRODUCTION

By the 1960s, technical proficiency had become an end in itself for modern dancers, rather than the means to an end. Technique became set and strict, codified in the style of the originator, with emphasis on greater and greater achievement. Only those teaching in the Laban-Wigman-Holm tradition included improvisation in their classes. Aspects of ballet were incorporated increasingly into modern dance classes, ballet barres were installed in modern dance studios, and many modern dancers took ballet classes regularly. Thus the wide philosophical gap between the two dance forms began to narrow.

In 1962 a new rebellion came which was the most far-reaching to date. This was the Judson Group, the first co-operative effort within modern dance since the Workers Dance League. The Group began with the composition students of Robert Dunn, a musician who had worked with Graham and Cunningham. Most of the students were from the Cunningham studio and company. One of them had studied with Anna Halprin, an avant-garde dancer on the West Coast who worked in improvisation (some of the others studied with her a few years later). The Judson Group, therefore, evolved from the existing avant-garde, extending their mentors' revolutionary theories farther than ever. This newest rebellion was against the established modern dance: their mentors' mentors.

The founding dancers included Trisha Brown, Judith Dunn, David Gordon, Deborah and Alex Hay, Steve Paxton, Yvonne Rainer, and James Waring. A place to perform was provided at the Judson Memorial Church in New York City by Al Carmines, associate minister and director of the arts program of the church. The first performance was held in the church gymnasium with borrowed technical equipment; later the performances were moved upstairs to the church sanctuary. All decisions affecting the group were made collectively. These dancers were not interested in repertory, the proscenium stage, or technique. They were interested in individual creativity.

At the same time the Judson Group began to take shape, other dancers and choreographers were erasing the dividing lines between modern dance and ballet. Ballet companies began to introduce into their repertory works that had been choreographed by modern dancers. One of the first such crossovers was the New York City Ballet's performance of Merce Cunningham's *Summerspace* as originally done by the Cunningham Company, with the addition of toe shoes for the ballerinas. Ironically, this occurred just when Cunningham's influence on the Judson Group was greatest. Later, other ballet companies, such as the Joffrey Ballet, the American Ballet Theatre, the Cincinnati Ballet, and the Hartford Ballet, added to their repertory works by José Limón, Lester Horton, and Twyla Tharp. The Connecticut College summer program became the American Dance Festival, which offered ballet and ethnic dance as well as modern dance. In 1978 the program moved again, this time to Duke University.

Meanwhile, the names of Clive Barnes, Marcia Siegel, Jill Johnston, Deborah Jowitt, Don McDonagh, Joseph Mazo, Anna Kisselgoff, Arlene Croce, and Walter Sorrell were added to the ranks of the critics. The tradition of dance books written by critics has continued, with a substantial amount of the newest literature on dance coming from these writers.

Another important development of the mid-sixties grew out of the political climate in America. Concurrent with the broadening of human rights for black people, black choreographers began to create dances that existed as works of art rather than as works of ethnic art. The dances were based on ethnic themes only at the will of the choreographers. Their predecessors, such as Pearl Primus, Katherine Dunham, and Geoffrey Holder had been limited entirely to African, Afro-Caribbean, and Afro-American themes. The new black dancers—Alvin Ailey, Donald McKayle, Rod Rodgers, Eleo Pomare, Raymond Johnson, Gus Solomons Jr., and others—choreographed dances on a wide range of subject matter for their companies.

The "Happenings" of the late sixties, which were an outgrowth of the Judson movement, seem in retrospect to have been a barometer for the temper of the young Americans at that time. Individualism was encouraged, but individuals banded together more cohesively than before. Some of the

major pop art painters and sculptors, such as Robert Rauch-
enberg and Robert Morris, began to choreograph. Audience
participation became standard. The emphasis of the Happenings was on spontaneous improvisation, natural movement, nonmovement, nondancers, nudity, street or second-
hand clothes (noncostume), and the use of ordinary objects.
Performances were often given in lofts, but were just as often
given any place, any time.

The far-out went as far as it could—performing in foun-
tains, in plazas and museums, and eventually on rooftops
and on walls.

Although the outward appearance differed from the dance
of Isadora, the spirit of the movement, in its rejection of all
dance that is not natural, was hers.

*In the early 1960s Anna Halprin was already in-
fluencing some of the dancers who later became key
figures in the Judson Dance Theater. She was working
independently in improvisation, using a complete
range of movement beyond dance technique and often
performing out of the theater.*

THE *A native of Winnetka, Illinois, she studied at the University of Wisconsin with*

PROCESS *Margaret H'Doubler.*

IS *After graduation she made her debut in*

THE *the 1944 Broadway musical* Sing Out

PURPOSE Sweet Land, *which was choreographed by Doris Humphrey and Charles Weid-*

*man. She worked with Barbara Mettler in New
Hampshire before moving to San Francisco, where
she had a joint studio with Welland Lathrop between
1948 and 1955. Her Dancers' Workshop was founded
in Marin County, California in 1955. Her husband,
landscape architect Lawrence Halprin, wrote* The
RSVP Cycles: Creative Process in the Human Environment *about her work.*

*In recent years her work has become a therapeutic
process in which the emphasis is on the experience of
creating art spontaneously within a group situation.
The value is for the participants, not the viewers.*

AN INTERVIEW
BY VERA MALETIC

*Anna
Halprin
(1920-)*

Maletic. It seems to me that your personal approach to movement has evolved from some specific needs of our contemporary life, particularly in the U.S.A. and [on] the West Coast. What do you aim for with your educational and performance activities in relation to the trainees and in relation to the audience?

Halprin. Of course, this is not the easiest question to answer. It's like asking what your whole life is about. But I think I can start with the first notion that comes into my head, and that is I have developed an enormous concern and interest in movement as it relates to a more natural outgrowth of expression. In other words, I am disinterested in movement so highly stylized that we must say this is a Dancer. Anybody's a dancer to me at any time when I am involved in communicating with that person through his movement. This has led me to a way of working with students that does not rely so much on traditional or conventional means, which tend to make the kind of dancer image that I'm really interested in for myself.

More and more I have begun to stress breathing as a base, because I find that the deeper the student can get into the breathing center, the more open he becomes to releasing areas in his body which become alive and accessible to him for his work. So this is a very important base of our work. You know, my training has been with Margaret H'Doubler from Wisconsin University. Of course she was always interested in movement as an expressive medium for communication and was never interested in style and patterns of movement. In a very convincing way she grounded me in a more biological approach to movement—movement that is more natural to the nervous system, to the bone structure, to the muscle action. I found that in my training with her, the stress in movement was on understanding your body as action and, at the same time, being able to appreciate feedback, so that the relationship of the feeling to the movement was complete. Now when you learn patterned movement, you're so involved in learning the pattern that the tendency is simply to cut off the feeling aspect. And by feeling, I'm not referring to a kind of free-style self-expression. I mean just the feeling that's inherent when you clench your fist in anger, or stamp your feet, or jump in exhilaration. These are all natural and the most expressive movement we do. And when you become aware of the movement and the feeling it's evoking, you begin to have the freedom to use it consciously and excitingly, and that's when you begin to become an artist in your material.

It's that approach to movement that I'm talking about. I've never taught classes in which I teach a style, or a pattern, or set progression. First of all, I keep changing from year to year. I keep finding new things that I keep incorporating. Recently I've gotten very involved in developing a new use of body training through principles that have to do with getting the body into positions of stress. And then— it's almost like isometric exercises—from the stress position it goes into a trembling that gets you into a kind of forced breathing. It must change the chemistry in the body, because it's as if your whole circulatory system just comes alive. This is something very new to me, because I've never been able to get at the circulatory system before. I'll show you some of the movements afterwards, if you'd like to see them. The efficiency is just incredible. By placing your body in a position, you get all the strength and a fantastic sense of your body as a totality. So we've been experimenting, as we constantly do, with new methods to get deeper and deeper into the body itself.

Maletic. I think you have answered my second question already. It was: how would you define your approach to education, art, and theatre, apart from traditional concepts?

Halprin. Well, I think this goes back to the way I have always related myself to dance and life. That is, I try not to separate the experiences of life, because we are in confrontation with our experiences, constantly, in art. And this brings me to an appreciation of, or an emphasis on, the relationship between personal growth and artistic growth. For the two must go hand in hand; otherwise there is no maturity that ever takes place. Since I've been working simultaneously in education and theatre all my life, it's hard for me to know the source for an idea. But I do know that in the theatre experiences, I want very much to deal with people on that stage who are identifying with very real experiences in life, in such a way that the audiences can identify themselves with the so-called performers. Rather than just looking at somebody doing something very unusual, I want the audience to be able to identify and realize that this is a person more than he is a dancer, a person who identifies with very real things.

We don't even accept the theatre as a conventional place where the audience is here and you're there, but it *is* a place, and whatever you do in that place is valid because it's the place. You don't have to be on the stage separating here from there. This desire to merge a very life-like situation into the concept of the dance is very true also in my training. Everything we do in dance somehow or other usually relates to who you are as a person, and this affects how you see things and feel things and relate to people. Again, it's this nonseparation of life and art, so that somehow or other it becomes a heightening process.

Maletic. Do you feel there is a difference between self-exploration or self-expression as individual therapeutic experience and as an artistic expression?

Halprin. This is a hard question to answer right now, because the word therapy is being used by so many different people in so many different ways. So is the word creativity. At one time, you could use the word creativity and feel fairly safe, but now there's creative merchandise. Everything's creative—you can get a creative ice cream cone. The word therapy is beginning to become like a tea party. You know, let's get together and have a little therapy session. So it gets a little difficult. But I would say that if you use the word therapy in terms of personal growth, any art experience that is valid to a person and that is based on personal experience certainly, automatically, must have therapeutic value. But if your attention as an artist is only on what you are getting therapeutically, you are not paying attention to the fact that essentially you're a craftsman, that essentially your job is to be a vehicle for other people.

To me, a performer is simply a vehicle, a submergence of the ego. Otherwise, you may as well stay in your studio. But when you take the responsibility for performing for an audience, you are then accepting the fact that you must go through some sort of distilling process in which the personal experience has become so zeroed and so heightened by a clarity that you know exactly what you're dealing with, in terms of an element. You have so much skill that you can get right down to the essence of that element. Then you find the movement—spatial, dynamic—essence of that idea inherent not only in how your body moves, but in an awareness of where you are in space, an awareness of the total thing. That has therapeutic value—that's OK—but that shouldn't be your concern.

Maletic. What is your criterion for determining whether a performance is true or genuine in involvement and feeling, or whether it is a phony? Also, what is your criterion for determining the choice of events for a public theatre performance?

Halprin. This is very difficult to answer, because we're in such a violent, explosive period of experimentation. At least I am, and certainly all the young artists I work with are. Yet I know that before I ever present a work in public, I've gone through two years' research, two years of going through many, many sketches. And I work very hard to have a score which externalizes the elements so I can get further and further detached from the source, so I can be detached from it and still be very much involved. Other than that, I don't know how to make any judgment about other people's work. First of all, being here on the West Coast, I don't see an awful lot, and what I have seen coming on tour is working in such a different direction from mine. It's hard to know. But because I've spent so many years in movement, I can, just intuitively, tell when a performance is lacking in what I call the audience dimension. And I usually can tell on the basis that the experience just hasn't been structured at all, that the individual is behaving, not moving. There's a difference.

Maletic. What are the concepts of your kinetic theatre?

Halprin. The theatre is based on the human expression which comes primarily from movement, from motion. But it goes into the other areas of human expression, which include the visual and the speaking and all of the things that represent a total kind of experience. And this is what I am most interested in developing, a theatre which uses the total resources of the human being. So, rather than call it dance, which seems always to be limited, I'd rather find a new word right now. Although it's basically what dance was in its more primitive time.

Maletic. Of the main streams in psychology, Jungian, Gestalt, Existential, etc., which do you feel the closest affinity with?

Halprin. I feel most closely aligned with the Gestalt therapy, but that may be because of my contact with Fritz Perls. When I read his book, *Gestalt Therapy,* or when I work with him, I'm continually reminded of similarities. It's the coming together of all the parts. That is important to me, and it seems this is what is stressed in the Gestalt. I feel very identified with it.

Maletic. Have you had any psychedelic experiences and, if so, have they influenced your creativity?

Halprin. Yes, I have had a psychedelic experience, only once, and it did get me in touch with a very deep breathing experience in which I was able to sense what the Chinese call the red spot. I was able to start the radiation all through my body, and this relaxation that set in was so profound, it completely changed my body structure. This happened at the University of California. Somebody was filming it. Afterwards, I felt very different in posture and alignment, and when I started to move I felt very different. But when I saw the film, I didn't even recognize myself. My body went into a very effortless type of alignment, and my movements had no effort. Without getting out of breath I was able to move with so much more strength and richness. I felt so much more alive. Because I was able to direct it towards the discovery of relaxation through breathing, the experience had very illuminating effects.

Maletic. Could you tell me something about your professional background and the persons who influenced you?

Halprin. I have been dancing ever since I was a little girl, in a very free and natural way. When I went to college, I studied with Margaret H'Doubler. I would say that she was my great teacher. The more I work on my own, the more I keep coming back and saying, oh, this is what she meant, of course. Even though I have gone into a slightly different emphasis, I still feel I'm her student and I'm still learning. She's such a wealth of ideas, it's taken me years to accumulate the information that substantiates what she was saying. My husband has been very much a teacher for me because of his work in landscape architecture. He's made me enormously aware of the choreography of space. A very important teacher in my life was Rabbi Kadushin, who made me very aware of philosophical concepts in Judaism which reinforced my belief in creativity as a means of strengthening a sense of self-affirmation, not only to oneself, but to the many layers penetrating from oneself to others. This cer-

tainly developed a desire for, and a belief in, human encounter on a creative level.

Maletic. Since I come from Europe, I wonder if you can
tell me if there are particular needs in this part of America
which create your kind of work. Is this kind of activity
specific to the West Coast?

Halprin. I suppose I again may sound a little biological,
but I think that the word is ecology and I think that there
is something so vital about our natural surroundings that we
have become, perhaps unconsciously. . . . How can you live
in this kind of landscape, with the ocean, with the cliffs, with
the vital forces of nature at your feet all the time, and not be
affected by the so-called nature-oriented point of view? You
become vitally concerned with the materials, the sensual
materials of our lives, and with the almost primitive naive-
ness of being an extension of your environment. This begins
to free you to appreciate the very characteristics of what a
human being is, and from there you start coming out again.
And when you start coming out and relaxing, you are working in a sort of nonintellectual way.

I'll speak for myself. I have a tremendous faith in the process of a human mechanism, and in creativity as an essential
attribute of all human beings. This creativity is stimulated
only when the sense organs are brought to life. This faith in
the process is the only goal or purpose I need. What happens
as a result creates and generates its own purpose. So I don't
question the purpose beforehand; I've already accepted the
process as the purpose. In this sense it's nonintellectual. I
don't get all sorts of intellectual theories that this dance work
or this new piece in this blah blah blah, but this is where we
are in our growth, this is where we are in our educational
commitment. The process is the purpose; let it be, let it keep
growing, and something will happen. And what happens
generates it's own purpose. I'm being very repetitive, but in
this sense it's nonintellectual and very nature-oriented.

WE DON'T TALK ABOUT IT. WE ENGAGE IN IT

Judith Dunn (1933-)

Judith Dunn earned a Master's Degree in dance from Sarah Lawrence College and taught for three years at Brandeis University before becoming a member of the Merce Cunningham Dance Company. She performed with Cunningham from 1958 to 1963 and was one of the original members of the Judson Dance Theater. Since that time she has collaborated and toured with musician-composer Bill Dixon. Presently, Ms. Dunn is on the faculty of Bennington College.

Artists for the most part don't think abstractly about communication. We study it. We engage in it. When asked, "Well, aren't you interested in communicating?" I usually answer that I don't think about it. This answer is almost always misunderstood.

I think about my work and the problems I have, both artistic and economic, getting it accomplished. I think about the position of artists in our society, why it is that way and how I am going to keep surviving as a practicing artist. I think about the ideas and energy I have for work, and how only a fraction of these plans will ever be realized. I think about artistic endeavor being as essential as science for life. I think about art processes and products as I do about social science. I think about composing and how it is defined. I think about training for artists and where the standards and definitions of a field arise, who they serve, what they preserve, and what they eliminate. I think often about the inevitability of change.

Artists choose to make public expression through exhibitions, performances, written words and the like. They are involved in the communicative process all the time. If you are an artist, that is what you mean to be doing. Otherwise you would never get out of bed. You would dream dances, poems, music, paintings, buildings. Every artist wants a response from his or her own time. This response and exchange is not achieved by plots and games. It is an insult to an audience to assume to know their limits, what they will understand or perceive. The emphasis must be on the work, esthetically, philosophically, socially, with which the artist means to communicate.

Artists are still suspect in our culture and hold a very tenuous place. The products of the artist circulate, for the most part, outside the mainstream of the lives of most people. This is caused by current definitions of art and artists as well as the economics of artistic existence.

The economics of artistic existence and the manner in which art is marketed have a large influence on the decisions that the artist makes, the resulting art produced and the way in which these products and performances are perceived as art or not by the consumer-audience. Mostly artists prefer to ignore this, yet are always bellyaching about it in disguised form. There is still among some a mistaken belief that making the right moves, receiving a status grant, being at the correct social gathering will bring the artist to the attention of the timely gallery owner, publisher or agent and then the doors to success will open. Although some have made it this way, it does not solve the problem by any means and certainly leaves a lot to be desired as a lifestyle. These economic pressures tend to produce a divorce between the artist and the large public. Much art in our time has become increasingly hermetic and the life an artist leads continues to be surrounded by various myths. The familiar ones deal with deprivation and suffering as necessary for artistic activity. Another is that artists, in order to function, must not lead ordinary lives, but engage in esoteric revels with inspiration and the muse. There is not much sense of art as work and, in that way at least, as an ordinary part of life.

This might be the place to talk about the impulse to art, or why, if it is all so awful, people choose to become artists. On that subject I am not able to do more than be descriptive. I do know that no artist can do more than express his or her time more or less perfectly. In fact that is what artists do. An artist organizes material that is available to everyone. There is a necessity to perform this act I'm calling organization. I know for myself the desire to put things together is irrepressible. Where, one might ask, does the imagination enter. Imagination is not mysterious. Permitting yourself to use it fully is not something we are encouraged to do and therein lies the mystery. Philosophy, history, science, the development of worldview, attention to detail and the overview. These are food for the imagination. I don't know why an artist chooses one medium over another. Perhaps it's opportunity.

The power of art lies in its ability and necessity to illuminate the time in which it is made. There are certain formal considerations to all the arts. Time, both in small units such as internal rhythm and phrases and longer ones such as the length of a work or the time factor involved in how a painting or sculpture draws your eyes over its surface. Space, both axial and immediate, also environmental. Structure, or the way in which a work is divided into parts and exists as a whole. Order, or the logic of the arrangement of materials and finally, "tone," or the expressive-emotional factor which is both intended and accidental. In practice these elements are bound together and are only separated for analysis.

In order to develop the uses of formal concepts suitably expressive of our own lives, we must be aware of the events and discoveries which influence our own times. I'm not speaking of a false hipness where tradition and the past are denigrated and only the new and faddish are extolled.

Current technology makes time and order good examples. If I can send a message and have it received as fast as I speak or think it, it is very different than if it takes me a year to deliver it by sail power or on foot. There are ways to condense messages, scramble them and have them instantly available. There are devices which can receive and store tremendous amounts of information and swiftly perform operations with this information which would take men and women many lifetimes to accomplish. Film is another example where, through technology, time and order can be dealt with in a non-linear fashion. We can also through

newly developed instruments know about the intimate structures of natural phenomena both organic and inorganic.
This knowledge affects art and changes it, gives the imagination new landscapes to range in. The arts that are most
readily affected are those where the potential for other
than descriptive expression is inherent in the non-verbal
character of the medium, such as contemporary dance,
music, visual arts. Speech is slow, dance is fast.

These formal elements and the concepts behind their use
give art the character it possesses and also place it in historical perspective. The notion of historical perspective saves
the individual from wasteful ideas of self-importance and
immutable concepts. Ideas do not belong to individuals,
but to everyone. No idea is so precious that it should be
hoarded. There is always another idea behind the one just
given away.

I used to keep very elaborate journals. In my mother's
garage there is a dresser, five drawers full of notebooks.
Essays and speculations about most of the things I have
done as a dancer. These books are elaborate far beyond
a workbook or record keeping. They also served as that.
Lately my appetite for this kind of journal keeping has
diminished. There was in my mind some confusion about
permanence, about capturing or keeping so I could savor it
at some future date. The problems of having work produced for independent artists are severe. Journal keeping
is a poor, but not totally unsatisfying translation. A dance
disappears as you see it. A movie of a dance is a dream.
A description of a dance is just that. The nature of dance
includes impermanence. This is both an opportunity and
a problem.

I have tried to make the most of the opportunities that the
nature of my field presents. To move away from the middle
neutral, that obvious set of moves and appearances which
define the field most narrowly. Eight years ago musician-
composer Bill Dixon and I began to collaborate in composing
and producing works involving both music and dance and in
teaching composition to musicians and dancers. We discussed, planned and developed together all the aspects of
the work we were composing. We practiced together, criticized each other and held workshops for the musicians

and dancers who worked with us. We considered the pieces
we composed as being created by both of us and not belonging to one another. Our collaborative position was
not readily accepted. We found ourselves involved in much
theoretical discussion and demand for explanation about our
competence to "invade" each other's field. We thought and
planned ways to organize artistic activities to benefit both the
artists and the public.

I began at that time to work seriously in improvisation,
not as a way of gathering material or making preparations
which would then be transformed by other means into a
"composition," but improvisation as the sole method of
composition. Improvisation as I see it means composing
and performing simultaneously. All the forming elements
and decisions which exist in the longer method apply here as
well. One considers structure, order, space, time, materials
and "tone," and one practices daily to make these decisions
quickly, consciously and with control. In the last three
years I have used this method exclusively.

At the beginning of this period there were many struggles.
I had to come to terms with all of my definitions of order
and structure. I had to expand my ideas of what dance
movement was and could be. What provided me with encouragement and material for study was the example of the
improvisational tradition of Black Music, particularly in
its most contemporary aspects as demonstrated by Bill
Dixon and others.

The methods used in work have implications beyond their
immediate artistic use. Improvisation depends very much
on the abilities of all the performers involved. They must
bring themselves to the task without reservation and they
must bring their decision-making power as well.

There are several ways in which decision making and control may be exercised in composition. Picture a scale ranging from total control in the hands of one individual, to a
situation of complete collaboration of all the performers
involved. After spending most of my career as a dancer-
choreographer at one end of the scale I have now moved
to the other. This move came out of the needs of work,
the benefit to the work and existence in general. I think
it is important to say there is no sacrifice of leadership, nor

is there any loss of "individuality." Quite the opposite.
Aspects of both come forward in a unique fashion from all
involved. Experience brings with it knowledge. This does
not disappear. Those who are in the earlier stages of their
career bring to decisions the knowledge of their time and
experiences. One does not negate the other. They fit together very neatly. It is not enough to agree to work col-
laboratively. It involves constant effort and a continuing
critical attention to the processes involved, both artistic
and social.

My current position has brought changes, but some ideas
remain fixed. I still retain opposition to journalistic criticism
and "higher criticism" as it currently affects artists and
audience. It seems mostly to serve the persons who write
it. In my experience it certainly does not help the artist
or inform the public in any serious way about the nature
of the work, the ideas involved or in many cases what actually took place. Criticism increasingly has come to mean
tearing works and performers apart in a negative and cynical
fashion. Too much store, especially by younger artists, is
placed on the words of the critics. In the formative part
of a career not only is it important to develop skills, to know
the history and evolution of the field, but also to achieve
a sense of the worth of your own ideas and judgment. In
dance, perhaps more than the other arts, the basic unit,
the tool is the self. That tool has to be sharpened and tested,
permitted to range in an atmosphere which encourages
examination and analysis, and is primarily non-judgmental,
which focuses on the development of standards rather than
having them superimposed as rules which must be first un-
questioningly followed and then, only as the grey hairs
begin to appear, be discarded. We must create situations
which encourage the release of the imagination, which makes
study natural and desirable and which brings artists into respectful and encouraging relationships with each other as opposed to the more competitive style of artists of the historical
past. It is important to create spaces where artist and audience can each do their communicative work with the greatest
interchange, mutual concern and benefit.

Yvonne Rainer, born in San Francisco, was one of the major avant-garde choreographers of the sixties and an original member of the Judson Dance Theater. She studied dance with Martha Graham, Merce Cunningham, Anna Halprin, and Edith Stephen. She was

THE MIND IS A MUSCLE

a composition student of Robert Dunn and began to choreograph in 1961. In addition to her own company and the Judson group, she has performed with several other choreographers, including James Waring and Judith Dunn.

Her works focus on natural movement and simple tasks. As one of the young rebels who moved away from rigid dance technique, Rainer choreographs within the scope of minimalist art. She has worked with artists Robert Morris and Robert Rauschenberg, and also with film.

Yvonne Rainer (1934-)

In 1975 she published a retrospective survey of her work entitled Work: 1961-73. *"The Mind is a Muscle," from the dance of the same name, was originally written in 1966.*

A Quasi Survey of Some "Minimalist" Tendencies in the Quantitatively Minimal Dance Activity Midst the Plethora, or an Analysis of Trio A

OBJECTS	DANCES

eliminate or minimize

1. role of artist's hand	1. phrasing
2. hierarchical relationships of parts	2. development and climax
3. texture	3. variation: rhythm, shape, dynamics
4. figure reference	4. character
5. illusionism	5. performance
6. complexity and detail	6. variety: phases and the spatial field
7. monumentality	7. the virtuosic feat and the fully extended body

substitute

1. factory fabrication	1. energy equality and "found" movement
2. unitary forms, modules	2. equality of parts, repetition
3. uninterrupted surface	3. repetition or discrete events
4. nonreferential forms	4. neutral performance
5. literalness	5. task or tasklike activity
6. simplicity	6. singular action, event, or tone
7. human scale	7. human scale

Although the benefit to be derived from making a one-to-one relationship between aspects of so-called minimal sculpture and recent dancing is questionable, I have drawn up a chart that does exactly that. Those who needed alternatives to subtle distinction making will be elated, but nevertheless such a device may serve as a shortcut to ploughing through some of the things that have been happening in a specialized area of dancing and once stated can be ignored or culled from at will.

It should not be thought that the two groups of elements are mutually exclusive ("eliminate" and "substitute"). Much work being done today—both in theater and art—has concerns in both categories. Neither should it be thought that the type of dance I shall discuss has been influenced exclusively by art. The changes in theater and dance reflect changes in ideas about man and his environment that have affected all the arts. That dance should reflect these changes at all is of interest, since for obvious reasons it has always been the most isolated and inbred of the arts. What is perhaps unprecedented in the short history of the modern dance is the close correspondence between concurrent developments in dance and the plastic arts.

Isadora Duncan went back to the Greeks; Humphrey and Graham* used primitive ritual and/or music for structuring, and although the people who came out of the Humphrey-Graham companies and were active during the thirties and forties shared socio-political concerns and activity in common with artists of the period, their work did not reflect any direct influence from or dialogue with the art so much as a reaction to the time. (Those who took off in their own directions in the forties and fifties—Cunningham, Shearer, Litz, Marsicano et al.—must be appraised individually. Such a task is beyond the scope of this article.) The one previous area of correspondence might be German Expressionism and Mary Wigman and her followers, but photographs and descriptions of the work show little connection.

---

*In the case of Graham, it is hardly possible to relate her work to anything outside of theatre, since it was usually dramatic and psychological necessity that determined it.

Within the realm of movement invention—and I am talking for the time being about movement generated by means
other than accomplishment of a task or dealing with an object—the most impressive change has been in the attitude to
phrasing, which can be defined as the way in which energy
is distributed in the execution of a movement or series of
movements. What makes one kind of movement different
from another is not so much variations in arrangements
of parts of the body as differences in energy investment.

It is important to distinguish between real energy and
what I shall call "apparent" energy. The former refers
to actual output in terms of physical expenditure on the
part of the performer. It is common to hear a dance teacher
tell a student that he is using "too much energy" or that
a particular movement does not require "so much energy."
This view of energy is related to a notion of economy and
ideal movement technique. Unless otherwise indicated,
what I shall be talking about here is "apparent" energy, or
what is seen in terms of motion and stillness rather than
of actual work, regardless of the physiological or kinesthetic
experience of the dancer. The two observations—that of the
performer and that of the spectator—do not always correspond. A vivid illustration of this is my *Trio A*: upon
completion two of us are always dripping with sweat while
the third is dry. The correct conclusion to draw is not that
the dry one is expending less energy, but that the dry one
is a "non-sweater."

Much of the western dancing we are familiar with can be
characterized by a particular distribution of energy: maximal
output or "attack" at the beginning of a phrase,* recovery at
the end, with energy often arrested somewhere in the middle.
This means that one part of the phrase—usually the part
that is the most still—becomes the focus of attention, reg-
istering like a photograph or suspended moment of climax.
In the Graham-oriented modern dance these climaxes can
come one on the heels of the other. In types of dancing
that depend on less impulsive controls, the climaxes are
farther apart and are not so dramatically "framed." Where

---

*The term "phrase" must be distinguished from "phrasing." A phrase is simply
two or more consecutive movements, while phrasing, as noted previously, refers
to the manner of execution.

extremes in tempi are imposed, this ebb-and-flow of effort is also pronounced: in the instance of speed the contrast between movement and rest is sharp, and in the adagio, or supposedly continuous kind of phrasing, the execution of transitions demonstrates more subtly the mechanics of getting from one point of still "registration" to another.

The term "phrase" can also serve as a metaphor for a longer or total duration containing beginning, middle, and end. Whatever the implications of a continuity that contains high points or focal climaxes, such an approach now seems to be excessively dramatic and more simply, unnecessary.

Energy has been used to implement heroic more-than-human technical feats and to maintain a more-than-human look of physical extension, which is familiar as the dancer's muscular "set." In the early days of the Judson Dance Theatre someone wrote an article and asked "Why are they so intent on just being themselves?" It is not accurate to say that everyone at that time had this in mind. (I certainly didn't; I was more involved in experiencing a lion's share of ecstasy and madness than in "being myself" or doing a job.) But where the question applies, it might be answered on two levels: 1) The artifice of performance has been re-evaluated in that action, or what one does, is more interesting and important than the exhibition of character and attitude, and that action can best be focused on through the submerging of the personality; so ideally one is not even oneself, one is a neutral "doer." 2) The display of technical virtuosity and the display of the dancer's specialized body no longer make any sense. Dancers have been driven to search for an alternative context that allows for a more matter-of-fact, more concrete, more banal quality of physical being in performance, a context wherein people are engaged in actions and movements making a less spectacular demand on the body and in which skill is hard to locate.

It is easy to see why the *grand jeté* (along with its ilk) had to be abandoned. One cannot "do" a *grand jeté;* one must "dance" it to get it done at all, i.e., invest it with all the necessary nuances of energy distribution that will produce the look of climax together with a still, suspended extension in the middle of the movement. Like a romantic, overblown plot this particular kind of display—with its emphasis on nuance and skilled accomplishment, its accessibility to comparison and interpretation, its involvement with connoisseurship, its introversion, narcissism, and self-congratulatoriness—has finally in this decade exhausted itself, closed back on itself, and perpetuates itself solely by consuming its own tail.

The alternatives that were explored now are obvious: stand, walk, run, eat, carry bricks, show movies, or move or be moved by some *thing* rather than oneself. Some of the early activity in the area of self-movement utilized games, "found" movement (walking, running, etc.), and people with no previous training. (One of the most notable of these early efforts was Steve Paxton's solo, *Transit,* in which he performed movement by "marking" it. "Marking" is what dancers do in rehearsal when they do not want to expend the full amount of energy required for the execution of a given movement. It has a very special look, tending to blur boundaries between consecutive movements.) These descriptions are not complete. Different people have sought different solutions.

Since I am primarily a dancer, I am interested in finding solutions primarily in the area of moving oneself, however many excursions I have made into pure and not-so-pure thing-moving. In 1964 I began to play around with simple one- and two-motion phrases that required no skill and little energy and contained few accents. The way in which they were put together was indeterminate, or decided upon in the act of performing, because at that time the idea of a different kind of continuity as embodied in transitions or connections between phrases did not seem to be as important as the material itself. The result was that the movements or phrases appeared as isolated bits framed by stoppages. Underscored by their smallness and separateness, they projected as perverse *tours de force.* Every time "elbow-wiggle" came up one felt like applauding. It was obvious that the idea of an unmodulated energy output as demonstrated in the movement was not being applied to the continuity. A continuum of energy was required. Duration and transition had to be considered.

Which brings me to *The Mind is a Muscle, Trio A.* Without giving an account of the drawn-out process through which this four-and-a-half-minute movement series (performed simultaneously by three people) was made, let me talk about its implications in the direction of movement-as-task or movement-as-object.

One of the most singular elements in it is that there are no pauses between phrases. The phrases themselves often consist of separate parts, such as consecutive limb articulations— "right leg, left leg, arms, jump," etc.—but the end of each phrase merges immediately into the beginning of the next with no observable accent. The limbs are never in a fixed, still relationship and they are stretched to their fullest extension only in transit, creating the impression that the body is constantly engaged in transitions.

Another factor contributing to the smoothness of the continuity is that no one part of the series is made any more important than any other. For four and a half minutes a great variety of movement shapes occur, but they are of equal weight and are equally emphasized. This is probably attributable both to the sameness of physical "tone" that colors all the movements and to the attention to the pacing. I can't talk about one without talking about the other.

The execution of each movement conveys a sense of unhurried control. The body is weighty without being completely relaxed. What is seen is a control that seems geared to the *actual* time it takes the *actual* weight of the body to go through the prescribed motions, rather than an adherence to an imposed ordering of time. In other words, the demands made on the body's (actual) energy resources appear to be commensurate with the task—be it getting up from the floor, raising an arm, tilting the pelvis, etc.—much as one would get out of a chair, reach for a high shelf, or walk down stairs when one is not in a hurry.* The movements are not mimetic, so they do not remind one of such actions, but I like to think that in their manner of execution they have the factual quality of such actions.

Of course, I have been talking about the "look" of the movements. In order to achieve this look in a continuity of

---

*I do not mean to imply that the demand of musical or metric phrasing makes dancing look effortless. What it produces is a different kind of effort, where the body looks more extended, "pulled up," highly energized, ready to go, etc. The dancer's "set" again.

separate phrases that does not allow for pauses, accents, or stillness, one must bring to bear many different degrees of effort just in getting from one thing to another. Endurance comes into play very much with its necessity for conserving (actual) energy (like the long-distance runner). The irony here is in the reversal of a kind of illusionism: I have exposed a type of effort where it has been traditionally concealed and have concealed phrasing where it has been traditionally displayed.

So much for phrasing. My *Trio A* contained other elements mentioned in the chart that have been touched on in passing, not being central to my concerns of the moment. For example, the "problem" of performance was dealt with by never permitting the performers to confront the audience. Either the gaze was averted or the head was engaged in movement. The desired effect was a worklike rather than exhibitionlike presentation.

I shall deal briefly with the remaining categories on the chart as they relate to *Trio A*. Variation was not a method of development. No one of the individual movements in the series was made by varying a quality of any other one. Each is intact and separate with respect to its nature. In a strict sense neither is there any repetition (with the exception of occasional consecutive traveling steps). The series progresses by the fact of one discrete thing following another. This procedure was consciously pursued as a change from my previous work, which often had one identical thing following another—either consecutively or recurrently. Naturally the question arises as to what constitutes repetition. In *Trio A*, where there is no consistent consecutive repetition, can the simultaneity of three identical sequences be called repetition? Or can the consistency of energy tone be called repetition? Or does repetition apply only to successive specific actions?

All of these considerations have supplanted the desire for dance structures wherein elements are connected thematically (through variation) and for a diversity in the use of phrases and space. I think two assumptions are implicit here: 1) A movement is a complete and self-contained event; elaboration in the sense of varying some aspect of it can only blur its distinctness; and 2) Dance is hard to see. It must either be made less fancy, or the fact of that intrinsic difficulty must be emphasized to the point that it becomes almost impossible to see.

Repetition can serve to enforce the discreteness of a movement, objectify it, make it more objectlike. It also offers an alternative way of ordering material, literally making the material easier to see. That most theatre audiences are irritated by it is not yet a disqualification.

My *Trio A* dealt with the "seeing" difficulty by dint of its continual and unremitting revelation of gestural detail that did *not* repeat itself, thereby focusing on the fact that the material could not easily be encompassed.

There is at least one circumstance that the chart does not include (because it does not relate to "minimization"), viz., the static singular object versus the object with interchangeable parts. The dance equivalent is the indeterminate performance that produces variations ranging from small details to a total image. Usually indeterminacy has been used to change the sequentialness—either phrases or larger sections— of a work, or to permute the details of a work. It has also been used with respect to timing. Where the duration of separate, simultaneous events is not prescribed exactly, variations in the relationship of these events occur. Such is the case with the trio I have been speaking about, in which small discrepancies in the tempo of individually executed phrases result in the three simultaneous performances constantly moving in and out of phase and in and out of synchronization. The overall look of it is constant from one performance to another, but the distribution of bodies in space at any given instant changes.

I am almost done. *Trio A* is the first section of *The Mind is a Muscle*. There are six people involved and four more sections. *Trio B* might be described as a VARIATION of *Trio A* in its use of unison with three people; they move in exact unison throughout. *Trio A* is about the EFFORTS of two men and a woman in getting each other aloft in VARIOUS ways while REPEATING the same diagonal SPACE pattern throughout. In *Horses* the group travels about as a unit, recurrently REPEATING six different ACTIONS. *Lecture* is a solo that REPEATS the MOVEMENT series of *Trio A*. There will be at least three more sections.*

There are many concerns in this dance. The concerns may appear to fall on my tidy chart as randomly dropped toothpicks might. However, I think there is sufficient separating-out in my work as well as that of certain of my contemporaries to justify an attempt at organizing those points of departure from previous work. Comparing the dance to Minimal Art provided a convenient method of organization. Omissions and overstatements are a hazard of any systematizing in art. I hope that some degree of redress will be offered by whatever clarification results from this essay.

*This article was written before the final version of *The Mind is a Muscle* had been made. (*Mat, Stairs,* and *Film* are not discussed.)

Pilobolus was born in the winter of the academic year 1970-1971 on the Dartmouth College campus. Four students in a modern dance class, with no previous dance experience, produced a unique, organic, eleven-minute dance, and named it Pilobolus for a fungus. Their early performances proved so successful that they quickly settled into a performing career. In December 1971 Pilobolus made its New York debut at the Louis-Nikolais Dance Theater Lab. In 1973 the four men added their former teacher, Alison Chase, and dancer Martha Clarke to the group. Since that time, despite the departure of one of the original members, the group has continued to attract acclaim and prizes with their innovative, athletic approach to dance.

The men originally substituted athleticism for traditional dance technique. They have since blended the two, as they continue to develop. The cooperative creative effect achieved by support of one another's weight in unusual ways allow the dancers to explore new possibilities of movement, new ways of performing old movement, and new images altogether. The result is an entirely new aesthetics, and an often sculpturesque effect. The excitement is in the dancer's daring and in their elimination of effort from the difficult and sometimes seemingly dangerous dances.

TALKING WITH PILOBOLUS

"Pilobolus has twelve legs but one soul." The trust and the unity is reflected in the following interview with Pilobolus, made in 1976.

An
Interview
by
Elvi
Moore

Elvi Moore. It sounds as though you constantly hear yourselves described as a gymnastic/acrobatic team, is that correct?

Martha Clarke. Yes, but none of us has any background in acrobatics or gymnastics.

Alison Chase. I think people use it because they don't know how to define us and it is an easy way of description. We don't use traditional dance vocabulary and so they think that it's mainly gymnastic vocabulary.

Moses Pendleton. We do use gymnastics and acrobatics, but it is also true that we draw from all kinds of movement, whether labeled modern dance or whatever. We don't have anything against being upside down or off vertically. People see that only as being gymnastic, but for us, it is a vehicle to show a particular image or something choreographically we feel works in the piece. I think the thing that bothers us is the fact that "gymnastic" usually means stunts and feats that are done simply for effect. We don't feel that we're just out there doing or showing tricks. There is something else, at least a concept, an idea, behind those particular movements.

Robby Barnett. Moreover, I think our new work is moving away from the earlier vocabulary that we have been more involved in up to now. Our last two pieces are not even gymnastic, and there is not much dancing in them.

Elvi. There certainly is evident an evolution, it seems to me, from the original pieces to *Monkshood Farewell* and the untitled piece. You are going into something completely different now, into more thematic works, is that correct?

Martha. Yes, with a more theatrical impulse. I think we now use the linked movement in the earlier techniques merely as a means to realize the images and maybe the theatrical ideas that we have. Whereas, before that, technique was an end in itself.

Moses. In the earlier pieces, like *Ciona,* we were more concerned simply with the movement, the shape, the designs and the musicality of the piece. This new untitled work, more than any of the previous pieces, is beginning to deal with the relationships between people and is much more a theater piece.

Elvi. Martha said that none of you have had acrobatic or gymnastic training. How did your whole style evolve? I know that the two ladies are dance trained, and were the rest of you trained by Alison?

Alison. Oh, I don't take any credit for their talent.

Robby. I think to a degree the reason it went the way it did was that there's a certain sort of release, almost athletic energy, and when we moved, it wasn't with a trained dancer's body. Because of our athletic background, instead of doing extensions and doing turns on center, we started by holding on to each other. We were interested in the design; it was something that we could control very easily without training.

Alison. The first dance of Pilobolus was the defining piece. I had never seen people use their bodies to create shapes in tension like that. I'd say that this was the piece that defined their early style.

Moses. When we first began, there was Jonathan, myself, and another fellow, Steve Johnson. The original piece that we did was titled *Pilobolus.* I felt very paranoid about just getting up and doing a dance. We felt that maybe we couldn't dance, so why try to? When we began, we didn't really feel free, moving in space individually. We literally *had* to hang onto each other. We all figured that we could at least do that much, and it was something larger than any one body could make. It wasn't so difficult if you did create this shape, a thing that moved. We began to play around by combining bodies.

Elvi. How do you go about keeping your bodies in shape; in a systematic training or all different ways?

Alison. We do nothing collectively in terms of training. Everybody does what they need to do for their own body. Some of the guys have started to do ballet barre and Martha and I try to help them with that.

Moses. The women now are jogging and lifting weights and working out in the gym and *we're* going to ballet classes!

Jonathan Wolken. We constantly wrestle on mats.

Moses. Alison runs four miles a day. I used to run all the time—now I never lift a foot or never break into stride.

Elvi. Why are you getting into ballet exercises now?

Jonathan. That's an individual thing. For example, *this* person [pointing to himself] is not getting into ballet classes yet. It's a totally open kind of thing in the company.

Martha. I think it helps to push the technical possibilities and to refine them.

Moses. In order to even develop or change the choreography sometimes you can work by thinking of a new dance. Another way to go about it is to simply train your body differently so that you can do new movements that offer a different vocabulary to make a new dance. If we worked to do things we weren't able to do before, then the next piece might involve a different vocabulary, therefore a different choreography.

Jonathan. The point I'm trying to make, probably in a backward way, is that despite the fact that one's movement possibilities are increased, the choreography seems to take a direction of its own. If we use training of any kind, it's more toward choreographic ends than for training itself.

Moses. We're also finding that the training for a particular piece, *Ciona,* for example, would be much more effective if people could stand on their own two feet a little better, could move more easily through space.

Martha. The more technical facility you have, the more you're able to explore. That's why I feel we should all be getting stronger and refining what we have. I think the company is dancing better each season. It's from doing work. It's from performing it all. Jonathan, you're the only one in the company who is not in favor of this, and that's your prerogative, but I think that the other people who are doing the barre would feel that they're improving.

Jonathan. Well, I feel that I'm improving without a barre. That's not to say I don't feel I'm improving. For that matter, I can't say that people would not normally improve anyway if they would just pay attention to their movements. It's not the barre, it's not the wall, it's not the set-up, it's the idea of concentrating on the movement.

Moses. It's not just the barre. I think the point is that you pay attention to your needs and you work on your body.

Elvi. You all feel, though, that some discipline in training your own bodies in your own way is very good in keeping sharp.

Jonathan. Without a doubt, even when we approach the barre in a different way. Martha might do a very traditional barre, sixteen of these, sixteen of those. Alison might do something of a traditional barre too. Whereas, if I went to the barre, and when I've seen the other men in the company go to the barre, I wouldn't use it in the same way. I might pull or tug against completely different things.

Alison. I think, given that the women are trained and the men are untrained, there might be an area between that we could explore if they had the training that approximated ours or tried to meet ours. I think that Martha and I have met the boys' way of moving. I think it would be nice if they could meet our way of moving at some point in time.

Moses. I think the point is that whether you do a barre, or stretch, or just hang upside down, the difference is the attention that you try to give your body to make it work bet-

ter each day. Somehow that will reflect itself in the choreography.

Elvi. What about choreography, the creative endeavors in
choreography, can you talk about that a little bit? How do
you start a new work? Does it always begin with a definite
movement idea?

Jonathan. Before we start talking about this, we should
probably add a word of precaution that everyone in this company has distinct and probably radically different ideas about
what is done, how it's done, and how it begins, so that people
will speak differently for themselves when they answer this.

Martha. I would say that with the new piece, we started
with the notion of a man under a woman's skirt and the idea
of being tall and small, of being able to just feel the movement possibilities within that structure of having somebody
under your skirt.

Alison. And the image possibility. There's that element
of fantasy of being street level and being twice that high, and
then this form, that shape have various other image suggestions.

Martha. The psychological line that the dance takes means
we find movements all of a sudden. We don't say we want to
make this apparent or that apparent; it's constructed rather
blindly in a way, and then all of a sudden certain things will
be revealed to both. This is what the relationship is about,
but it happens after the movement has been invented and
sewn together.

Moses. To continue what Martha was saying, when we
first begin a piece, we might have a vague idea of what we
want to do. We may spend a couple of weeks on what we
call gathering material; in a way it's like an improvisation.
We go into a studio and just work and play on various moves.
Eventually one move may link to another or you may find a
particular image that will allow you to start thinking in terms
of where a piece may go, or it might develop. In the process
of those three weeks you might find three or four sets—bits
of material for different pieces. Eventually we begin to focus
in on one particular idea from the movement, from the
images that emerge from the movement. Then the piece begins to develop. After a couple of weeks the ideas become

formed, and you begin to work more seriously on movement that has something to do with that original idea which came out of a certain type of improvisation.

Martha. Then there might also be phrases that don't seem to have any home. The dance might go fine A to F, then suddenly you've got M-N-O, and you have to then think of an idea that would make a legitimate connection theatrically.

Moses. Further on, the ideas become more manifest, and you almost start making movements out of the ideas. Whereas, as Martha says, to fill in particular gaps, you start thinking of certain types of movement to complete a concept.

Alison. With this new piece, there is a lot of material that we just haven't developed yet. We have a whole bar scene, a saloon scene, and we become dwarves with these skirts that are very long. Martha and I are transformed into dwarves by putting our knees up into our tops, while the guys would still be inside the skirt, but there's no torso and they move out gradually, but we have not used it yet.

Robby. It can be very frustrating, to have material that's marvelous, but it just doesn't fit. As Alison said, we have a whole range of terrifically comedic movements using these big women as tops and street ladies, a lot of very funny slapstick stuff that we don't feel is appropriate the way the piece is going.

Elvi. Are you satisfied with the new piece as it is now?

Jonathan. We're in the process of beginning to mount a lot of free choreography into our things. As soon as we get the time to go at it again, we'll change it because there are problems in this piece, especially because of the score, which is for us much more liquid. It has been composed for an orchestra, it's been recorded by an orchestra. If it's going to be amended, it has to be assembled. It can be done for sure, but it's a much more difficult process and one has to look at editing in a different way.

Robby. I think we'll attempt to make our piece fit the score at this point. It's perfectly possible for them to make room beyond what the score holds. We will have to extend the score, but I think certainly we're going to try to fit whatever changes we do inside that.

Moses. We worked on it furiously, and even unfinished,

it was very helpful to gain a perspective on it by performing it. Even in the rough stage, because it gives us a chance to get away from it and look at it and have a certain response to it. It allows us to see the piece a bit more objectively.

Elvi. Where do you foresee yourselves going now, more into the theatrical works like the new untitled one?

Robby. I think for the next year, as we hone this piece and change it, we are going to be involved in smaller works that will give us each a chance to explore the things that we happen to be particularly interested in. I think it's hard to tell what [the] company will turn out next. It's hard to say what out direction will be. For example, when the original four decided to ask the women to join. At the time, we thought we'd just try it out and see how it went, thinking at least it would keep things moving forward, rather than sort of stymying us all. So they came along with us, and after a certain period of time we all sort of melted together.

Martha. In the beginning, Allison and I were not well integrated in the group. It took a year and a half, nearly two years, to make it work where everyone was on kind of equal footing.

Moses. One of the difficulties was that they had their pieces that they were doing and we had ours. Obviously, it doesn't look like an integrated company if the women want to do their business and the men come on and want to do theirs. Then we began to try to fit the women into a man's vocabulary, which they have done wonderfully. It's unbelievable. Alison would come in and simply do a male role in obviously a very strong man-type dance. Both of them have done that very well and now we're beginning to evolve, like this new piece, which is very much a woman's theme. It's about women, and Robby and I, for instance, are trying to think in terms of women's psychology, which is different from the women trying to do men's movement.

Elvi. I think the integration is quite clear. In your first appearance at the University of Chicago a year and a half ago, and again in January, I felt a tremendous difference in the way the company now handles its work.

Moses. *Monkshood* was the first piece that we, as a company of four men and two women, began to choreograph from the start. Obviously, when you make a piece, if you begin the choreography with the people who are going to be in the piece, everything is integrated because it's wedded at the start.

Martha. Also, we had a year under our belts. We knew about each other's sense of humor, the kind of twist that we wanted to take.

Elvi. How do you handle requests from other dancers to join your company?

Jonathan. Bringing people into the company, this is an interesting subject. We think about it a lot, talk about it some too. Our company, because it's different, because of the fact that there is no central thing, and because we work cooperatively, the idea of bringing an outside influence into the company is not just a lark. It's a temporary release, as we've mentioned before—you know, it gives us all a kind of release of tension. But the long-run effect is really a serious consideration of how we'll get along as an expanded family. The interaction of the company is very intense, and complete.

Martha. Also, we've achieved a group aesthetic. We all have different ideas about the dances, but when something good happens, we all know it's good. The minute you bring a new element in on a more or less permanent basis, it risks this.

Robby. We're also somewhat resistant to people who are almost too full of energy and too full of ideas because there is a certain personal subjugation that goes into being a corporate entity.

Jonathan. If all of us spoke all of our ideas all of the time, the confusion would be totally out of hand. So we have a collective filter, and it's really a pretty involved process.

Elvi. Part of the whole difference appears to be that, not only are you talking about making dances, but you're also talking about a whole lifestyle which certainly makes Pilobolus very unique, and would make someone coming in go through a difficult adjustment period.

Moses. We try to function on a type of self-discipline and sort of democratic situation and at times, I suppose, try to take advantage of it.

Jonathan. It's idealistically an approach. Just the fact that we manage to eke out an existence and keep centered without falling apart is a remarkable feat.

Moses. You wonder sometimes why people get themselves into group situations in the first place; maybe because they find energy and ideas from it, and the fact that they can't really feel that they function well by themselves. It certainly happens in many groups as the group matures and establishes itself. People, after a while, growing older, begin to have their own sensibility and need for individuality, and I think *that* is even happening in our company. There comes a point where you wonder whether the group is actually feeding the individual, which it must do always. I don't think a group works simply because you're doing it totally for the group; you're doing it for yourself also. That's the thing that becomes more and more difficult in this company as people begin to have a certain sense of their own aesthetic sensibility. To constantly compromise in a group in which individuals are trying very hard to develop as individuals: that's the tension we're always working on.

Martha. I hope that what we'll achieve is an objectivity about the work itself, with the individual adding to the work and gaining from the work in order to expand the individual's career. Each person has to grow within the framework, everybody has to be given the chance to grow.

Moses. At times, for some people in the group it becomes threatening because they feel that they see another individual in the group taking off. That for me is not too much of a threat to Pilobolus, but a necessary course for it to take. Although it may not be the most efficient way to keep this company together, it has to allow itself to become inefficient, allow itself to accommodate, to listen to personal needs as best it can.

Jonathan. The only thing that can be said in all truth is that the relationship between the individual and the company is constantly fluctuating and changing and re-establishing new balances. Sometimes the thing is out of control, sometimes it's totally in control. Individuals are always related to Pilobolus, this third entity, in fluctuating ways. So it's really quite a boiling pot. You never can say exactly where it is or exactly where it's going or where it might go.

Elvi. I think that's really an amazing feat, four and a half years with only one change in personnel. Let me wish you continued success as you continue to grow as individuals and as a group. Many of us will certainly be watching and hoping to enjoy your expanding talents for a long time to come.

*Born in Aberdeen, Washington, Trisha Brown studied
with Anna Halprin while a dance major at Mills
College. She went to New York in 1960, and in 1962
became a founding member of the Judson Dance
Theater. A few years later she organized her own
company, which was incorporated in 1970. In that
same year she also became a founding member of the
Grand Union, an improvisational dance theater
company.*

*In her dances, Brown uses ordinary movements in ex-
traordinary circumstances: on New York City
rooftops, in rafts on a lake, on walls. She works in
structured improvisation and describes her choreographic approach as similar to that of "a brick-
layer with a sense of humor."*

DIALOGUE ON DANCE

*Douglas Dunn was born and
grew up in Palo Alto, California. With a strong background
in athletics and ballet, he went
to New York to dance
in 1968. He performed*
*with Yvonne Rainer and Group from 1968 to 1970,
and with Merce Cunningham and Dance Company
from 1969 to 1973.*

*Dunn was also a founding member of the Grand
Union and performed with it from 1970 to 1975. In
1971 he began his own choreography, working both
independently and in collaboration with others.
He is presently performing "Douglas Dunn: Solo
Film and Dance" in the U.S. and Europe.*

*Trisha
Brown
(1936-)*

This self-interview, conducted for Ballet Review,
*is another indication of the cooperative spirit found
among the members of the avant-garde of the sixties
and seventies.*

*Douglas
Dunn
(1942-)*

Dunn. For *Lazy Madge* I'm working with
nine dancers, one at a time, spending about
eight to ten hours making about five to ten
minutes of material on each person. And I am
making duets for myself with several of the
people. This seems to come only after I've

made solo material for the person. I'm also thinking about making trios using them without me. The dancers I'm working with are people who've studied dance—and they're dancers who're all very different, have different techniques, and strikingly different personalities which becomes very obvious when they're on the space together. I made a solo on each of two women who'd never met. They did their two solos on the space at the same time. They had a strong reaction to one another and the result was very exciting on a \dog-meets-dog level as well as on a dance level.\ I'm trying to *not* think about all the things I used to think about—that's been my main instruction to myself for this work. Not to pay attention to most of the formal things. So I end up paying attention to simply what I have to tell a person to do and go through movement that they can remember and keep. So far there is a very strong formality to my work and it's coming out different than if I had paid attention to it.

Brown. What do you mean by formality?

Dunn. Everything. The time, the space, the rhythm, the movement. . .plus any general shape of the piece. I never lay out floor patterns. I try not to have any ideas before I start working with a person. I focus on that person and not just physically; I try to generate imagery off paying attention to them.

Brown. So you make a solo on them.

Dunn. Very specifically. I don't work at all until the people come in. There is also some amount of material which I consider stylistic because it repeats. I just found myself using certain movements more than others.

Brown. How do you do that?

Dunn. For example, the first person I worked with is a short, squarish woman and for some reason when I thought of her certain images came to mind. The second position, for one. I'm allowing imagery to come back into my work. The other formal thing that's going on in the work is that there are very, very short phrases which are almost always stopped. Each phrase is a little rhythmic invention which eventually stops. Then something else begins.

Brown. Is that because you were making the piece in that size segment and stopping and teaching it to them?

Dunn. Not really. It's about having to undercut all the re-presentational imagery that's coming in. Physical imagery—dance movement imagery as well as mime imagery. At this point I don't think of myself as someone with a personal dance style. That's irrelevant to me. What I'm dealing with is what I know about the outside world. So this piece is about that. . . . I'm still relatively dedicated to being functional about getting in and out of things unless there's a specific imagistic reason not to do so. The things that I do which are specifically awkward are made to be awkward. I don't really say I want to make an image of something. I start to make steps, then think of the imagistic possibilities. So it's not as if the imagery comes first. The feeling in the image area develops later. This is new to me.

Brown. I call what you're talking about a position.

Dunn. I'm just making a difference in the degree of atten-tion to images in my work.

Brown. I was wondering if you're allowing that a movement has more meaning than just pure physical imagery.

Dunn. A lot more. But I'm not asking people to perform in a way that they add to that at all. In fact, I'm making dif-ficult movements, so that the dancers struggle with them. That's also one of the things I'm working with.

Brown. What happens if they can't achieve it?

Dunn. Everybody can try to do something of what it is.

Brown. What do you settle for?

Dunn. I haven't yet taken anything away from anybody be-cause they can't do it. Watching them try to do it interests me a lot. I also see the experience of people who have that attitude for learning how to do something. That experience amazes me more and more because it's faded somewhat in me. Having this appetite to learn how to do things they can't do at first helps. They do it.

Whether they do it or not is irrelevent because there is a line of something going on that makes it feel necessary to do the next thing. Sometimes it requires something very awk-ward. By awkward I mean something difficult, physically or otherwise. People have an appetite for trying to do it, and as long as they have that energy, I'm going to be there. All it accepts is that people come and go. I haven't set up a sche-

dule with nine people and said this is what we're working on
and so on. This is going to be some kind of on-going situation until we know whether to keep going.

Brown. But do you intend to have them performing all together at one time in one place?

Dunn. Yeah. And I tend to leave a lot of decisions unde-
ceded. I've been making these duets and I haven't been
setting at all what I do. It's really that forgetting, not knowing I guess, that is new to me. I've never been in such a dance
situation. This approach is for *Lazy Madge:* this is not my
approach.

Brown. Right now I'm just at the beginning stage of making
a new piece. [*Structured Pieces V* was performed in France
at the Fêtes Musicales de la Sainte-Baume in August, 1976.]
I don't know how much of what I say will be in the piece.
But I've made a section of material which is something like
functional movement. Not functional movement, but a
logical progression where one movement follows another.
Movement B is an obvious movement after A, C is obvious
after B. No big jumps. I try not to leave anything out.
There are little flashes of eccentricity along the way. This
movement goes backward as well as forward. I now have
two people who are doing it.

There are points in the phrase (like standing up, sitting,
etc.) that are like possible intersections for other obvious
moves to go in other directions. I intend to make alternate
phrases branching off this main phrase. They will all back up
and go forward and possibly even to the right and the left. At
this point two people go forward and backward in a three-
minute phrase. They start out and go forward. I verbally stop
them, back them up, bring them forward, put them in sync
with each other. . . . I try to get interesting combinations of
the phrase, visually and rhythmically, by verbally mani-
pulating them.

At this point I'd like to put this movement, and a greatly
extended phrase of 20 minutes, on to at least four people
and try to direct them from outside during the performance.
I don't think I'll be dancing in this piece. I've been sitting
more and watching my dancers work in front of me, but then
I get up to do things and it's hard for me to stay warm. I was

thinking about some sort of platform that could be built for me so I could stretch while I'm watching them. When they need me I could get right up. Then I thought I should put pillows on this platform. Then I saw myself sinking down into the pillows, sending messages like paper airplanes out to the dancers.

Dunn. It's very interesting that you should direct the new piece. When I got out of the Merce Cunningham Company and started watching pieces, one of the things I disliked was the frequent modern dance theme of the choreographer as. . . choreographer. I thought I was certainly not going to get involved in *that!* And I'm very involved in it. *Lazy Madge* is about that. It shocks me to death.

Brown. Is the dancing more virtuosic?

Dunn. No. It's much easier to do physically.

Brown. Are you thinking of a dramatic character?

Dunn. No. Not that strong. . . . I don't want to use movement manipulations as a source of invention. I'm involved in retrograde work. . . .I'm thinking of movement in an imagistic way—images that interrupt the line of movement.

Brown. I start with a structure and make movement to fit my concept. . . .I used to always improvise, to have some sort of improvisation in my work—which was purely dealing with my personal resources on the fly in front of the audience. When I began dancing with the Grand Union, I didn't have to do that any more. There was a marked transition in my own work from improvisation, large constructions, and language to movement.

So when I got back into making movement, I used a simple form which was to make 1 movement, repeat it several times and add 2, repeat 1 and 2 several times and add 3, then 4, etc. Movements were wedged in between earlier additions which upset the linear scheme and caused the dance to fatten rather than lengthen—and often in a lopsided manner. I was learning about the form by doing it. It was a messy construction job but I would never go back and correct it. *Primary Accumulation* was only one movement at a time— one, one-two, one-two-three, etc. A pared down and less emotive version, although viewers were emotionally stirred.

Dunn. I think your answer indicates something general which is that there is an interest in dance as an area to experiment with movement problems or performance problems as possibilities—as opposed to a vehicle for expressing what you think about the world. It's like talking—through your dancing—about the kinds of things that interest you about movement, how you put a dance together. What is it about? Your titles suggest that you look at dance as a formal structure. *Accumulation* as a title as opposed to your *Pamplona Stones* points to the structural basis of the piece.

Brown. Pamplona Stones was put together through free association which was a break from the more austere *Accumulation* pieces I had been doing. I scripted it before teaching it to the other dancers. It is an imaginary dialogue based on some drawings I had made. It turned out that there was a constant inner dramatic thread in the piece. It was referring back to itself through words and questioning and actions. It got its name through sounds. We were using stones as material very early in the piece and Pamplona rhymed with stones—somewhat. One performer was Spanish and Pamplona is a Spanish town I remembered.

Dunn. The question of what to call one's work is a problem. I think everybody looks around the environment, sees how terms are being used and tries to represent their work as clearly as possible. This was a problem with the Grand Union. We wanted to think of ourselves as doing everything, and just wanted to know how to say that. We didn't call ourselves "dancers" because that was too limited. We chose not to use words like "theatre" or "drama" because we didn't like the association with other theatre. We definitely wanted to be connected with an art position. We used to say "Grand Union is a collaboration of individual artists." People choose the words "dance" or "theatre" according to the elements in their work.

Brown. In the sixties, a trained dancer was a person with a puffed-out ribcage who was designed to project across the footlights in a proscenium arch stage. He or she couldn't necessarily do a natural kind of movement, even a simple one. So what I looked for was a person with a natural, well-coordinated, instinctive ability to move. At that time the whole dance vocabulary was open. It was no longer selected movement or chosen gestures for telling a story within the formal vocabulary of ballet movement. All movement became available for choreographing. . . . *Walking on the Wall* gave the illusion that the audience was overhead, looking down on the tops of the heads of the performers walking and standing below. It also showed what it was, the performance of a simple activity against the principles of gravity. The rigging and technical business of getting up there was in clear view.

Dunn. It was stylized movement in extraordinary circumstances, or ordinary movement in extraordinary circumstances.

Brown. That was developing a skill for an occasion—appearing to be natural in a completely un-natural situation. The "happenings" people used non-actors to do performances and that came before Judson. Also there is a certain look or personality of trained dancers of traditional schools. They train for alikeness, a certain conformity. It was interesting to have people of different personalities and posture and looks about them on the stage. I've been working with combinations of other kinds of movement than natural movement. I've been working with unnatural movement.

Dunn. If we talk historically, what wasn't present as available material for dances in the sixties and which later became available material was stylization. Before the sixties there was no consciousness of certain things as being dance.

Brown. I think the "Twist" helped a lot in the sixties.

Dunn. Rock dancing was a bridge between your daily life, which was still unconscious perhaps, and part of your classroom dance life which was not making available that possibility . . . . When I came to New York in 1968 and Yvonne Rainer was looking for people fresh off the farm and people who didn't know how to point their feet, I was in front of the line. It seemed to me the most normal thing possible. I thought why not? I wasn't in touch with the issues of the time at all. I just enjoyed doing what I was used to doing in a much more conscious way. At the same time I was training like hell to do those things I couldn't do. When I started to make work a few years later, a broader range of movement possibilities were somehow made accessible. I feel very grateful for all of that because I don't feel at all that I have a revolutionary sensibility.

It may be true that neither critics nor audiences absorbed what happened in the sixties but I don't think I'd be doing what I'm doing now if that hadn't happened.

I've been thinking about the influences of other artists a lot lately—more than I ever have. Even wanting to begin to talk about people's work in those terms. I'm very interested in the overall energy or undertone of a work. Is there a positive or negative energy of a work? What are the generative forces of a piece of work? How is the energy being structured? I used to watch dancing like I watched people just walking on the street. Now I am more interested in the relationship of the performer to what he or she is doing.

Brown. The word "energy" throws me. It's one of those words like "vibes." It has no meaning for me. Are you talking about the humanness of the people?

Dunn. I'm talking about emphasis. Is there a craftsman-like approach, an inspirational approach, a hard-nosed approach, a consciously avant-garde approach to the work? What is coming to the fore?

Brown. I think that it comes into the category of naturalness or natural movements. Doing things in a straight way. The human way of doing something is often preferred when I give instructions to my performers to do something.

Born in Detroit, with a background in jazz dance and choreography for night clubs and resorts, Rod Rodgers went to New York in 1963. He performed there during the next few years with several dance groups, including the Erick Hawkins Dance Company. A year after his arrival in New York, the Rod Rodgers Dance Company was formed.

DON'T TELL ME WHO I AM

During the following fifteen years, the company established an eclectic repertoire of abstract, dance-drama, jazz, and modern dance works. It was one of the first American dance companies under the direction of a black artist to establish a base of recognition for something other than exclusively ethnic or traditional Afro-American styles. Choreography for the company is by Mr. Rodgers and guest artists. Rod Rodgers also has choreographed for television and off-Broadway productions.

"Don't Tell Me Who I Am," a succinct statement of purpose, first appeared in The Negro Digest.

Rod Rodgers (1938–)

(On several occasions I have been asked if I felt that my dance art is affected by my being Afro-American. This question surprises me because I am aware of the way my present work has evolved from my early experience and basic technique in Afro-Cuban and jazz dance. But in an art like dance, people have no way of seeing where you are coming from unless you have managed to retain examples of your early work in your repertoire, and I have not found this practical. So the question persists from blacks and whites who strongly feel that the most important thing a black artist can do today is to help establish a black cultural identity by emphasizing traditional Afro-American thematic material. The following statement from my point of view clarifies the role of non-traditional, experimental "black art.")

***

I am not looking for any over-simplified answer to the question: Who am I? It is obvious by now that I am not going to be a great white American dancer. But I have little patience with people who suggest that to be a black choreographer one must limit one's scope and deal exclusively with traditional Afro-American material.

The question of an artist's identity is one that he continually asks. He asks it through his chosen medium by experimentally probing into different aspects of his identity and environment. Whether one functions as a choreographer who also happens to be black, or as a black man who happens to be a choreographer is determined by one's point of view at a given moment. The ideal point of view at any given moment, for the individual artist, is the one which best allows him to create the most profoundly exciting art. If he cannot produce beautiful and exciting art, there is no point in discussing his political or ideological commitments in relation to art.

The militant black revolutionary may think of art in terms of the whole machinery of the revolution, as a means of bringing forth the rich heritage of the African in America and of creating a sense of identity for the sake of the revolution. Most of the existing dance companies which are instruments of black choreographers have placed their emphasis on traditional Afro-American material. They are exploring through their artistry the proud Afro-American heritage, and they can evoke poignant images which will encourage intolerance of racial suppression. But these images are not the only means of communicating a black consciousness. While traditional black art is playing a vital role in the awakening of a black cultural identity, now it is equally important for black artists to discourage the crystallization of new limiting stereotypes by not confining themselves to over-simplified traditional images.

I am not suggesting that black artists should or could cut themselves off from Afro-American tradition. Artist or layman, our past experience inevitably affects our articulation of present ideas. But if an artist's sense of immediacy is to vitalize his work, he should have freedom to decide which ideas he feels a need to communicate at a particular time. Artists have felt compelled to create images calling for social changes long before their own people were ready to initiate such changes. Other artists might never be moved to focus their art on socio-historic events. It is not a question of art for art's sake; it is a need to be true to one's own feelings. Although masterpieces *have* been created on commission, in the process of fulfilling some sponsor's vision, far more often the product of artists working with ideas which are devoid of deep personal relevance has tended to be poor art.

An artist's assumption that he knows exactly what his audience "needs" often results in art that is, at best, patronizing. The highest compliment an artist can pay his audience is to invite them to witness his exploration of the maximum possibilities of his art, based on his total experience.

The dance that I do is Afro-American, simply because I am Afro-American. My blackness is part of my identity as a human being, and my dance exploration is evolving in relation to my total experience as a man. It is simply a question of what takes precedence in the creative act: my total living experience, or those experiences which I consider particularly relevent to my blackness. Both white and black Americans have long been conditioned to accept the myth that Afro-Americans function well only in certain predictable areas. This myth must be dispelled. The refusal of black artists to confine their work to convenient categories will contribute to the destruction of this limited notion. Each dance that I create has grown out of my personal experience as a black American. Each movement that I explore is part of my own personal heritage.

My emphasis is on exploring through my medium, experimenting with dance, trying to find fresh ways of evoking physical and spiritual images to make new poetic comments about man's eternal beauty and pathos. My function in the revolution will be to share my personal experience—a vital and growing experience—through dance: it will not be to show only old stereotypes or create new ones.

CONCLUSION

The avant-garde of the sixties has sustained its influence through the seventies, at the same time giving rise to younger, even more experimental dancers, still performing in lofts and off-Broadway theaters in New York City and on the college circuit.

Their groups, in the tradition of the Judson group, are collective, cooperative enterprises, usually without a single director, as is often reflected in their names: the Grand Union, the Multigravitional Aeordance Group, and the Pilobolus Dance Theatre, among others. Some avant-garde groups more traditionally use the name of the originator-director, including the Trisha Brown Company, the Laura Dean Dancers and Musicians, and the Laura Foreman Dance Theatre.

The experiment with nontechnical movement, nonmovement, nondancers, no fixed repertory, and performance out of the theater has continued. Its impact, however, has lessened considerably during the decade of the seventies. The pendulum has begun to swing back to formality, technique, ideational content, expressiveness, and costumes—even skirts on the female dancers. As the country simmered down from the Viet Nam War, the student rebellion, and the black rebellion of the late sixties and early seventies, a more secure, positive outlook manifested itself. This atmosphere was reflected by artists as the use of formal elements began to reappear in their compositions.

Federal support for the arts has created a more stable financial picture. The Coordinated Residency Touring Program, the artists-in-residence programs at colleges, the Artists in the Schools programs, and federally funded grants to individual artists and companies have meant more performing, larger audiences, and greater remuneration for the artists. There has also been an astounding increase in the number of dance companies; there were 115 in New York City alone in 1978 (encompassing all dance forms).

Just as dance has flourished in New York City, so, has it mushroomed across the country. Although New York remains the dance center, an increasing number of companies have sprung up in other locations, fed by burgeoning college dance departments. Among them are: Pilobolus Dance Theater, Washington, Connecticut; Nancy Hauser Dance Company, St. Paul, Minnesota; Repertory Dance Theater, Salt Lake City, Utah; the Bill Evans Dance Company, Seattle, Washington; and the Bella Lewitzky Dance Company and the Gloria Newman Dance Theater, Los Angeles, California.

At the same time, the established modern dance has incorporated more ballet in its techniques, training, and works. In 1976 Martha Graham celebrated the fiftieth anniversary of her first independent concert by creating a new work, *Lucifer*, for two of the most respected ballet dancers of the twentieth century, Margot Fonteyn and Rudolf Nureyev of the Royal Ballet. In 1977, in celebration of the centennial anniversary of the birth of Isadora Duncan, Lynn Seymour of the Royal Ballet danced in Sir Frederick Ashton's "Five Brahms Waltzes in the Manner of Isadora Duncan." Modern dancers Annabelle Gamson and Joyce Trisler also presented performances in honor of Isadora Duncan.

The scope of modern dancers, once fixed on their rebellion from ballet and all other established forms of dance, has become broader. In fact, the trend toward extensive ballet training for modern dancers has brought a balletic look to modern dance companies. Several exist as repertory companies, offering a wide range of dance styles. That of Twyla Tharp is itself a microcosm of the new eclecticism: a blend of ballet, jazz, and modern dance. With all three dance styles, as well as tap and baton, in her background, she has choreographed for ballet companies as well as for her own, and for film, television, and even an ice skater, John Curry.

Modern dance thrives within the context of rebellion because of the continuing and absolute respect for the individual's right to creative expression. The result is an immense diversity.

Historically, modern dance arose within the milieu of Art Nouveau, vaudeville, and exoticism. The early avant-garde created revolutionary art by using simplicity, often to the point of severity. A new aesthetics was produced by integrating meaning and movement through three-dimensional asymmetrical design. Along the way, the rebellion became codified, systematized, and oriented toward trends and techniques. The new avant-garde has returned to simplicity in the current leaning toward minimal art.

The original rebellion came full circle, gave rise to a new one which came full circle, which gave rise . . .—and so modern dance has evolved, and in all probability will continue to evolve in the future. It is likely that there will always be an established center and a radical fringe, with most dancers found somewhere in between.

BIBLIOGRAPHY

I Artists

● Isadora Duncan

Duncan, Irma. *Duncan Dancer.* Middletown, Conn.: Wesleyan University Press, 1966.

———. *Isadora Duncan: Pioneer in the Art of Dance.* New York: The New York Public Library, 1958.

———. *The Technique of Isadora Duncan.* New York: Kamin Publishers, 1937. (Brooklyn: Dance Horizons, 1970.)

Duncan, Isadora. *The Art of the Dance.* New York: Theatre Arts Books, 1970.

———. *My Life.* New York: Boni & Liveright, 1927. (New York: Liveright, 1955.)

Desti, Mary. *The Untold Story: The Life of Isadora Duncan 1921-1927.* New York: Horace Liveright, 1929.

MacDougall, Allan Ross. *Isadora: A Revolutionary in Art and Love.* New York: Thomas Nelson & Sons, 1960.

Magriel, Paul David. *Isadora Duncan.* New York: Henry Holt & Co., 1947.

Maria-Theresa. "The Spirit of Isadora Duncan." In Myron Howard Nadel and Constance Gwen Nadel, eds., *The Dance Experience: Readings in Dance Appreciation.* New York: Praeger Publishers, 1970.

Roslavleva, Natalia. "Prechistenka 20: The Isadora Duncan School in Moscow." *Dance Perspectives* 64 (1975).

Schneider, Ilya Ilyich. *Isadora Duncan: The Russian Years.* Translated by David Magershack. London: MacDonald, 1968.

Seroff, Victor. *The Real Isadora.* London: Hutchinson, 1972.

Sorell, Walter. "Two Rebels, Two Giants: Isadora and Martha." In Walter Sorell, ed., *The Dance Has Many Faces.* 2d ed. rev. New York: Columbia University Press, 1966.

Steegmuller, Francis, ed. *Your Isadora: The Love Story of Isadora Duncan and Gordon Craig.* New York: Random House and The New York Public Library, 1974.

Terry, Walter. *Isadora Duncan: Her Life, Her Art, Her Legacy.* New York: Dodd, Mead & Co., 1963.

_____. "The Legacy of Ìsadora Duncan and Ruth St. Denis." *Dance Perspectives* 5 (1960).

● Loie Fuller

DeMorini, Claire. "Loie Fuller, The Fairy of Light." In Paul Magriel, ed., *Chronicles of American Dance.* New York: Henry Holt & Co., 1948.

Fuller, Loie. *Fifteen Years of a Dancer's Life.* Boston: Small, Maynard & Co., 1913. (Brooklyn: Dance Horizons, 1976.)

Kermode, Frank. "Loie Fuller and the Dance Before Diaghilev." *Theatre Arts* 46, no. 9 (1962) pp 6-21.

● Ruth St. Denis

St. Denis, Ruth, and Shawn, Ted. *Denishawn Magazine* 1-3 (1924-1925).

_____. *Lotus Light.* Boston and New York: Houghton, Mifflin & Co., 1932.

_____. "Religious Manifestations in the Dance." In Walter Sorell, ed., *The Dance Has Many Faces.* 2d ed. rev. New York: Columbia University Press, 1966.

_____. *An Unfinished Life.* New York and London: Harper & Bros., 1939. (Brooklyn: Dance Horizons, 1969.)

Schlundt, Christena. "Into the Mystic with Miss Ruth." *Dance Perspectives* 47 (1971).

_____. *The Professional Appearances of Ruth St. Denis and Ted Shawn.* New York: The New York Public Library, 1962.

Shawn, Ted. *Ruth St. Denis.* San Francisco: J. H. Nash, 1920.

Terry, Walter. "The Legacy of Isadora Duncan and Ruth St. Denis." *Dance Perspectives* 5 (1960).

_____. *Miss Ruth: The More Living Life of Ruth St. Denis.* New York: Dodd, Mead & Co., 1969.

● Ted Shawn

Dreier, Katherine Sophie. *Shawn the Dancer.* London: J. M. Dent & Son, Ltd., 1933.

Schlundt, Christena. *The Professional Appearances of Ruth St. Denis and Ted Shawn.* New York: The New York Public Library, 1962.

_____. *The Professional Appearances of Ted Shawn and His Men Dancers.* New York: The New York Public Library, 1967.

● Shawn, Ted. *The American Ballet.* New York: Henry Holt & Co., 1926.

———. *Dance We Must.* Pittsfield, Mass.: Eagle Printing & Binding Co., 1940, 1950, 1963. (New York: Haskell House, 1974.)

———. *Every Little Movement.* Pittsfield, Mass.: Eagle Printing & Binding Co., 1954, 1963. (Brooklyn: Dance Horizons, 1968.)

———. *One Thousand and One Night Stands.* With Grace Poole. New York: Doubleday, 1960.

———. *Ruth St. Denis.* San Francisco: J. H. Nash, 1920.

———. *33 Years of American Dance.* Pittsfield, Mass.: Eagle Printing & Binding Co., 1959.

Terry, Walter. *Ted Shawn: Father of American Dance.* New York: Dial Press, 1977.

● Mary Wigman

Holm, Hanya. "The Mary Wigman I Know." In Walter Sorell, ed., *The Dance Has Many Faces.* 2d ed. rev. New York: Columbia University Press, 1966.

Scheyer, Ernst. "The Shape of Space: The Art of Mary Wigman and Oskar Schlemmer." *Dance Perspectives* 41 (1970).

Wigman, Mary. *The Language of Dance.* Translated by Walter Sorell. Middletown, Conn.: Wesleyan University Press, 1966.

———. *The Mary Wigman Book.* Edited and translated by Walter Sorell. Middletown, Conn.: Wesleyan University Press, 1975.

———. "The New German Dance." In Virginia Stewart and Merle Armitage, eds., *The Modern Dance.* New York: E. Weyhe, 1935. (Brooklyn: Dance Horizons, 1970.)

———. "The Philosophy of Modern Dance." In Selma Jeanne Cohen, ed., *Dance as a Theatre Art.* New York: Dodd, Mead & Co., 1974.

● Martha Graham

Anderson, Jack. "Some Personal Grumbles About Martha Graham." *Ballet Review* 2, no. 1 (1967) p. 25.

Armitage, Merle, ed. *Martha Graham.* Los Angeles: privately printed, 1937. (Brooklyn: Dance Horizons, 1966.)

Borek, Tom. "Graham." *Eddy* 4 (1974) pp. 28-37.

Graham, Martha. "The American Dance." In Virginia Stewart and Merle Armitage, eds., *The Modern Dance.* New York: E. Weyhe, 1935. (Brooklyn: Dance Horizons, 1970.)

____. "A Dancer's World." *Dance Observer* 25, no. 1 (1958) p. 5.

____. "How I Became a Dancer." In Myron Howard Nadel and Constance Gwen Nadel, eds., *The Dance Experience: Readings in Dance Appreciation.* New York: Praeger Publishers, 1970.

____. "Martha Graham Speaks." *Dance Observer* 30, no. 4 (1963) pp. 53-55.

____. "A Modern Dancer's Primer for Action." Edited by Frederick R. Rogers. In *Dance: A Basic Educational Technique.* New York: Macmillan, 1941.

____. *The Notebooks of Martha Graham.* Introduction by Nancy Wilson Ross. New York: Harcourt, Brace, Jovanovich, 1973.

Leatherman, Leroy. *Martha Graham: Portrait of the Lady as an Artist.* New York: Alfred A. Knopf, 1966.

McDonagh, Don. *Martha Graham.* New York: Praeger Publishers, 1974.

Morgan, Barbara. *Martha Graham: Sixteen Dances in Photographs.* New York: Duel, Sloan, and Pearce, 1941.

Sorell, Walter. "Two Rebels, Two Giants: Isadora and Martha." In Walter Sorell, ed., *The Dance Has Many Faces.* 2d ed. rev. New York: Columbia University Press, 1966.

Terry, Walter. *Frontiers of Life: The Life of Martha Graham.* New York: Thomas Y. Crowell Co., 1975.

Trowbridge, Charlotte. *Dance Drawings of Martha Graham.* Forward by Martha Graham; preface by James Johnson Sweeney. New York: Dance Observer, 1945.

● Doris Humphrey

Cohen, Selma Jeanne. *Doris Humphrey: An Artist First.* Middletown, Conn.: Wesleyan University Press, 1972.

Humphrey, Doris. "America's Modern Dance." In Myron Howard Nadel and Constance Gwen Nadel, eds., *The Dance Experience: Readings in Dance Appreciation.* New York: Praeger Publishers, 1970.

____. *The Art of Making Dances.* Edited by Barbara Pollack. New York and Toronto: Rinehart & Company, Inc., 1959.

____, and Love, Paul. "The Dance of Doris Humphrey." In Virginia Stewart and Merle Armitage, eds., *The Modern Dance.* New York: E. Weyhe, 1935. (Brooklyn: Dance Horizons, 1970.)

____. "Dance Drama." In Walter Sorell, ed., *The Dance Has Many Faces.* 2d ed. rev. New York: Columbia University Press, 1966.

____. "New Dance: An Unfinished Autobiography." *Dance Perspectives*. 25 (1966).

Stodelle, Ernestine. *The Dance Technique of Doris Humphrey and Its Creative Potential.* Princeton, N. J.: Princeton Book Company, Publishers, 1978.

● Charles Weidman

Manasevit, Shirley D. "A Last Interview with Charles Weidman." *Dance Scope* 10, no. 1 (1975-1976) pp. 32-50.

Weidman, Charles. "Random Remarks." In Walter Sorell, ed., *The Dance Has Many Faces.* 2d ed. rev. New York: Columbia University Press, 1966.

____, and Love, Paul. "The Work of Charles Weidman." In Virginia Stewart and Merle Armitage, eds., *The Modern Dance.* New York: E. Weyhe, 1935. (Brooklyn: Dance Horizons, 1970.)

Wynne, David. "Three Years With Charles Weidman." *Dance Perspectives* 60 (1974).

● Hanya Holm

Holm, Hanya. "The German Dance in the American Scene." In Virginia Stewart and Merle Armitage, eds., *The Modern Dance.* New York: E. Weyhe, 1935. (Brooklyn: Dance Horizons, 1970.)

____. "The Mary Wigman I Know." In Walter Sorell, ed., *The Dance Has Many Faces.* 2d ed. rev. New York: Columbia University Press, 1966.

Sorell, Walter. *Hanya Holm: Biography of an Artist.* Middletown, Conn.: Wesleyan University Press, 1969.

● Merce Cunningham

Brown, Carolyn, et al. "Tir.. 'n Walk in Space." *Dance Perspectives* 34 (1968).

Cunningham, Merce. *Changes: Notes on Choreography.* New York: Something Else Press, 1968.

____. "The Function of a Technique for Dance." In Walter Sorell, ed., *The Dance Has Many Faces.* Cleveland and New York: World Publishing Co., 1951.

____. "The Impermanent Art." In Fernando Puma, ed., *Seven Arts 3.* Indian Hills, Colo.: Falcon's Riding Press, 1955.

____. "Choreography and the Dance." In Stanley Rosner and Lawrence E. Abt, eds., *The Creative Experience.* New York: Grossman Publications, 1970. (New York: Dell Publishing Co., 1972.)

Klosty, James, ed. *Merce Cunningham.* New York: Saturday Review Press, E. P. Dutton & Co., Inc., 1975.

Snell, Michael. "Cunningham and the Critics." *Ballet Review* 3, no. 6 (1971) pp. 16-39.

Yates, Peter. "Merce Cunningham Restores the Dance to Dance." *Impulse* (1965) pp. 13-17.

● Erick Hawkins

Hawkins, Erick. "Erick Hawkins Addresses a New-to-Dance Audience." In Myron Howard Nadel and Constance Gwen Nadel, eds., *The Dance Experience: Readings in Dance Appreciation.* New York: Praeger Publishers, 1970.

——. "Pure Fact in Movement Technique and Choreography." *Dance Observer* 25, no. 9 (1958) pp. 133-134.

——. "Pure Poetry." In Selma Jeanne Cohen, ed., *The Modern Dance: Seven Statements of Belief.* Middletown, Conn.: Wesleyan University Press, 1965.

——. "What is the Most Beautiful Dance?" In Walter Sorell, ed., *The Dance Has Many Faces.* 2d ed. rev. New York: Columbia University Press, 1966.

——. "Why Does a Man Dance and What Does He Dance, and Who Should Watch Him?" In Myron Howard Nadel and Constance Gwen Nadel, eds., *The Dance Experience: Readings in Dance Appreciation.* New York: Praeger Publishers, 1970.

Rochlein, Harvey. *Notes on Contemporary American Dance 1964.* Baltimore: University Extension Press, 1964.

● José Limón

Limón, José. "An American Accent." In Selma Jeanne Cohen, ed., *The Modern Dance: Seven Statements of Belief.* Middletown, Conn.: Wesleyan University Press, 1965.

——. "American Dance on Tour." *Juilliard Review* 6 (1958) pp. 8-11.

——. "Composing a Dance." *Juilliard Review* 2 (1955) pp. 17-23.

——. "Dancers Are Musicians Are Dancers." *Juilliard Review Annual* (1966-1967).

——. "Music Is the Strongest Ally to a Dancer's Way of Life." In Myron Howard Nadel and Constance Gwen Nadel, eds., *The Dance Experience: Readings in Dance Appreciation.* New York: Praeger Publishers, 1970.

___. "On Dance." In Fernando Puma, ed., *Seven Arts 1.* Garden City, N. Y.: Permabooks, Doubleday & Company, Inc., 1953.

___. "The Universities and the Arts." *Dance Scope* 1, no. 2 (1965) pp. 23-27.

___. "The Virile Dance." In Walter Sorell, ed., *The Dance Has Many Faces.* 2d ed. rev. New York: Columbia University Press, 1966.

___. "Young Dancers State Their Views." *Dance Observer* 13, no. 1 (1946) p. 7.

Siegel, Marcia B. "José Limón 1908-1972." *Ballet Review* 4, no. 4 (1973) pp. 100-104.

Anna Sokolow

Sokolow, Anna. "Talking to Dance and Dancers." *Dance and Dancers* 5 (1967) pp. 18-19.

Winter, Rhoda. "Conversation with Anna Sokolow." *Impulse* (1958) pp. 43-46.

Alwin Nikolais

Coleman, Martha. "On the Teaching of Choreography: An Interview with Alwin Nikolais." *Dance Observer* 17, no. 10 (1950) pp. 148-150.

Copeland, Roger. "A Conversation with Alwin Nikolais." *Dance Scope* 8, no. 1 (1973-1974) pp. 41-46.

Louis, Murray. "The Contemporary Dance Theatre of Alwin Nikolais." *Dance Observer* 27, no. 2 (1960) pp. 24-26.

Nikolais, Alwin. "An Art of Magic: Interview with Dance and Dancers." *Dance and Dancers* 7 (1969) pp. 24-26.

___. "A New Method of Dance Notation." In Myron Howard Nadel and Constance Gwen Nadel, eds., *The Dance Experience: Readings in Dance Appreciation.* New York: Praeger Publishers, 1970.

___. "Growth of a Theme." In Walter Sorell, ed., *The Dance Has Many Faces.* 2d ed. rev. New York: Columbia University Press, 1966.

___. "The New Dimension of Dance." *Impulse* (1958) pp. 43-46.

___. "No Man from Mars." In Selma Jeanne Cohen, ed., *The Modern Dance: Seven Statements of Belief.* Middletown, Conn.: Wesleyan University Press, 1966.

___. "What Is the Most Beautiful Dance." In Walter Sorell, ed., *The Dance Has Many Faces.* Cleveland and New York: World Publishing Co., 1951.

● Anna Halprin

Halprin, Anna. "Intuition and Improvisation." In Marian van Tuyl, ed., *Anthology of Impulse.* Brooklyn: Dance Horizons, 1969.

——. "Yvonne Rainer Interviews Anna Halprin." *Drama Review* (T30), 10, no. 2 (1965) pp. 168-178.

Halprin, Lawrence. *The RSVP Cycles: Creative Processes in the Human Environment.* New York: George Braziller, Inc., 1969.

● Judith Dunn

Dunn, Judith. "My Work and Judson's." *Ballet Review* 1, no. 6 (1967) pp. 22-26.

Siegel, Marcia B., ed. "Dancer's Notes." *Dance Perspectives* 38 (1969).

● Yvonne Rainer

Hecht, Robin Silver. "Reflections on the Career of Yvonne Rainer and the Values of Minimal Dance." *Dance Scope* 8, no. 1 (1973-1974). pp. 12-25.

Rainer, Yvonne, et al. "Conversation in Manhattan." *Impulse* (1967) pp. 57-64.

——. "The Dwarf Syndrome." In Walter Sorell, ed., *The Dance Has Many Faces.* 2d ed. rev. New York: Columbia University Press, 1966.

——. "Some Retrospective Notes on a Dance for 10 People and 12 Mattresses Called 'Parts of Some Sextets.' " *Tulane Drama Review* (T30) 10, no. 2 (1965) pp. 142-166.

——. *Work, 1961-73.* Halifax: The Press of The Nova Scotia College of Art and Design; New York: New York University Press, 1974.

——. "Yvonne Rainer Interviews Anna Halprin." *Drama Review* (T30), 10, no. 2 (1965) pp. 168-178.

● Rod Rodgers

Rodgers, Rod. "For the Celebration of Our Blackness." *Dance Scope* 3, no. 2 (1967) pp. 6-10.

——. "Is it just for jobs?" *Dance Magazine* 41, no. 4 (1967) p. 26.

——. "Men and dance: why do we question the image?" *Dance Magazine* 40, no. 4 (1966) pp. 35-36.

● Pilobolus

Fanger, Iris M. "Pilobolus." *Dance Magazine* 48, no. 7 (1974) pp. 38-42.

●Trisha Brown

Brown, Trisha, et al. "Conversation in Manhattan." *Impulse* (1967) pp. 57-64.

___. "Three Pieces." *Drama Review* (T65) 19, no. 1 (1975) pp. 26-32.

Siegel, Marcia B. "New Dance: Individuality, Image, and the Demise of the Coterie." *Dance Magazine* 48, no. 4 (1974) pp. 39-44.

Sommer, Sally R. "Trisha Brown Making Dances." *Dance Scope* 11, no. 2 (1977) pp. 7-18.

●Douglas Dunn

Dunn, Douglas. "Notes on Playing Myself." *Eddy* 4 (1974) pp. 28-37.

Logos, Fanny. "Hide and Seek." *Eddy* 7 (1975-1976) pp. 67-69.

II TOPICS

● Choreography

Cunningham, Merce. *Changes: Notes on Choreography.* New York: Something Else Press, 1968.

Ellfeldt, Lois V. *A Primer for Choreographers.* Palo Alto, Calif.: National Press Books, 1967.

Gray, Miriam, ed. *Focus on Dance V.* Washington, D.C.: American Association for Health, Physical Education and Recreation, 1969.

Halprin, Lawrence. *The RSVP Cycles: Creative Processes in the Human Environment.* New York: George Braziller, Inc., 1969.

Hawkins, Alma M. *Creating Through Dance.* Englewood Cliffs, N.J.: Prentice-Hall, Inc., 1966.

Horst, Louis. *Modern Forms In Relation to the Other Arts.* With Carol Russell. San Francisco: Impulse Publications, 1961, 1963.

___. *Pre-Classic Forms.* New York: Kamin Dance Publishers, 1953. (Brooklyn: Dance Horizons, 1968.)

Humphrey, Doris. *The Art of Making Dances.* Edited by Barbara Pollack. New York and Toronto: Rinehart & Company, Inc., 1959. (New York: Grove Press, 1962.)

Turner, Margery J. *New Dance: Approaches to Nonliteral Choreography.* With Ruth Grauert and Arlene Zallman. Pittsburgh: University of Pittsburgh Press, 1971.

● Criticism

Battock, Gregory, ed. *The New Art: A Critical Anthology.* New York: E. P. Dutton & Co., 1966.

Croce, Arlene. *Afterimages.* New York: Alfred A. Knopf, 1978.

Denby, Edwin. *Looking at the Dance.* New York: Horizon Press, 1968.

Johnston, Jill. *Marmalade Me.* New York: E. P. Dutton & Co., 1971.

Jowitt, Deborah. *Dance Beat: Selected Views and Reviews 1967-1976.* New York: Marcel Dekker, Inc., 1977.

Siegel, Marica B. *At the Vanishing Point.* New York: Saturday Review Press, 1972.

——. *Watching the Dance Go By.* New York: Houghton Mifflin Co., 1977.

● Films

Durkin, Kathleen, and Levesque, Paul, eds. *Catalog of Dance Films.* Compiled by Susan Braun and Dorothy H. Currie. New York: Dance Films Association, Inc., 1974.

Mueller, John. *Dance Film Directory: An Annotated and Evaluative Guide to Films on Ballet and Modern Dance.* Princeton, N. J.: Princeton Book Company, Publishers, 1979.

● History

Anderson, Jack. *Dance.* New York: Newsweek Books, 1974.

Armitage, Merle. *Dance Memoranda.* Edited by Edwin Corle. New York: Duell, Sloan and Pearce, 1949.

Cohen, Selma Jeanne, ed. *Dance as a Theatre Art.* New York: Dodd, Mead and Co., 1974.

de Mille, Agnes. *The Book of the Dance.* New York: Golden Press, 1963.

Emery, Lynne Fauley. *Black Dance in the United States from 1619 to 1970.* Palo Alto, Calif.: National Press Books, 1972.

Hering, Doris. *Twenty-Five Years of American Dance.* Rev. ed. New York: Rudolf Orthwine, 1954.

Kirstein, Lincoln. *Dance: A Short History of Classical Theatrical Dancing.* New York: G. P. Putnam & Sons, 1935. (Brooklyn: Dance Horizons, 1974.)

Kraus, Richard. *History of the Dance.* Englewood Cliffs, N. J.: Prentice-Hall, Inc., 1969.

Lloyd, Margaret. *The Borzoi Book of Modern Dance.* New York: Alfred A. Knopf, 1949. (Brooklyn: Dance Horizons, 1970.)

McDonagh, Don. *The Complete Guide to Modern Dance.* Garden City, N. Y.: Doubleday & Co., Inc., 1976. (New York: Popular Library, 1977.)

____. *The Rise and Fall and Rise of Modern Dance.* New York: Outerbridge and Dienstfrey, 1970. (New York: New American Library, Inc., 1971.)

Magriel, Paul. *Chronicles of the American Dance.* New York: Henry Holt & Co., 1948.

Martin, John. *America Dancing.* New York: Dodge Publishing Co., 1936. (Brooklyn: Dance Horizons, 1968.)

____. *The Dance.* New York: Tudor Publishing Co., 1946.

____. *Introduction to the Dance.* New York: A. S. Barnes, 1933. (Brooklyn: Dance Horizons, 1965.)

____. *John Martin's Book of the Dance.* New York: Tudor Publishing Co., 1963.

Maynard, Olga. *American Modern Dancers: The Pioneers.* Boston and Toronto: Little, Brown and Co., 1965.

Mazo, Joseph H. *Prime Movers: The Makers of Modern Dance in America.* New York: William Morrow and Co., Inc., 1977.

Palmer, Winthrop. *Theatrical Dancing in America.* New York: Bernard Ackerman, 1945. (2d ed. rev. New York: A. S. Barnes and Co., 1978.)

Sherman, Jane. *Soaring.* Middletown, Conn.: Wesleyan University Press, 1976.

____. *The Drama of Denishawn Dance.* Middletown, Conn.: Wesleyan University Press, 1979.

Siegel, Marcia B. *The Shapes of Change: Images of American Dance.* Boston: Houghton Mifflin Co., 1979.

Sorell, Walter. *The Dance Through the Ages.* New York: Grosset and Dunlap, 1967.

Stebbins, Genevieve. *The Delsarte System of Expression.* Brooklyn: Dance Horizons, 1978.

Terry, Walter. *The Dance in America.* New York: Harper and Bros., 1956. (Rev. ed. New York: Harper & Row, 1973.)

___. *I Was There: Selected Dance Reviews and Articles, 1936-1976.* Compiled and edited by Andrew Mark Wentink. New York: Marcel Dekker Press, 1978.

Warren, Larry. *Lester Horton: Modern Dance Pioneer.* New York: Marcel Dekker Press, 1977.

●Theory

Arnheim, Rudolf. *Toward a Psychology of Art.* Berkeley and Los Angeles: University of California Press, 1967.

Cage, John. *Silence.* Middletown, Conn.: Wesleyan University Press, 1961.

Cohen, Selma Jeanne, ed. *The Modern Dance: Seven Statements of Belief.* Middletown, Conn.: Wesleyan University Press, 1966.

Forti, Simone. *Handbook in Motion.* Halifax, Canada: The Press of the Nova Scotia College of Art and Design, 1973.

H'Doubler, Margaret. *Dance: A Creative Art Experience.* New York: Appleton-Century-Crofts, 1940. (Madison: University of Wisconsin Press, 1959, 1966.)

Kinney, Troy. *The Dance: Its Place in Art and Life.* New York: F. A. Stokes Co., 1924.

Langer, Suzanne K. *Feeling and Form.* New York: Charles Scribner's Sons, 1953.

___. *Problems of Art.* New York: Charles Scribner's Sons, 1957.

___. *Reflections on Art.* Baltimore: John Hopkins University Press, 1959.

Livet, Anne, ed. *Contemporary Dance.* New York: Abbeville Press, Inc., 1978.

Lyle, Cynthia. *Dancers on Dancing.* New York and London: Drake Publishers, 1977.

Martin, John. *The Modern Dance.* New York: A. S. Barnes Co., 1936. (Brooklyn: Dance Horizons, 1965.)

Nadel, Myron Howard, and Nadel, Constance Gwen, eds. *The Dance Experience: Readings in Dance Appreciation.* New York: Praeger Publishers, 1970.

Percival, John. *Experimental Dance.* New York: Universe Books, 1971.

Selden, Elizabeth. *The Dancer's Quest.* Berkeley and Los Angeles: University of California Press, 1935.

___. *Elements of the Free Dance.* New York: A. S. Barnes, 1930.

Sheets, Maxine. *The Phenomenology of Dance.* Madison: University of Wisconsin Press, 1966.

Sorell, Walter, ed. *The Dance Has Many Faces.* Cleveland and New York: World Publishing Co., 1951. (2d ed. rev.; New York: Columbia University Press, 1966.)

___. *The Dancer's Image: Points and Counterpoints.* New York: Columbia University Press, 1971.

___. *The Duality of Vision: Genius and Versatility in the Arts.* New York: Bobbs-Merrill Co., 1970.

Stewart, Virginia, and Armitage, Merle, eds. *The Modern Dance.* New York: E. Weyhe, 1935. (Brooklyn: Dance Horizons, 1970.)

van Tuyl, Marian, ed. *Anthology of Impulse.* Brooklyn: Dance Horizons, 1970.

von Laban, Rudolf. *Choreutics.* Edited by Lisa Ullman. London: MacDonald & Evans, 1966.
, and Lawrence, F.C. *Effort.* London: MacDonald & Evans, 1947.

___. *A Life For Dance.* New York: Theatre Arts Books, 1975.

___. *The Mastery of Movement.* 2d ed. London: MacDonald & Evans, 1960.

___. *Principles of Dance and Movement Notation.* London: Mac-Donald & Evans, 1956.

● Reference Material

Beaumont, Cyril, ed. *A Bibliography of the Dance Collection of Doris Niles and Serge Leslie.* Annotated by Serge Leslie. 3 vols. London: C.W. Beaumont, 1966-1974.

Clarke, Mary, and Vaughan, David, eds., *The Encyclopedia of Dance and Ballet.* New York: G.P. Putnam's Sons, 1977.

Chujoy, Anatole. *Dance Encyclopedia.* New York: A. S. Barnes and Co. Inc., 1949. (Rev. and enlarged by Anatole Chujoy and P.W. Manchester; New York: Simon and Schuster, 1967.)

Dance Index. Reprint. 7 vols. Arno Press, 1971.

Kaprelian, Mary H., comp. and ed. *Aesthetics for Dancers: A Selected Annotated Bibliography.* Washington, D. C.: American Alliance for Health, Physical Education and Recreation, 1976.

McDonagh, Don. *The Complete Guide to Modern Dance.* Garden City, N.Y.: Doubleday & Co. Inc., 1976.

Magriel, Paul David. *A Bibliography of Dancing.* New York: M. W. Wilson, 1936. (New York: Benjamin, 1966.)

New York Public Library. *Dictionary Catalog: New York Public Library Dance Collection.* 10 vols. New York: The New York Public Library, Astor, Lenox, and Tilden Foundation, distributed by G. K. Hall, Boston, 1974. Supplemental issues 1975, 1976, 1977.